T0306119

Economic Networks

It has become increasingly clear that economies can fruitfully be viewed as networks, consisting of millions of nodes (households, firms, banks, etc.) connected by business, social, and legal relationships. These relationships shape many outcomes that economists measure. Over the past few years, research on economic networks has flourished, as economists try to understand supply-side dynamics, default cascades, aggregate fluctuations, and many other phenomena. *Economic Networks* provides a brisk introduction to network analysis that is self-contained, rigorous, and illustrated with many figures, diagrams and listings with computer code. Network methods are put to work analyzing production networks, financial networks, and other related topics (including optimal transport, another highly active research field). Visualizations using recent data bring key ideas to life.

Thomas J. Sargent is a Nobel Prize–winning economist and Professor of Economics at New York University. He has held positions at Stanford, Minnesota, Chicago, and Princeton, and served as President of the Econometric Society and of the American Economic Association. He is renowned for his influential research on macroeconomics, rational expectations, and policy analysis.

John Stachurski is a professor at the Australian National University who has made influential contributions to the study of Markov models and dynamic optimization. He is an economist specializing in mathematical and computational economics and is also a co-founder of QuantEcon, a popular platform for open-source economic modeling.

Structural Analysis in the Social Sciences

Edited by Mark Granovetter

The series Structural Analysis in the Social Sciences presents studies that analyze social behavior and institutions by reference to relations among such concrete social entities as persons, organizations, and nations. Relational analysis contrasts on the one hand with reductionist methodological individualism and on the other with macro-level determinism, whether based on technology, material conditions, economic conflict, adaptive evolution, or functional imperatives. In this more intellectually flexible, structural middle ground, analysts situate actors and their relations in a variety of contexts. Since the series began in 1987, its authors have variously focused on small groups, history, culture, politics, kinship, aesthetics, economics, and complex organizations, creatively theorizing how these shape and in turn are shaped by social relations. Their style and methods have ranged widely, from intense, long-term ethnographic observation to highly abstract mathematical models. Their disciplinary affiliations have included history, anthropology, sociology, political science, business, economics, mathematics, and computer science. Some have made explicit use of social network analysis, including many of the cutting-edge and standard works of that approach, whereas others have kept formal analysis in the background and used "networks" as a fruitful orienting metaphor. All have in common a sophisticated and revealing approach that forcefully illuminates our complex social world.

Recent Books in the Series

Economic Networks

Theory and Computation

THOMAS J. SARGENT
New York University

JOHN STACHURSKI
Australian National University

CAMBRIDGE
UNIVERSITY PRESS

Shaftesbury Road, Cambridge CB2 8EA, United Kingdom

One Liberty Plaza, 20th Floor, New York, NY 10006, USA

477 Williamstown Road, Port Melbourne, VIC 3207, Australia

314–321, 3rd Floor, Plot 3, Splendor Forum, Jasola District Centre, New Delhi – 110025, India

103 Penang Road, #05–06/07, Visioncrest Commercial, Singapore 238467

Cambridge University Press is part of Cambridge University Press & Assessment,
a department of the University of Cambridge.

We share the University's mission to contribute to society through the pursuit of
education, learning and research at the highest international levels of excellence.

www.cambridge.org
Information on this title: www.cambridge.org/9781009456357

DOI: 10.1017/9781009456340

First published 2024

A catalogue record for this publication is available from the British Library

Library of Congress Cataloging-in-Publication Data
Names: Stachurski, John, 1969- author. | Sargent, Thomas J, author.
Title: Economic networks : theory and computation : Quantecon Book I /
    Thomas J Sargent and John Stachurski.
Description: 1 edition. | New York : Cambridge University Press, [2024] |
    Includes bibliographical references and index.
Identifiers: LCCN 2023045874 | ISBN 9781009456357 (hardback) |
    ISBN 9781009456364 (paperback)
Subjects: LCSH: Business networks. | Social networks–Economic aspects. |
    Economics–Sociological aspects. | Economics–Mathematical models.
Classification: LCC HD69.S8 S713 2024 | DDC 302.4–dc23/eng/20231201
LC record available at https://lccn.loc.gov/2023045874

ISBN 978-1-009-45635-7 Hardback
ISBN 978-1-009-45636-4 Paperback

To Nina and Finn

Contents

Figures

Tables

Preface

The development and use of network science has grown exponentially since the beginning of the twenty-first century. The ideas and techniques found in this field are already core tools for analyzing a vast range of phenomena, from epidemics and disinformation campaigns to chemical reactions and brain function.

In economics, network theory is typically taught as a specialized subfield, available to students as one of many elective courses toward the end of their program. However, we are rapidly approaching the stage where every aspiring scientist – including social scientists and economists – wants to know the foundations of this field. It is arguably the case that, just as every well-trained economist learns the basics of convex optimization, maximum likelihood, and linear regression, so too should every graduate student in economics learn the fundamental ideas of network theory.

This book is an introduction to economic networks, intended for students and researchers in the fields of economics and applied mathematics. The book emphasizes quantitative modeling, with the main underlying tools being graph theory, linear algebra, fixed-point theory, and programming. Most mathematical tools are covered from first principles, with two main technical results – the Neumann series lemma and the Perron–Frobenius theorem – playing a central role.

The book is suitable for a one-semester course, taught either to advanced undergraduate students who are comfortable with linear algebra or to beginning graduate students. (For example, although we define eigenvalues, an ideal student would already know what eigenvalues and eigenvectors are, so that concepts like "eigenvector centrality" or results like the Neumann series lemma are readily absorbed.) The text will also suit students from mathematics, engineering, computer science, and other related fields who wish to learn about the connection between economics and networks.

Several excellent books on network theory in economics and social science already exist, including Easley et al. (2010), Jackson (2010), Borgatti et al. (2018), and Goyal (2023), as well as the handbook by Bramoullé et al. (2016). These texts have broad scope and treat many useful applications. In contrast, our book is narrower and more technical. It provides the mathematical, computational, and graph-theoretic foundations that are required to understand and apply network theory, along with a treatment of some of the most important network applications in economics, finance, and operations research. It can be used as a complementary resource or as a preliminary course that facilitates understanding of the alternative texts listed above, as well as research papers in the area.

Our book contains a mix of Python and Julia code. The majority is in Python because the libraries are more stable at the time of writing, although Julia also has strong graph manipulation and optimization libraries. Code for the figures is available from the authors. There are many solved exercises, ranging from simple to quite hard. At the end of each chapter, we provide notes, informal comments, and references.

We are greatly indebted to Jim Savage and Schmidt Futures for generous financial support, as well as to Shu Hu and Chien Yeh for their outstanding research assistance. QuantEcon research fellow Matthew McKay generously lent us his time and expertise in data analysis, networks, and visualization. QuantEcon research assistant Mark Dawkins turned an unstructured collection of code files into an elegant companion Jupyter Book.

Qianbin Dou has prepared a Chinese translation of this book, with assistance from his colleagues Meilu Sun and Ling Hu. In the process, Qianbin raised many important points that greatly enhanced the quality of all chapters. We thank Qianbin and his colleagues for their extremely valuable help.

For many additional fixes, comments, and suggestions, we thank Quentin Batista, Rolf Campos, Fernando Cirelli, Rebekah Dix, Saya Ikegawa, Fazeleh Kazemian, Dawie van Lill, Simon Mishricky, Pietro Monticone, Flint O'Neil, Akshay Shanker, Zejin Shi, Arnav Sood, Natasha Watkins, Chao Wei, and Zhuoying Ye. Finally, Chase Coleman, Alfred Galichon, Spencer Lyon, Daisuke Oyama, and Jesse Perla are collaborators at QuantEcon, and almost everything we write has benefited from their input. This text is no exception.

Common Symbols

$P \implies Q$	P implies Q
$P \iff Q$	$P \implies Q$ and $Q \implies P$
$[n]$	the set $\{1, \ldots, n\}$
$\alpha := 1$	α is defined as equal to 1
$f \equiv 1$	function f is everywhere equal to 1
$\wp(A)$	the power set of A; that is, the collection of all subsets of set A
$\mathbb{N}$, $\mathbb{Z}$, and $\mathbb{R}$	the natural numbers, integers, and real numbers respectively
$\mathbb{C}$	the set of complex numbers (see Section A.1.8)
$\mathbb{Z}_+$, $\mathbb{R}_+$, etc.	the nonnegative elements of $\mathbb{Z}$, $\mathbb{R}$, etc.
$\mathbb{M}^{n \times k}$	all $n \times k$ matrices
$\mathrm{diag}(a_1, \ldots, a_n)$	the diagonal matrix with $a_1, \ldots a_n$ on the principal diagonal
$|x|$	the absolute value of $x \in \mathbb{R}$
$|B|$	the cardinality of (number of elements in) set B
$f : A \rightarrow B$	f is a function from set A to set B
$x \mapsto y$	x is mapped to y (under some given function)
$\mathbb{R}^S$	the set of all functions from S to $\mathbb{R}$
$\mathbb{R}^n$	all n-tuples of real numbers
$\|x\|_1$	the ℓ_1 norm $\sum_i |x_i|$ (see Section 2.3.1.1)
$\|x\|_\infty$	the ℓ_∞ norm $\max_i |x_i|$ (see Section 2.3.1.1)
$\|A\|$ when $A \in \mathbb{M}^{n \times k}$	the operator norm of A (see Section 2.3.2.3)
$\langle a, b \rangle$	the inner product of a and b
$a \vee b$	the maximum of a and b (pointwise if they are vectors)
$a \wedge b$	the minimum of a and b (pointwise if they are vectors)
$g \ll h$	function (or vector) g is everwhere strictly less than h

$\mathbb{1}$	vector of ones or function everywhere equal to one
$\mathbb{1}\{P\}$	indicator, equal to 1 if statement P is true and 0 otherwise
$i_d(v)$	in-degree of node v
$o_d(v)$	out-degree of node v
$\mathscr{I}(v)$	set of direct predecessors of node v
$\mathscr{O}(v)$	set of direct successors of node v
$u \rightarrow v$	node v is accessible from node u
IID	independent and identically distributed
iff	if and only if
$\forall$	for all
$\exists$	there exist(s)
δ_x	the probability distribution concentrated on point x
$\mathscr{D}(S)$	the set of distributions on S
$X \overset{d}{=} Y$	X and Y have the same distribution
$X \sim F$	X has distribution F
$\Pi(\varphi, \psi)$	the set of all couplings of (φ, ψ)
$f \circ g$	the composition of functions f and g

1   Introduction

Relations are the fundamental fabric of reality.

(Michele Coscia)

1.1   Motivation

Alongside the exponential growth of computer networks over the last few decades, we have witnessed concurrent and equally rapid growth in a field called *network science*. Once computer networks brought network structure into clearer focus, scientists began to recognize networks almost everywhere, even in phenomena that had already received centuries of attention using other methods, and to apply network theory to organize and expand knowledge right throughout the sciences, in every field and discipline.

The set of possible examples is vast, and sources mentioning or treating hundreds of different applications of network methods and graph theory are listed in the reading notes at the end of the chapter. In computer science and machine learning alone, we see computational graphs, graphical networks, neural networks, and deep learning. In operations research, network analysis focuses on minimum cost flow, traveling salesman, shortest path, and assignment problems. In biology, networks are a standard way to represent interactions between bioentities.

In this book, our interest lies in economic and social phenomena. Here, too, networks are pervasive. Important examples include financial networks, production networks, trade networks, transport networks, and social networks. For example, social and information networks affect trends in sentiments and opinions, consumer decisions, and a range of peer effects. The topology of financial networks helps to determine the relative fragility of the financial system, while the structure of production networks affects trade, innovation, and the propagation of local shocks.

Figures 1.1 and 1.2 show two examples of trade networks. Figure 1.1 is called a *Sankey diagram*, which is a kind of figure used to represent flows. Oil flows from left to right. The countries on the left and below are the top 10 exporters of crude oil, while the countries on the right are the top 20 consumers. The figure relates to one of our

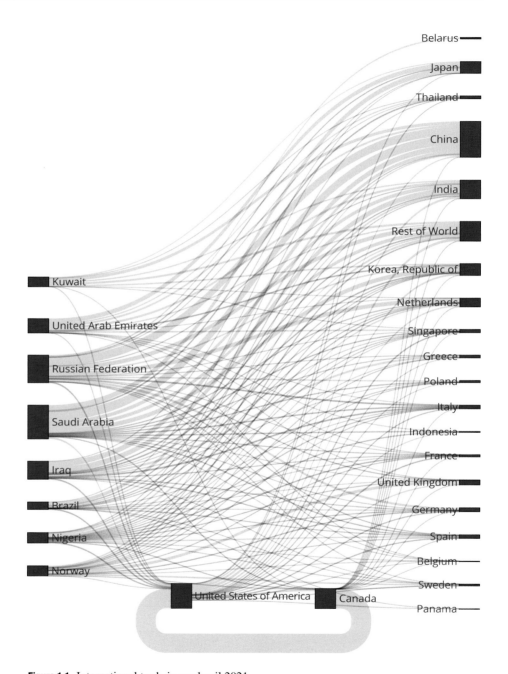

Figure 1.1 International trade in crude oil 2021

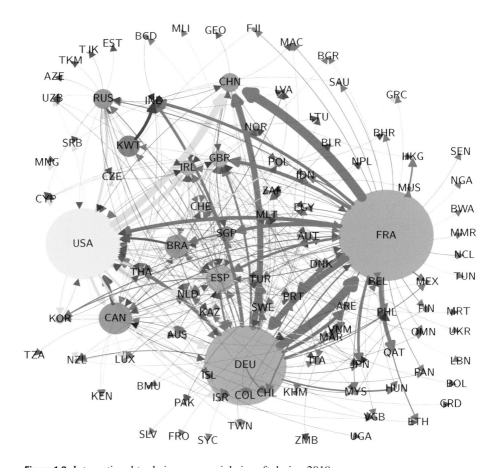

Figure 1.2 International trade in commercial aircraft during 2019

core topics: optimal (and equilibrium) flows across networks. We treat optimal flows at length in Chapter 3.[1]

Figure 1.2 shows international trade in large commercial aircraft in 2019.[2] Node size is proportional to total exports, and link width is proportional to exports to the target country. The USA, France, and Germany are revealed as major export hubs.

While some readers viewing Figures 1.1 and 1.2 might at first suspect that the network perspective adds little more than an attractive technique for visualizing data, it actually adds much more. For example, in Figure 1.2, node colors are based on a ranking of "importance" in the network called *eigenvector centrality*, which we introduce in §1.4.3.4. Such rankings and centrality measures are an active area of

[1] This figure was constructed by QuantEcon research fellow Matthew McKay, using International Trade Data (SITC, Rev 2) collected by The Growth Lab at Harvard University.
[2] This figure was also constructed by Matthew McKay, using data 2019 International Trade Data SITC Revision 2, code 7924. The data pertain to trade in commercial aircraft weighing at least 15,000 kg. It was sourced from CID Dataverse.

research among network scientists. Eigenvector and other forms of centrality feature throughout the text. For example, we will see that these concepts are closely connected to – and shed new light on – fundamental ideas first developed many years ago by researchers in the field of input–output economics.

In addition, in production networks, it turns out that the nature of shock propagation is heavily dependent on the underlying structure of the network. For example, for a few highly connected nodes, shocks occurring within one firm or sector can have an outsized influence on aggregate-level fluctuations. Economists are currently racing to understand these relationships, their interactions with various centrality measures, and other closely related phenomena.

To understand this line of work, as well as other applications of network methods to economics and finance, some technical foundations are required. For example, to define eigenvector centrality, we need to be familiar with eigenvectors, spectral decompositions, and the Perron–Frobenius theorem. To work with *Katz centrality*, which also features regularly in network science and economics, we require a sound understanding of the Neumann series lemma. The Perron–Frobenius theorem and the Neumann series lemma form much of the technical foundation of this textbook. We review them in detail in §1.2 and develop extensions throughout the remaining chapters.

One reason that analysis of networks is challenging is high dimensionality. To see why, consider implementing a model with n economic agents. This requires n times more data than one representative agent in a setting where agents are atomistic or coordinated by a fixed number of prices. For example, Carvalho and Grassi (2019) model the dynamics of $n = 6 \times 10^6$ firms, all of which need to be tracked when running a simulation. However, if we wish to model interactions between each pair i, j (supply linkages, liabilities, etc.), then, absent sparsity conditions, the data processing requirement grows like $O(n^2)$.[3] In the Carvalho and Grassi (2019) example, n^2 is 3.6×10^{13}, which is very large even for modern computers. One lesson is that network models can be hard to solve, even with powerful computers, unless we think carefully about algorithms.

In general, to obtain a good grasp on the workings of economic networks, we will need computational skills plus a firm understanding of linear algebra, probability, and a field of discrete mathematics called graph theory. The rest of this chapter provides relevant background in these topics. Before tackling this background, we recommend that readers skim the list of common symbols on page xix, as well the mathematical topics in the appendix, which starts on page 180. (The appendix is not intended for sequential reading but rather as a source of definitions and fundamental results to be drawn on in what follows.)

---

[3] See §A.3 for a discussion of big O notation.

1.2 Spectral Theory

In this section we review some linear algebra needed for the study of graphs and networks. Highlights include the spectral decomposition of diagonalizable matrices, the Neumann series lemma, and the theorem of Perron and Frobenius.

1.2.1 Eigendecompositions

Our first task is to cover spectral decompositions and the spectral theorem. We begin with a brief review of eigenvalues and their properties. (If you are not familiar with eigenvalues and eigenvectors, please consult an elementary treatment first. See, for example, Cohen (2021).)

1.2.1.1 Eigenvalues

Fix A in $\mathbb{M}^{n \times n}$. A scalar $\lambda \in \mathbb{C}$ is called an **eigenvalue** of A if there exists a nonzero complex vector $e \in \mathbb{C}^n$ such that $Ae = \lambda e$. A vector e satisfying this equality is called an **eigenvector** corresponding to the eigenvalue λ. (Notice that eigenvalues and eigenvectors are allowed to be complex, even though we restrict elements of A to be real.) The set of all eigenvalues of A is called the **spectrum** of A and written as $\sigma(A)$. As we show below, A has at most n distinct eigenvalues.

In Julia, we can check for the eigenvalues of a given square matrix A via `eigvals(A)`. Here is one example

```
using LinearAlgebra
A = [0 -1;
     1  0]
eigenvals = eigvals(A)
```

Running this code in a Jupyter cell (with Julia kernel) produces

```
2-element Vector{ComplexF64}:
 0.0 - 1.0im
 0.0 + 1.0im
```

Here `im` stands for i, the imaginary unit (i.e., $i^2 = -1$).

EXERCISE 1.2.1. Using pencil and paper, confirm that Julia's output is correct. In particular, show that

$$A = \begin{pmatrix} 0 & -1 \\ 1 & 0 \end{pmatrix} \implies \sigma(A) = \{i, -i\},$$

with corresponding eigenvectors $(-1, i)^\top$ and $(-1, -i)^\top$.

If $\lambda \in \sigma(A)$ and e is an eigenvector for λ, then (λ, e) is called an **eigenpair**.

EXERCISE 1.2.2. Prove: if (λ, e) is an eigenpair of A and α is a nonzero scalar, then $(\lambda, \alpha e)$ is also an eigenpair of A.

LEMMA 1.2.1 $\lambda \in \mathbb{C}$ *is an eigenvalue of A if and only if* $\det(A - \lambda I) = 0$.

Proof If $\lambda \in \mathbb{R}$, then Lemma 1.2.1 follows directly from Theorem A.4.8 on page 201, since $\det(A - \lambda I) = 0$ is equivalent to the existence of a nonzero vector e such that $(A - \lambda I)e = 0$, which in turn says that λ is an eigenvalue of A. The same arguments extend to the case $\lambda \in \mathbb{C}$ because the statements in Theorem A.4.8 are also valid for complex-valued matrices (see, e.g., Jänich (1994)).   □

It can be shown that $p(\lambda) := \det(A - \lambda I)$ is a polynomial of degree n.[4] This polynomial is called the **characteristic polynomial** of A. By the fundamental theorem of algebra, there are n roots (i.e., solutions in $\mathbb{C}$ to the equation $p(\lambda) = 0$), although some may be repeated as in the complete factorization of $p(\lambda)$. By Lemma 1.2.1,

(i) each of these roots is an eigenvalue, and
(ii) no other eigenvalues exist besides these n roots.

If $\lambda \in \sigma(A)$ appears k times in the factorization of the polynomial $p(\lambda)$, then λ is said to have **algebraic multiplicity** k. An eigenvalue with algebraic multiplicity one is called **simple**. A simple eigenvalue λ has the property that its eigenvector is unique up to a scalar multiple, in the sense of Exercise 1.2.2. In other words, the linear span of $\{e \in \mathbb{C}^n : (\lambda, e) \text{ is an eigenpair}\}$ (called the **eigenspace** of λ) is one-dimensional.

EXERCISE 1.2.3. For $A \in \mathbb{M}^{n \times n}$, show that $\lambda \in \sigma(A)$ iff $\tau \lambda \in \sigma(\tau A)$ for all $\tau > 0$.

EXERCISE 1.2.4. A useful fact concerning eigenvectors is that if the characteristic polynomial $p(\lambda) := \det(A - \lambda I)$ has n distinct roots, then the n corresponding eigenvectors form a basis of $\mathbb{C}^n$. Prove this for the case where all eigenvectors are real – that is, show that the n (real) eigenvectors form a basis of $\mathbb{R}^n$. (Bases are defined in §A.4.2. Proving this for $n = 2$ is also a good exercise.)

1.2.1.2   The Eigendecomposition

What are the easiest matrices to work with? An obvious answer to this question is: diagonal matrices. For example, when $D = \text{diag}(\lambda_i)$ with $i \in [n]$,

- the linear system $Dx = b$ reduces to n completely independent scalar equations;
- the t-th power D^t is just $\text{diag}(\lambda_i^t)$; and
- the inverse D^{-1} is just $\text{diag}(\lambda_i^{-1})$, assuming all λ_i's are nonzero.

While most matrices are not diagonal, there is a way that "almost any" matrix can be viewed as a diagonal matrix, after translation of the usual coordinates in $\mathbb{R}^n$ via an alternative basis. This can be extremely useful. The key ideas are described below.

---

[4] See, for example, Jänich (1994), chapter 6.

$A \in \mathbb{M}^{n \times n}$ is called **diagonalizable** if

$$A = PDP^{-1} \text{ for some } D = \text{diag}(\lambda_1, \ldots, \lambda_n) \text{ and nonsingular matrix } P.$$

We allow both D and P to contain complex values. The representation PDP^{-1} is called the **eigendecomposition** or the **spectral decomposition** of A.

One way to think about diagonalization is in terms of maps, as in

$$
\begin{array}{ccc}
\mathbb{R}^n & \xrightarrow{\;A\;} & \mathbb{R}^n \\
{\scriptstyle P^{-1}}\downarrow & & \uparrow{\scriptstyle P} \\
\mathbb{C}^n & \xrightarrow{\;D\;} & \mathbb{C}^n
\end{array}
$$

Either we can map directly with A or, alternatively, we can shift to $\mathbb{C}^n$ via P^{-1}, apply the diagonal matrix D, and then shift back to $\mathbb{R}^n$ via P.

The equality $A = PDP^{-1}$ can also be written as $AP = PD$. Decomposed across column vectors, this equation says that each column of P is an eigenvector of A, and each element along the principal diagonal of D is an eigenvalue.

EXERCISE 1.2.5. Confirm this. Why are column vectors taken from P nonzero, as required by the definition of eigenvalues?

EXERCISE 1.2.6. The trace of a matrix is equal to the sum of its eigenvalues, and the determinant is their product. Prove this fact in the case where A is diagonalizable.

EXERCISE 1.2.7. The asymptotic properties of the map $m \mapsto A^m$ are determined by the eigenvalues of A. This is clearest in the diagonalizable case, where $A = P \text{diag}(\lambda_i) P^{-1}$. To illustrate, use induction to show that

$$A = P \text{diag}(\lambda_i) P^{-1} \implies A^m = P \text{diag}(\lambda_i^m) P^{-1} \text{ for all } m \in \mathbb{N}. \tag{1.1}$$

When does diagonalizability hold?

While diagonalizability is not universal, the set of matrices in $\mathbb{M}^{n \times n}$ that fail to be diagonalizable has "Lebesgue measure zero" in $\mathbb{M}^{n \times n}$. (Loosely speaking, only special or carefully constructed examples will fail to be diagonalizable.) The next results provide conditions for the property.

THEOREM 1.2.2 *A matrix $A \in \mathbb{M}^{n \times n}$ is diagonalizable if and only if its eigenvectors form a basis of $\mathbb{C}^n$.*

This result is intuitive: for $A = PDP^{-1}$ to hold, we need P to be invertible, which requires that its n columns are linearly independent. Since $\mathbb{C}^n$ is n-dimensional, this means that the columns form a basis of $\mathbb{C}^n$.

COROLLARY 1.2.3 *If $A \in \mathbb{M}^{n \times n}$ has n distinct eigenvalues, then A is diagonalizable.*

Proof See Exercise 1.2.4. □

EXERCISE 1.2.8. Give a counterexample to the statement that the condition in Corollary 1.2.3 is necessary as well as sufficient.

There is another way that we can establish diagonalizability, based on symmetry. Symmetry also lends the diagonalization certain properties that turn out to be very useful in applications. We are referring to the following celebrated theorem.

THEOREM 1.2.4 (Spectral theorem)   *If $A \in \mathbb{M}^{n \times n}$ is symmetric, then there exists a real orthonormal $n \times n$ matrix U such that*

$$A = U D U^\top \quad \text{with} \quad \lambda_i \in \mathbb{R}_+ \text{ for all } i, \text{ where } D = \mathrm{diag}(\lambda_1, \dots, \lambda_n).$$

Since, for the orthonormal matrix U, we have $U^\top = U^{-1}$ (see Lemma A.4.9), one consequence of the spectral theorem is that A is diagonalizable. For obvious reasons, we often say that A is **orthogonally diagonalizable**.

1.2.1.3   Worker Dynamics

Let's study a small application of eigendecomposition. Suppose that, each month, workers are hired at rate α and fired at rate β. Their two states are unemployment (state 1) and employment (state 2). Figure 1.3 shows the transition probabilities for a given worker in each of these two states.

We translate these dynamics into the matrix

$$P_w = \begin{pmatrix} 1 - \alpha & \alpha \\ \beta & 1 - \beta \end{pmatrix}, \quad \text{where} \quad 0 \leqslant \alpha, \beta \leqslant 1. \tag{1.2}$$

- Row 1 of P_w gives probabilities for unemployment and employment, respectively, when currently unemployed.
- Row 2 of P_w gives probabilities for unemployment and employment, respectively, when currently employed.

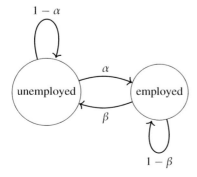

Figure 1.3 Worker transition dynamics

EXERCISE 1.2.9. Using Lemma 1.2.1, show that the two eigenvalues of P_w are $\lambda_1 := 1$ and $\lambda_2 := 1 - \alpha - \beta$. Show that, when $\min\{\alpha, \beta\} > 0$,

$$e_1 := \begin{pmatrix} 1 \\ 1 \end{pmatrix} \quad \text{and} \quad e_2 := \begin{pmatrix} -\alpha \\ \beta \end{pmatrix}$$

are two corresponding eigenvectors and that λ_1 and λ_2 are simple.

EXERCISE 1.2.10. Show that, when $\alpha = \beta = 0$, the eigenvalue λ_1 is not simple.

Below we demonstrate that the m-th power of P_w provides m-step transition probabilities for workers. Anticipating this discussion, we now seek an expression for P_w^m at arbitrary $m \in \mathbb{N}$. This problem is simplified if we use diagonalization.

EXERCISE 1.2.11. Assume that $\min\{\alpha, \beta\} > 0$. (When $\alpha = \beta = 0$, computing the powers of P_w is trivial.) Show that

$$P_w = EDE^{-1} \quad \text{when} \quad D = \begin{pmatrix} 1 & 0 \\ 0 & \lambda_2 \end{pmatrix} \quad \text{and} \quad E = \begin{pmatrix} 1 & -\alpha \\ 1 & \beta \end{pmatrix}.$$

Using (1.1), prove that

$$P_w^m = \frac{1}{\alpha + \beta} \begin{pmatrix} \beta + \alpha(1 - \alpha - \beta)^m & \alpha(1 - (1 - \alpha - \beta)^m) \\ \beta(1 - (1 - \alpha - \beta)^m) & \alpha + \beta(1 - \alpha - \beta)^m \end{pmatrix} \tag{1.3}$$

for every $m \in \mathbb{N}$.

1.2.1.4 Left Eigenvectors

A vector $\varepsilon \in \mathbb{C}^n$ is called a **left eigenvector** of $A \in \mathbb{M}^{n \times n}$ if ε is an eigenvector of $A^\top$. In other words, ε is nonzero, and there exists a $\lambda \in \mathbb{C}$ such that $A^\top \varepsilon = \lambda \varepsilon$. We can alternatively write the expression as $\varepsilon^\top A = \lambda \varepsilon^\top$, which is where the name "left" eigenvector originates.

Left eigenvectors will play important roles in what follows, including that of stochastic steady states for dynamic models under a Markov assumption. To help distinguish between ordinary and left eigenvectors, we will at times call (ordinary) eigenvectors of A **right eigenvectors** of A.

If A is diagonalizable, then so is $A^\top$. To show this, let $A = PDP^{-1}$ with $D = \text{diag}(\lambda_i)$. We know from earlier discussion that the columns of P are the (right) eigenvectors of A.

EXERCISE 1.2.12. Let $Q = (P^\top)^{-1}$. Prove that $Q^\top P = I$ and $A^\top = QDQ^{-1}$.

The results of the last exercise show that, when $A = PDP^{-1}$, the columns of $(P^\top)^{-1}$ coincide with the left eigenvectors of A. (Why?) Equivalently, $A = PDQ^\top$, where $Q = (\varepsilon_1, \ldots, \varepsilon_n)$ is the $n \times n$ matrix with i-th column equal to the i-th left eigenvector of A.

EXERCISE 1.2.13. Let $(e_i)_{i=1}^n$ be right eigenvectors of A, and let $(\varepsilon_i)_{i=1}^n$ be the left eigenvectors. Prove that

$$\langle \varepsilon_i, e_j \rangle = \mathbb{1}\{i = j\} \qquad (i, j \in [n]). \tag{1.4}$$

[Hint: Use the results of Exercise 1.2.12.]

EXERCISE 1.2.14. Continuing with the notation defined above and continuing to assume that A is diagonalizable, prove that

$$A = \sum_{i=1}^n \lambda_i e_i \varepsilon_i^\top \quad \text{and} \quad A^m = \sum_{i=1}^n \lambda_i^m e_i \varepsilon_i^\top \tag{1.5}$$

for all $m \in \mathbb{N}$. The expression for A on the left-hand side of (1.5) is called the **spectral representation** of A.

EXERCISE 1.2.15. Prove that each $n \times n$ matrix $\lambda_i e_i \varepsilon_i^\top$ in the sum $\sum_{i=1}^n \lambda_i e_i \varepsilon_i^\top$ is rank 1.

1.2.1.5 Similar Matrices

Diagonalizability is a special case of a more general concept: $A \in \mathbb{M}^{n \times n}$ is called **similar** to $B \in \mathbb{M}^{n \times n}$ if there exists an invertible matrix P such that $A = PBP^{-1}$. In this terminology, A is diagonalizable if and only if it is similar to a diagonal matrix.

EXERCISE 1.2.16. Prove that similarity between matrices is an equivalence relation (see §A.1.2) on $\mathbb{M}^{n \times n}$.

EXERCISE 1.2.17. The fact that similarity is an equivalence relation on $\mathbb{M}^{n \times n}$ implies that this relation partitions $\mathbb{M}^{n \times n}$ into disjoint equivalence classes, elements of which are all similar. Prove that all matrices in each equivalence class share the same eigenvalues.

EXERCISE 1.2.18. Prove: If A is similar to B, then A^m is similar to B^m. In particular

$$A = PBP^{-1} \implies A^m = PB^m P^{-1} \text{ for all } m \in \mathbb{N}.$$

The last result is a generalization of (1.1). When A is large, calculating the powers A^k can be computationally expensive or infeasible. If, however, A is similar to some simpler matrix B, then we can take powers of B instead, and then transition back to A using the similarity relation.[5]

---

[5] The only concern with this shift process is that P can be ill-conditioned, implying that the inverse is numerically unstable.

1.2.2   The Neumann Series Lemma

Most high school students learn that, if a is a number with $|a| < 1$, then

$$\sum_{i \geqslant 0} a^i = \frac{1}{1-a}. \tag{1.6}$$

This geometric series representation extends to matrices: If A is a matrix satisfying a certain condition, then (1.6) holds, in the sense that $\sum_{i \geqslant 0} A^i = (I - A)^{-1}$. (Here I is the identity matrix.) But what is the "certain condition" that we need to place on A, which generalizes the concept $|a| < 1$ to matrices? The answer to this question involves the "spectral radius" of a matrix, which we now describe.

1.2.2.1   Spectral Radius

Fix $A \in \mathbb{M}^{n \times n}$. With $|z|$ indicating the modulus of a complex number z, the **spectral radius** of A is defined as

$$r(A) := \max\{|\lambda| : \lambda \text{ is an eigenvalue of } A\}. \tag{1.7}$$

Within economics, the spectral radius has important applications in dynamics, asset pricing, and numerous other fields. As we will see, the same concept also plays a key role in network analysis.

REMARK 1.2.1 *For any square matrix A, we have $r(A^\top) = r(A)$. This follows from the fact that A and $A^\top$ always have the same eigenvalues.*

Example 1.2.1: As usual, diagonal matrices supply the simplest example: If $D = \operatorname{diag}(d_i)$, then the spectrum $\sigma(D)$ is just $\{d_i\}_{i \in [n]}$, and hence $r(D) = \max_i |d_i|$.

After executing

```
import numpy as np
```

The following Python code computes the spectral radius of a square matrix M:

```
def spec_rad(M):
    return np.max(np.abs(np.linalg.eigvals(M)))
```

1.2.2.2   Geometric Series

We can now return to the matrix extension of (1.6) and state a formal result.

THEOREM 1.2.5 (Neumann series lemma (NSL))   *If A is in $\mathbb{M}^{n \times n}$ and $r(A) < 1$, then $I - A$ is nonsingular and*

$$(I - A)^{-1} = \sum_{m=0}^{\infty} A^m. \tag{1.8}$$

     The sum $\sum_{m=0}^{\infty} A^m$ is called the **power series** representation of $(I - A)^{-1}$. Convergence of the matrix series is understood as element-by-element convergence.

A full proof of Theorem 1.2.5 can be found in Cheney (2013) and many other sources. The core idea is simple: if $S = I + A + A^2 + \cdots$ then $I + AS = S$. Reorganizing gives $(I - A)S = I$, which is equivalent to (1.8). The main technical issue is showing that the power series converges. The full proof shows that this always holds when $r(A) < 1$.

EXERCISE 1.2.19. Fix $A \in \mathbb{M}^{n \times n}$. Prove the following: if $r(A) < 1$, then, for each $b \in \mathbb{R}^n$, the linear system $x = Ax + b$ has the unique solution $x^* \in \mathbb{R}^n$ given by

$$x^* = \sum_{m=0}^{\infty} A^m b. \tag{1.9}$$

1.2.3   The Perron–Frobenius Theorem

In this section we state and discuss a suprisingly far-reaching theorem due to Oskar Perron and Ferdinand Frobenius, which has applications in network theory, machine learning, asset pricing, Markov dynamics, nonlinear dynamics, input–output analysis, and many other fields. In essence, the theorem provides additional information about eigenvalues and eigenvectors when the matrix in question is positive in some sense.

1.2.3.1   Order in Matrix Space
We require some definitions. In what follows, for $A \in \mathbb{M}^{n \times k}$, we write

- $A \geqslant 0$ if all elements of A are nonnegative and
- $A \gg 0$ if all elements of A are strictly positive.

It's easy to imagine how nonnegativity and positivity are important notions for matrices, just as they are for numbers. However, strict positivity of every element of a matrix is hard to satisfy, especially for a large matrix. As a result, mathematicians routinely use two notions of "predominantly strictly positive," which sometimes provide sufficient positivity for the theorems that we need.

Regarding these two notions, for $A \in \mathbb{M}^{n \times n}$, we say that $A \geqslant 0$ is

- **irreducible** if $\sum_{m=0}^{\infty} A^m \gg 0$ and
- **primitive** if there exists an $m \in \mathbb{N}$ such that $A^m \gg 0$.

Evidently, for $A \in \mathbb{M}^{n \times n}$ we have

$$A \gg 0 \quad \Longrightarrow \quad A \text{ primitive} \quad \Longrightarrow \quad A \text{ irreducible} \quad \Longrightarrow \quad A \geqslant 0.$$

A nonnegative matrix is called **reducible** if it fails to be irreducible.

EXERCISE 1.2.20. By examining the expression for P_w^m in (1.3), show that P_w is

(i) irreducible if and only if $0 < \alpha, \beta \leqslant 1$; and
(ii) primitive if and only if $0 < \alpha, \beta \leqslant 1$ and $\min\{\alpha, \beta\} < 1$.

In addition to the above notation, for $A, B \in \mathbb{M}^{n \times k}$, we also write

- $A \geqslant B$ if $A - B \geqslant 0$ and $A \gg B$ if $A - B \gg 0$,
- $A \leqslant 0$ if $-A \geqslant 0$, etc.

EXERCISE 1.2.21. Show that $\leqslant$ is a partial order (see §A.2.1) on $\mathbb{M}^{n \times k}$.

The partial order $\leqslant$ discussed in Exercise 1.2.21 is usually called the **pointwise partial order** on $\mathbb{M}^{n \times k}$. Analogous notation and terminology are used for vectors.

The following exercise shows that nonnegative matrices are order-preserving maps (see §A.2.3) on vector space under the pointwise partial order – a fact we shall exploit many times.

EXERCISE 1.2.22. Show that the map $x \mapsto Ax$ is order-preserving (see §A.2.3) whenever $A \geqslant 0$ (i.e., $x \leqslant y$ implies $Ax \leqslant Ay$ for any conformable vectors x, y).

1.2.3.2   Statement of the Theorem

Let A be in $\mathbb{M}^{n \times n}$. In general, $r(A)$ is not an eigenvalue of A. For example,

$$A = \text{diag}(-1, 0) \implies \sigma(A) = \{-1, 0\} \text{ while } r(A) = 1.$$

But $r(A)$ is always an eigenvalue when $A \geqslant 0$. This is just one implication of the following famous theorem.

THEOREM 1.2.6 (Perron–Frobenius)   *If $A \geqslant 0$, then $r(A)$ is an eigenvalue of A with nonnegative real right and left eigenvectors:*

$$\exists \text{ nonzero } e, \varepsilon \in \mathbb{R}^n_+ \text{ such that } Ae = r(A)e \text{ and } \varepsilon^\top A = r(A)\varepsilon^\top. \qquad (1.10)$$

If A is irreducible, then, in addition,

(i) $r(A)$ is strictly positive and a simple eigenvalue;
(ii) the eigenvectors e and ε are everywhere positive; and
(iii) eigenvectors of A associated with other eigenvalues fail to be nonnegative.

If A is primitive, then, in addition,

(i) the inequality $|\lambda| \leqslant r(A)$ is strict for all eigenvalues λ of A distinct from $r(A)$; and
(ii) with e and ε normalized so that $\langle \varepsilon, e \rangle = 1$, we have

$$r(A)^{-m} A^m \to e\,\varepsilon^\top \qquad (m \to \infty). \qquad (1.11)$$

The fact that $r(A)$ is simple under irreducibility means that its eigenvectors are unique up to scalar multiples. We will exploit this property in several important uniqueness proofs.

In the present context, $r(A)$ is called the **dominant eigenvalue** or **Perron root** of A, while ε and e are called the **dominant left and right eigenvectors** of A, respectively.

Why do we use the word "dominant" here? To help illustrate, let us suppose that $A \in \mathbb{M}^{n \times n}$ is primitive and fix any $x \in \mathbb{R}^n$. Consider what happens to the point $x_m := A^m x$ as m grows. By (1.11) we have $A^m x \approx r(A)^m c e$ for large m, where $c = \varepsilon^\top x$. In other words, asymptotically, the sequence $(A^m x)_{m \in \mathbb{N}}$ is just scalar multiples of e, growing at rate $\ln r(A)$. Thus, $r(A)$ dominates other eigenvalues in controlling the growth rate of $A^m x$, while e dominates other eigenvectors in controlling the direction of growth.

EXERCISE 1.2.23. The $n \times n$ matrix $P := e\varepsilon^\top$ in (1.11) is called the **Perron projection** of A. Prove that $P^2 = P$ (a property that is often used to define projection matrices) and rank $P = 1$. Describe the one-dimensional space that P projects all of $\mathbb{R}^n$ into.

Example 1.2.2: Fix $A \geq 0$. If $r(A) = 1$, then $I - A$ is not invertible. To see this, observe that, by Theorem 1.2.6, since $r(A)$ is an eigenvalue of A, there exists a nonzero vector e such that $(I - A)e = 0$. The claim follows. (Why?)

1.2.3.3 Worker Dynamics II

We omit the full proof of Theorem 1.2.6, which is quite long and can be found in Meyer (2000), Seneta (2006b), or Meyer-Nieberg (2012).[6] Instead, to build intuition, let us prove the theorem in a rather simple special case.

The special case we will consider is the class of matrices

$$P_w = \begin{pmatrix} 1 - \alpha & \alpha \\ \beta & 1 - \beta \end{pmatrix} \quad \text{with} \quad 0 \leq \alpha, \beta \leq 1.$$

This example is drawn from the study of worker dynamics in §1.2.1.3.

You might recall from §1.2.1.3 that $\lambda_1 = 1$ and $\lambda_2 = 1 - \alpha - \beta$. Clearly $r(A) = 1$, so $r(A)$ is an eigenvalue, as claimed by the first part of the Perron–Frobenius theorem.

From now on we assume that $\min\{\alpha, \beta\} > 0$, which just means that we are excluding the identity matrix in order to avoid some tedious qualifying remarks.

The two right eigenvectors (e_1, e_2) and two left eigenvectors $(\varepsilon_1, \varepsilon_2)$ are, respectively,

$$e_1 := \begin{pmatrix} 1 \\ 1 \end{pmatrix}, \quad e_2 := \begin{pmatrix} -\alpha \\ \beta \end{pmatrix}, \quad \varepsilon_1 := \frac{1}{\alpha + \beta}\begin{pmatrix} \alpha \\ \beta \end{pmatrix}, \quad \text{and} \quad \varepsilon_2 := \begin{pmatrix} \alpha \\ -\alpha \end{pmatrix}.$$

EXERCISE 1.2.24. Verify these claims. (The right eigenvectors were treated in §1.2.1.3.)

EXERCISE 1.2.25. Recall from Exercise 1.2.20 that P_w is irreducible if and only if both α and β are strictly positive. Show that all the claims about irreducible

---

[6] See also Glynn and Desai (2018), which provides a new proof of the main results, based on probabilistic arguments, including extensions to infinite state spaces.

matrices in the Perron–Frobenius theorem are valid for P_w under this irreducibility condition.

EXERCISE 1.2.26. Recall from Exercise 1.2.20 that P_w is primitive if and only if $0 < \alpha, \beta \leqslant 1$ and $\min\{\alpha, \beta\} < 1$. Verify the claim (1.11) for P_w under these conditions. In doing so, you can use the expression for P_w^m in (1.3).

1.2.3.4 Bounding the Spectral Radius

Using the Perron–Frobenius theorem, we can provide useful bounds on the spectral radius of a nonnegative matrix. In what follows, fix $A = (a_{ij}) \in \mathbb{M}^{n \times n}$ and set

- $\text{rowsum}_i(A) := \sum_j a_{ij}$ = the i-th row sum of A and
- $\text{colsum}_j(A) := \sum_i a_{ij}$ = the j-th column sum of A.

LEMMA 1.2.7   *If $A \geqslant 0$, then*

(i) $\min_i \text{rowsum}_i(A) \leqslant r(A) \leqslant \max_i \text{rowsum}_i(A)$ *and*
(ii) $\min_j \text{colsum}_j(A) \leqslant r(A) \leqslant \max_j \text{colsum}_j(A)$.

Proof Let A be as stated and let e be the right eigenvector in (1.10). Since e is nonnegative and nonzero, we can and do assume that $\sum_j e_j = 1$. From $Ae = r(A)e$, we have $\sum_j a_{ij} e_j = r(A) e_i$ for all i. Summing with respect to i gives $\sum_j \text{colsum}_j(A) e_j = r(A)$. Since the elements of e are nonnegative and sum to one, $r(A)$ is a weighted average of the column sums. Hence the second pair of bounds in Lemma 1.2.7 holds. The remaining proof is similar (use the left eigenvector). □

1.3 Probability

Next we review some elements of probability that will be required for analysis of networks.

1.3.1 Discrete Probability

We first introduce probability models on finite sets and then consider sampling methods and stochastic matrices.

1.3.1.1 Probability on Finite Sets

Throughout this text, if S is a finite set, then we set

$$\mathscr{D}(S) := \left\{ \varphi \in \mathbb{R}_+^S : \sum_{x \in S} \varphi(x) = 1 \right\}$$

and call $\mathscr{D}(S)$ the set of **distributions** on S. We say that a random variable X taking values in S has distribution $\varphi \in \mathscr{D}(S)$ and write $X \overset{d}{=} \varphi$ if

$$\mathbb{P}\{X = x\} = \varphi(x) \quad \text{for all } x \in S.$$

$(0, 0, 1)$

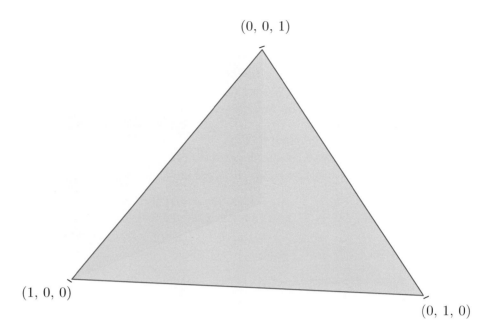

$(1, 0, 0)$

$(0, 1, 0)$

Figure 1.4 If $S = \{1, 2, 3\}$, then $\mathscr{D}(S)$ is the unit simplex in $\mathbb{R}^3$

A distribution φ can also be understood as a vector $(\varphi(x_i))_{i=1}^{n} \in \mathbb{R}^n$ (see Lemma A.1.2 in §A.1.3). As a result, $\mathscr{D}(S)$ can be viewed as a subset of $\mathbb{R}^n$. Figure 1.4 provides a visualization when $S = \{1, 2, 3\}$. Each $\varphi \in \mathscr{D}(S)$ is identified by the point $(\varphi(1), \varphi(2), \varphi(3))$ in $\mathbb{R}^3$.

More generally, if $|S| = n$, then $\mathscr{D}(S)$ can be identified with the **unit simplex** in $\mathbb{R}^n$, which is the set of all n-vectors that are nonnegative and sum to one.

Throughout, given $x \in S$, we use the symbol δ_x to represent the element of $\mathscr{D}(S)$ that puts all mass on x. In other words, $\delta_x(y) = \mathbb{1}\{y = x\}$ for all $y \in S$. In Figure 1.4, each δ_x is a vertex of the unit simplex.

We frequently make use of the **law of total probability**, which states that, for a random variable X on S and arbitrary $A \subset S$,

$$\mathbb{P}\{X \in A\} = \sum_i \mathbb{P}\{X \in A \mid X \in B_i\}\mathbb{P}\{X \in B_i\}, \qquad (1.12)$$

where $\{B_i\}$ is a partition of S (i.e., finite collection of disjoint subsets of S such that their union equals S).

EXERCISE 1.3.1. Prove (1.12) assuming $\mathbb{P}\{X \in B_i\} > 0$ for all i.

1.3.1.2   Inverse Transform Sampling

Let S be a finite set. Suppose we have the ability to generate random variables that are uniformly distributed on $(0, 1]$. We now want to generate random draws from S that are distributed according to arbitrary $\varphi \in \mathscr{D}(S)$.

Let W be uniformly distributed on $(0, 1]$, so that, for any $a \leqslant b \in (0, 1]$, we have $\mathbb{P}\{a < W \leqslant b\} = b - a$, which is the length of the interval $(a, b]$.[7] Our problem will be solved if we can create a function $z \mapsto \kappa(z)$ from $(0, 1]$ to S such that $\kappa(W)$ has distribution φ. One technique is as follows. First we divide the unit interval $(0, 1]$ into disjoint subintervals, one for each $x \in S$. The interval corresponding to x is denoted $I(x)$ and is chosen to have length $\varphi(x)$. More specifically, when $S = \{x_1, \ldots, x_N\}$, we take

$$I(x_i) := (q_{i-1}, q_i], \quad \text{where} \quad q_i := \varphi(x_1) + \cdots + \varphi(x_i) \quad \text{and} \quad q_0 := 0.$$

You can easily confirm that the length of $I(x_i)$ is $\varphi(x_i)$ for all i.

Now consider the function $z \mapsto \kappa(z)$ defined by

$$\kappa(z) := \sum_{x \in S} x \mathbb{1}\{z \in I(x)\} \qquad (z \in (0, 1]), \tag{1.13}$$

where $\mathbb{1}\{z \in I(x)\}$ is one when $z \in I(x)$ and zero otherwise. It turns out that $\kappa(W)$ has the distribution we desire.

EXERCISE 1.3.2. Prove:

(i) For all $x \in S$, we have $\kappa(z) = x$ if and only if $z \in I(x)$.
(ii) The random variable $\kappa(W)$ has distribution φ.

EXERCISE 1.3.3. Let φ, κ, and W be as defined above. Prove that $\mathbb{E}\mathbb{1}\{\kappa(W) = j\} = \varphi(j)$ holds for all $j \in [n]$.

EXERCISE 1.3.4. Using Julia or another language of your choice, implement the inverse transform sampling procedure described above when $S = \{1, 2, 3\}$ and $\varphi = (0.2, 0.1, 0.7)$. Generate $1,000,000$ (quasi)independent draws (X_i) from φ, and confirm that $(1/n) \sum_{i=1}^{n} \mathbb{1}\{X_i = j\} \approx \varphi(j)$ for $j \in \{1, 2, 3\}$.

The last exercise tells us that the law of large numbers holds in this setting, since, under this law, we expect that

$$\frac{1}{n} \sum_{i=1}^{n} \mathbb{1}\{X_i = j\} \to \mathbb{E}\mathbb{1}\{X_i = j\}$$

with probability one as $n \to \infty$. In view of Exercise 1.3.3, the right-hand side equals $\varphi(j)$.

---

[7] The probability is the same no matter whether inequalities are weak or strict.

EXERCISE 1.3.5. Suppose that, on a computer, you can generate only uniform random variables on $(0, 1]$, and you wish to simulate a flip of a biased coin with heads probability $\delta \in (0, 1)$. Propose a method.

EXERCISE 1.3.6. Suppose that, on a computer, you are able to sample from distributions φ and ψ defined on some set S. The set S can be discrete or continuous and, in the latter case, the distributions are understood as densities. Propose a method to sample on a computer from the convex combination $f(s) = \delta\varphi(s) + (1 - \delta)\psi(s)$, where $\delta \in (0, 1)$.

1.3.1.3   Stochastic Matrices

A matrix $P = (p_{ij}) \in \mathbb{M}^{n \times n}$ is called a **stochastic matrix** if

$$P \geqslant 0 \quad \text{and} \quad P\mathbb{1} = \mathbb{1}, \text{ where } \mathbb{1} \in \mathbb{R}^n \text{ is a column vector of ones.}$$

In other words, P is nonnegative and has unit row sums.

We will see many applications of stochastic matrices in this text. Often the applications are probabilistic, where each row of P is interpreted as a distribution over a finite set.

EXERCISE 1.3.7. Let P, Q be $n \times n$ stochastic matrices. Prove the following facts.

(i) PQ is also stochastic.
(ii) $r(P) = 1$.
(iii) There exists a row vector $\psi \in \mathbb{R}_+^n$ such that $\psi\mathbb{1} = 1$ and $\psi P = \psi$.

The vector ψ in part (iii) of Exercise 1.3.7 is called the *PageRank vector* by some authors, due to its prominence in Google's PageRank algorithm. We will call it a **stationary distribution** instead.[8] Stationary distributions play a key role in the theory of Markov chains, to be treated in §4.1. Ranking methods are discussed again in §1.4.3. PageRank is treated in more detail in §4.2.3.3.

1.3.2   Power Laws

Next we discuss distributions on the (nondiscrete) sets $\mathbb{R}$ and $\mathbb{R}_+$. We are particularly interested in a certain class of distributions that are apparently nonstandard and yet appear with surprising regularity in economics, social science, and the study of networks. We refer to distributions that are said to obey a "power law."

In what follows, given a real-valued random variable X, the function

$$F(t) := \mathbb{P}\{X \leqslant t\} \qquad (t \in \mathbb{R})$$

---

[8] Stationary distributions of stochastic matrices were intensively studied by many mathematicians well over a century before Larry Page and Sergey Brin patented the PageRank algorithm, so it seems unfair to allow them to appropriate the name.

is called the **cumulative distribution function** (CDF) of X. The **counter** CDF (CCDF) of X is the function $G(t) := \mathbb{P}\{X > t\} = 1 - F(t)$.

A useful property that holds for any nonnegative random variable X and $p \in \mathbb{R}_+$ is the identity

$$\mathbb{E} X^p = \int_0^\infty p t^{p-1} \mathbb{P}\{X > t\} \, dt. \tag{1.14}$$

See, for example, Çınlar (2011), p. 63.

1.3.2.1 Heavy Tails

Recall that a random variable X on $\mathbb{R}$ is said to be **normally distributed** with mean μ and variance σ^2, and we write $X \stackrel{d}{=} N(\mu, \sigma^2)$, if X has density

$$\varphi(t) := \sqrt{\frac{1}{2\pi\sigma^2}} \exp\left(\frac{-(t - \mu)^2}{2\sigma^2}\right) \qquad (t \in \mathbb{R}).$$

One notable feature of the normal density is that the tails of the density approach zero quickly. For example, $\varphi(t)$ goes to zero like $\exp(-t^2)$ as $t \to \infty$, which is extremely fast.

A random variable X on $\mathbb{R}_+$ is called **exponentially distributed** and we write $X \stackrel{d}{=} \mathrm{Exp}(\lambda)$ if, for some $\lambda > 0$, X has density

$$p(t) = \lambda e^{-\lambda t} \qquad (t \geqslant 0).$$

The tails of the exponential density go to zero like $\exp(-t)$ as $t \to \infty$, which is also relatively fast.

When a distribution is relatively light-tailed, in the sense that its tails go to zero quickly, draws rarely deviate more than a few standard deviations from the mean. In the case of a normal random variable, the probability of observing a draw more than three standard deviations above the mean is around 0.0014. For six standard deviations, the probability falls to 10^{-11}.

In contrast, for some distributions, "extreme" outcomes occur relatively frequently. The left panel of Figure 1.5 helps to illustrate this by simulating 1,000 independent draws from Student's t-distribution, with 1.5 degrees of freedom. For comparison, the right subfigure shows an equal number of independent draws from the $N(0,4)$ distribution. The Student's t draws reveal tight clustering around zero combined with a few large deviations.

Formally, a random variable X on $\mathbb{R}$ is called **light-tailed** if its **moment generating function**

$$m(t) := \mathbb{E} e^{tX} \qquad (t \geqslant 0) \tag{1.15}$$

is finite for at least one $t > 0$. Otherwise X is called **heavy-tailed**.[9]

---

[9] Terminology on heavy tails varies across the literature, but our choice is increasingly standard. See, for example, Foss et al. (2011) or Nair et al. (2021).

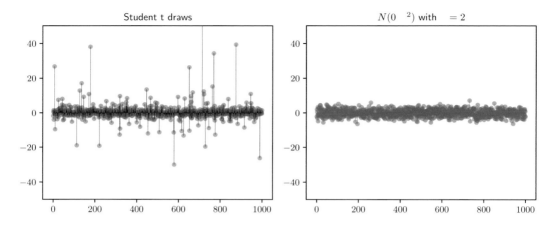

Figure 1.5 Independent draws from Student's t- and normal distributions

Example 1.3.1: If $X \stackrel{d}{=} N(\mu, \sigma^2)$, the moment generating function of X is known to be

$$m(t) = \exp\left(\mu t + \frac{t^2 \sigma^2}{2}\right) \qquad (t \geqslant 0).$$

Hence X is light-tailed.

Example 1.3.2: A random variable X on $(0, \infty)$ is said to have **lognormal density** and we write $X \stackrel{d}{=} LN(\mu, \sigma^2)$ if $\ln X \stackrel{d}{=} N(\mu, \sigma^2)$. The mean and variance of this distribution are, respectively,

$$\mathbb{E} X = \exp(\mu + \sigma^2/2) \quad \text{and} \quad \text{Var } X = (\exp(\sigma^2) - 1) \exp(2\mu + \sigma^2).$$

The moment generating function $m(t)$ is known to be infinite for all $t > 0$, so any lognormally distributed random variable is heavy-tailed.

For any random variable X and any $r \geqslant 0$, the (possibly infinite) expectation $\mathbb{E}|X|^r$ called the r-th **moment** of X.

LEMMA 1.3.1 *Let X be a random variable on $\mathbb{R}_+$. If X is light-tailed, then all of its moments are finite.*

Proof Pick any $r > 0$. We will show that $\mathbb{E} X^r < \infty$. Since X is light-tailed, there exists a $t > 0$ such that $m(t) = \mathbb{E} \exp(t X) < \infty$. For a sufficiently large constant $\bar{x}$ we have $\exp(tx) \geqslant x^r$ whenever $x \geqslant \bar{x}$. As a consequence, with F as the distribution of X, we have

$$\mathbb{E} X^r = \int_0^{\bar{x}} x^r F(\mathrm{d}x) + \int_{\bar{x}}^{\infty} x^r F(\mathrm{d}x) \leqslant \bar{x}^r + m(t) < \infty. \qquad \square$$

EXERCISE 1.3.8. Prove that the lognormal distribution has finite moments of every order.

Together with Lemma 1.3.1, Exercise 1.3.8 shows that existence of an infinite moment is a sufficient but not necessary condition for heavy tails.

1.3.2.2   Pareto Tails

Given $\alpha > 0$, a nonnegative random variable X is said to have a **Pareto tail** with **tail index** α if there exists a $c > 0$ such that

$$\lim_{t \to \infty} t^{\alpha} \, \mathbb{P}\{X > t\} = c. \tag{1.16}$$

In other words, the CCDF G of X satisfies

$$G(t) \approx ct^{-\alpha} \text{ for large } t. \tag{1.17}$$

If X has a Pareto tail for some $\alpha > 0$, then X is also said to obey a **power law**.

Example 1.3.3: A random variable X on $\mathbb{R}_+$ is said to have a **Pareto distribution** with parameters $\bar{x}, \alpha > 0$ if its CCDF obeys

$$G(t) = \begin{cases} 1 & \text{if } t < \bar{x} \\ (\bar{x}/t)^{\alpha} & \text{if } t \geqslant \bar{x} \end{cases}. \tag{1.18}$$

It should be clear that such an X has a Pareto tail with tail index α.

Regarding Example 1.3.3, note that the converse is not true: Pareto-tailed random variables are not necessarily Pareto-distributed, since the Pareto tail property only restricts the far right-hand tail.

EXERCISE 1.3.9. Show that, if X has a Pareto tail with tail index α, then $\mathbb{E}[X^r] = \infty$ for all $r \geqslant \alpha$. [Hint: Use (1.14).]

From Exercise 1.3.9 and Lemma 1.3.1, we see that every Pareto-tailed random variable is heavy-tailed. The converse is not true, since the Pareto tail property (1.16) is very specific. Despite this, it turns out that many heavy-tailed distributions encountered in the study of networks are, in fact, Pareto-tailed.

EXERCISE 1.3.10. Prove: If $X \overset{d}{=} \mathrm{Exp}(\lambda)$ for some $\lambda > 0$, then X does not obey a power law.

1.3.2.3   Empirical Power Law Plots

When the Pareto tail property holds, the CCDF satisfies $\ln G(t) \approx \ln c - \alpha \ln t$ for large t. In other words, G is eventually log linear. Figure 1.6 illustrates this using a Pareto distribution. For comparison, the CCDF of an exponential distribution is also shown.

If we replace the CCDF G with its empirical counterpart – which returns, for each x, the fraction of the sample with values greater than x – we should also obtain an approximation to a straight line under the Pareto tail assumption.

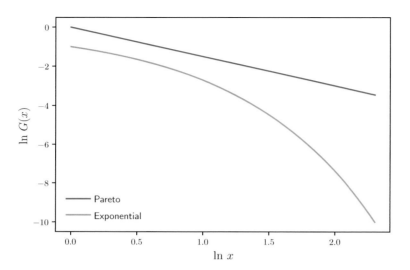

Figure 1.6 CCDF plots for the Pareto and exponential distributions

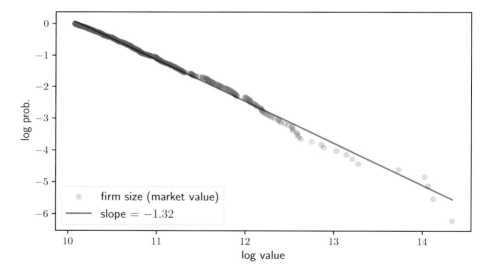

Figure 1.7 Empirical CCDF plots for largest firms (Forbes)

For example, consider the cross-sectional distribution of firm sizes. While the precise nature of this distribution depends on the measure of firm size, the sample of firms, and other factors, the typical picture is one of extreme heavy tails. As an illustration, Figure 1.7 shows an empirical CCDF log–log plot for market values of the largest 500 firms in the Forbes Global 2000 list, as of March 2021. The slope estimate and data distribution are consistent with a Pareto tail and infinite population variance.

1.3.2.4 **Discrete Power Laws**

Let X be a random variable with the Pareto distribution, as described in Example 1.3.3. The density of this random variable on the set $[\bar{x}, \infty)$ is $p(t) = ct^{-\gamma}$ with $c := \alpha \bar{x}^\alpha$ and $\gamma := \alpha + 1$. The next exercise extends this idea.

EXERCISE 1.3.11. Let X be a random variable with density p on $\mathbb{R}_+$. Suppose that, for some constants $c > 0$, $\gamma > 1$, and $\bar{x} \in \mathbb{R}_+$, we have

$$p(t) = ct^{-\gamma} \quad \text{whenever} \quad t \geqslant \bar{x}. \tag{1.19}$$

Prove that X is Pareto-tailed with tail index $\alpha := \gamma - 1$.

The discrete analog of (1.19) is a distribution on the positive integers with

$$f(k) = ck^{-\gamma} \tag{1.20}$$

for large k. In the special case where this equality holds for all $k \in \mathbb{N}$, and c is chosen so that $\sum_{k \in \mathbb{N}} f(k) = 1$, we obtain the **zeta distribution**.[10]

In general, when we see a probability mass function with the specification (1.20) for large k, we can identify this with a Pareto tail, with tail index $\alpha = \gamma - 1$. Figure 1.8 illustrates with $\gamma = 2$.

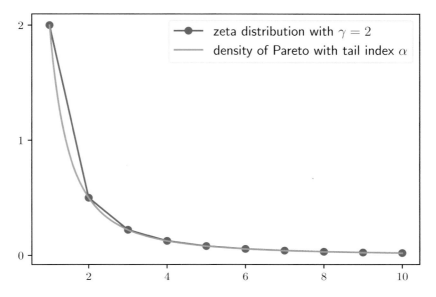

Figure 1.8 Zeta and Pareto distributions

---

[10] Obviously the correct value of c depends on γ, so we can write $c = H(\gamma)$ for some suitable function H. The correct function for this normalization is called the Riemann zeta function.

1.4   Graph Theory

Graph theory is a major branch of discrete mathematics. It plays an essential role in this text because it forms the foundations of network analysis. This section provides a concise introduction to graph theory suitable for our purposes.[11]

Graph theory has another closely related use: Many economic models are stochastic and dynamic, which means that they specify states of the world and rates of transition between them. One of the most natural ways to conceptualize these notions is to view states as vertices in a graph and transition rates as relationships between them.

We begin with definitions and fundamental concepts. We focus on directed graphs, where there is a natural asymmetry in relationships (bank A lends money to bank B, firm A supplies goods to firm B, etc.). This costs no generality, since undirected graphs (where relationships are symmetric two-way connections) can be recovered by insisting on symmetry (i.e., existence of a connection from A to B implies existence of a connection from B to A).

1.4.1   Unweighted Directed Graphs

We begin with unweighted directed graphs and examine standard properties, such as connectedness and aperiodicity.

1.4.1.1   Definition and Examples
A **directed graph** or **digraph** is a pair $\mathscr{G} = (V, E)$, where

- V is a finite nonempty set and
- E is a collection of ordered pairs $(u, v) \in V \times V$ called **edges**.

Elements of V are called the **vertices** or **nodes** of $\mathscr{G}$. Intuitively and visually, an edge (u, v) is understood as an arrow from vertex u to vertex v.

Two graphs are given in Figures 1.9 and 1.10. Each graph has three vertices. In these cases, the arrows (edges) could be thought of as representing positive possibility of transition over a given unit of time.

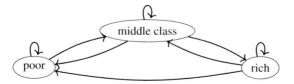

Figure 1.9 A digraph of classes

[11] Graph theory is often regarded as originating from work by the brilliant Swiss mathematician Leonhard Euler (1707–1783), including his famous paper on the "Seven Bridges of Königsberg."

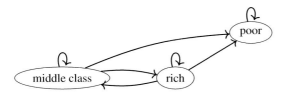

Figure 1.10 An alternative edge list

For a given edge (u, v), the vertex u is called the **tail** of the edge, while v is called the **head**. Also, u is called a **direct predecessor** of v, and v is called a **direct successor** of u. For $v \in V$, we use the following notation:

- $\mathscr{I}(v) :=$ the set of all direct predecessors of v
- $\mathscr{O}(v) :=$ the set of all direct successors of v

Also, the **in-degree** and **out-degree** of $v \in V$ are defined by

- the $i_d(v) := |\mathscr{I}(v)|$ and
- the $o_d(v) := |\mathscr{O}(v)|$, respectively.

If $i_d(v) = 0$ and $o_d(v) > 0$, then v is called a **source**. If either $\mathscr{O}(v) = \emptyset$ or $\mathscr{O}(v) = \{v\}$, then v is called a **sink**. For example, in Figure 1.10, "poor" is a sink with an in-degree of 3.

1.4.1.2 Digraphs in NetworkX

Both Python and Julia provide valuable interfaces to numerical computing with graphs. Of these libraries, the Python package NetworkX is probably the most mature and fully developed. It provides a convenient data structure for representing digraphs and implements many common routines for analyzing them. To import it into Python we run

```
import networkx as nx
```

In all of the code snippets shown below, we assume readers have executed this import statement, as well as

```
import numpy as np
import matplotlib.pyplot as plt
```

As an example, let us create the digraph in Figure 1.10, which we denote henceforth by $\mathscr{G}_p$. To do so, we first create an empty `DiGraph` object:

```
G_p = nx.DiGraph()
```

Next we populate it with nodes and edges. To do this we write down a list of all edges, with `poor` represented by `p` and so on:

```
edge_list = [
    ('p', 'p'),
    ('m', 'p'), ('m', 'm'), ('m', 'r'),
    ('r', 'p'), ('r', 'm'), ('r', 'r')
]
```

Finally, we add the edges to our `DiGraph` object:

```
for e in edge_list:
    u, v = e
    G_p.add_edge(u, v)
```

Adding the edges automatically adds the nodes, so `G_p` is now a correct representation of $\mathscr{G}_p$. For our small digraph we can verify this by plotting the graph via NetworkX with the following code:

```
fig, ax = plt.subplots()
nx.draw_spring(G_p, ax=ax, node_size=500, with_labels=True,
               font_weight='bold', arrows=True, alpha=0.8,
               connectionstyle='arc3,rad=0.25', arrowsize=20)
plt.show()
```

This code produces Figure 1.11, which matches the original digraph in Figure 1.10.

`DiGraph` objects have methods that calculate the in-degrees and out-degrees of vertices. For example,

```
G_p.in_degree('p')
```

prints 3.

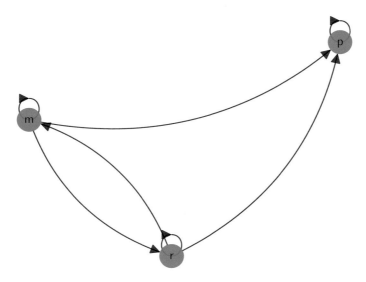

Figure 1.11 NetworkX digraph plot

1.4.1.3   Communication

Next we study communication and connectedness, which have important implications for production, financial, transportation, and other networks, as well as for dynamic properties of Markov chains.

A **directed walk** from vertex u to vertex v of a digraph $\mathscr{G}$ is a finite sequence of vertices, starting with u and ending with v, such that any consecutive pair in the sequence is an edge of $\mathscr{G}$. A **directed path** from u to v is a directed walk from u to v such that all vertices in the path are distinct. For example, in Figure 1.12, $(3, 2, 3, 2, 1)$ is a directed walk from 3 to 1 but not a directed path, while $(3, 2, 1)$ is both a directed path and a directed walk from 3 to 1.

As is standard, the **length** of a directed walk (or path) counts the number of edges rather than vertices. For example, the directed path $(3, 2, 1)$ from 3 to 1 in Figure 1.12 is said to have length 2.

Vertex v is called **accessible** (or **reachable**) from vertex u, and we write $u \to v$, if either $u = v$ or there exists a directed path from u to v. A set $U \subset V$ is called **absorbing** for the directed graph (V, E) if no element of $V \setminus U$ is accessible from U.

Example 1.4.1: Let $\mathscr{G} = (V, E)$ be a digraph representing a production network, where elements of V are sectors, and $(i, j) \in E$ means that i supplies products or services to j. Then sector m is an upstream supplier of sector ℓ whenever $m \to \ell$.

Example 1.4.2: The vertex {poor} in the Markov digraph displayed in Figure 1.10 is absorbing, since {middle, rich} is not accessible from {poor}.

Two vertices u and v are said to **communicate** if $u \to v$ and $v \to u$.

EXERCISE 1.4.1. Let (V, E) be a directed graph, and write $u \sim v$ if u and v communicate. Show that $\sim$ is an equivalence relation (see §A.1.2).

Since communication is an equivalence relation, it induces a partition of V into a finite collection of equivalence classes. Within each of these classes, all elements communicate. These classes are called **strongly connected components**. The graph itself is called **strongly connected** if there is only one such component; that is, v is accessible from u for any pair $(u, v) \in V \times V$. This corresponds to the idea that any node can be reached from any other.

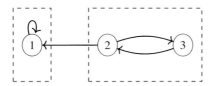

Figure 1.12 Strongly connected components of a digraph (rectangles)

Example 1.4.3: Figure 1.12 shows a digraph with strongly connected components {1} and {2, 3}. The digraph is not strongly connected.

Example 1.4.4: In Figure 1.9, the digraph is strongly connected. In contrast, in Figure 1.10, rich is not accessible from poor, so the graph is not strongly connected.

NetworkX can be used to test for communication and strong connectedness, as well as to compute strongly connected components. For example, applied to the digraph in Figure 1.12, the code

```
G = nx.DiGraph()
G.add_edge(1, 1)
G.add_edge(2, 1)
G.add_edge(2, 3)
G.add_edge(3, 2)

list(nx.strongly_connected_components(G))
```

prints [{1}, {2, 3}].

1.4.1.4   Aperiodicity

A **cycle** $(u, v, w, \ldots, u)$ of a directed graph $\mathcal{G} = (V, E)$ is a directed walk in $\mathcal{G}$ such that (i) the first and last vertices are equal and (ii) no other vertex is repeated. The graph is called a **directed acyclic graph** if it contains no cycles. The graph is called **periodic** if it contains at least one cycle and, moreover, there exists a $k > 1$ such that the length of every cycle is a multiple of k. The graph is called **aperiodic** if it is not periodic.

Example 1.4.5: In Figure 1.13, the cycles are (a, b, a), (b, a, b), (b, c, b), (c, b, c), (c, d, c) and (d, c, d). Hence the length of every cycle is 2 and the graph is periodic.

EXERCISE 1.4.2. Prove the following: If $\mathcal{G}$ is a directed acyclic graph, then, for any node u in $\mathcal{G}$, there exists a node v such that $u \to v$ and $o_d(v) = 0$.

An obvious sufficient condition for aperiodicity is existence of even one self-loop. The digraphs in Figures 1.9–1.12 are aperiodic for this reason.

The next result provides an easy way to understand aperiodicity for connected graphs. Proofs can be found in Norris (1998) and Häggström et al. (2002).

Figure 1.13 A periodic digraph

LEMMA 1.4.1 *Let $\mathcal{G} = (V, E)$ be a digraph. If $\mathcal{G}$ is strongly connected, then $\mathcal{G}$ is aperiodic if and only if, for all $v \in V$, there exists a $q \in \mathbb{N}$ such that, for all $k \geqslant q$, there exists a directed walk of length k from v to v.*

It is common to call a vertex v satisfying the condition in Lemma 1.4.1 **aperiodic**. With this terminology, Lemma 1.4.1 states that a strongly connected digraph is aperiodic if and only if every vertex is aperiodic.

NetworkX can be used to check for aperiodicity of vertices or graphs. For example, if G is a `DiGraph` object, then `nx.is_aperiodic(G)` returns `True` or `False` depending on the aperiodicity of G.

1.4.1.5 Adjacency Matrices

There is a simple map between edges of a graph with fixed vertices and a binary matrix called an adjacency matrix. The benefit of viewing connections through adjacency matrices is that they bring the power of linear algebra to the analysis of digraphs. We illustrate this briefly here and extensively in §1.4.2.

If $\mathcal{G} = (V, E)$ is a digraph with $V = \{v_1, \ldots, v_n\}$, then the $n \times n$ **adjacency matrix** corresponding to (V, E) is defined by[12]

$$A = (a_{ij})_{1 \leqslant i, j \leqslant n} \quad \text{with} \quad a_{ij} = \mathbb{1}\{(v_i, v_j) \in E\}. \tag{1.21}$$

For example, with {poor, middle, rich} mapped to $(1, 2, 3)$, the adjacency matrix corresponding to the digraph in Figure 1.10 is

$$A = \begin{pmatrix} 1 & 0 & 0 \\ 1 & 1 & 1 \\ 1 & 1 & 1 \end{pmatrix}. \tag{1.22}$$

An adjacency matrix provides us with enough information to recover the edges of a graph. More generally, given a set of vertices $V = \{v_1, \ldots, v_n\}$, an $n \times n$ matrix $A = (a_{ij})_{1 \leqslant i, j \leqslant n}$ with binary entries generates a digraph $\mathcal{G}$ with vertices V and edges

$$E = \{(v_i, v_j) \in V \times V : a_{ij} = 1\}.$$

The adjacency matrix of this graph (V, E) is A.

EXERCISE 1.4.3. A digraph (V, E) is called **undirected** if $(u, v) \in E$ implies $(v, u) \in E$. What property does this imply on the adjacency matrix?

REMARK 1.4.1 *The idea that a digraph can be undirected, presented in Exercise 1.4.3, seems contradictory. After all, a digraph is a* directed *graph. Another way to introduce undirected graphs is to define them as a vertex-edge pair (V, E), where each edge $\{u, v\} \in E$ is an unordered pair, rather than an ordered pair (u, v). However,*

---

[12] Note that, in some applied fields, the adjacency matrix is transposed: $a_{ij} = 1$ if there is an edge from j to i, rather than from i to j. We will avoid this odd and confusing definition (which contradicts both standard graph theory and standard notational conventions in the study of Markov chains).

the definition in Exercise 1.4.3 is essentially equivalent and more convenient for our purposes, since we mainly study directed graphs.

Like NetworkX, the Python library `quantecon` provides a graph object that supplies certain graph-theoretic algorithms. In the case of QuantEcon's `DiGraph` object, algorithms are implemented by interfacing with routines in SciPy, and an instance is created by supplying an adjacency matrix. For example, to construct a digraph corresponding to Figure 1.10, we use the corresponding adjacency matrix (1.22):

```
import quantecon as qe
import numpy as np


A = ((1, 0, 0),
     (1, 1, 1,),
     (1, 1, 1))
A = np.array(A)          # Convert to NumPy array
G = qe.DiGraph(A)
```

Let's print the set of strongly connected components, as a list of NumPy arrays:

```
G.strongly_connected_components
```

The output is `[array([0]), array([1, 2])]`.

1.4.2   Weighted Digraphs

Early quantitative work on networks tended to focus on unweighted digraphs, where the existence or absence of an edge is treated as sufficient information (e.g., following or not following on social media, existence or absence of a road connecting two towns). However, for some networks, this binary measure is less significant than the size or strength of the connection.

As one illustration, consider Figure 1.14, which shows flows of funds (i.e., loans) between private banks, grouped by country of origin. An arrow from Japan to the USA, say, indicates aggregate claims held by Japanese banks on all US-registered banks, as collected by the Bank of International Settlements (BIS). The size of each node in the figure is increasing in the total foreign claims of all other nodes on this node. The widths of the arrows are proportional to the foreign claims they represent.[13] The country codes are given in Table 1.1.

In this network, an edge (u, v) exists for almost every choice of u and v (i.e., almost every country in the network).[14] Hence existence of an edge is not particularly informative. To understand the network, we need to record not just the existence or

---

[13] Data for the figure was obtained from the BIS consolidated banking statistics, for Q4 of 2022. Our calculations used the immediate counterparty basis for financial claims of domestic and foreign banks, which calculates the sum of cross-border claims and local claims of foreign affiliates in both foreign and local currencies. The foreign claim of a node to itself is set to zero.

[14] In fact arrows representing foreign claims less than US$10 million are cut from Figure 1.14, so the network is even denser than it appears.

Table 1.1 Codes for the 16-country financial network

AU	Australia	DE	Germany	CL	Chile	ES	Spain
PT	Portugal	FR	France	TR	Turkey	GB	United Kingdom
US	United States	IE	Ireland	AT	Austria	IT	Italy
BE	Belgium	JP	Japan	SW	Switzerland	SE	Sweden

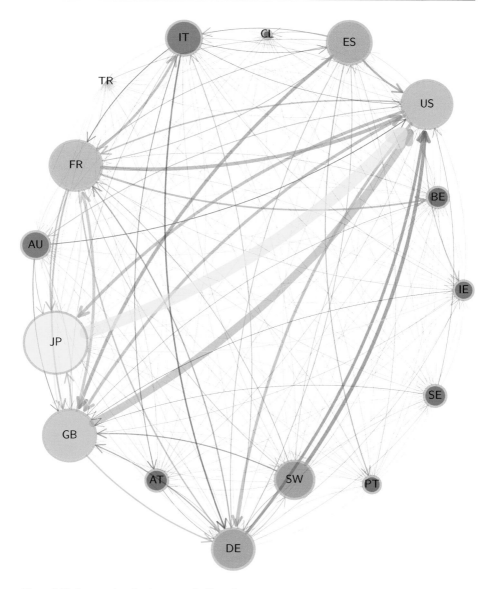

Figure 1.14 International private credit flows by country

absence of a credit flow, but also the size of the flow. The correct data structure for recording this information is a "weighted directed graph," or "weighted digraph." In this section we define this object and investigate its properties.

1.4.2.1   Definitions

A **weighted digraph** $\mathscr{G}$ is a triple (V, E, w) such that (V, E) is a digraph and w is a function from E to $(0, \infty)$, called the **weight function**.

REMARK 1.4.2   *Weights are traditionally regarded as nonnegative. In this text we insist that weights are also positive, in the sense that $w(u, v) > 0$ for all $(u, v) \in E$. The reason is that the intuitive notion of zero weight is understood, here and below, as absence of a connection. In other words, if (u, v) has "zero weight," then (u, v) is not in E, so w is not defined on (u, v).*

Example 1.4.6: As suggested by the discussion above, the graph shown in Figure 1.14 can be viewed as a weighted digraph. Vertices are countries of origin, and an edge exists between country u and country v when private banks in u lend nonzero quantities to banks in v. The weight assigned to edge (u, v) gives total loans from u to v as measured according to the discussion of Figure 1.14.

Example 1.4.7: Figure 1.15 shows a weighted digraph, with arrows representing edges of the induced digraph (compare with the unweighted digraph in Figure 1.9). The numbers next to the edges are the weights. In this case, you can think of the numbers on the arrows as transition probabilities for a household over, say, one year. For example, a rich household has a 10% chance of becoming poor.

The definitions of **accessibility, communication, periodicity,** and **connectedness** extend to any weighted digraph $\mathscr{G} = (V, E, w)$ by applying them to (V, E). For example, (V, E, w) is called strongly connected if (V, E) is strongly connected. The weighted digraph in Figure 1.15 is strongly connected.

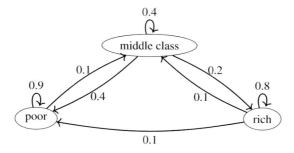

Figure 1.15 A weighted digraph

1.4.2.2 Adjacency Matrices of Weighted Digraphs

In §1.4.1.5 we discussed adjacency matrices of unweighted digraphs. The **adjacency matrix** of a *weighted* digraph (V, E, w) with vertices $\{v_1, \ldots, v_n\}$ is the matrix

$$A = (a_{ij})_{1 \leqslant i, j \leqslant n} \quad \text{with} \quad a_{ij} = \begin{cases} w(v_i, v_j) & \text{if } (v_i, v_j) \in E \\ 0 & \text{otherwise.} \end{cases}$$

Clearly, once the vertices in V are enumerated, the weight function and adjacency matrix provide the same information. We often work with the latter, since it facilitates computations.

Example 1.4.8: With {poor, middle, rich} mapped to $(1, 2, 3)$, the adjacency matrix corresponding to the weighted digraph in Figure 1.15 is

$$A = \begin{pmatrix} 0.9 & 0.1 & 0 \\ 0.4 & 0.4 & 0.2 \\ 0.1 & 0.1 & 0.8 \end{pmatrix}. \tag{1.23}$$

In QuantEcon's `DiGraph` implementation, weights are recorded via the keyword `weighted`:

```
A = ((0.9, 0.1, 0.0),
     (0.4, 0.4, 0.2),
     (0.1, 0.1, 0.8))
A = np.array(A)
G = qe.DiGraph(A, weighted=True)    # Store weights
```

REMARK 1.4.3 *Every unweighted digraph can be regarded as a weighted digraph by introducing a weight function that assigns unit weight to each edge. The resulting adjacency matrix is binary and agrees with our original definition for unweighted digraphs in* (1.21). *In this sense, the set of unweighted digraphs is a subset of the set of all weighted digraphs.*

One of the key points to remember about adjacency matrices is that taking the transpose "reverses all the arrows" in the associated digraph.

Example 1.4.9: The digraph in Figure 1.16 can be interpreted as a stylized version of a financial network, with vertices as banks and edges showing flow of funds, similar to Figure 1.14 on page 31. For example, we see that bank 2 extends a loan of size 200 to bank 3. The corresponding adjacency matrix is

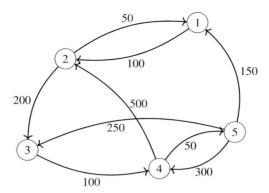

Figure 1.16 A network of credit flows across institutions

$$A = \begin{pmatrix} 0 & 100 & 0 & 0 & 0 \\ 50 & 0 & 200 & 0 & 0 \\ 0 & 0 & 0 & 100 & 0 \\ 0 & 500 & 0 & 0 & 50 \\ 150 & 0 & 250 & 300 & 0 \end{pmatrix}. \tag{1.24}$$

The transposition is

$$A^\top = \begin{pmatrix} 0 & 50 & 0 & 0 & 150 \\ 100 & 0 & 0 & 500 & 0 \\ 0 & 200 & 0 & 0 & 250 \\ 0 & 0 & 100 & 0 & 300 \\ 0 & 0 & 0 & 50 & 0 \end{pmatrix}. \tag{1.25}$$

The corresponding network is visualized in Figure 1.17. This figure shows the network of liabilities after the loans have been granted. Both of these networks (original and transpose) are useful for the analysis of financial markets (see, e.g., Chapter 5).

It is not difficult to see that each nonnegative $n \times n$ matrix $A = (a_{ij})$ can be viewed as the adjacency matrix of a weighted digraph with vertices equal to $[n]$. The weighted digraph $\mathscr{G} = (V, E, w)$ in question is formed by setting

$$V = [n], \quad E = \{(i, j) \in V \times V : a_{ij} > 0\} \quad \text{and} \quad w(i, j) = a_{ij} \text{ for all } (i, j) \in E.$$

We call $\mathscr{G}$ the **weighted digraph induced by** A.

The next exercise helps to reinforce the point that transposes reverse the edges.

EXERCISE 1.4.4. Let $A = (a_{ij})$ be a nonnegative $n \times n$ matrix, and let $\mathscr{G} = ([n], E, w)$ and $\mathscr{G}' = ([n], E', w')$ be the weighted digraphs induced by A and $A^\top$, respectively. Show that

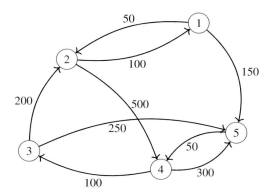

Figure 1.17 The transpose: a network of liabilities

(i) $(j, k) \in E'$ if and only if $(k, j) \in E$.

(ii) $j \rightarrow k$ in $\mathscr{G}'$ if and only if $k \rightarrow j$ in $\mathscr{G}$.

1.4.2.3 Application: Quadratic Network Games

Acemoglu et al. (2016) and Zenou (2016) consider quadratic games with n agents where agent k seeks to maximize

$$u_k(x) := -\frac{1}{2}x_k^2 + \alpha x^\top A x + x_k \varepsilon_k. \tag{1.26}$$

Here $x = (x_i)_{i=1}^n$, A is a symmetric matrix with $a_{ii} = 0$ for all i, $\alpha \in (0, 1)$ is a parameter, and $\varepsilon = (\varepsilon_i)_{i=1}^n$ is a random vector. (This is the set up for the quadratic game in §21.2.1 of Acemoglu et al. (2016).) The k-th agent takes the decisions x_j as given for all $j \neq k$ when maximizing (1.26).

In this context, A is understood as the adjacency matrix of a graph with vertices $V = [n]$, where each vertex is one agent. We can reconstruct the weighted digraph (V, E, w) by setting $w(i, j) = a_{ij}$ and letting E be all (i, j) pairs in $[n] \times [n]$ with $a_{ij} > 0$. The weights identify some form of relationship between the agents, such as influence or friendship.

EXERCISE 1.4.5. A **Nash equilibrium** for the quadratic network game is a vector $x^* \in \mathbb{R}^n$ such that, for all $i \in [n]$, the choice x_i^* of agent i maximizes (1.26) taking x_j^* as given for all $j \neq i$. Show that, whenever $r(A) < 1/\alpha$, a unique Nash equilibrium x^* exists in $\mathbb{R}^n$ and, moreover, $x^* := (I - \alpha A)^{-1} \varepsilon$.

The network game described in this section has many interesting applications, including social networks, crime networks and peer networks. References are provided in §1.5.

1.4.2.4   Properties

In this section, we examine some of the fundamental properties of and relationships among digraphs, weight functions, and adjacency matrices. Throughout this section, without loss of generality, we consider a weighted digraph with $V = [n]$.

As an additional convention, if A is an adjacency matrix, and A^k is the k-th power of A, then we write a^k_{ij} for a typical element of A^k. With this notation, we observe that, since $A^{(s+t)} = A^s A^t$, the rules of matrix multiplication imply

$$a^{s+t}_{ij} = \sum_{\ell=1}^{n} a^s_{i\ell}\, a^t_{\ell j} \qquad (i,j \in [n], \;\; s,t \in \mathbb{N}). \tag{1.27}$$

(A^0 is the identity.) The next proposition explains the significance of the powers.

PROPOSITION 1.4.2   *Let $\mathcal{G}$ be a weighted digraph with adjacency matrix A. For distinct vertices $i, j \in [n]$ and $k \in \mathbb{N}$, we have*

$$a^k_{ij} > 0 \quad \Longleftrightarrow \quad \text{there exists a directed walk of length } k \text{ from } i \text{ to } j.$$

Proof   ($\Leftarrow$) The statement is true by definition when $k = 1$. Suppose in addition that $\Leftarrow$ holds at $k - 1$, and suppose there exists a directed walk $(i, \ell, m, \ldots, n, j)$ of length k from i to j. By the induction hypothesis we have $a^{k-1}_{in} > 0$. Moreover, (n, j) is part of a directed walk, so $a_{nj} > 0$. Applying (1.27) now gives $a^k_{ij} > 0$.

($\Rightarrow$) Left as an exercise (just use the same logic).   □

Example 1.4.10: In §4.1 we show that if elements of A represent one-step transition probabilities across states, then elements of A^t, the t-th power of A, provide t-step transition probabilities. In Markov process theory, (1.27) is called the *Chapman–Kolmogorov equation.*

In this context, the next result is fundamental.

THEOREM 1.4.3   *Let $\mathcal{G}$ be a weighted digraph. The following statements are equivalent:*

(i) *$\mathcal{G}$ is strongly connected.*
(ii) *The adjacency matrix generated by $\mathcal{G}$ is irreducible.*

Proof   Let $\mathcal{G}$ be a weighted digraph with adjacency matrix A. By Proposition 1.4.2, strong connectedness of $\mathcal{G}$ is equivalent to the statement that, for each $i, j \in V$, we can find a $k \geqslant 0$ such that $a^k_{ij} > 0$. (If $i = j$ then set $k = 0$.) This, in turn, is equivalent to $\sum_{m=0}^{\infty} A^m \gg 0$, which is irreducibility of A.   □

Example 1.4.11: Strong connectivity fails in the digraph in Figure 1.18, since vertex 4 is a source. By Theorem 1.4.3, the adjacency matrix must be reducible.

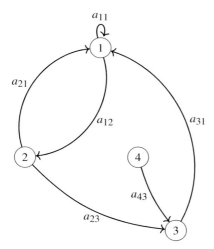

Figure 1.18 Failure of strong connectivity

We will find that the property of being primitive is valuable for analysis. (The Perron–Frobenius theorem hints at this.) What do we need to add to strong connectedness to obtain primitiveness?

THEOREM 1.4.4 *For a weighted digraph $\mathcal{G} = (V, E, w)$, the following statements are equivalent:*

(i) *$\mathcal{G}$ is strongly connected and aperiodic.*
(ii) *The adjacency matrix generated by $\mathcal{G}$ is primitive.*

Proof of Theorem 1.4.4 First we show that, if $\mathcal{G}$ is aperiodic and strongly connected, then, for all $i, j \in V$, there exists a $q \in \mathbb{N}$ such that $a_{ij}^k > 0$ whenever $k \geqslant q$. To this end, pick any i, j in V. Since $\mathcal{G}$ is strongly connected, there exists an $s \in \mathbb{N}$ such that $a_{ij}^s > 0$. Since $\mathcal{G}$ is aperiodic, we can find an $m \in \mathbb{N}$ such that $\ell \geqslant m$ implies $a_{jj}^\ell > 0$. Picking $\ell \geqslant m$ and applying (1.27), we have

$$a_{ij}^{s+\ell} = \sum_{r \in V} a_{ir}^s a_{rj}^\ell \geqslant a_{ij}^s a_{jj}^\ell > 0.$$

Thus, with $t = s + m$, we have $a_{ij}^k > 0$ whenever $k \geqslant t$.

((i) $\Rightarrow$ (ii)). By the preceding argument, given any $i, j \in V$, there exists an $s(i, j) \in \mathbb{N}$ such that $a_{ij}^m > 0$ whenever $m \geqslant s(i, j)$. Setting $k := \max s(i, j)$ over all (i, j) yields $A^k \gg 0$.

((ii) $\Rightarrow$ (i)). Suppose that A is primitive. Then, for some $k \in \mathbb{N}$, we have $A^k \gg 0$. Strong connectedness of the digraph follows directly from Proposition 1.4.2. It remains to check aperiodicity.

Aperiodicity will hold if we can establish that $a_{11}^{k+1} > 0$, since then we have a cycle of length k and another of length $k + 1$. To show that this holds, we use (1.27) to write

$$a_{11}^{k+1} = \sum_{\ell \in V} a_{1\ell} a_{\ell 1}^k \geqslant \bar{a} \sum_{\ell \in V} a_{i\ell},$$

where $\bar{a} := \min_{\ell \in V} a_{\ell 1}^k > 0$. The proof will be done if $\sum_{\ell \in V} a_{1\ell} > 0$. But this must be true, since otherwise vertex 1 is a sink, which contradicts strong connectedness. □

Example 1.4.12: In Exercise 1.2.20 we worked hard to show that P_w is irreducible if and only if $0 < \alpha, \beta \leqslant 1$, using the approach of calculating and then examining the powers of P_w (as shown in (1.3)). However, the result is trivial when we examine the corresponding digraph in Figure 1.3 and use the fact that irreducibility is equivalent to strong connectivity. Similarly, the result in Exercise 1.2.20 that P_w is primitive if and only if $0 < \alpha, \beta \leqslant 1$ and $\min\{\alpha, \beta\} < 1$ becomes much easier to establish if we examine the digraph and use Theorem 1.4.4.

1.4.3   Network Centrality

When studying networks of all varieties, a recurring topic is the relative "centrality" or "importance" of different nodes. One classic application is the ranking of web pages by search engines. Here are some examples related to economics:

- In which industry will one dollar of additional demand have the most impact on aggregate production, once we take into account all the backward linkages? In which sector will a rise in productivity have the largest effect on national output?
- A negative shock endangers the solvency of the entire banking sector. Which institutions should the government rescue, if any?
- In the network games considered in §1.4.2.3, the Nash equilibrium is $x^* = (I - \alpha A)^{-1} \varepsilon$. Players' actions are dependent on the topology of the network, as encoded in A. A common finding is that the level of activity or effort exerted by an agent (e.g., severity of criminal activity by a participant in a criminal network) can be predicted from their "centrality" within the network.

In this section we review essential concepts related to network centrality.[15]

1.4.3.1   Centrality Measures

Let G be the set of weighted digraphs. A **centrality measure** associates to each $\mathscr{G} = (V, E, w)$ in G a vector $m(\mathscr{G}) \in \mathbb{R}^{|V|}$, where the i-th element of $m(\mathscr{G})$ is interpreted as the centrality (or rank) of vertex v_i. In most cases $m(\mathscr{G})$ is nonnegative. In what follows, to simplify notation, we take $V = [n]$.

---

[15] Centrality measures are sometimes called "influence measures," particularly in connection with social networks.

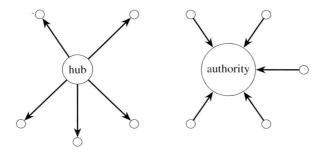

Figure 1.19 Hub vs. authority

(Unfortunately, the definitions and terminology associated with even the most common centrality measures vary widely across the applied literature. Our convention is to follow the mathematicians, rather than the physicists. For example, our terminology is consistent with Benzi and Klymko (2015).)

1.4.3.2 Authorities vs. Hubs

Search engine designers recognize that web pages can be important in two different ways. Some pages have high **hub centrality**, meaning that they *link to* valuable sources of information (e.g., news aggregation sites). Other pages have high **authority centrality**, meaning that they contain valuable information, as indicated by the number and significance of *incoming* links (e.g., websites of respected news organizations). Figure 1.19 helps to visualize the difference.

Similar ideas can be and have been applied to economic networks (often using different terminology). For example, in the production networks we study below, high hub centrality is related to upstreamness: Such sectors tend to supply intermediate goods to many important industries. Conversely, a high authority ranking will coincide with downstreamness.

In what follows we discuss both hub-based and authority-based centrality measures, providing definitions and illustrating the relationship between them.

1.4.3.3 Degree Centrality

Two of the most elementary measures of "importance" of a vertex in a given digraph $\mathcal{G} = (V, E)$ are its in-degree and out-degree. Both of these provide a centrality measure. **In-degree centrality** $i(\mathcal{G})$ is defined as the vector $(i_d(v))_{v \in V}$. **Out-degree centrality** $o(\mathcal{G})$ is defined as $(o_d(v))_{v \in V}$. If $\mathcal{G}$ is expressed as a NetworkX `DiGraph` called G (see, e.g., §1.4.1.2), then $i(\mathcal{G})$ can be calculated via

```
iG = [G.in_degree(v) for v in G.nodes()]
```

This method is relatively slow when $\mathcal{G}$ is a large digraph. Since vectorized operations are generally faster, let's look at an alternative method using operations on arrays.

To illustrate the method, recall the network of financial institutions in Figure 1.16. We can compute the in-degree and out-degree centrality measures by first converting the adjacency matrix, which is shown in (1.24), to a binary matrix that corresponds to the adjacency matrix of the same network viewed as an unweighted graph:

$$U = \begin{pmatrix} 0 & 1 & 0 & 0 & 0 \\ 1 & 0 & 1 & 0 & 0 \\ 0 & 0 & 0 & 1 & 0 \\ 0 & 1 & 0 & 0 & 1 \\ 1 & 0 & 1 & 1 & 0 \end{pmatrix}. \tag{1.28}$$

Now $U(i, j) = 1$ if and only if i points to j. The out-degree and in-degree centrality measures can be computed as

$$o(\mathcal{G}) = U\mathbb{1} \quad \text{and} \quad i(\mathcal{G}) = U^{\top}\mathbb{1}, \tag{1.29}$$

respectively. That is, summing the rows of U gives the out-degree centrality measure, while summing the columns gives the in-degree measure.

The out-degree centrality measure is a hub-based ranking, while the vector of in-degrees is an authority-based ranking. For the financial network in Figure 1.16, a high out-degree for a given institution means that it lends to many other institutions; a high in-degree indicates that many institutions lend to it.

Notice that, to switch from a hub-based ranking to an authority-based ranking, we need only transpose the (binary) adjacency matrix U. We will see that the same is true for other centrality measures. This is intuitive, since transposing the adjacency matrices reverses the directions of the edges (Exercise 1.4.4).

For a weighted digraph $\mathcal{G} = (V, E, w)$ with adjacency matrix A, the **weighted out-degree centrality** and **weighted in-degree centrality** measures are defined as

$$o(\mathcal{G}) = A\mathbb{1} \quad \text{and} \quad i(\mathcal{G}) = A^{\top}\mathbb{1}, \tag{1.30}$$

respectively, by analogy with (1.29). We present some intuition for these measures in applications below.

Unfortunately, while in- and out-degree measures of centrality are simple to calculate, they are not always informative. As an example, consider again the international credit network shown in Figure 1.14. There, an edge exists between almost every node, so the in- or out-degree-based centrality ranking fails to effectively separate the countries. This can be seen in the out-degree ranking of countries corresponding to that network in the top left panel of Figure 1.20 and in the in-degree ranking in the top right.

There are other limitations of degree-based centrality rankings. For example, suppose web page A has many inbound links, while page B has fewer. Even though page A dominates in terms of in-degree, it might be less important than web page B to, say, a potential advertiser, when the links into B are from more heavily trafficked pages. Thinking about this point suggests that importance can be recursive: The importance of a given node depends on the importance of other nodes that link to it. The next set of centrality measures we turn to has this recursive property.

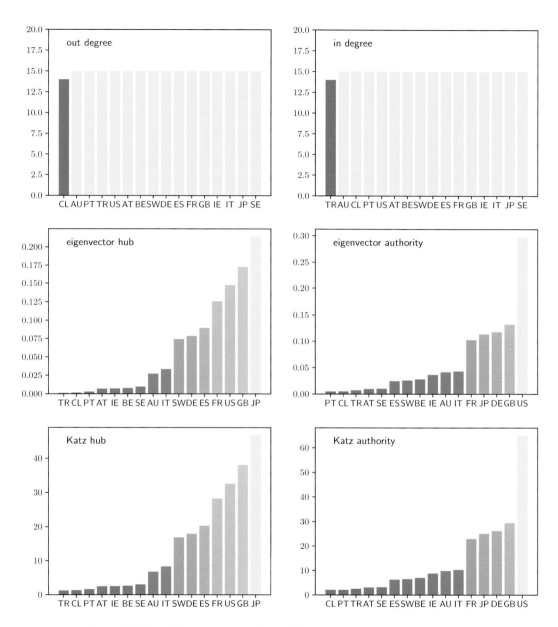

Figure 1.20 Centrality measures for the credit network

1.4.3.4   Eigenvector Centrality

Let $\mathscr{G} = (V, E, w)$ be a weighted digraph with adjacency matrix A. Recalling that $r(A)$ is the spectral radius of A, the **hub-based eigenvector centrality** of $\mathscr{G}$ is defined as the $e \in \mathbb{R}^n_+$ that solves

$$e = \frac{1}{r(A)} Ae. \tag{1.31}$$

Element-by-element, this is

$$e_i = \frac{1}{r(A)} \sum_{j \in [n]} a_{ij} e_j \qquad \text{for all } i \in [n].\qquad (1.32)$$

Note the recursive nature of the definition: The centrality obtained by vertex i is proportional to a sum of the centralities of all vertices, weighted by the "rates of flow" from i into these vertices. A vertex i is highly ranked if (a) there are many edges leaving i, (b) these edges have large weights, and (c) the edges point to other highly ranked vertices.

When we study demand shocks in §2.1.3, we will provide a more concrete interpretation of eigenvector centrality. We will see that, in production networks, sectors with high hub-based eigenvector centrality are important *suppliers*. In particular, they are activated by a wide array of demand shocks once orders flow backwards through the network.

EXERCISE 1.4.6. Show that (1.32) has a unique solution, up to a positive scalar multiple, whenever A is strongly connected.[16]

As the name suggests, hub-based eigenvector centrality is a measure of hub centrality: Vertices are awarded high rankings when they *point to* important vertices. The next two exercises help to reinforce this point.

EXERCISE 1.4.7. Show that nodes with zero out-degree always have zero hub-based eigenvector centrality.

To compute eigenvector centrality when the adjacency matrix A is primitive, we can employ the Perron–Frobenius theorem, which tells us that $r(A)^{-m} A^m \to e\,\varepsilon^\top$ as $m \to \infty$, where ε and e are the dominant left and right eigenvectors of A. This implies

$$r(A)^{-m} A^m \mathbb{1} \to ce, \quad \text{where } c := \varepsilon^\top \mathbb{1}.\qquad (1.33)$$

Thus, evaluating $r(A)^{-m} A^m \mathbb{1}$ at large m returns a scalar multiple of e. The package NetworkX provides a function for computing eigenvector centrality via (1.33).

One issue with this method is the assumption of primitivity, since the convergence in (1.33) can fail without it. The following function uses an alternative technique, based on Arnoldi iteration, which typically works even when primitivity fails. (The `authority` option is explained below.)

```
import numpy as np
from scipy.sparse import linalg

def eigenvector_centrality(A, m=40, authority=False):
    """
    Computes and normalizes the dominant eigenvector of A.
    """
```

---

[16] While the dominant eigenvector is only defined up to a positive scaling constant, this is no reason for concern, since positive scaling has no impact on the ranking. In most cases, users of this centrality ranking choose the dominant eigenvector e satisfying $\|e\| = 1$.

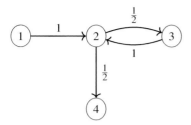

Figure 1.21 A network with a source and a sink

```
A_temp = A.T if authority else A
r, vec_r = linalg.eigs(A_temp, k=1, which='LR')
e = vec_r.flatten().real
return e / np.sum(e)
```

EXERCISE 1.4.8. Show that the digraph in Figure 1.21 is not primitive. Using the code above or another suitable routine, compute the hub-based eigenvector centrality rankings. You should obtain values close to $e = (0.3694, 0.2612, 0.3694, 0)$. Note that the sink vertex (vertex 4) obtains the lowest rank.

The middle left panel of Figure 1.20 shows the hub-based eigenvector centrality ranking for the international credit network shown in Figure 1.14. Countries that are rated highly according to this rank tend to be important players in terms of supply of credit. Japan takes the highest rank according to this measure, although countries with large financial sectors, such as Great Britain and France, are not far behind. (The color scheme in Figure 1.14 is also matched to hub-based eigenvector centrality.)

The **authority-based eigenvector centrality** of $\mathscr{G}$ is defined as the $e \in \mathbb{R}^n_+$ solving

$$e = \frac{1}{r(A)} A^\top e. \qquad (1.34)$$

The difference between (1.34) and (1.32) is just transposition of A. (Transposes do not affect the spectral radius of a matrix.) Element-by-element, this is

$$e_j = \frac{1}{r(A)} \sum_{i \in [n]} a_{ij} e_i \qquad \text{for all } j \in [n]. \qquad (1.35)$$

We see e_j will be high if many nodes with high authority rankings link to j.

The middle right panel of Figure 1.20 shows the authority-based eigenvector centrality ranking for the international credit network shown in Figure 1.14. Highly ranked countries are those that attract large inflows of credit, or credit inflows from other major players. The USA clearly dominates the rankings as a target of inter-bank credit.

EXERCISE 1.4.9. Assume that A is strongly connected. Show that authority-based eigenvector centrality is uniquely defined up to a positive scaling constant and equal to the dominant *left* eigenvector of A.

1.4.3.5   **Katz Centrality**

Eigenvector centrality can be problematic. Although the definition in (1.32) makes sense when A is strongly connected (so that, by the Perron–Frobenius theorem, $r(A) > 0$), strong connectedness fails in many real world networks. We will see examples of this in §2.1, for production networks defined by input–output matrices.

In addition, while strong connectedness yields strict positivity of the dominant eigenvector, many vertices can be assigned a zero ranking when it fails (see, e.g., Exercise 1.4.7). This zero ranking often runs counter to our intuition when we examine specific networks.

Considerations such as these encourage the use of an alternative notion of centrality for networks called Katz centrality, originally due to Katz (1953), which is positive under weaker conditions and uniquely defined up to a tuning parameter. Fixing β in $(0, 1/r(A))$, the **hub-based Katz centrality** of weighted digraph $\mathscr{G}$ with adjacency matrix A, at parameter β, is defined as the vector $\kappa := \kappa(\beta, A) \in \mathbb{R}^n_+$ that solves

$$\kappa_i = \beta \sum_{j \in [n]} a_{ij} \kappa_j + 1 \qquad \text{for all } i \in [n]. \tag{1.36}$$

The intuition is very similar to that provided for eigenvector centrality: High centrality is conferred on i when it is linked to by vertices that themselves have high centrality. The difference between (1.36) and (1.32) is just in the additive constant 1.

EXERCISE 1.4.10. Show that, under the stated condition $0 < \beta < 1/r(A)$, hub-based Katz centrality is always finite and uniquely defined by

$$\kappa = (I - \beta A)^{-1} \mathbb{1} = \sum_{\ell \geqslant 0} (\beta A)^\ell \mathbb{1}, \tag{1.37}$$

where $\mathbb{1}$ is a column vector of ones.

EXERCISE 1.4.11. We know from the Perron–Frobenius theorem that the eigenvector centrality measure will be everywhere positive when the digraph is strongly connected. A condition weaker than strong connectivity is that every vertex has positive out-degree. Show that the Katz measure of centrality is strictly positive on each vertex under this condition.

The attenuation parameter β is used to ensure that κ is finite and uniquely defined under the condition $0 < \beta < 1/r(A)$. It can be proved that, when the graph is strongly connected, hub-based (resp., authority-based) Katz centrality converges to the hub-based (resp., authority-based) eigenvector centrality as $\beta \uparrow 1/r(A)$.[17] This is why, in the bottom two panels of Figure 1.20, the hub-based (resp., authority-based) Katz centrality ranking is seen to be close to its eigenvector-based counterpart.

When $r(A) < 1$, we use $\beta = 1$ as the default for Katz centrality computations.

EXERCISE 1.4.12. Compute the hub-based Katz centrality rankings for the simple digraph in Figure 1.21 when $\beta = 1$. You should obtain $\kappa = (5, 4, 5, 1)$. Hence, the

---

[17] See, for example, Benzi and Klymko (2015).

source vertex (vertex 1) obtains equal highest rank, and the sink vertex (vertex 4) obtains the lowest rank.

Analogously, the **authority-based Katz centrality** of $\mathscr{G}$ is defined as the $\kappa \in \mathbb{R}_+^n$ that solves

$$\kappa_j = \beta \sum_{i \in [n]} a_{ij} \kappa_i + 1 \qquad \text{for all } j \in [n]. \tag{1.38}$$

EXERCISE 1.4.13. Show that, under the restriction $0 < \beta < 1/r(A)$, the unique solution to (1.38) is given by

$$\kappa = (I - \beta A^\top)^{-1} \mathbb{1} \qquad \Longleftrightarrow \qquad \kappa^\top = \mathbb{1}^\top (I - \beta A)^{-1}. \tag{1.39}$$

(Verify the stated equivalence.)

EXERCISE 1.4.14. Compute the authority-based Katz centrality rankings for the digraph in Figure 1.21 when $\beta = 1$. You should obtain $\kappa = (1, 6, 4, 4)$. Notice that the source vertex now has the lowest rank. This is due to the fact that hubs are devalued relative to authorities.

1.4.4 Scale-Free Networks

What kinds of properties do large, complex networks typically possess? One of the most striking facts about complex networks is that many exhibit the **scale-free** property, which means, loosely speaking, that the number of connections possessed by each vertex in the network follows a power law. The scale-free property is remarkable because it holds for a wide variety of networks, from social networks to citation, sales, financial, and production networks, each of which is generated by different underlying mechanisms. Nonetheless, they share this specific statistical structure.

We begin this section by defining the degree distribution and then discuss its properties, including possible power law behavior.

1.4.4.1 Empirical Degree Distributions

Let $\mathscr{G} = (V, E)$ be a digraph. Assuming without loss of generality that $V = [n]$ for some $n \in \mathbb{N}$, the **in-degree distribution** of G is the sequence $(\varphi_{in}(k))_{k=0}^n$ defined by

$$\varphi_{in}(k) = \frac{\sum_{v \in V} \mathbb{1}\{i_d(v) = k\}}{n} \qquad (k = 0, \ldots, n), \tag{1.40}$$

where $i_d(v)$ is the in-degree of vertex v. In other words, the in-degree distribution evaluated at k is the fraction of nodes in the network that have in-degree k. In Python, when $\mathscr{G}$ is expressed as a NetworkX `DiGraph` called G and `import numpy as np` has been executed, the in-degree distribution can be calculated via

```
def in_degree_dist(G):
    n = G.number_of_nodes()
    iG = np.array([G.in_degree(v) for v in G.nodes()])
```

```
phi = [np.mean(iG == k) for k in range(n+1)]
return phi
```

The **out-degree distribution** is defined analogously, replacing i_d with o_d in (1.40), and denoted by $(\varphi_{out}(k))_{k=0}^{n}$.

Recall that a digraph $\mathscr{G} = (V, E)$ is called undirected if $(u, v) \in E$ implies $(v, u) \in E$. If $\mathscr{G}$ is undirected, then $i_d(v) = o_d(v)$ for all $v \in V$. In this case we usually write φ instead of φ_{in} or φ_{out} and refer simply to the **degree-distribution** of the digraph.

A **scale-free network** is a network whose degree distribution obeys a power law, in the sense that there exist positive constants c and γ with

$$\varphi(k) \approx ck^{-\gamma} \quad \text{for large } k. \tag{1.41}$$

Here $\varphi(k)$ can refer to the in-degree or the out-degree (or both), depending on our interest. In view of the discussion in §1.3.2.4, this can be identified with the idea that the degree distribution is Pareto-tailed with tail index $\alpha = \gamma - 1$.

Although we omit formal tests, the degree distribution for the commercial aircraft international trade network shown in Figure 1.2 on page 3 is approximately scale-free. Figure 1.22 illustrates this by plotting the degree distribution alongside $f(x) = cx^{-\gamma}$ with $c = 0.2$ and $\gamma = 1.1$. (In this calculation of the degree distribution, performed by the NetworkX function `degree_histogram`, directions are ignored and the network is treated as an undirected graph.)

Attention was drawn to the scale-free nature of many networks by Barabási and Albert (1999). They found, for example, that the in-degree and out-degree distributions for internet pages connected by hyperlinks both follow power laws. In subsequent years, many networks have been found to have the scale-free property, up to a first

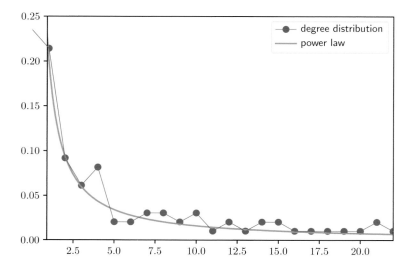

Figure 1.22 Degree distribution for international aircraft trade

approximation, including networks of followers on Twitter (Pearce, 2017; Punel and Ermagun, 2018), other social networks (Rybski et al., 2009), and academic collaboration networks (e.g., papers plus citations).

Within economics and finance, Carvalho (2014) shows that the weighted out-degree distribution for US input–output data (discussed further in Chapter 2) obeys a power law, as does the Katz centrality measure. Carvalho et al. (2021) document power law tails for the in-degree (suppliers) and out-degree (customers) distributions in a Japanese network of interacting firms. Scale-free degree distributions have also been observed in a number of financial and inter-bank credit networks (Kim et al., 2007; Ou et al., 2007; De Masi et al., 2011).

In many cases, the scale-free property of a given network has significant implications for economic outcomes and welfare. For example, a power law in input–output networks often typically indicates dominance by a small number of very large sectors or firms. This in turn affects both the dynamism of the industry and the likelihood of aggregate instability caused by firm-level shocks. We explore some of these issues in Chapter 2.

1.4.4.2   Random Graphs

One way to explore the implications of different dynamics for the degree distribution of graphs is to specify a law for generating graphs randomly and then examine the degree distribution that results. This methodology leads to insights on the kinds of mechanisms that can generate scale-free networks.

We begin with one of the most popular and elementary ways of randomly generating an undirected graph, originally examined by Erdös and Rényi (1960). The process to generate a graph $\mathcal{G} = (V, E)$ is

(i)   fix an integer $n \in \mathbb{N}$ and a $p \in (0, 1)$;
(ii) view $V := [n]$ as a collection of vertices;
(iii) let $E = \{\emptyset\}$; and
(iv) for each $(i, j) \in V \times V$ with $i \neq j$, add the undirected edge $\{i, j\}$ to the set of edges E with probability p.

In the last step additions are independent – each time, we flip an unbiased IID coin with head probability p and add the edge if the coin comes up heads.

The Python code below provides a function that can be called to randomly generate an undirected graph using this procedure. It applies the `combinations` function from the `itertools` library, which, for the call `combinations(A, k)`, returns a list of all subsets of A of size k. For example,

```
import itertools
letters = 'a', 'b', 'c'
list(itertools.combinations(letters, 2))
```

returns `[('a', 'b'), ('a', 'c'), ('b', 'c')]`.

We use `combinations` to produce the set of all possible edges and then add them to the graph with probability p:

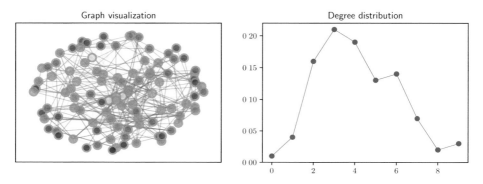

Figure 1.23   An instance of an Erdos–Renyi random graph

```
def erdos_renyi_graph(n=100, p=0.5, seed=1234):
    "Returns an Erdos-Renyi random graph."
    np.random.seed(seed)
    edges = itertools.combinations(range(n), 2)
    G = nx.Graph()

    for e in edges:
        if np.random.rand() < p:
            G.add_edge(*e)
    return G
```

(The code presented here is a simplified version of functionality provided by the library NetworkX. It is written for clarity rather than efficiency. More efficient versions can be found both in NetworkX and in Julia's Graphs.jl library.)

The left-hand side of Figure 1.23 shows one instance of a graph that was generated by the `erdos_renyi_graph` function, with $n = 100$ and $p = 0.05$. Lighter colors on a node indicate higher degree (more connections). The right-hand side shows the degree distribution, which exhibits a bell-shaped curve typical for Erdos–Renyi random graphs. In fact one can show (see, e.g., Bollobás (1999) or Durrett (2007)) that the degree distribution is binomial, with

$$\varphi(k) = \binom{n-1}{k} p^k (1-p)^{n-1-k} \qquad (k = 0, \dots, n-1).$$

1.4.4.3   Preferential Attachment

Clearly Erdos–Renyi random graphs fail to replicate the heavy right-hand tail of the degree distribution observed in many networks. In response to this, Barabási and Albert (1999) proposed a mechanism for randomly generating graphs that feature the scale-free property.

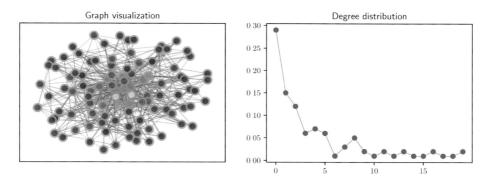

Figure 1.24 An instance of a preferential attachment random graph

The stochastic mechanism they proposed is called **preferential attachment**. In essence, each time a new vertex is added to an undirected graph, it is attached by edges to m of the existing vertices, where the probability of vertex v being selected is proportional to the degree of v. Barabási and Albert (1999) showed that the resulting degree distribution exhibits a Pareto tail in the limit as the number of vertices converges to $+\infty$. A careful proof can be found in Chapter 4 of Durrett (2007).

Although we omit details of the proof, we can see the power law emerge in simulations. For example, Figure 1.24 shows a random graph with 100 nodes generated by NetworkX's `barabasi_albert_graph` function. The number of attachments m is set to 5. The simulated degree distribution on the right-hand side of Figure 1.24 already exhibits a long right tail.

The preferential attachment model is popular not just because it replicates the scale-free property of many real-world networks but also because its mechanism is simple and plausible. For example, in citation networks, we can imagine that a well-cited paper is more likely to attract additional citations than a poorly cited paper. Similar intuition can be applied to an individual on a social network, where the number of links is measured in terms of the number of followers.

1.5   Chapter Notes

The Perron–Frobenius theorem is due to Oskar Perron (1880–1975) and Ferdinand Georg Frobenius (1849–1917). The main results were proved by 1912. As early as 1915, Dénes König (1884–1944) saw the connection between the Perron–Frobenius theorem and graph theory, and provided an alternative proof using bipartite graphs. Some of the history is discussed in Schrijver (2005).

We have already mentioned the textbooks on economic and social networks by Jackson (2010), Easley et al. (2010), Borgatti et al. (2018), and Goyal (2023), as well as the handbook by Bramoullé et al. (2016). Jackson (2014) gives a survey of the literature. Within the realm of network science, the high level texts by Newman (2018), Menczer et al. (2020), and Coscia (2021) are excellent.

One good text on graphs and graph-theoretic algorithms is Kepner and Gilbert (2011). Ballester et al. (2006) provide an interpretation of Katz centrality (which they call Bonacich centrality) in terms of Nash equilibria of quadratic games. Sharkey (2017) presents a new interpretation of Katz centrality using control theory. Polovnikov et al. (2022) use Katz centrality to uncover hidden ultimate owners in firm ownership data. Du et al. (2015) show how PageRank can be obtained as a competitive equilibrium of an economic problem. Calvó-Armengol et al. (2009) develop a model in which the outcomes for agents embedded in a network are proportional to the Katz centrality. Elliott and Golub (2019) show that, in a setting where agents can create nonrival, heterogeneous public goods, an important set of efficient solutions are characterized by contributions being proportional to agents' eigenvector centralities in the network.

Kumamoto and Kamihigashi (2018) provide a detailed survey of power laws in economics and the social sciences, including a discussion of the preferential attachment model of Barabási and Albert (1999). Newman (2005) is also highly readable. The textbook of Durrett (2007) is rigorous, carefully written, and contains interesting motivational background, as well as an extensive citation list for studies of scale-free networks.

It should be clear from the symbol $\approx$ in (1.41) that the definition of scale-free networks is not entirely rigorous. Moreover, when connecting the definition to observed networks, we cannot obtain complete clarity by taking a limit, as we did when we defined power laws in §1.3.2, since the number of vertices is always finite. This imprecision in the definition has led to heated debate (see, e.g., Holme (2019)). Given the preponderance of positive empirical studies, we take the view that, up to a reasonable degree of approximation, the scale-free property is remarkably widespread.

In §1.4.2.3 we briefly mentioned network games, social networks, and key players. These topics deserve more attention than we are able to provide. An excellent overview is given in Zenou (2016). Amarasinghe et al. (2020) apply these ideas to problems in economic development. Valuable related papers include Allouch (2015), Belhaj et al. (2016), Demange (2017), Belhaj and Deroïan (2019), and Galeotti et al. (2020).

Another topic we reluctantly omit in order to keep the textbook short is endogenous network formation in economic environments. Influential papers in this field include Jackson and Wolinsky (1996), Bala and Goyal (2000), Watts (2001), Hojman and Szeidl (2008), Galeotti and Goyal (2010), and Graham (2017).

Finally, Candogan et al. (2012) study the profit maximization problem for a monopolist who sells items to participants in a social network. The main idea is that, in certain settings, the monopolist will find it profitable to offer discounts to key players in the network. Atalay et al. (2011) argue that in-degrees observed in US buyer–supplier networks have lighter tails than a power law and supply a model that better fits their data.

2 Production

In this chapter we study production in multisector environments. The basic framework is input–output analysis, which was initiated by Wassily Leontief (1905–1999) and popularized in Leontief (1941). Input–output analysis is routinely used to organize national accounts and study inter-industry relationships. In 1973, Leontief received the Nobel Prize in Economic Sciences for his work on input–output systems.

  Input–output analysis is currently being incorporated into modern theories of trade, growth, shock propagation, and aggregate fluctuations in multisector models (§2.4 provides a detailed list of references). One of the reasons for the renewed interest is that the introduction of concepts from network analysis and graph theory has yielded new insights. This chapter provides an introduction to the main ideas.

2.1 Multisector Models

In this section we introduce the basic input–output model, explain the network interpretation of the model, and connect traditional questions, such as the relative impact of demand shocks across sectors, to network topology and network centrality.

2.1.1 Production Networks

We begin with the foundational concepts of input–output tables and how they relate to production networks. To simplify the exposition, we ignore imports and exports in what follows. (References for the general case are discussed in §2.4.)

2.1.1.1 Input–Output Analysis

Agencies tasked with gathering national and regional production accounts (such as the US Bureau of Economic Analysis) compile input–output data based on the structure set out by Leontief (1941). Firms are divided across n sectors, each of which produces a single homogeneous good. These sectors are organized into an input–output table, a highly simplified example of which is

	sector 1	sector 2	sector 3
sector 1	a_{11}	a_{12}	a_{13}
sector 2	a_{21}	a_{22}	a_{23}
sector 3	a_{31}	a_{32}	a_{33}

Entries a_{ij} are called the **input–output coefficients**;

$$a_{ij} = \frac{\text{value of sector } j\text{'s inputs purchased from sector } i}{\text{total sales of sector } j}.$$

Thus, a_{ij} is large if sector i is an important supplier of intermediate goods to sector j. The sum of the j-th column of the table gives the value of all inputs to sector j. The i-th row shows how intensively each sector uses good i as an intermediate good.

The **production coefficient matrix** $A = (a_{ij})$ induces a weighted digraph $\mathscr{G} = (V, E, w)$, where $V = [n]$ is the list of sectors and

$$E := \{(i, j) \in V \times V : a_{ij} > 0\}$$

is the edge set. The values a_{ij} show backward linkages across sectors.

Given $i \in V$, the set $\mathscr{O}(i)$ of direct successors of i is all sectors to which i supplies a positive quantity of output. The set $\mathscr{I}(i)$ is all sectors that supply a positive quantity to i.

Figure 2.1 illustrates the weighted digraph associated with the 15-sector version of the input–output tables provided by the Bureau of Economic Analysis for the year 2021.[1] An arrow from i to j indicates a positive weight a_{ij}. Weights are indicated by the widths of the arrows, which are proportional to the corresponding input–output coefficients. The sector codes are provided in Table 2.1. The sizes of vertices are proportional to their share of total sales across all sectors.

A quick look at Figure 2.1 shows that manufacturing (ma) is an important supplier for many sectors, including construction (co) and agriculture (ag). Similarly, the financial sector (fi) and professional services (pr) supply services to a broad range of sectors. On the other hand, education (ed) is relatively downstream and only a minor supplier of intermediate goods to other sectors.

The color scheme for the nodes is by hub-based eigenvector centrality, with hotter colors indicating higher centrality. Later, in §2.1.3, we will give an interpretation of hub-based eigenvector centrality for this setting that connects to the relative impact of demand shocks.

2.1.1.2   Connectedness

We will gain insights into input–output networks by applying some of the graph-theoretic notions studied in Chapter 1.4. One elementary property we can investigate is connectedness. We can imagine that demand and productivity shocks diffuse more widely through a given production network when the network is relatively connected.

---

[1] We obtain input expenditures and total sales for each sector from the Make-Use Tables of the Input–Output Accounts Data. The figure was created using Python's NetworkX library.

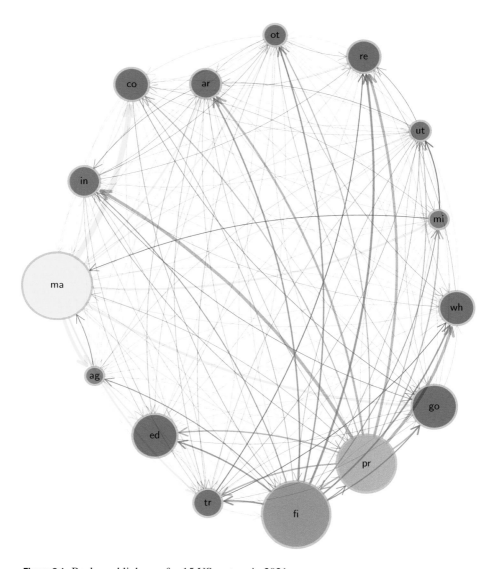

Figure 2.1 Backward linkages for 15 US sectors in 2021

Conversely, the impact of a demand shock occurring within an absorbing set will be
isolated to sectors in that set.

The 15-sector network in Figure 2.1 is strongly connected. Checking this visually
is hard, so instead we use a graph-theoretic algorithm that finds strongly connected
components from QuantEcon's `DiGraph` class. (This class is convenient for the
current problem because instances are created directly from the adjacency matrix.)
Examining the attributes of this class when the weights are given by the 15-sector
input–output model confirms its strong connectedness. The same class can be used to

Table 2.1 Sector codes for the 15-good case

Label	Sector
ag	Agriculture, forestry, fishing, and hunting
ar	Arts, entertainment, accommodation, and food services
co	Construction
ed	Educational services, health care, and social assistance
fi	Finance, insurance, real estate, rental, and leasing
go	Government
in	Information
ma	Manufacturing
mi	Mining
ot	Other services, except government
pr	Professional and business services
re	Retail trade
tr	Transportation and warehousing
ut	Utilities
wh	Wholesale trade

verify that the network is also aperiodic. Hence, the input–output matrix A is primitive. This fact will be used in computations below.

2.1.1.3   Disaggregation

Figure 2.2 repeats the graphical representation for the more disaggregated 71-sector case. Sector codes are provided in Table 2.2. Input–output coefficients below 0.01 were rounded to zero to increase visual clarity. As in the 15-sector case, the sizes of vertices and edges are proportional to share of sales and input–output coefficients, respectively. Hotter colors indicate higher hub-based eigenvector centrality (which we link to propagation of demand shocks in §2.1.3).

Unlike the 15-sector case, the 71-sector 2021 input–output matrix is not strongly connected. This is because it contains sinks (sectors with zero out-degree). For example, according to the data, sector 441 "motor vehicle and parts dealers" do not supply any intermediate inputs, although they do, of course, supply products to final consumers.

2.1.2   Equilibrium

Equilibrium in Leontief models involves tracing the impact of final demand as it flows backward through different sectors in the economy. To illustrate the challenges this generates, consider the simplified network shown in Figure 2.3. Suppose sector 3 receives a positive demand shock. Meeting this demand will require greater output from its immediate suppliers, which are sectors 2 and 4. However, an increase in production in sector 2 requires more output from sector 1, which then requires more output from sector 3, where the initial shock occurred. This, in turn, requires more

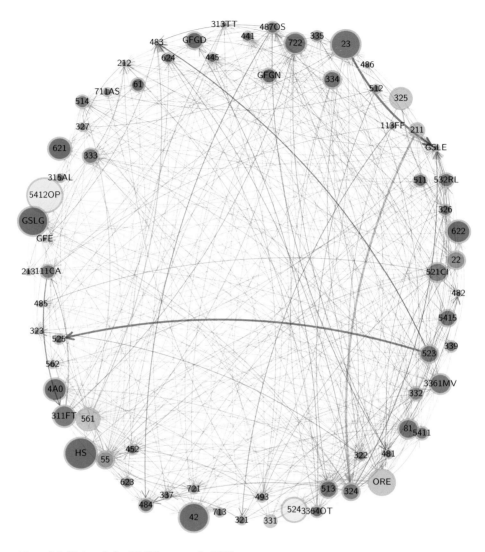

Figure 2.2 Network for 71 US sectors in 2021

output from sectors 2 and 4, and so on. Thus, the chain of backward linkages leads to an infinite loop. Resolving this tail-chasing problem requires some analysis.

2.1.2.1 Identities

To start our search for equilibria, we set

- $d_i :=$ final consumer demand for good i.
- $x_i :=$ total sales of sector i.
- $z_{ij} :=$ inter-industry sales from sector i to sector j.

Table 2.2 Sector codes for the 71-good case

IO Code	Sector	IO Code	Sector
111CA	Farms	486	Pipeline transportation
113FF	Forestry, fishing	487OS	Other transportation
211	Oil and gas extraction	493	Warehousing and storage
212	Mining, except oil, gas	511	Publishing industries
213	Mining support activities	512	Motion picture and sound
22	Utilities	513	Broadcasting, telecommunications
23	Construction	514	Data processing, internet publishing
311FT	Food, beverage, tobacco	521CI	Reserve banks, credit intermediation
313TT	Textile mills and products	523	Securities and investments
315AL	Apparel and leather	524	Insurance carriers
321	Wood products	525	Funds, trusts, financial vehicles
322	Paper products	532RL	Rental and leasing services
323	Printing	5411	Legal services
324	Petroleum and coal	5412OP	Miscellaneous technical services
325	Chemical products	5415	Computer systems design
326	Plastics, rubber	55	Firm management
327	Nonmetallic mineral products	561	Administrative
331	Primary metals	562	Waste management
332	Fabricated metal products	61	Educational services
333	Machinery	621	Ambulatory health care services
334	Computer & electronic products	622	Hospitals
335	Electrical equipment	623	Nursing and residential care facilities
3361MV	Motor vehicles, parts	624	Social assistance
3364OT	Other transportation equipment	711AS	Arts, spectator sports, museums
337	Furniture	713	Amusements, gambling, recreation
339	Miscellaneous manufacturing	721	Accommodation
4A0	Other retail	722	Food services and drinking places
42	Wholesale trade	81	Other services, except government
441	Motor vehicle and parts dealers	GFE	Federal government enterprises
445	Food and beverage stores	GFGD	Federal government (defense)
452	General merchandise stores	GFGN	Federal government (nondefense)
481	Air transportation	GSLE	State and local government enterprises
482	Rail transportation	GSLG	State and local government
483	Water transportation	HS	Housing
484	Truck transportation	ORE	Other real estate
485	Passenger transportation		

All numbers are understood to be in units of national currency – dollars, say. For each sector i, we have the accounting identity

$$x_i = \sum_{j=1}^{n} z_{ij} + d_i, \tag{2.1}$$

which states that total sales are divided between sales to other industries and sales to final consumers.

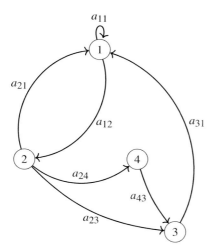

Figure 2.3 A simple production network

Notice that

$$\frac{z_{ij}}{x_j} = \text{dollar value of inputs from } i \text{ per dollar output from } j = a_{ij}, \tag{2.2}$$

where the values a_{ij} are the the input–output coefficients discussed in §2.1.1.1. Using the coefficients, (2.1) can be rewritten as

$$x_i = \sum_{j=1}^{n} a_{ij} x_j + d_i, \qquad i = 1, \dots n. \tag{2.3}$$

The first term on the right-hand side is the amount of good i required as input when the output vector is $x := (x_i)_{i=1}^n$. We can combine the n equations in (2.3) into the linear system

$$x = Ax + d. \tag{2.4}$$

2.1.2.2 Existence and Uniqueness

So far we have used no more than accounting identities and definitions. However, we would also like to use (2.4) to determine output vector x given demand vector d, taking A as fixed. As a first step, we seek conditions under which nonnegative solutions to (2.4) exist and are unique.

The **value added** of sector j is defined as sales minus spending on intermediate goods, or

$$v_j := x_j - \sum_{i=1}^{n} z_{ij}.$$

ASSUMPTION 2.1.1   *The input–output adjacency matrix A obeys*

$$\eta_j := \sum_{i=1}^{n} a_{ij} < 1 \quad \text{for all } j \in [n]. \tag{2.5}$$

EXERCISE 2.1.1. Prove that Assumption 2.1.1 holds whenever value added is strictly positive in each sector.

Exercise 2.1.1 shows that Assumption 2.1.1 is very mild. For example, in a competitive equilibrium, where firms make zero profits, positive value added means that payments to factors of production other than intermediate goods (labor, land, etc.) are strictly positive.

EXERCISE 2.1.2. Let $\eta(A) := \max_{j \in [n]} \eta_j$. Prove that $r(A) \leqslant \eta(A) < 1$ whenever Assumption 2.1.1 holds.

PROPOSITION 2.1.1   *If Assumption 2.1.1 holds, then, for each $d \geqslant 0$, the production system (2.4) has the unique nonnegative output solution*

$$x^* = Ld, \quad \text{where } L := (I - A)^{-1}. \tag{2.6}$$

Proof   By Exercise 2.1.2 and Assumption 2.1.1, we have $r(A) < 1$. Hence the Neumann series lemma (NSL) implies x^* in (2.6) is the unique solution in $\mathbb{R}^n$. Regarding nonnegativity, since A is nonnegative, so is A^i for all i. Hence $x^* \geqslant 0$, by the power series representation $L = \sum_{i=0}^{\infty} A^i$ provided by the NSL.   □

The matrix $L = (\ell_{ij})$ in (2.6) is called the **Leontief inverse** associated with the coefficient matrix A. We discuss its interpretation in §2.1.3.

EXERCISE 2.1.3. A demand vector is called nontrivial if $d \neq 0$. Let d be nontrivial, and suppose that $r(A) < 1$. Show that, in equilibrium, every sector is active (i.e., $x^* \gg 0$) when A is irreducible.

EXERCISE 2.1.4. A *closed* input–output system is one where $d = 0$. A nontrivial solution of a closed system $x = Ax$ is a nonzero $x \in \mathbb{R}_+^n$ such that $Ax^* = x^*$. Let A be irreducible. Show that no nontrivial solution exists when $r(A) < 1$. Show that a nontrivial solution exists and is unique up to constant multiples when $r(A) = 1$.

EXERCISE 2.1.5. Consider a closed input–output system defined by input matrix A. Let A be primitive. Show that every nontrivial solution is everywhere positive. Show that no nontrivial solution exists when $r(A) > 1$.

2.1.2.3   Assumptions

It is common to interpret the expression $x^* = (I - A)^{-1}d$ from (2.6) as meaning that supply is driven by demand. While this is not a universal truth, it does have plausibility in some settings, such as when analyzing demand shifts in the short run.

Changes in demand lead to changes in inventories, which typically cause firms to modify production quantities. We investigate these ideas in depth in §2.1.3.

Another assumption concerns the production function in each sector. You might recall from elementary microeconomics that the **Leontief production function** takes the form

$$x = f(z_1, \ldots, z_n) = \min\{\gamma_1 z_1, \ldots, \gamma_n z_n\}. \tag{2.7}$$

Here x is the output in a given sector, $\{\gamma_i\}$ is a set of parameters, and $\{z_i\}$ is a set of inputs. To understand why (2.7) is called a Leontief production function, note that by (2.2) we have

$$x_j = \frac{z_{ij}}{a_{ij}} \quad \text{for all } i \in [n] \text{ such that } a_{ij} > 0. \tag{2.8}$$

If we interpret $z/0 = \infty$ for all $z \geq 0$, then (2.8) implies $x_j = \min_{i \in [n]} z_{ij}/a_{ij}$. This is a version of (2.7) specialized to sector j. Hence (2.7) arises naturally from Leontief input–output analysis.

A final comment on assumptions is that, while the Leontief model is too simple for some purposes, it serves as a useful building block for more sophisticated models. We discuss one such model in §2.2.1.

2.1.3 Demand Shocks

In this section we study the impacts of changes in demand via a power series representation $\sum_{i \geq 0} A^i$ of the Leontief inverse L. We assume throughout that $r(A) < 1$, so that the series and L are finite and equal.

2.1.3.1 Response to Demand Shocks

Consider the impact of a demand shock of size Δd, so that demand shifts from d_0 to $d_1 = d_0 + \Delta d$. The equilibrium output vector shifts from $x_0 = L d_0$ to $x_1 = L d_1$. Subtracting the first of these equations from the second and expressing the result in terms of differences gives $\Delta x = L \Delta d$. Using the geometric sum version of the Leontief inverse yields

$$\Delta x = \Delta d + A(\Delta d) + A^2(\Delta d) + \cdots. \tag{2.9}$$

The sums in this term show how the shock propagates backward through the production network:

(i) Δd is the initial response in each sector;
(ii) $A(\Delta d)$ is the response generated by the first round of backward linkages;
(iii) $A^2(\Delta d)$ is the response generated by the second round; and so on.

The total response is the sum of responses at all rounds.

We can summarize the above by stating that a typical element ℓ_{ij} of $L = \sum_{m \geq 0} A^m$ shows the total impact on sector i of a unit change in demand for good j, after taking

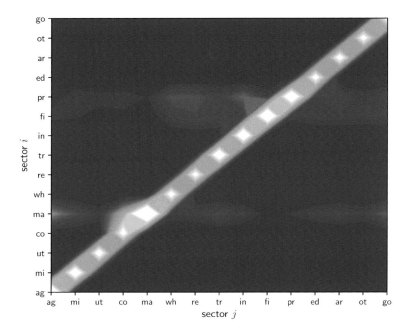

Figure 2.4 The Leontief inverse L (hotter colors indicate larger values)

into account all direct and indirect effects. L itself is reminiscent of a Keynesian multiplier: Changes in demand are multiplied by this matrix to generate the final output.

Figure 2.4 helps visualize the Leontief inverse computed from the 15-sector network. Hotter colors indicate larger values for ℓ_{ij}, with i on the vertical axis and j on the horizontal axis. We see, for example, that an increase in demand in almost any sector generates a rise in manufacturing output.

2.1.3.2   Shock Propagation

Figure 2.5 shows the impact of a given vector of demand shocks Δd on the 15-sector input–output model. In this simulation, each element of Δd was drawn independently from a uniform distribution. The vector Δd is shown visually in the panel titled "round 0," with hotter colors indicating larger values. The shock draw was relatively large in retail (re) and information (in).

The remaining rounds then show the values $A^2(\Delta d)$, $A^4(\Delta d)$, etc., with hotter colors indicating higher values. In each round, to make the within-round comparison between sectors clearer, values of the vector $A^i(\Delta d)$ are rescaled into the $[0, 1]$ interval before the color map is applied.

Note that, by round 6, the values of $A^i(\Delta d)$ have settled into a fixed pattern. (This is only up to a scaling constant, since values are rescaled into $[0, 1]$ as just discussed.) Manufacturing is the most active sector, while finance and professional services are

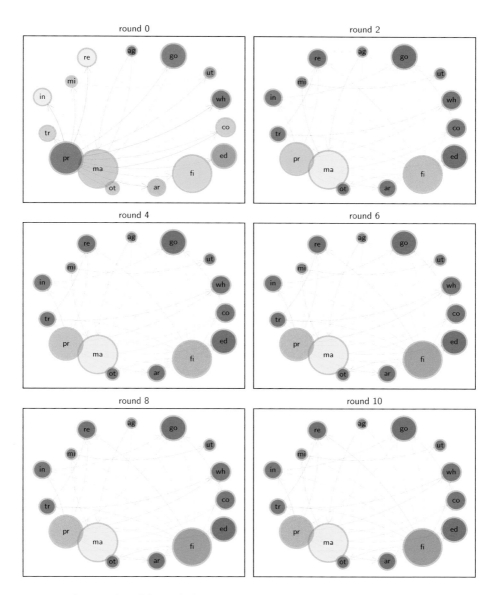

Figure 2.5 Propagation of demand shocks via backward linkages

also quite active. In fact, if we repeat the simulation with a new draw for Δd, the pattern of active sectors quickly converges to exactly the same configuration.

We can explain this phenomenon using the Perron–Frobenius theorem. Since A is primitive (in the 15-sector case), we know that $r(A)^{-m} A^m$ converges to $e\varepsilon^\top$ as $m \to \infty$, where e and ε are the dominant left and right eigenvectors, respectively, normalized so that $\langle \varepsilon, e \rangle = 1$. It follows that, for large m, we have

$$A^m(\Delta d) \approx r(A)^m \langle \varepsilon, \Delta d \rangle e. \tag{2.10}$$

In other words, up to a scaling constant, the shock response $A^m(\Delta d)$ converges to the dominant right eigenvector, which is also the hub-based eigenvector centrality measure.

In Figure 2.5, the scaling constant is not visible because the values are rescaled to a fixed interval before the color map is applied. However, (2.10) shows us its value, as well as the fact that the scaling constant converges to zero like $r(A)^m$. Hence, the dominant eigenpair $(r(A), e)$ gives us both the configuration of the response to an arbitrary demand shock and the rate at which the response dies out as we travel back through the linkages.

At this point, we recall that the sectors in Figure 2.1 were colored according to hub-based eigenvector centrality. If you compare this figure to Figure 2.5, you will be able to confirm that, at least for later rounds, the color schemes line up, as predicted by the theory. Finance (fi) and manufacturing (ma) rank highly, as does the professional services sector (pr), which includes consulting, accounting, and law.

2.1.3.3   Eigenvector Centrality

Let's look at hub-based eigenvector centrality more closely. In a production network, the hub property translates into being an important supplier. Our study of demand shocks in §2.1.3 highlighted the significance of the eigenvector measure of hub-based centrality: If sector i has high rank under this measure, then it becomes active after a large variety of different shocks. Figure 2.6 shows hub-based eigenvector centrality as a bar graph for the 15-sector case. By this measure, manufacturing is by far the most dominant sector in the US economy.

Reviewing the color scheme in Figure 2.2 based on our current understanding of eigenvector centrality, we see that technical servies (54120P), insurance (524),

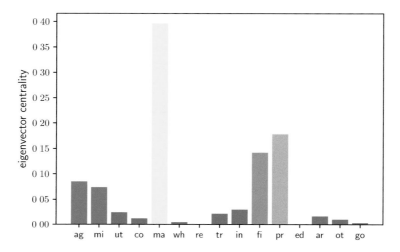

Figure 2.6 Eigenvector centrality across US industrial sectors

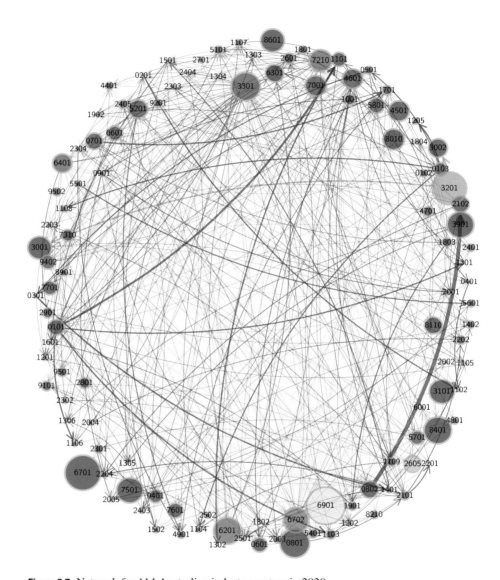

Figure 2.7 Network for 114 Australian industry sectors in 2020

chemical products (325), and primary metals (331) are among the most highly ranked, and hence a wide range of demand shocks generate high activity in these sectors.

To provide some extra context, we show the analogous figure using Australian 2020 input–output data, collected by the Australian Bureau of Statistics (Figure 2.7). Node size is proportional to sales share, and arrow width is proportional to the input–output coefficient. The color map shows hub-based eigenvector centrality.

By this measure, the highest-ranked sector is 6901, which is "professional, scientific, and technical services." This includes scientific research, engineering, computer systems design, law, accountancy, advertising, market research, and management consultancy. The next-highest sectors are construction and electricity generation.

2.1.3.4   Output Multipliers

One way to rank sectors that has a long tradition in input–output analysis is via output multipliers. The **output multiplier** of sector j, denoted below by μ_j, is usually defined as the "total sector-wide impact of an extra dollar of demand in sector j," where total means taking into account backward linkages. This measure has historically been of interest to policy makers considering the impacts of fiscal stimuli.

Recalling from §2.1.3.1 that ℓ_{ij} shows the total impact on sector i of a unit change in demand for good j, we come to the definition

$$\mu_j = \sum_{i=1}^{n} \ell_{ij} \qquad (j \in [n]).$$

In vector notation, this is $\mu^\top = \mathbb{1}^\top L$, or

$$\mu^\top = \mathbb{1}^\top (I - A)^{-1}. \tag{2.11}$$

Comparing this with (1.39), we see that the vector of output multipliers is equal to the authority-based Katz centrality measure (with the parameter β defaulting to unity).

The connection between the two measures makes sense: High authority-based centrality means that a sector has many inward links and that those links are from other important sectors. Loosely speaking, such a sector is an important buyer of intermediate inputs. A sector highly ranked by this measure that receives a demand shock will cause a large impact on the whole production network.

Figure 2.8 shows the sizes of output multipiers across 15 US industrial sectors, calculated from the same input–output data as the previous 15-sector figures, using (2.11). The highest ranks are assigned to manufacturing, agriculture, and construction.

2.1.4   Forward Linkages

Several economic questions connect to the relative "upstreamness" of a sector or production good. For example, Olabisi (2020) finds that upstreamness is related to sectoral volatility, while Antràs et al. (2012) examine the relationship between upstreamness and tendency to export. Tariff changes tend to have different aggregate effects when applied to upstream rather than downstream industries (Martin & Otto, 2020). Finally, since WWII, many developing countries have systematically supported and encouraged upstream industries (Liu, 2019).

In order to study upstreamness, we first introduce the Ghosh model for forward linkages, which uses a rearrangement of terms from the original Leontief model.

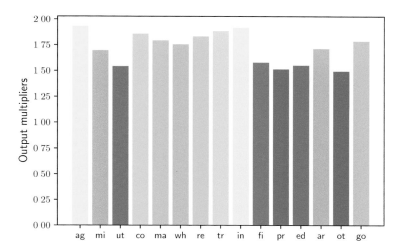

Figure 2.8 Output multipliers across 15 US industrial sectors

2.1.4.1 The Ghosh Model

Recall that $a_{ij} = z_{ij}/x_j =$ the dollar value of inputs from i per dollar of sales from j. Consider now the related quantities

$$f_{ij} := \frac{z_{ij}}{x_i} = \text{value of inputs from } i \text{ to } j \text{ per dollar output from } i. \qquad (2.12)$$

Let $F := (f_{ij})_{i,j\in[n]}$. The matrix F is called the **direct-output** matrix or the **Ghosh matrix**. Element f_{ij} can be interpreted as the size of the "forward linkage" from i to j. Analogous to A, the matrix F can be viewed as a weight function over output sectors and visualized as in Figure 2.9. This digraph uses the same data source as Figure 2.1.

EXERCISE 2.1.6. Prove that A and F are similar matrices (see §1.2.1.5) when $x \gg 0$.

Let v_j be value added in sector j (i.e., payments to factors of production other than intermediate goods). We have

$$x_j = \sum_{i=1}^{n} z_{ij} + v_j \qquad (j \in [n]). \qquad (2.13)$$

This states that (under perfect competition), the revenue of sector j is divided between spending on intermediate goods, which is the first term $\sum_{i=1}^{n} z_{ij}$, and payments to other factors of production (value added).

Using the forward linkages, we can rewrite (2.13) as $x_j = \sum_i f_{ij}x_i + v_j$ for all j or, in matrix form,

$$x^\top = x^\top F + v^\top. \qquad (2.14)$$

Taking transposes and solving under the assumption $r(F) < 1$ gives

$$x^* = (I - F^\top)^{-1}v. \qquad (2.15)$$

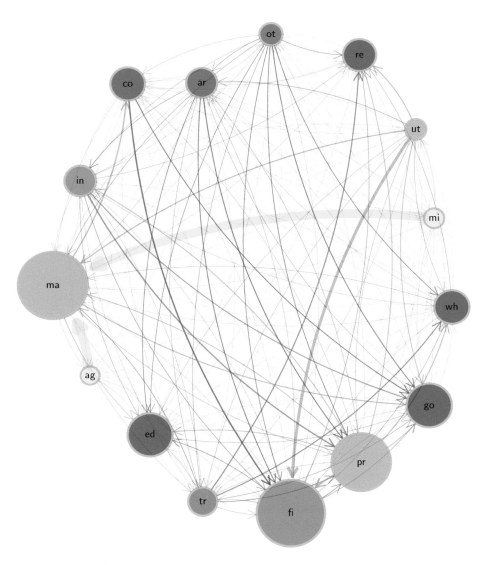

Figure 2.9 Forward linkages and upstreamness over US industrial sectors

We can think of the solution x^* in (2.15) as the amount of output necessary to acquire a given amount of value added. Since payments of value added are made to underlying factors of production, the Ghosh model is also called a "supply-side input–output model."

EXERCISE 2.1.7. In §2.1.2.2 we argued that $r(A) < 1$ will almost always hold. This carries over to $r(F)$, since $r(A) = r(F)$ whenever $x \gg 0$. Provide a proof of the last statement.

We omit a discussion of the relative merits of supply- and demand-driven input–output models. Our main interest in forward linkages is due to their connection to the topic of ranking sectors by relative upstreamness.

2.1.4.2 Upstreamness

Which industries are relatively upstream? One proposed measure of upstreamness can be found in Antràs et al. (2012). With f_{ij} as defined in (2.12), the upstreamness u_i of sector i is defined recursively by

$$u_i = 1 + \sum_{j=1}^{n} f_{ij} u_j. \tag{2.16}$$

The recursive definition of the vector u in (2.16) stems from the idea that those sectors selling a large share of their output to upstream industries should be upstream themselves.

We can write (2.16) in vector form as $u = \mathbb{1} + Fu$ and solve for u as

$$u = (I - F)^{-1} \mathbb{1}. \tag{2.17}$$

A unique nonnegative solution exists provided that $r(F) < 1$. We expect this to hold in general, due to the findings in Exercise 2.1.7.

Maintaining the convention $\beta = 1$, we see that the upstreamness measure (2.17) proposed by Antràs et al. (2012) is identical to the hub-based Katz centrality measure (1.37) for the production network with weights allocated by the forward linkage matrix F.

Figure 2.10 shows the result of computing u via (2.17), plotted as a bar graph, for the 15-sector input–output network. Consistent with expectations, the primary

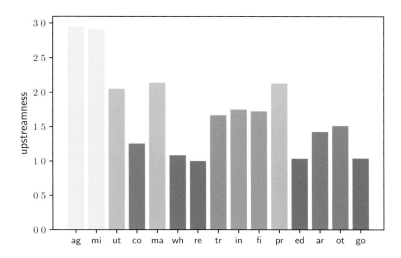

Figure 2.10 Relative upstreamness of US industrial sectors

commodity producers (agriculture and mining) are the most upstream, while retail and education are typical downstream sectors.

The nodes in Figure 2.9 are also colored by upstreamness.

2.2 General Equilibrium

One limitation of the Leontief input–output analysis from §2.1 is that demand is fixed and exogenous. In this section we embed Leontief's model in an equilibrium setting where output and prices are determined by a combination of supply and demand. One objective is to understand how an input–output structure interacts with firm-level shocks to shape aggregate volatility.

2.2.1 Supply and Demand

Our first step is to introduce and solve a multisector general equilibrium model based on Acemoglu et al. (2012) and Carvalho and Tahbaz-Salehi (2019).

2.2.1.1 Production and Prices

As in the Leontief economy, there are n sectors, also called industries, each of which produces one good. Real output in sector j is given by

$$y_j = s_j \ell_j^\alpha \prod_{i=1}^n q_{ij}^{a_{ij}}. \tag{2.18}$$

Here

- s_j is a sector-specific shock (independent across sectors);
- ℓ_j is labor input to sector j;
- q_{ij} is the amount of good i used in the production of good j; and
- α and a_{ij} take values in $(0, 1)$ and satisfy $\alpha + \sum_i a_{ij} = 1$ for all $j \in [n]$.

The last condition implies constant returns to scale (CRS) in each sector.[2]

EXERCISE 2.2.1. Let $A = (a_{ij})$ be the $n \times n$ matrix of **technical coefficients** from the Cobb–Douglas production function in (2.18). Using the stated assumptions and the results in §1.2.3.4, show that $r(A) < 1$.[3]

EXERCISE 2.2.2. Prove that $\sum_i \sum_j a_{ij}^{(m)} = n(1 - \alpha)^m$ for all $m \in \mathbb{N}$, where $a_{ij}^{(m)}$ is the (i, j)-th element of A^m.

---

[2] In order to be consistent with traditional input–output notation (see §2.1), we transpose i and j relative to sources such as Acemoglu et al. (2012) and Carvalho and Tahbaz-Salehi (2019). This is just a matter of convention.

[3] Later, in §2.3, we use additional spectral theory to prove the exact result $r(A) = 1 - \alpha$.

Firms are price takers. With p_j being the price of good j, a firm in sector j maximizes profits

$$\pi_j := p_j y_j - w\ell_j - \sum_i p_i q_{ij} \tag{2.19}$$

with respect to the $n + 1$ controls ℓ_j and $q_{1j}, \ldots, q_{nj}$.

EXERCISE 2.2.3. Show that, when prices and wages are taken as given, the unique global maximizers of (2.19) are

$$\ell_j = \alpha \frac{p_j y_j}{w} \quad \text{and} \quad q_{ij} = a_{ij} \frac{p_j y_j}{p_i} \quad (i, j \in [n]). \tag{2.20}$$

REMARK 2.2.1 *From (2.20) we have $a_{ij} = (p_i q_{ij})/(p_j y_j)$, which states that the i, j-th technical coefficient is the dollar value of inputs from i per dollar of sales from j. This coincides with the definition of a_{ij} from the discussion of input–output tables in §2.1.1.1. Hence, in the current setting, the (unobservable) technical coefficient matrix equals the (observable) input–output coefficient matrix defined in §2.1.*

Substituting the maximizers (2.20) into the production function gives

$$y_j = cs_j \left(\frac{p_j y_j}{w} \right)^\alpha \prod_{i=1}^n \left(\frac{p_j y_j}{p_i} \right)^{a_{ij}}, \tag{2.21}$$

where c is a positive constant depending only on parameters.

EXERCISE 2.2.4. Using (2.21), show that

$$\rho_j = \sum_i a_{ij} \rho_i - \varepsilon_j, \quad \text{where } \rho_j := \ln \frac{p_j}{w} \quad \text{and} \quad \varepsilon_j := \ln(cs_j).$$

Let ρ and ε be the column vectors $(\rho_i)_{i=1}^n$ and $(\varepsilon_i)_{i=1}^n$ of normalized prices and log shocks from Exericse 2.2.4. Collecting the equations stated there leads to $\rho^\top = \rho^\top A - \varepsilon^\top$, or

$$\rho = A^\top \rho - \varepsilon. \tag{2.22}$$

EXERCISE 2.2.5. Prove that

$$\rho_j = -\sum_i \varepsilon_i \ell_{ij}, \quad \text{where } L := (\ell_{ij}) := (I - A)^{-1}. \tag{2.23}$$

Why is L well defined?

As in Chapter 2, the matrix L is the Leontief inverse generated by A.

2.2.1.2 Consumption

Wages are paid to a representative household who chooses consumption to maximize utility $\sum_i \ln c_i$. In equilibrium, profits are zero, so the only income accruing to the household consists of wage income. The household supplies one unit of labor inelastically. Hence, the budget constraint is $\sum_i p_i c_i = w$.

EXERCISE 2.2.6. Show that the unique utility maximizer is the vector $(c_1, \ldots, c_n)$ that satisfies $p_i c_i = w/n$ for all $i \in [n]$. (Equal amounts are spent on each good.)

2.2.1.3   Aggregate Output

In this economy, aggregate value added (defined in §2.1.4) is equal to the wage bill. This quantity is identified with real aggregate output and referred to as GDP. The **Domar weight** of each sector is defined as its sales as a fraction of GDP:

$$h_i := \frac{p_i y_i}{w}.$$

From the closed economy market clearing condition $y_i = c_i + \sum_j q_{ij}$ and the optimality conditions, we obtain

$$y_i = \frac{w}{n p_i} + \sum_j a_{ij} \frac{p_j y_j}{p_i}. \qquad (2.24)$$

EXERCISE 2.2.7. Letting $L = (\ell_{ij})$ be the Leontief inverse and using (2.24), show that Domar weights satisfy

$$h_i = \frac{1}{n} \sum_j \ell_{ij} \qquad \text{for all } i \in [n].$$

EXERCISE 2.2.8. Prove that $\sum_{i=1}^n h_i = 1/\alpha$.

From the results of Exercise 2.2.4 we obtain $\ln w = \ln p_j + \sum_i \varepsilon_i \ell_{ij}$. Setting $g := \ln w$ and summing yields

$$ng = \sum_j \ln p_j + \sum_i \varepsilon_i \sum_j \ell_{ij}.$$

Normalizing prices so that $\sum_i \ln p_i = 0$, this simplifies to

$$g = \sum_i \varepsilon_i h_i. \qquad (2.25)$$

Thus, log GDP is the inner product of sectoral shocks and the Domar weights.

2.2.2   The Granular Hypothesis

We have just constructed a multisector model of production and output. We plan to use this model to study shock propagation and aggregate fluctuations. Before doing so, however, we provide a relatively simple and network-free discussion of shock propagation. The first step is to connect the propagation of shocks to the firm size distribution. Later, in §2.2.3, we will see how these ideas relate to the general equilibrium model and the topology of the production network.

2.2.2.1 Aggregate vs. Idiosyncratic Shocks

Some fluctuations in aggregate variables, such as GDP growth and the unemployment rate, can be tied directly to large exogenous changes in the aggregate environment. One obvious example is the jump in the US unemployment rate from 3.5% to 14.8% between February and April 2020, which was initiated by the onset of the COVID pandemic and the resulting economic shutdown.

Other significant fluctuations lack clear macro-level causes. For example, researchers offer mixed explanations for the 1990 US recession, including "technology shocks," "consumption shocks," and loss of "confidence" (Cochrane, 1994). However, these explanations are either difficult to verify on the basis of observable outcomes or require exogenous shifts in variables that should probably be treated as endogenous.

One way to account for at least some of the variability observed in output growth across most countries is on the basis of firm-level and sector-specific productivity and supply shocks. Examples of sector-specific shocks include

(i) the spread of African Swine Fever to China in 2018;
(ii) the Great East Japan Earthquake of 2011 and resulting tsunami, which triggered meltdowns at three reactors in the Fukushima Daiichi Nuclear Power Plant; and
(iii) the destruction of Asahi Kasei Microdevices' large scale integrated circuit factory in Miyazaki Prefecture in October 2020.

In the discussion below, we investigate the extent to which firm-level shocks can drive fluctuations in aggregate productivity.

2.2.2.2 The Case of Many Small Firms

It has been argued that idiosyncratic, firm-level shocks can only account for a very small fraction of aggregate volatility (see, e.g., Dupor (1999)). The logical heart of this argument is the dampening effect of averaging over independent random variables. To illustrate the main idea, we follow a simple model of production without linkages across firms by Gabaix (2011).

Suppose there are n firms, with the size of the i-th firm, measured by sales, denoted by S_i. Since all sales fulfill final demand, GDP is given by $Y := \sum_{i=1}^{n} S_i$. We use primes for next period values and Δ for first differences (e.g., $\Delta S_i = S_i' - S_i$). We assume that firm growth $\Delta S_i / S_i$ is equal to $\sigma_F \varepsilon_i$, where $\{\varepsilon_i\}$ is a collection of IID random variables corresponding to firm-level idiosyncratic shocks. We also assume that $\text{Var}(\varepsilon_i) = 1$, so that σ_F represents firm-level growth volatility.

GDP growth is then

$$G := \frac{\Delta Y}{Y} = \frac{\sum_{i=1}^{n} \Delta S_i}{Y} = \sigma_F \sum_{i=1}^{n} \frac{S_i}{Y} \varepsilon_i.$$

EXERCISE 2.2.9. Treating the current firm size distribution $\{S_i\}$ and hence GDP as given, show that, under the stated assumptions, the standard deviation of GDP growth $\sigma_G := (\operatorname{Var} G)^{1/2}$ is

$$\sigma_G = \sigma_F H_n, \quad \text{where} \quad H_n := \left(\sum_{i=1}^{n} \left(\frac{S_i}{Y} \right)^2 \right)^{1/2}. \tag{2.26}$$

If, say, all firms are equal size, so that $n S_i = Y$, this means that $\sigma_G = \sigma_F / \sqrt{n}$, so volatility at the aggregate level is very small when the number of firms is large. For example, if the number of firms n is 10^6, which roughly matches US data, then

$$\frac{\sigma_G}{\sigma_F} = H_n = \left(\frac{1}{10^6} \right)^{1/2} = 10^{-3} = 0.001. \tag{2.27}$$

Hence firm-level volatility accounts for only 0.1% of aggregate volatility.

To be more concrete, Gabaix (2011) calculates $\sigma_F = 12$, which means that, by (2.27), $\sigma_G = 0.012\%$. But the volatility of GDP growth is actually far higher. Indeed, Figure 2.11 reports that, for the USA, σ_G is approximately 2%, which is two orders of magnitude greater. The core message is that, under the stated assumptions, firm-level shocks explain only a tiny part of aggregate volatility.

2.2.2.3 The Effect of Heavy Tails

There are some obvious problems with the line of reasoning used in §2.2.2.2. One is that firms are assumed to be of identical size. In reality, most firms are small to medium, while a relative few are enormous. For example, in the USA, sectors such as technology, electronics, and retail are each dominated by a small number of very large firms.

Gabaix (2011) emphasized that we can get closer to actual GDP volatility by more thoughtful specification of the firm size distribution. Altering the distribution $\{S_i\}_{i=1}^n$ changes the value H_n in (2.27), which is called the **Herfindahl index**. This index is often applied to a group of firms in a sector to measure industry concentration. For given aggregate output Y, the Herfindahl index is minimized when $S_i = S_j$ for all i, j. This is the case we considered above. The index is maximized at $H_n = 1$ when a single firm dominates all sales. By (2.27), a larger Herfindahl index will increase σ_G relative to σ_F, which allows firm-level shocks to account for more of aggregate volatility.

Calculation of H_n is challenging because the entire firm size distribution $\{S_i\}_{i=1}^n$ is difficult to observe. Nonetheless, we can estimate H_n by (a) estimating a population probability distribution that fits the empirical distribution $\{S_i\}_{i=1}^n$ and (b) using analysis or Monte Carlo simulations to calculate typical values of H_n.

For step (a), Gabaix (2011) cites the study of Axtell (2001), which finds the firm size distribution to be Pareto with tail index 1.059. If we repeatedly draw $\{S_i\}_{i=1}^n$ from a Pareto distribution with $\alpha = 1.059$ and $n = 10^6$, record the value of H_n after

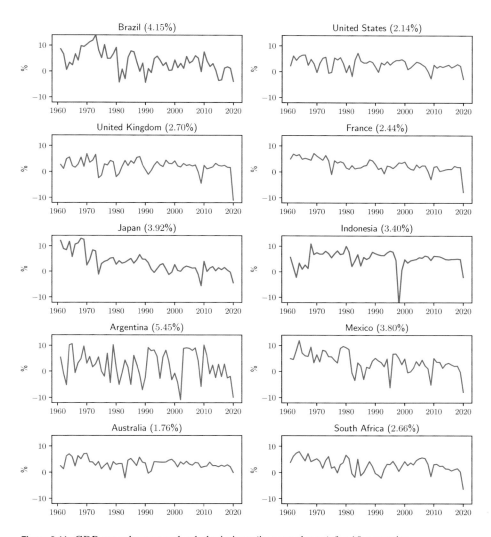

Figure 2.11 GDP growth rates and std. deviations (in parentheses) for 10 countries

each draw, and then take the median value as our estimate, we obtain $H_n \approx 0.88$. In other words, under the Pareto assumption just stated, firm-level volatility accounts for almost 90% of aggregate volatility. In essence, this means that, to explain aggregate volatility, we need to look no further than firm-level shocks.

2.2.2.4 Sensitivity Analysis

The finding in the previous paragraph is quite striking. How seriously should we take it?

One issue is that the figure $H_n \approx 0.88$ is not robust to small changes in assumptions. For example, the regression in Figure 1.7 suggests that we take 1.32 as our estimate for the tail index α, rather than Axtell's value of 1.059. If we rerun the same calculation with $\alpha = 1.32$, the estimated value of H_n falls to 0.018. In other words, firm-level shocks account for only 1.8% of aggregate volatility.

Another issue is that the large value for H_n obtained under Axtell's parameterization is very sensitive to the parametric family chosen for the firm size distribution. The next exercise illustrates this.

EXERCISE 2.2.10. Figure 1.7 suggests only that the far right tail of the firm size distribution obeys a Pareto law. In fact, some authors argue that the lognormal distribution provides a better fit than the Pareto distribution (Kondo et al. (2020) provide a recent discussion). So suppose now that $\{S_i\}$ is n IID draws from the $LN(\mu, \sigma^2)$ distribution (as given in Example 1.3.2), where μ, σ are parameters.[4] Implement and run Algorithm 1. Set $m = 10^3$ and $n = 10^6$. Choose μ and σ so that the mean and median of the $LN(\mu, \sigma^2)$ distribution agree with that of the standard Pareto distribution with tail index α, which are $\alpha/(\alpha - 1)$ and $2^{1/\alpha}$, respectively. As in Gabaix (2011), set $\alpha = 1.059$. What estimate do you obtain for H_n? How much of aggregate volatility is explained?

1　**for** j *in* $1, \ldots, m$ **do**
2　　| 　generate n independent draws $\{S_i^j\}$ from the $LN(\mu, \sigma^2)$ distribution ;
3　　| 　compute the Herfindahl index H_n^j corresponding to $\{S_i^j\}$;
4　**end**
5　set H_n equal to the median value of $\{H_n^j\}_{j=1}^m$;
6　**return** H_n

Algorithm 1: Generate an estimate of H_n under lognormality

2.2.3　Network Structure and Shock Propagation

The sensitivity analysis in §2.2.2.4 suggests we should be skeptical of the claim that firm-level shocks explain most aggregate-level shocks that we observe. This means that either micro-level shocks account for only a small fraction of aggregate volatility or, alternatively, that the model is too simple, and micro-level shocks are amplified through some other mechanism.

An obvious way to explore this further is to allow linkages between firms, in the sense that the inputs for some firms are outputs for others. Such an extension opens up the possibility that shocks propagate through the network. This seems plausible even for the sector-specific shocks listed above, such as the Great East Japan Earthquake.

---

[4] In other words, each S_i is an independent copy of the random variable $S := \exp(\mu + \sigma Z)$, where Z is standard normal.

Although the initial impact was focused on electricity generation, the flow-on effects for other sectors were rapid and substantial (Carvalho et al., 2021).

To investigate more deeply, we connect our discussion of the granular hypothesis back to the multisector models with linkages studied above, allowing us to study flow-on and multiplier effects across industries.

2.2.3.1   Industry Concentration and Shocks

From (2.25) and the independence of sectoral shocks, the standard deviation σ_g of log GDP is given by

$$\sigma_g = \sigma H_n, \quad \text{where} \quad H_n := \left(\sum_{i=1}^n h_i^2 \right)^{1/2}, \tag{2.28}$$

where σ is the standard deviation of each ε_i.

Note that the expression for aggregate volatility takes the same form as (2.26) from our discussion of the granular hypothesis in §2.2.2, where H_n was called the Herfindahl index. Once again, this index is the critical determinant of how much firm-level volatility passes through to aggregate volatility. In particular, as discussed in §2.2.2.3, independent firm-level shocks cannot explain aggregate volatility unless H_n is large, which in turn requires that the components of the vector h are relatively concentrated in a single or small number of sectors.

To investigate an extreme case, we recall from Exercise 2.2.8 that $\sum_{i=1}^n h_i = 1/\alpha$. The Herfindahl index is $H_n := \|h\|$, where $\| \cdot \|$ is the Euclidean norm.

EXERCISE 2.2.11. Show that the minimizer of $\|h\|$ given $\sum_{i=1}^n h_i = 1/\alpha$ is the constant vector where $h_i = 1/(\alpha n)$ for all i.

Under this configuration of sector shares,

$$H_n = \frac{1}{n\alpha} \|\mathbb{1}\| = \frac{1}{n\alpha} \sqrt{n} = O\left(\frac{1}{\sqrt{n}} \right).$$

Hence, by (2.28), we have $\sigma_g = O(n^{-1/2})$. This is the classic diversification result. The standard deviation of log GDP goes to zero like $n^{-1/2}$, as in the identical firm size case in §2.2.2.2.

Now let's consider the other extreme:

EXERCISE 2.2.12. Show that the maximum of $H_n = \|h\|$ under the constraint $\sum_{i=1}^n h_i = 1/\alpha$ is $1/\alpha$, attained by setting $h_k = 1/\alpha$ for some k and $h_j = 0$ for other indices.

This is the extreme case of zero diversification. By (2.25), log GDP is then

$$g = \sum_i \varepsilon_i h_i = \frac{1}{\alpha} \varepsilon_k.$$

The volatility of log GDP is constant in n, rather than declining in the number of sectors. In other words, idiosyncratic and aggregate shocks are identical.

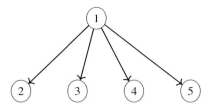

Figure 2.12 Star network with single hub

2.2.3.2   The Role of Network Topology

In the previous section we looked at two extreme cases, neither of which is realistic. Now we look at intermediate cases. In doing so, we note an interesting new feature: Unlike the analysis in §2.2.2, where the sector shares were chosen from some fixed distribution, the Herfindahl index is now determined by the network structure of production.

To see this, we can use the results of Exercise 2.2.7 to obtain

$$h = \frac{1}{n} L \mathbb{1} = \frac{1}{n} \sum_{m \geqslant 0} A^m \mathbb{1}.$$

Recalling our discussion in §1.4.3.5, we see that the vector of Domar weights is just a rescaling of the vector of hub-based Katz centrality rankings for the input–output matrix. Thus, the propagation of sector-specific productivity shocks up to the aggregate level depends on the distribution of Katz centrality across sectors. The more "unequal" this distribution, the larger the pass through.

Figures 2.12 and 2.13 show some examples of different network configurations, each of which is associated with a different Katz centrality vector. Not surprisingly, the symmetric network has a constant centrality vector, so that all sectors have equal centrality. This is the maximum diversification case, as discussed in §2.2.3.1. The other two cases have nonconstant centrality vectors and hence greater aggregate volatility.[5]

EXERCISE 2.2.13. Let the nonzero input–output coefficients a_{ij} shown by the arrows in Figures 2.12 and 2.13 all have equal value 0.2. Show computationally that the hub-based Katz centrality vectors for the hub and star networks are

$$\kappa_h = (1.8, 1, 1, 1, 1) \quad \text{and} \quad \kappa_s = (1.2, 1.2, 1.2, 1.2, 1),$$

respectively (for nodes $1, \ldots, 5$).

The results of Exercise 2.2.13 show that the hub network has the more unequal Katz centrality vector. Not surprisingly, the source node in the hub has a high hub-

---

[5] The captions in Figure 2.13 refer to these two cases as "star networks," in line with recent usage in multisector production models. In graph theory, a star network is an *un*directed graph that (a) is strongly connected and (b) has only one node with degree greater than one.

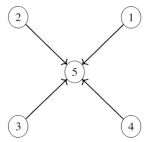

(a) Star network with single authority

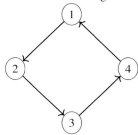

(b) Symmetric network

Figure 2.13 Symmetric and asymmetric networks

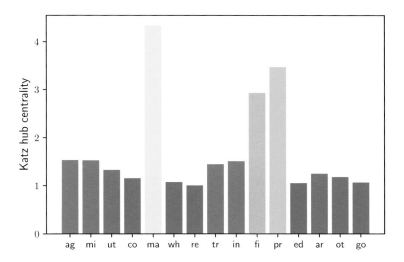

Figure 2.14 Hub-based Katz centrality across 15 US industrial sectors

based centrality ranking. Productivity shocks affecting this sector have a large effect on aggregate GDP.

Figure 2.14 shows hub-based Katz centrality computed from the 15-sector input–output data for 2021. We can see that productivity shocks in manufacturing will have a significantly larger impact on aggregate output than shocks in, say, retail or education.

2.2.3.3   Supply Shocks vs. Demand Shocks

In the previous section we saw that the degree to which a productivity shock propagates through the economy depends on the hub-based centrality ranking of the relevant sector. This is intuitive. Sectors that act like hubs supply many sectors, so changes in productivity in these sectors will have large flow-on effects.

This is in contrast to what we learned in §2.1.3.4, where a high authority-based centrality measure leads to high shock propagation. The difference can be explained by the source of the shocks: In §2.1.3.4, we were concerned with the impact of demand shocks. Demand shocks to sector i have large flow-on effects when many sectors purchase inputs from sector i. Hence, authority-based centrality measures are appropriate for studying this case.

2.3   More Spectral Theory

This is a relatively technical section, which analyzes aspects of vector dynamics and spectral theory in more depth. It is aimed at readers who are interested in further mathematical discussion of the theory treated above. The ideas studied here are applied to production problems to generate additional insights into the existence and uniqueness of equilibria, as well as later topics such as convergence of distributions for Markov models on networks.

2.3.1   Vector Norms

In this section we learn about abstract vector norms on $\mathbb{R}^n$ and provide several examples. Later we will see how the different norms are related and how they can be useful for some kinds of network analysis.

2.3.1.1   Norms

A function $\| \cdot \| \colon \mathbb{R}^n \to \mathbb{R}$ is called a **norm** on $\mathbb{R}^n$ if, for any $\alpha \in \mathbb{R}$ and $u, v \in \mathbb{R}^n$,

(a) $\|u\| \geqslant 0$ (nonnegativity)
(b) $\|u\| = 0 \iff u = 0$ (positive definiteness)
(c) $\|\alpha u\| = |\alpha| \|u\|$ and   (positive homogeneity)
(d) $\|u + v\| \leqslant \|u\| + \|v\|$ (triangle inequality)

The Euclidean norm is a norm on $\mathbb{R}^n$, as suggested by its name.

Example 2.3.1: The ℓ_1 **norm** of a vector $u \in \mathbb{R}^n$ is defined by

$$u = (u_1, \ldots, u_n) \mapsto \|u\|_1 := \sum_{i=1}^{n} |u_i|. \tag{2.29}$$

In machine learning applications, $\|\cdot\|_1$ is sometimes called the "Manhattan norm," and $d_1(u, v) := \|u - v\|_1$ is called the "Manhattan distance" or "taxicab distance" between vectors u and v. We will refer to it more simply as the ℓ_1 **distance** or ℓ_1 **deviation**.

EXERCISE 2.3.1. Verify that the ℓ_1 norm on $\mathbb{R}^n$ satisfies (a)–(d) above.

The ℓ_1 norm and the Euclidean norm are special cases of the so-called ℓ_p **norm**, which is defined for $p \geqslant 1$ by

$$u = (u_1, \ldots, u_n) \mapsto \|u\|_p := \left(\sum_{i=1}^{n} |u_i|^p \right)^{1/p}. \tag{2.30}$$

It can be shown that $u \mapsto \|u\|_p$ is a norm for all $p \geqslant 1$, as suggested by the name (see, e.g., Kreyszig (1978)). For this norm, the subadditivity in (d) is called **Minkowski's inequality**.

Since the Euclidean case is obtained by setting $p = 2$, the Euclidean norm is also called the ℓ_2 norm, and we write $\|\cdot\|_2$ rather than $\|\cdot\|$ when extra clarity is required.

EXERCISE 2.3.2. Prove that $u \mapsto \|u\|_\infty := \max_{i=1}^{n} |u_i|$ is also a norm on $\mathbb{R}^n$.

(The symbol $\|u\|_\infty$ is used because, $\forall u \in \mathbb{R}^n$, we have $\|u\|_p \to \|u\|_\infty$ as $p \to \infty$.) This norm is called the **supremum norm**.

EXERCISE 2.3.3. The so-called ℓ_0 "norm" $\|u\|_0 := \sum_{i=1}^{n} \mathbb{1}\{u_i \neq 0\}$, routinely used in data science applications, is *not* in fact a norm on $\mathbb{R}^n$. Prove this.

2.3.1.2 Equivalence of Vector Norms

When u and $(u_m) := (u_m)_{m \in \mathbb{N}}$ are all elements of $\mathbb{R}^n$, we say that (u_m) **converges** to u and write $u_m \to u$ if

$$\|u_m - u\| \to 0 \text{ as } m \to \infty \text{ for some norm } \|\cdot\| \text{ on } \mathbb{R}^n.$$

It might seem that this definition is imprecise. Don't we need to clarify that the convergence is with respect to a particular norm?

In fact we do not. This is because any two norms $\|\cdot\|_a$ and $\|\cdot\|_b$ on $\mathbb{R}^n$ are **equivalent**, in the sense that there exist finite constants M, N such that

$$M\|u\|_a \leqslant \|u\|_b \leqslant N\|u\|_a \quad \text{for all } u \in \mathbb{R}^n. \tag{2.31}$$

EXERCISE 2.3.4. Let us write $\|\cdot\|_a \sim \|\cdot\|_b$ if there exist finite M, N such that (2.31) holds. Prove that $\sim$ is an equivalence relation on the set of norms on $\mathbb{R}^n$.

EXERCISE 2.3.5. Let $\|\cdot\|_a$ and $\|\cdot\|_b$ be any two norms on $\mathbb{R}^n$. Given a point u in $\mathbb{R}^n$ and a sequence (u_m) in $\mathbb{R}^n$, use (2.31) to confirm that $\|u_m - u\|_a \to 0$ implies $\|u_m - u\|_b \to 0$ as $m \to \infty$.

Another way to understand $u_m \to u$ is via **pointwise convergence**: Each element of the vector sequence u_m converges to the corresponding element of u. Pointwise and norm convergence are equivalent, as the next result makes clear.

LEMMA 2.3.1   *Fix $(u_m) \subset \mathbb{R}^n$, $u \in \mathbb{R}^n$, and norm $\| \cdot \|$ on $\mathbb{R}^n$. Taking $m \to \infty$, the following statements are equivalent:*

(i) $\|u_m - u\| \to 0$;

(ii) $\langle a, u_m \rangle \to \langle a, u \rangle$ *for all $a \in \mathbb{R}^n$; and*

(iii) (u_m) *converges pointwise to u.*

EXERCISE 2.3.6. Prove Lemma 2.3.1.

EXERCISE 2.3.7. Using Lemma 2.3.1, provide a simple proof of the fact that convergence in $\mathbb{R}^n$ is preserved under addition and scalar multiplication: If $u_m \to x$ and $v_m \to y$ in $\mathbb{R}^n$, while $\alpha_m \to \alpha$ in $\mathbb{R}$, then $u_m + v_m \to x + y$ and $\alpha_m u_m \to \alpha x$.

2.3.2   Matrix Norms

In some applications, the number of vertices n of a given digraph is measured in millions or billions. This means that the adjacency matrix A is enormous. To control complexity, A must often be replaced by a sparse approximation A_s. It is natural to require that A and A_s are close. But how should we define this?

More generally, how can we impose a metric on a set of matrices to determine similarity or distance between them? One option is to follow the example of vectors on $\mathbb{R}^n$ and introduce a norm on $\mathbb{M}^{n \times k}$. With such a norm $\| \cdot \|$ in hand, we can regard A and A_s as close when $\|A - A_s\|$ is small.

For this and other reasons, we now introduce the notion of a matrix norm.

2.3.2.1   Definition

Analogous to vectors on $\mathbb{R}^n$, we will call a function $\| \cdot \|$ from $\mathbb{M}^{n \times k}$ to $\mathbb{R}_+$ a **norm** if for any $A, B \in \mathbb{M}^{n \times k}$,

(a) $\|A\| \geqslant 0$ (nonnegativity)

(b) $\|A\| = 0 \iff u = 0$ (positive definiteness)

(c) $\|\alpha A\| = |\alpha| \|A\|$ and   (positive homogeneity)

(d) $\|A + B\| \leqslant \|A\| + \|B\|$ (triangle inequality)

The distance between two matrices A, B is then specified as $\|A - B\|$.

Unlike vectors, matrices have a product operation defined over all conformable matrix pairs. We want matrix norms to interact with this product in a predictable way. For example, it is helpful for analysis when a matrix norm $\| \cdot \|$ is **submultiplicative**, meaning that

$$\|AB\| \leqslant \|A\| \cdot \|B\| \quad \text{for all conformable matrices } A, B. \tag{2.32}$$

A useful implication of (2.32) is that $\|A^i\| \leqslant \|A\|^i$ for any $i \in \mathbb{N}$ and $A \in \mathbb{M}^{n \times n}$, where A^i is the i-th power of A.

2.3.2.2   The Frobenius Norm

One way to construct a norm on matrix space $\mathbb{M}^{n \times k}$ is to first introduce the **Frobenius inner product** of matrices $A = (a_{ij}), B = (b_{ij})$ as

$$\langle A, B \rangle_F := \sum_{i=1}^{n} \sum_{j=1}^{n} a_{ij} b_{ij} = \text{trace}(AB^\top) = \text{trace}(BA^\top). \tag{2.33}$$

From this inner product, the **Frobenius norm** of $A \in \mathbb{M}^{n \times k}$ is defined as

$$\|A\|_F := \langle A, A \rangle_F^{1/2}. \tag{2.34}$$

In essence, the Frobenius norm converts an $n \times k$ matrix into an nk vector and computes the Euclidean norm.

The Frobenius norm is submultiplicative. The next exercise asks you to prove this in one special case.

EXERCISE 2.3.8. Suppose that A is a row vector and B is a column vector. Show that (2.32) holds in this case when $\| \cdot \|$ is the Frobenius norm.

2.3.2.3   The Operator Norm

Another important matrix norm is the **operator norm**, defined at $A \in \mathbb{M}^{n \times k}$ by

$$\|A\| := \sup\{\|Au\| : u \in \mathbb{R}^k \text{ and } \|u\| = 1\}, \tag{2.35}$$

where the norm $\| \cdot \|$ on the right hand size of (2.35) is the Euclidean norm on $\mathbb{R}^n$.

Example 2.3.2: If $A = \text{diag}(a_i)$, then, for any $u \in \mathbb{R}^n$ we have $\|Au\|^2 = \sum_i (a_i u_i)^2$. To maximize this value subject to $\sum_i u_i^2 = 1$, we pick j such that $a_j^2 \geqslant a_i^2$ for all i and set $u_i = \mathbb{1}\{i = j\}$. The maximized value of $\|Au\|$ is then

$$\|A\| = \sqrt{a_j^2} = \max_{i \in [n]} |a_i|.$$

EXERCISE 2.3.9. Show that $\|A\|$ equals the supremum of $\|Au\|/\|u\|$ over all $u \neq 0$.

EXERCISE 2.3.10. It is immediate from the definition of the operator norm that

$$\|Au\| \leqslant \|A\| \cdot \|u\| \qquad \forall u \in \mathbb{R}^n. \tag{2.36}$$

Using this fact, prove that the operator norm is submultiplicative.

EXERCISE 2.3.11. Let $\| \cdot \|$ be the operator norm on $\mathbb{M}^{n \times n}$. Show that, for each $A \in \mathbb{M}^{n \times n}$, we have

(i) $\|A\|^2 = r(A^\top A)$;
(ii) $r(A)^k \leqslant \|A^k\|$ for all $k \in \mathbb{N}$; and
(iii) $\|A^\top\| = \|A\|$.

2.3.2.4   Other Matrix Norms

Two other useful matrix norms are the ℓ_1 and ℓ_∞ norms given by

$$\|A\|_1 := \sum_{i=1}^{n} \sum_{j=1}^{k} |a_{ij}| \quad \text{and} \quad \|A\|_\infty := \max_{i \in [n], \, j \in [k]} |a_{ij}|.$$

EXERCISE 2.3.12. Prove that both are norms on $\mathbb{M}^{n \times k}$.

EXERCISE 2.3.13. Prove that both norms are submultiplicative.

2.3.2.5   Equivalence of Matrix Norms

In §2.3.1.2 we saw that all norms on $\mathbb{R}^n$ are equivalent. Exactly the same result holds true for matrix norms: Any two norms $\| \cdot \|_a$ and $\| \cdot \|_b$ on $\mathbb{M}^{n \times k}$ are **equivalent**, in the sense that there exist finite constants M, N such that

$$M\|A\|_a \leqslant \|A\|_b \leqslant N\|A\|_a \quad \text{for all } A \in \mathbb{M}^{n \times k}. \tag{2.37}$$

A proof can be found (for abstract finite-dimensional vector space) in Bollobás (1999).

Analogous to the vector case, given A and $(A_m) := (A_m)_{m \in \mathbb{N}}$ in $\mathbb{M}^{n \times k}$, we say that (A_m) **converges** to A and write $A_m \to A$ if $\|A_m - A\| \to 0$ as $m \to \infty$, where $\| \cdot \|$ is a matrix norm. Once again, we do not need to clarify the norm due to the equivalence property. Also, norm convergence is equivalent to pointwise convergence:

EXERCISE 2.3.14. Prove that, given A and (A_m) in $\mathbb{M}^{n \times k}$, we have $A_m \to A$ as $m \to \infty$ if and only if every element a_{ij}^m of A_m converges to the corresponding element a_{ij} of A.

EXERCISE 2.3.15. Prove the following result for matrices A, B, C and matrix sequences $(A_m), (B_m)$, taking $m \to \infty$ and assuming sizes are conformable:

(i) If $B_m \to A$ and $A_m - B_m \to 0$, then $A_m \to A$.
(ii) If $A_m \to A$, then $B A_m C \to B A C$.

Example 2.3.3: Convergence of the Perron projection in (1.11) of the Perron–Frobenius theorem was defined using pointwise convergence. By Exercise 2.3.14, norm convergence also holds. One of the advantages of working with norms is that we can give rates of convergence for norm deviation. This idea is discussed further in §2.3.3.3.

EXERCISE 2.3.16. Given A and (A_m) in $\mathbb{M}^{n \times n}$, prove that $A_m \to A$ as $m \to \infty$ if and only if $s^\top A_m s \to s^\top A s$ for every $s \in \mathbb{R}^n$.

2.3.3   Iteration in Matrix Space

Results such as Proposition 1.4.2 on page 36 already showed us the significance of powers of adjacency matrices. The Perron–Frobenius theorem revealed connections between spectral radii, dominant eigenvectors, and powers of positive matrices. In this section we investigate powers of matrices in more depth.

2.3.3.1   Gelfand's Formula

One very general connection between matrix powers and spectral radii is **Gelfand's formula** for the spectral radius:

THEOREM 2.3.2   *For any matrix norm* $\| \cdot \|$ *and* $A \in \mathbb{M}^{n \times n}$, *we have*

$$r(A) = \lim_{k \to \infty} \|A^k\|^{1/k}. \tag{2.38}$$

Proofs can be found in Bollobás (1999) or Kreyszig (1978).

EXERCISE 2.3.17. The references above show that the limit (2.38) always exists. Using this fact, prove that every choice of norm over $\mathbb{M}^{n \times n}$ yields the same value for this limit.

The next exercise shows that $r(A) < 1$ implies $\|A^k\| \to 0$ at a geometric rate.

EXERCISE 2.3.18. Using (2.38), show that $r(A) < 1$ implies the existence of a constant $\delta < 1$ and an $M < \infty$ such that $\|A^k\| \leqslant \delta^k M$ for all $k \in \mathbb{N}$.

EXERCISE 2.3.19. Consider the dynamic system $x_t = A x_{t-1} + d$ with x_0 given, where each x_t and d are vectors in $\mathbb{R}^n$, and A is $n \times n$. (If you like, you can think of this process as orders flowing backwards through a production network.) Show that, when $r(A) < 1$, the sequence $(x_t)_{t \geqslant 0}$ converges to $x^* := (I - A)^{-1} d$, independent of the choice of x_0.

EXERCISE 2.3.20. In §2.2.1 we studied a production coefficient matrix of the form $A = (a_{ij})$ in $\mathbb{M}^{n \times n}$, where each a_{ij} takes values in $(0, \infty)$, and, for each j, $\alpha + \sum_i a_{ij} = 1$ for some $\alpha > 0$. We can calculate $r(A)$ using the following strategy. In Exercise 2.2.2 we saw that $\sum_i \sum_j a_{ij}^{(m)} = n(1 - \alpha)^m$ for all $m \in \mathbb{N}$, where $a_{ij}^{(m)}$ is the (i, j)-th element of A^m. Using the fact that $\|B\|_1 := \sum_i \sum_j |b_{ij}|$ is a matrix norm, apply Gelfand's formula to obtain $r(A) = 1 - \alpha$.

2.3.3.2   A Local Spectral Radius Theorem

The next theorem is a "local" version of Gelfand's formula that relies on positivity. It replaces matrix norms with vector norms, which are easier to compute.

THEOREM 2.3.3   *Fix $A \in \mathbb{M}^{n \times n}$ and let $\| \cdot \|$ be any norm on $\mathbb{R}^n$. If $A \geqslant 0$ and $x \gg 0$, then*

$$\| A^m x \|^{1/m} \to r(A) \qquad (m \to \infty). \tag{2.39}$$

Theorem 2.3.3 tells us that, eventually, for any positive x, the norm of the vector $A^m x$ grows at rate $r(A)$. A proof can be found in Krasnoselskii (1964).[6]

Example 2.3.4: In §2.1.3 we studied how the impact of a given demand shock Δd flows backward through a production network, with $A^m(\Delta d)$ giving the impact on sectors at m steps (backward linkages). When $\Delta d \gg 0$ and $r(A) < 1$, Theorem 2.3.3 tells us that $\| A^m \Delta d \| = O(r(A)^m)$. If we set the norm to $\| \cdot \|_\infty$, this tells us that the maximal impact of demand shocks through backward linkages fades at rate $r(A)$.

EXERCISE 2.3.21. Prove Theorem 2.3.3 in the case where A is primitive.

2.3.3.3   Convergence to the Perron Projection

The local spectral radius theorem assumes $A \geqslant 0$. Now we further strengthen this assumption by requiring that A is primitive. In this case, $r(A)^{-m} A^m$ converges to the Perron projection as $m \to \infty$ (see (1.11)). We want *rates* of convergence in high-dimensional settings.

We fix $A \in \mathbb{M}^{n \times n}$ and label the eigenvalues so that $|\lambda_{i+1}| \leqslant |\lambda_i|$ for all i. Note that $|\lambda_1| = \lambda_1 = r(A)$. Let $E := e\,\varepsilon^\top$ be the Perron projection.

PROPOSITION 2.3.4   *If A is diagonalizable and primitive, then $\alpha := |\lambda_2/\lambda_1| < 1$ and*

$$\| r(A)^{-m} A^m - E \| = O\left(\alpha^m\right). \tag{2.40}$$

Thus, an upper bound on the rate of convergence to the Perron projection is determined by the modulus of the ratio of the first two eigenvalues.

Proof   We saw in (1.5) that $A^m = \sum_{i=1}^n \lambda_i^m e_i \varepsilon_i^\top$ for all $m \in \mathbb{N}$. From this spectral representation we obtain

$$r(A)^{-m} A^m - e_1 \varepsilon_1^\top = r(A)^{-m} \left(A^m - r(A)^m e_1 \varepsilon_1^\top \right) = \sum_{i=2}^n \theta_i^m e_i \varepsilon_i^\top$$

when $\theta_i := \lambda_i / r(A)$. Let $\| \cdot \|$ be the operator norm on $\mathbb{M}^{n \times n}$. The triangle inequality gives

[6] A direct proof of a generalized version of Theorem 2.3.3 is provided in Theorem B1 of Borovička and Stachurski (2020).

$$\|r(A)^{-m}A^m - e_1\varepsilon_1^\top\| \leqslant \sum_{i=2}^{n}|\theta_i|^m\|e_i\varepsilon_i^\top\| \leqslant |\theta_2|^m\sum_{i=2}^{n}\|e_i\varepsilon_i^\top\|.$$

Since A is primitive, the Perron–Frobenius theorem tells us that $|\lambda_2| < r(A)$. Hence $\alpha := |\theta_2| < 1$. The proof is now complete. ☐

2.3.4   Exact Stability Conditions

The Neumann series lemma tells us that the linear system $x = Ax + d$ has a unique solution whenever $r(A) < 1$. We also saw that, in the input–output model, where A is the adjacency matrix, the condition $r(A) < 1$ holds whenever every sector has positive value added (Assumption 2.1.1 and Exercise 2.1.2). Hence we have sufficient conditions for stability.

This analysis, while important, leaves open the question of how tight the conditions are and what happens when they fail. For example, we might ask

 (i) To obtain $r(A) < 1$, is it necessary that each sector has positive value added? Or can we obtain the same result under weaker conditions?
 (ii) What happens when $r(A) < 1$ fails? Do we always lose existence of a solution, or uniqueness, or both?

In §2.3.4.1 and §2.3.4.2 below we address these two questions.

2.3.4.1   Spectral Radii of Substochastic Matrices

To reiterate, the results in §5.1.3 relied on the assumption that every sector has positive value added, which in turn gave us the property $r(A) < 1$ for the adjacency matrix of the input–output production network. Positive value added in every sector is not necessary, however. Here we investigate a weaker condition that is exactly necessary and sufficient for $r(A) < 1$. This weaker condition is very helpful for understanding other kinds of networks too, including financial networks, as discussed in §5.2.

To begin, recall that a matrix $P \in \mathbb{M}^{n\times n}$ is called stochastic if $P \geqslant 0$ and $P\mathbb{1} = \mathbb{1}$. Similarly, $P \in \mathbb{M}^{n\times n}$ is called **substochastic** if $P \geqslant 0$ and $P\mathbb{1} \leqslant \mathbb{1}$. Thus, a substochastic matrix is a nonnegative matrix with less than unit row sums. Clearly the transpose $Q^\top$ of a nonnegative matrix Q is substochastic if and only if Q has less than unit column sums.

A natural example of a substochastic matrix is the transpose $A^\top$ of an adjacency matrix A of an input–output network. Indeed, such an A is nonnegative and, for the j-th column sum we have

$$\sum_i a_{ij} = \frac{\sum_i z_{ij}}{x_j} = \frac{\text{spending on inputs by sector } j}{\text{total sales of sector } j}.$$

Hence $\sum_i a_{ij} \leqslant 1$, which says that spending on intermediate goods and services by a given industry does not exceed total sales revenue, is a necessary condition for nonnegative profits in sector j. When this holds for all j, the adjacency matrix has less than unit column sums.

From Lemma 1.2.7 on page 15, we see that any substochastic matrix P has

$$r(P) \leqslant \max_i \text{rowsum}_i(P) \leqslant 1. \tag{2.41}$$

We wish to know when we can tighten this to $r(P) < 1$.

From (2.41), one obvious sufficient condition is that $\text{rowsum}_i(P) < 1$ for all i. This is, in essence, how we used Assumption 2.1.1 (every sector has positive value added) in the input–output model. Under that condition, we have $\sum_i a_{ij} < 1$ for all j, which says all column sums are strictly less than one. Hence

$$\max_i \text{colsum}_i(A) < 1 \iff \max_i \text{rowsum}_i(A^\top) < 1 \implies r(A^\top) < 1 \iff r(A) < 1,$$

where the middle implication is by (2.41), and the last equivalence is by $r(A) = r(A^\top)$.

Now we provide a weaker – in fact necessary and sufficient – condition for $r(P) < 1$, based on network structure. To do so, we define an $n \times n$ substochastic matrix $P = (p_{ij})$ to be **weakly chained substochastic** if, for all $m \in [n]$, there exists an $i \in [n]$ such that $m \to i$ and $\sum_j p_{ij} < 1$. Here accessibility of i from m is in terms of the induced weighted digraph.[7]

EXERCISE 2.3.22. Let $A = (a_{ij}) \in \mathbb{M}^{n \times n}$ be nonnegative. Show that $A^\top$ is weakly chained substochastic if and only if A has less than unit column sums and, for each $m \in [n]$, there exists an $i \in [n]$ such that $i \to m$ under (the digraph induced by) A and $\sum_k a_{ki} < 1$.

PROPOSITION 2.3.5   *For a substochastic matrix P, we have*

$$r(P) < 1 \iff P \text{ is weakly chained substochastic.}$$

A proof can be found in Corollary 2.6 of Azimzadeh (2019).

Now we return to the input–output model. Let's agree to say that sector i is an **upstream supplier** to sector j if $i \to j$ in the input–output network. By Proposition 1.4.2 on page 36, an equivalent statement is that there exists a $k \in \mathbb{N}$ such that $a_{ij}^k > 0$.

EXERCISE 2.3.23. Let A be the adjacency matrix of an input–output network, and assume that value added is nonnegative in each sector. Using Proposition 2.3.5, show that $r(A) < 1$ if and only if each sector in the network has an upstream supplier with positive value added.

---

[7] Induced weighted digraphs are defined in §1.4.2.1. By Proposition 1.4.2, accessibility of i from m is equivalent to existence of a $k \geqslant 0$ with $p_{mi}^k > 0$, where p_{mi}^k is the m,i-th element of P^k (and $P^0 = I$).

2.3.4.2   A Converse to the Neumann Series Lemma

Since the Neumann series lemma is a foundational result with many economic applications, we want to know what happens when the conditions of the lemma fail. Here is a partial converse:

THEOREM 2.3.6   *Fix $A \in \mathbb{M}^{n \times n}$ with $A \geq 0$. If A is irreducible, then the following statements are equivalent:*

(i) $r(A) < 1$.
(ii) $x = Ax + b$ has a unique everywhere positive solution for all $b \geq 0$ with $b \neq 0$.
(iii) $x = Ax + b$ has a nonnegative solution for at least one $b \geq 0$ with $b \neq 0$.
(iv) There exists an $x \gg 0$ such that $Ax \ll x$.

REMARK 2.3.1   *If A is irreducible and one of (and hence all of) items (i)–(iv) are true, then, by the Neumann series lemma, the unique solution is $x^* := \sum_{m \geq 0} A^m b$.*

REMARK 2.3.2   *Statement (iii) is obviously weaker than statement (ii). It is important, however, in the case where $r(A) < 1$ fails. In this setting, from the negation of (iii), we can conclude that there is* not *even one* nontrivial *b in $\mathbb{R}_+^n$ such that a nonnegative solution to $x = Ax + b$ exists.*

Proof of Theorem 2.3.6   We show (i) $\iff$ (iv) and then (i) $\iff$ (ii) $\iff$ (iii).

((i) $\Rightarrow$ (iv)). For x in (iv) we can use the Perron–Frobenius theorem to obtain a real eigenvector e satisfying $Ae = r(A)e \ll e$ and $e \gg 0$.

((iv) $\Rightarrow$ (i)). Fix $x \gg 0$ such that $x \gg Ax$. Through positive scaling, we can assume that $\|x\| = 1$. Choose $\lambda < 1$ such that $\lambda x \geq Ax$. Iterating on this inequality gives, for all $k \in \mathbb{N}$,

$$\lambda^k x \geq A^k x \quad \implies \quad \lambda^k = \lambda^k \|x\| \geq \|A^k x\| \quad \iff \quad \|A^k x\|^{1/k} \leq \lambda.$$

Hence, by the local spectral radius result in Theorem 2.3.3, $r(A) \leq \lambda < 1$.

((i) $\Rightarrow$ (ii)). Existence of a unique solution $x^* = \sum_{i \geq 0} A^i b$ follows from the NSL. Positivity follows from irreducibility of A, since $b \neq 0$ and $\sum_i A^i \gg 0$.

((ii) $\Rightarrow$ (iii)). Obvious.

((iii) $\Rightarrow$ (i)). Suppose there is a $b \geq 0$ with $b \neq 0$ and an $x \geq 0$ such that $x = Ax + b$. By the Perron–Frobenius theorem, we can select a left eigenvector e such that $e \gg 0$ and $e^\top A = r(A)e^\top$. For this e we have

$$e^\top x = e^\top Ax + e^\top b = r(A)e^\top x + e^\top b.$$

Since $e \gg 0$ and $b \neq 0$, we must have $e^\top b > 0$. In addition, $x \neq 0$ because $b \neq 0$ and $x = Ax + b$, so $e^\top x > 0$. Therefore $r(A)$ satisfies $(1 - r(A))\alpha = \beta$ for positive constants α, β. Hence $r(A) < 1$. $\square$

EXERCISE 2.3.24.   For the production system $x = Ax + d$, what do we require on A for the condition $r(A) < 1$ to be necessary for existence of a nonnegative output solution x^*, for each nontrivial d?

EXERCISE 2.3.25. Irreducibility cannot be dropped from Theorem 2.3.6. Provide an example demonstrating that, without irreducibility, we can have $r(A) \geqslant 1$ for some $A \geqslant 0$ and yet find a nonzero $b \geqslant 0$ and an $x \geqslant 0$ such that $x = Ax + b$.

2.4   Chapter Notes

High-quality foundational textbooks on input–output analysis and multisector production networks include Nikaido (1968), Miller and Blair (2009), and Antràs (2020). References on production networks and aggregate shocks include Acemoglu et al. (2012), Antràs et al. (2012), Di Giovanni et al. (2014), Carvalho (2014), Barrot and Sauvagnat (2016), Baqaee (2018), Carvalho and Tahbaz-Salehi (2019), Acemoglu and Azar (2020), Liu and Tsyvinski (2020), Miranda-Pinto (2021), and Carvalho et al. (2021).

For other network-centric analysis of multisector models, see, for example, Bernard et al. (2019), who use buyer–supplier relationship data from Belgium to investigate the origins of firm size heterogeneity when firms are interconnected in a production network. Herskovic (2018) analyzes asset pricing implications of production networks. Cai and Szeidl (2018) consider the effect of inter-firm relationships on business performance. La'O and Tahbaz-Salehi (2022) study optimal monetary policy in a production network. Dew-Becker (2022) analyzes tail risk and aggregate fluctuations in a nonlinear production network. Elliott et al. (2022) show that complex supply networks can greatly amplify small idiosyncratic shocks. Elliott and Golub (2022) provide a survey of network fragility that includes a discussion of production networks and the impact of sectoral shocks.

3 Optimal Flows

Up until now we have analyzed problems where network structure is either fixed or generated by some specified random process. In this chapter, we investigate networks where connections are determined endogenously via equilibrium or optimality conditions. In the process, we cover some of the most powerful methods available for solving optimization problems in networks and beyond, with applications ranging from traditional graph and network problems, such as trade, matching, and communication, through to machine learning, econometrics, and finance.

3.1 Shortest Paths

As a preliminary step, we study the **shortest path** problem – a topic that has applications in production, network design, artificial intelligence, transportation, and many other fields. The solution method we adopt also happens to be one of the clearest illustrations of Bellman's principle of optimality, which is one of the cornerstones of optimization theory and modern economic analysis.

3.1.1 Definition and Examples

We start proceedings by introducing simple examples. (In the next section we will formalize the problem and consider solution methods.)

3.1.1.1 Set Up

Consider a firm that wishes to ship a container from A to G at minimum cost, where A and G are vertices of the weighted digraph $\mathcal{G}$ shown in Figure 3.1. Arrows (edges) indicate paths that can be used for freight, while weights indicate costs of traversing them. In this context, the weight function is also called the **cost function**, and we denote it by c. For example, $c(A, B)$ is the cost of traveling from vertex A to vertex B.

Since this graph is small, we can find the minimum cost path visually. A quick scan shows that the minimum attainable cost is 8. Two paths realize this cost: (A, C, F, G) and (A, D, F, G), as shown in Figure 3.2 and Figure 3.3, respectively.

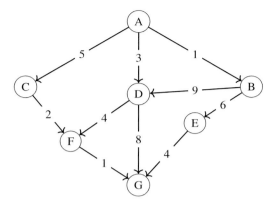

Figure 3.1 Graph for the shortest path problem

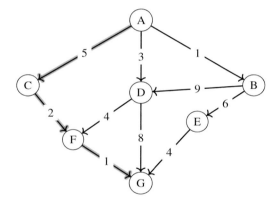

Figure 3.2 Solution 1

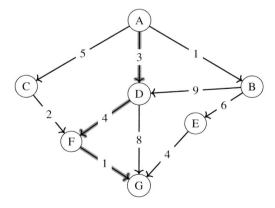

Figure 3.3 Solution 2

3.1.1.2 A Recursive View

Let's now consider a systematic solution that can be applied to larger graphs. Let $q^*(x)$ denote the **minimum cost-to-go** from vertex x. That is, $q^*(x)$ is the total cost of traveling from x to G *if* we take the best route. Its values are shown at each vertex in Figure 3.4. We can represent q^* in vector form via

$$(q^*(A), q^*(B), q^*(C), q^*(D), q^*(E), q^*(F), q^*(G)) = (8, 10, 3, 5, 4, 1, 0) \in \mathbb{R}^7. \quad (3.1)$$

As is clear from studying Figure 3.4, once q^* is known, the least-cost path can be computed as follows: Start at A and, from then on, at arbitrary vertex x, move to any y that solves

$$\min_{y \in \mathcal{O}(x)} \{c(x, y) + q^*(y)\}. \quad (3.2)$$

Here $\mathcal{O}(x) = \{y \in V : (x, y) \in E\}$ is the set of direct successors of x, as defined in §1.4.1, while $c(x, y)$ is the cost of traveling from x to y. In other words, to minimize the cost-to-go, we choose the next path to minimize current traveling cost plus cost-to-go from the resulting location.

Thus, if we know $q^*(x)$ at each x, then finding the best path reduces to the simple two stage optimization problem in (3.2).

But now another problem arises: how to find q^* in more complicated cases, where the graph is large. One approach to this problem is to exploit the fact that

$$q^*(x) = \min_{y \in \mathcal{O}(x)} \{c(x, y) + q^*(y)\} \quad (3.3)$$

must hold for every vertex x in the graph apart from G (where $q^*(G) = 0$).

Take the time to convince yourself that, for our example, the function q^* satisfies (3.3). In particular, check that (3.3) holds at each nonterminal x in Figure 3.4.

We can understand (3.3), which is usually called the **Bellman equation**, as a restriction on q^* that helps us identify this vector. The main difficulty with our plan is that

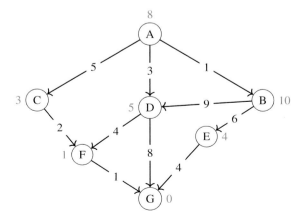

Figure 3.4 The cost-to-go function, with $q^*(x)$ indicated by red digits at each x

the Bellman equation is nonlinear in the unknown function q^*. Our strategy will be to convert this nonlinear equation into a fixed point problem, so that fixed point theory can be applied.

We do this in the context of a more general version of the shortest path problem.

3.1.2   Bellman's Method

We consider a generic shortest path problem on a **flow network**, which consists of a weighted digraph $\mathscr{G} = (V, E, c)$ with a sink $d \in V$ called the **destination** and a weight function $c \colon E \to (0, \infty)$ that associates a positive cost to each edge $(x, y) \in E$. In what follows, we take $|V| = n$.

We consider how to find the shortest (i.e., minimum cost) path from x to d for every $x \in V$. In doing so we impose the following assumption.

ASSUMPTION 3.1.1 $\mathscr{G}$ *is a directed acyclic graph. Moreover, for each* $x \in V$ *with* $x \neq d$, *there exists a directed path from* x *to* d.

To simplify the arguments below, we consider a second digraph $\mathscr{G}' = (V, E')$, where V is unchanged and $E' = E \cup \{(d, d)\}$. In other words, E' extends E by adding a self-loop at d. We also extend c to this self-loop by setting $c(d, d) = 0$. This just means that "terminating at d" is the same as "staying at d," since no more cost accrues after arrival at the destination. Figure 3.5 illustrates this in the context of the previous example.

EXERCISE 3.1.1. Prove that, for the extended digraph $\mathscr{G}'$, every infinite directed path $x_1, x_2, \ldots$ obeys $x_i = d$ for all $i \geqslant n$.

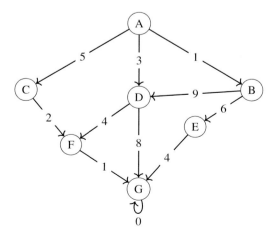

Figure 3.5 Addition of a self loop to the destination

We will use the intuition from the previous section, based around the Bellman equation, to construct a solution method.

3.1.2.1 Policies

Instead of optimal paths, it turns out to be more convenient to aim for optimal *policies*. In general, a policy is a specification of how to act in every state. In the present setting, a **policy** is a map $\sigma \colon V \to V$ with $\sigma(x) = y$ understood as meaning "when at vertex x, go to y." A policy is called **feasible** if $\sigma(x) \in \mathcal{O}(x)$ for all $x \in V$.

For any feasible policy σ and $x \in V$, the **trajectory** of x under σ is the path from x to the destination indicated by the feasible policy. In other words, it is the sequence $(p_0, p_1, p_2, \ldots)$ defined by $p_0 = x$ and $p_i = \sigma(p_{i-1})$ for all $i \in \mathbb{N}$. It can also be expressed as $(\sigma^i(x)) := (\sigma^i(x))_{i \geqslant 0}$, where σ^i is the i-th composition of σ with itself.

Let Σ be the set of all feasible policies. In view of Exercise 3.1.1, policies in Σ have the property that every trajectory they generate reaches d in n steps and stays there. In other words,

$$\sigma^i(x) = d \text{ for all } i \geqslant n \text{ and all } x \in V. \tag{3.4}$$

Given $q \in \mathbb{R}^V_+$, we call $\sigma \in \Sigma$ q-**greedy** if

$$\sigma(x) \in \operatorname*{argmin}_{y \in \mathcal{O}(x)} \{c(x, y) + q(y)\} \quad \text{for all } x \in V.$$

In essence, a greedy policy treats q as the minimum cost-to-go function and picks out an optimal path under that assumption.

Using our new terminology, we can rephrase the discussion in §3.1.1.2 as follows: The shortest-path problem can be solved by finding the true minimum cost-to-go function q^* and then following a q^*-greedy policy. In the remainder of this section, we prove this claim more carefully.

3.1.2.2 Cost of Policies

We need to be able to assess the cost of any given policy. To this end, for each $x \in V$ and $\sigma \in \Sigma$, let $q_\sigma(x)$ denote the cost of following σ from x. That is,

$$q_\sigma(x) = \sum_{i=0}^{\infty} c(\sigma^i(x), \sigma^{i+1}(x)) = \sum_{i=0}^{n-1} c(\sigma^i(x), \sigma^{i+1}(x)). \tag{3.5}$$

This second equality holds because $\sigma^i(x) = d$ for all $i \geqslant n$ and $c(d, d) = 0$. The function $q_\sigma \in \mathbb{R}^V_+$ is called the **cost-to-go** under σ.

It will be helpful in what follows to design an operator such that q_σ is a fixed point. For this purpose we let U be all $q \in \mathbb{R}^V_+$ with $q(d) = 0$ and define $T_\sigma \colon U \to U$ by

$$(T_\sigma q)(x) = c(x, \sigma(x)) + q(\sigma(x)) \qquad (x \in V).$$

Here and below, with $k \in \mathbb{N}$, the expression T_σ^k indicates the k-th composition of T_σ with itself (i.e., T_σ is applied k times).

EXERCISE 3.1.2. Prove that T_σ is a self-map on U for all $\sigma \in \Sigma$.

PROPOSITION 3.1.1   *For each $\sigma \in \Sigma$, the function q_σ is the unique fixed point of T_σ in U, and $T_\sigma^k q = q_\sigma$ for all $k \geqslant n$ and all $q \in U$.*

Proof   Fix $\sigma \in \Sigma$ and $q \in U$. For each $x \in V$ we have

$$(T_\sigma^2 q)(x) = c(x, \sigma(x)) + (T_\sigma q)(\sigma(x)) = c(x, \sigma(x)) + c(\sigma(x), \sigma^2(x)) + q(\sigma^2(x)).$$

More generally, for $k \geqslant n$, we have

$$(T_\sigma^k q)(x) = \sum_{i=0}^{k-1} c(\sigma^i(x), \sigma^{i+1}(x)) + q(\sigma^k(x)) = \sum_{i=0}^{n-1} c(\sigma^i(x), \sigma^{i+1}(x)).$$

The second equality holds because $\sigma^k(x) = d$ for all $k \geqslant n$ and $q(d) = 0$. Hence $(T_\sigma^k q)(x) = q_\sigma(x)$ by (3.5). The fact that q_σ is the unique fixed point of T_σ now follows from Exercise A.1.3 in the appendix (page 185).   □

3.1.2.3   Optimality

The **minimum cost-to-go** function q^* is defined by

$$q^*(x) = \min_{\sigma \in \Sigma} q_\sigma(x) \qquad (x \in V).$$

The definition of q^* matches our intuitive definition from §3.1.1.2, in the sense that $q^*(x)$ is, for each $x \in V$, the minimum cost of traveling from x to the destination d.

A policy $\sigma^* \in \Sigma$ is called **optimal** if it attains the minimum in the definition of q^*, so that $q^* = q_{\sigma^*}$ on V. Our main aims are to

(i) obtain a method for calculating q^* and
(ii) prove that a q^*-greedy policy is optimal, as suggested in our informal discussion above.

Regarding the first step, we claim that q^* satisfies the Bellman equation (3.3). To prove this claim, we introduce the **Bellman operator** T via

$$(Tq)(x) = \min_{y \in \mathcal{O}(x)} \{c(x, y) + q(y)\} \qquad (x \in V). \tag{3.6}$$

By construction, q^* satisfies the Bellman equation (3.3) if and only if $Tq^* = q^*$.

EXERCISE 3.1.3. Show that T is a self-map on U and, moreover, $Tq \leqslant T_\sigma q$ for all $q \in U$ and $\sigma \in \Sigma$.

EXERCISE 3.1.4. Show that T and T_σ are both order-preserving on $\mathbb{R}_+^V$ with respect to the pointwise partial order $\leqslant$. Prove that $T^k q \leqslant T_\sigma^k q$ for all $q \in U$, $\sigma \in \Sigma$, and $k \in \mathbb{N}$.

EXERCISE 3.1.5. Fix $q \in U$ and let σ be a q-greedy policy. Show that $Tq = T_\sigma q$.

The next result is central. It confirms that the minimum cost-to-go function satisfies the Bellman equation and also provides us with a means to compute it: Pick any q in U and then iterate with T.

PROPOSITION 3.1.2   *The function q^* is the unique fixed point of T in U and, in addition, $T^k q \to q^*$ as $k \to \infty$ for all $q \in U$.*

Proof   In view of Exercise A.1.3 in the appendix (page 185), it suffices to verify the existence of an $m \in \mathbb{N}$ such that $T^k q = q^*$ for all $k \geq m$ and all $q \in U$. To this end, let γ be the minimum of $c(x, y)$ over all $(x, y) \in E$. Since c is positive on such edges and E is finite, $\gamma > 0$.

Fix $q \in U$. We claim first that $T^k q \geq q^*$ for sufficiently large k. To see this, fix $k \in \mathbb{N}$ and iterate with T to get

$$(T^k q)(x) = c(x, p_1) + c(p_1, p_2) + \cdots + c(p_{k-1}, p_k) + q(p_k)$$

for some path $(x, p_1, \ldots, p_k)$. By Exercise 3.1.1, this path leads to d in n steps. This means that $(T^k q)(x) \geq q^*(x)$ when $k \geq n$, since $q^*(x)$ is the minimum cost of reaching d from x.

For the reverse inequality, fix $k \geq n$ and observe that, by Proposition 3.1.1 and the inequality from Exercise 3.1.4,

$$T^k q \leq T_{\sigma^*}^k q = q_{\sigma^*} = q^*.$$

We have now shown that $T^k q = q^*$ for sufficiently large k, as required.   □

We now have a means to compute the minimum cost-to-go function (by iterating with T, starting at any $q \in U$) and, in addition, a way to verify the following key result.

THEOREM 3.1.3   *A policy $\sigma \in \Sigma$ is optimal if and only if σ is q^*-greedy.*

Proof   By the definition of greedy policies,

$$\sigma \text{ is } q^*\text{-greedy} \quad \Longleftrightarrow \quad c(x, \sigma(x)) + q^*(\sigma(x)) = \min_{y \in \mathcal{O}(x)} \{c(x, y) + q^*(y)\}, \quad \forall x \in V.$$

Since q^* satisfies the Bellman equation, we then have

$$\sigma \text{ is } q^*\text{-greedy} \quad \Longleftrightarrow \quad c(x, \sigma(x)) + q^*(\sigma(x)) = q^*(x), \quad \forall x \in V.$$

The right-hand side is equivalent to $T_\sigma q^* = q^*$. At the same time, T_σ has only one fixed point in U, which is q_σ. Hence $q_\sigma = q^*$. Hence, by this chain of logic and the definition of optimality,

$$\sigma \text{ is } q^*\text{-greedy} \quad \Longleftrightarrow \quad q^* = q_\sigma \quad \Longleftrightarrow \quad \sigma \text{ is optimal.} \qquad □$$

3.1.2.4   An Implementation in Julia

Let's use the ideas set out above to solve the original shortest-path problem, concerning shipping, which we introduced in §3.1.1.1. We will implement in Julia.

Our first step is to set up the cost function, which we store as an array called `c`. We identify the vertices $A, \ldots, G$, with the integers $1, \ldots, 7$. We set `c[i, j]` = `Inf` when no edge exists from `i` to `j`, so that such a path is never chosen when evaluating the Bellman operator, as defined in (3.3). When an edge does exist, we enter the cost shown in Figure 3.1:

```
c = fill(Inf, (7, 7))

c[1, 2], c[1, 3], c[1, 4] = 1, 5, 3
c[2, 4], c[2, 5] = 9, 6
c[3, 6] = 2
c[4, 6] = 4
c[5, 7] = 4
c[6, 7] = 1
c[7, 7] = 0
```

Next we define the Bellman operator:

```
function T(q)
    Tq = similar(q)
    n = length(q)
    for x in 1:n
        Tq[x] = minimum(c[x, :] + q[:])
    end
    return Tq
end
```

Now we arbitrarily set $q \equiv 0$, generate the sequence of iterations Tq, T^2q, T^3q, and plot them:

```
using PyPlot
fig, ax = plt.subplots()

n = 7
q = zeros(n)
ax.plot(1:n, q)

for i in 1:3
    new_q = T(q)
    ax.plot(1:n, new_q, "-o", alpha=0.7)
    q = new_q
end
```

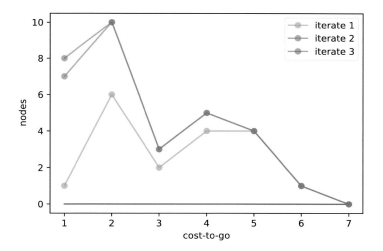

Figure 3.6 Shortest path Bellman iteration

After adding some labels, the output looks like the image in Figure 3.6. Notice that, by T^3q, we have already converged on q^*. You can confirm this by checking that the values of T^3q line up with those we obtained manually in Figure 3.4.

3.1.3 Betweenness Centrality

In §1.4.3 we discussed a range of centrality measures for networks, including degree, eigenvector, and Katz centrality. Aside from these, there is another well-known centrality measure, called betweenness centrality, which builds on the notion of shortest paths and is particularly popular in analysis of social and peer networks.

Formally, for a given graph $\mathcal{G} = (V, E)$, directed or undirected, the **betweenness centrality** of vertex $v \in V$ is

$$b(v) := \sum_{x, y \in V \setminus \{v\}} \frac{|S(x, v, y)|}{|S(x, y)|},$$

where $S(x, y)$ is the set of all shortest paths from x to y, and $S(x, v, y)$ is the set of all shortest paths from x to y that pass through v. (As usual, $|A|$ is the cardinality of A.) Thus, $b(v)$ is proportional to the probability that, for a randomly selected pair of nodes x, y, a randomly selected shortest path from x to y contains v. Thus, the measure will be high for nodes that "lie between" a large number of node pairs.

For example, NetworkX stores a graph called `florentine_families_graph` that details the marriage relationships between 15 prominent Florentine families during the fifteenth century. The data can be accessed via

```
import networkx as nx
G = nx.florentine_families_graph()
```

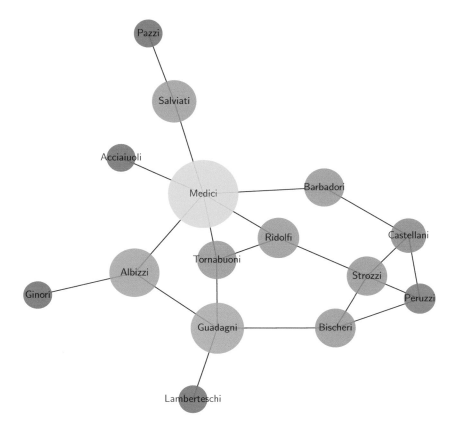

Figure 3.7 Betweenness centrality (by color and node size) for Florentine families

The network is shown in Figure 3.7, which was created using

```
nx.draw_networkx(G, [params])
```

where `[params]` stands for parameters listing node size, node color, and other features. For this graph, node size and node color are scaled by betweenness centrality, which is calculated via

```
nx.betweenness_centrality(G)
```

Although this graph is very simple, the output helps to illustrate the prominent role of the Medici family, consistent with their great wealth and influence in Florence and beyond.

3.2   Linear Programming and Duality

Our study of shortest paths in §3.1 used a relatively specialized optimization method. In this section we cover more general results in optimization and duality, which will then be applied to endogenous networks, optimal transport, and optimal flows. Part of the strategy is to take challenging optimization problems and regularize them, often by some form of convexification.

Before diving into theory, we use §3.2.1 below to provide motivation via one very specific application. This application involves what is typically called *matching* in economics and *linear assignment* in mathematics. We illustrate the key ideas in the context of matching workers to jobs. Later, when we discuss how to solve the problem, we will see the power of linear programming, convexification, and duality.

3.2.1 Linear Assignment

Behold the town of Springfield. A local employer is shutting down, and 40 workers stand idle. Fortunately for these workers, Springfield lies within a political battle-ground state, and, as a result, the mayor receives backing to attract a new employer. She succeeds by promising a certain firm that the 40 workers will be retrained for the new skills they require. For mathematical convenience, let us suppose that there are exactly 40 new positions, each with distinct skill requirements.

The team set up by the mayor records the individual skills of the 40 workers, along with the requirements of the new positions, and estimates the cost $c(i, j)$ of retraining individual i for position j. The team's challenge is to minimize the total cost of retraining. In particular, they wish to solve

$$\min_{\sigma \in \mathcal{P}} \sum_{i=1}^{40} c(i, \sigma(i)), \tag{3.7}$$

where $\mathcal{P}$ is the set of all permutations (i.e., bijective self-maps) on the integers $1, \ldots, 40$. Figure 3.8 illustrates one possible permutation.

The problem is discrete, so first-order conditions are unavailable. Unsure of how to proceed but possessing a powerful computer, the team instructs its workstation to step through all possible permutations and record the one that leads to the lowest total retraining cost. The instruction set is given in Algorithm 2.

After five days of constant execution, the workstation is still running and the mayor grows impatient. The team starts to calculate how long execution will take. The main determinant is the size of the set $\mathcal{P}$. Elementary combinatorics tells us that the number

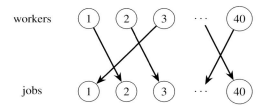

Figure 3.8 One possible assignment (i.e., permutation of [40])

```
1  set m = +∞ ;
2  for σ in 𝒫 do
3  │   set t(σ) = Σ⁴⁰ᵢ₌₁ c(i, σ(i)) ;
4  │   if t(σ) < m then
5  │   │   set m = t(σ) ;
6  │   │   set σ* = σ ;
7  │   end
8  end
9  return σ*
```

Algorithm 2: Minimizing total cost by testing all permutations

of permutations of a set of size n is $n!$. Quick calculations show that $40!$ exceeds 8×10^{47}. A helpful team member points out that this is much less than the number of possible AES-256 password keys (approximately 10^{77}). The mayor is not appeased and demands a runtime estimate.

Further calculations reveal the following: If, for each σ in $\mathcal{P}$, the workstation can evaluate the cost $t(\sigma) = \sum_{i=1}^{40} c(i, \sigma(i))$ in 10^{-10}-th of a second (which is extremely optimistic), then the total run time would be

$$10^{-10} \times 8 \times 10^{47} = 8 \times 10^{37} \text{ seconds} \approx 2.5 \times 10^{30} \text{ years.}$$

Another helpful team member provides perspective by noting that the sun will expand into a red giant and vaporize planet Earth in less than 10^{10} years.

The great computational cost of solving this problem by direct calculations is an example of what is often called the *curse of dimensionality*. This phrase, coined by Richard Bellman (1920–1984) during his fundamental research into dynamic optimization, refers to the exponential increase in processor cycles needed to solve computational problems to a given level of accuracy as the number of dimensions increases. The matching problem we have just described is high-dimensional because the choice variable σ, a permutation in $\mathcal{P}$, is naturally associated with the vector $(\sigma(1), \ldots, \sigma(40))$. This, in turn, is a point in 40-dimensional vector space.[1]

Fortunately, clever algorithms for this matching problem have been found, and, for problems such as this one, useful approximations to the optimal allocation can be calculated relatively quickly. For example, Dantzig (1951) showed how such problems can be cast as a *linear program*, which we discuss below. Further progress has been

---

[1] Readers familiar with high-performance computing techniques might suggest that the curse of dimensionality is no cause for concern for the matching problem, since the search algorithm can be parallelized. Unfortunately, even the best parallelization methods cannot save the workstation from being vaporized by the sun with the calculation incomplete. The best-case scenario is that adding another execution thread doubles effective computations per second and hence halves execution time. However, even with 10^{10} such threads (an enormous number), the execution time would still be 2.5×10^{20} years.

made in recent years by adding regularization terms to the optimization problem that admit derivative-based methods.

In the sections that follow, we place matching problems in a more general setting and show how they can be solved efficiently. Our first step is to review the basics of linear programming.

3.2.2 Linear Programming

A linear program is an optimization problem with a linear objective function and linear constraints. If your prior belief is that all interesting problems are nonlinear, then let us reassure you that linear programming is applicable to a *vast* array of interesting applications. One of these is, somewhat surprisingly, the assignment problem in §3.2.1, as famously demonstrated by the American mathematician George Bernard Dantzig (1914–2005) in Dantzig (1951). Other applications include optimal flows on networks and optimal transport problems, which in turn have diverse applications in economics, finance, engineering, and machine learning.

We explain the key ideas below, beginning with an introduction to linear programming.

3.2.2.1 A Firm Problem

One way to define linear programs is in terms of what open source and commercial solvers for linear programming problems handle. Typically, for these solvers, the problem takes the form

$$\min_{x \in \mathbb{R}^n} c^\top x \tag{3.8}$$

$$\text{subject to } A_1 x = b_1, \ A_2 x \leqslant b_2, \text{ and } d_\ell \leqslant x \leqslant d_u. \tag{3.9}$$

Here each A_i is a matrix with n columns, and c, b_1, b_2, d_ℓ, and d_u are conformable column vectors.

To illustrate, let's consider a simple example, which concerns a firm that fabricates products labeled $1, \ldots, n$. To make each product requires machine hours and labor. Product i requires m_i machine hours and ℓ_i labor hours per unit of output, as shown in the table below

product	machine hours	labor hours	unit price
1	m_1	ℓ_1	p_1
$\vdots$	$\vdots$	$\vdots$	$\vdots$
n	m_n	ℓ_n	p_n

A total of M machine hours and L labor hours are available. Letting q_i denote output of product i, the firm's problem is

$$\max_{q_1,\dots,q_n} \pi(q_1,\dots,q_n) := \sum_{i=1}^{n} p_i q_i - wL - rM$$

subject to

$$\sum_{i=1}^{n} m_i q_i \leqslant M, \quad \sum_{i=1}^{n} \ell_i q_i \leqslant L \text{ and } q_1,\dots,q_n \geqslant 0. \tag{3.10}$$

Here π is profits, and w and r are the wage rate and rental rate of capital. We are taking these values as fixed, along with L and M, so choosing the $q \in \mathbb{R}_+^n$ that maximizes profits is the same as choosing the q that maximizes revenue $\sum_{i=1}^{n} p_i q_i$. This will be our objective in what follows.

(Why are total labor supply and machine hours held fixed here? We might think of this problem as one of designing a daily or weekly production plan, which optimally allocates existing resources, given current prices.)

Figure 3.9 shows an illustration of a simple case with two products. Consistent with Exercise 3.2.3, the feasible set is a polyhedron, shaded in blue. The green lines are contour lines of the revenue function $(q_1, q_2) \mapsto p_1 q_1 + p_2 q_2$, with $p_1 = 3$ and $p_2 = 4$. By inspecting this problem visually and recognizing that the contour lines are increasing as we move to the northeast, it is clear that the maximum is obtained at the extreme point indicated in the figure.

Maximizing revenue is equivalent to minimizing $\sum_i (-p_i) q_i$, so with $c = (-p_1, -p_2)$, we have a linear programming problem to which we can apply a solver.

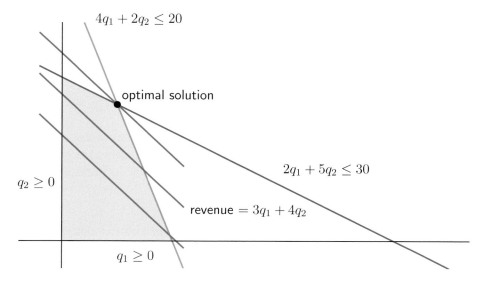

Figure 3.9 Revenue maximizing quantities

3.2.2.2   A Python Implementation

Let's look at one option for solving this problem with Python, via SciPy's open-source solver `linprog`. For the simple two-product firm problem, we ignore the unnecessary equality constraint in (3.9) and set

$$A_2 = \begin{pmatrix} m_1 & m_2 \\ \ell_1 & \ell_2 \end{pmatrix} \quad \text{and} \quad b_2 = \begin{pmatrix} M \\ L \end{pmatrix}.$$

The bound $0 \leqslant q$ is imposed by default, so we do not need to specify d_ℓ and d_u.

We apply the numbers in Figure 3.9, so the maximization version of the problem is

$$\max_{q_1, q_2} 3q_1 + 4q_2 \ \text{s.t.} \ q_1 \geqslant 0, \ q_2 \geqslant 0, \ 2q_1 + 5q_2 \leqslant 30 \text{ and } 4q_1 + 2q_2 \leqslant 20. \quad (3.11)$$

Now we set up primitives and call `linprog` as follows:

```
A = ((2,  5),
     (4,  2))
b = (30,  20)
c = (-3,  -4)    # minus in order to minimize
```

```
from scipy.optimize import linprog
result = linprog(c, A_ub=A, b_ub=b)
print(result.x)
```

The output is `[2.5,  5.0]`, indicating that we should set $q_1 = 2.5$ and $q_2 = 5.0$. The result is obtained via the simplex algorithm, discussed in §3.2.2.8.

EXERCISE 3.2.1. As a way to cross-check the solver's output, try to derive the solution $q = (2.5, 5.0)$ in a more intuitive way, by examining Figure 3.9.

EXERCISE 3.2.2. Consider the same problem with the same parameters, but suppose now that, in addition to the previous constraints, output of q_2 is bounded above by 4. Use `linprog` or another numerical linear solver to obtain the new solution.

3.2.2.3   A Julia Implementation

When solving linear programs, one option is to use a domain-specific modeling language to set out the objective and constraints in the optimization problem. In Python this can be accomplished using open source libraries, such as Pyomo and Google's OR-Tools. In Julia we can use JuMP.

The following code illustrates the Julia case, using JuMP, applied to the firm problem (3.11).

```
using JuMP
using GLPK
```

```
m = Model()
set_optimizer(m, GLPK.Optimizer)

@variable(m, q1 >= 0)
@variable(m, q2 >= 0)
@constraint(m, 2q1 + 5q2 <= 30)
@constraint(m, 4q1 + 2q2 <= 20)
@objective(m, Max, 3q1 + 4q2)

optimize!(m)
```

Notice how the JuMP modeling language allows us to write objectives and constraints as expressions, such as `2q1 + 5q2 <= 30`. This brings the code closer to the mathematics and makes it highly readable.

If we now run `value.(q1)` and `value.(q2)`, we get 2.5 and 5.0, respectively, which are the same as our previous solution.

3.2.2.4   Standard Linear Programs

The programming problem in (3.8)–(3.9) is convenient for applications but somewhat cumbersome for theory. A more canonical version of the linear programming problem is

$$P := \min_{x \in \mathbb{R}^n} \; c^\top x \; \text{ subject to } \; Ax = b \text{ and } x \geqslant 0. \tag{3.12}$$

Here x is interpreted as a column vector in $\mathbb{R}^n$, c is also a column vector in $\mathbb{R}^n$, A is $m \times n$, and b is $m \times 1$. A linear program in the form of (3.12) is said to be in **standard equality form**. In preparation for our discussion of duality below, we also call (3.12) the **primal problem**.

EXERCISE 3.2.3. Prove that the **feasible set** $F = \{x \in \mathbb{R}^n : Ax = b \text{ and } x \geqslant 0\}$ for the linear program (3.12) is a polyhedron.

Standard equality form is more general than it first appears. In fact the original formulation (3.8)–(3.9) can be manipulated into standard equality form via a sequence of transformations. Hence, when treating the theory below, we can specialize to standard equality form without losing generality.

Although we omit full details on the set of necessary transformations (which can be found in Bertsimas and Tsitsiklis (1997) and many other sources), let's gain some understanding by converting the firm optimization problem into standard equality form. To simplify notation, we address this task when $n = 3$, although the general case is almost identical.

As above, we switch to minimization of a linear constraint by using the fact that maximizing revenue is equivalent to minimizing $\sum_i (-p_i) q_i$. Next, we need to convert the two inequality constraints (3.10) into equality constraints. We do this by introducing **slack variables** s_m and s_ℓ and rewriting the constraints as

$$\sum_{i=1}^{3} m_i q_i + s_m = M, \quad \sum_{i=1}^{3} \ell_i q_i + s_\ell = L \quad \text{and} \quad q_1, q_2, q_3, s_m, s_\ell \geqslant 0.$$

Indeed, we can see that requiring $\sum_{i=1}^{3} m_i q_i + s_m = M$ and $s_m \geqslant 0$ is the same as imposing $\sum_{i=1}^{3} m_i q_i \leqslant M$, and the same logic extends to the labor constraint.

Setting $x := (q_1, q_2, q_3, s_m, s_\ell)$, we can now express the problem as

$$\min_{x} c^\top x, \quad \text{where} \quad c^\top := (-p_1, -p_2, -p_3, 0, 0)$$

subject to

$$\begin{pmatrix} m_1 & m_2 & m_3 & 1 & 0 \\ \ell_1 & \ell_2 & \ell_3 & 0 & 1 \end{pmatrix} \begin{pmatrix} q_1 \\ q_2 \\ q_3 \\ s_m \\ s_\ell \end{pmatrix} = \begin{pmatrix} M \\ L \end{pmatrix} \quad \text{and} \quad x \geqslant 0.$$

This is a linear program in standard equality form.

3.2.2.5   Duality for Linear Programs

One of the most important facts concerning linear programming is that strong duality always holds. Let us state the key results. The **dual problem** corresponding to the standard equality form linear program (3.12) is

$$D = \max_{\theta \in \mathbb{R}^m} b^\top \theta \text{ subject to } A^\top \theta \leqslant c. \tag{3.13}$$

Readers who have covered §A.7 in the appendix will be able to see the origins of this expression. In particular, by formula (A.19) in the appendix, the dual problem corresponding to the standard equality form linear program (3.12) can be expressed as

$$D = \max_{\theta \in \mathbb{R}^m} \min_{x \in E} L(x, \theta), \quad \text{where} \quad L(x, \theta) := c^\top x + \theta^\top (b - Ax) \tag{3.14}$$

and $E = \mathbb{R}^n_+$. (We can also treat the inequality $x \geqslant 0$ via a multiplier, but this turns out to be unnecessary.) Now observe that

$$\min_{x \in E} L(x, \theta) = b^\top \theta + \min_{x \geqslant 0} x^\top (c - A^\top \theta) = \begin{cases} b^\top \theta & \text{if } A^\top \theta \leqslant c \\ -\infty & \text{otherwise} \end{cases}.$$

Since the dual problem is to maximize this expression over $\theta \in \mathbb{R}^n$, we see immediately that a θ violating $A^\top \theta \leqslant c$ will never be chosen. Hence the dual to the primal problem (3.12) is (3.13).

3.2.2.6   Strong Duality

As shown in §A.7.1 of the appendix, the inequality $D \leqslant P$ always holds, where P is the primal value in (3.12). This is called **weak duality**. If $P = D$, then **strong**

duality is said to hold. Unlike weak duality, strong duality requires conditions on the primitives.

The next theorem states that, for linear programs, strong duality holds whenever a solution exists. A proof can be obtained either through Dantzig's simplex method or via Farkas' Lemma. See, for example, chapter 4 of Bertsimas and Tsitsiklis (1997) or chapter 6 of Matousek and Gärtner (2007).

THEOREM 3.2.1 (Strong duality for linear programs)   *The primal problem* (3.12) *has a finite minimizer* x^* *if and only if the dual problem* (3.13) *has a finite maximizer* θ^*. *If these solutions exist, then* $c^\top x^* = b^\top \theta^*$.

Strong duality of linear programs has many important roles. Some of these are algorithmic: Duality can be used to devise efficient solution methods for linear programming problems. Another way that duality matters for economists is that it provides deep links between optimality and competitive equilibria, as we show below.

3.2.2.7   Complementary Slackness

We say that $x^* \geqslant 0$ and $\theta^* \in \mathbb{R}^m$ satisfy the **complementary slackness** conditions for the linear program (3.12) when

$$\theta_i^* \left(b_i - \sum_{j=1}^n a_{ij} x_j^* \right) = 0 \quad \text{for all } i \in [m] \tag{3.15}$$

$$x_j^* \left(c_j - \sum_{i=1}^m a_{ij} \theta_i^* \right) = 0 \quad \text{for all } j \in [n]. \tag{3.16}$$

While it is possible to derive these expressions from the complementary slackness in the KKT conditions in §A.7.3, a better approach is to connect them directly to the saddle-point condition.

To see how this works, suppose that $x^* \geqslant 0$ is feasible for the primal problem, and $\theta^* \in \mathbb{R}^m$ is feasible for the dual problem. If (x^*, θ^*) is a saddle point of L, then the complementary slackness conditions (3.15)–(3.16) must hold. Indeed, (3.15) is trivial when x^* is feasible, since $Ax^* = b$. At the same time, (3.16) must be true because violation implies that

$$x_j^* \left(c_j - \sum_{i=1}^m a_{ij} \theta_i^* \right) > 0 \quad \text{for some } j \in [n],$$

due to dual feasibility (i.e., $A^\top \theta^* \leqslant c$) and $x^* \geqslant 0$. But then (x^*, θ^*) is not a saddle point of L, since changing the j-th element of x^* to zero strictly reduces the Lagrangian

$$L(x, \theta) = c^\top x + \theta^\top (b - Ax) = x^\top (c - A^\top \theta) + \theta^\top b.$$

By sharpening this argument, it is possible to show that, for linear programs, the complementary slackness conditions are the exact necessary and sufficient conditions for a saddle point of the Lagrangian. This leads to the next theorem.

THEOREM 3.2.2   *If $x^* \geqslant 0$ is feasible for the primal problem and θ^* is feasible for the dual problem, then the following statements are equivalent:*

(i) x^* is optimal for the primal problem and θ^* is optimal for the dual problem.
(ii) The pair (x^*, θ^*) obeys the complementary slackness conditions (3.15)–(3.16).

Chapter 4 of Bertsimas and Tsitsiklis (1997) provides more discussion and a full proof of Theorem 3.2.2. Below, we illustrate some of the elegant connections between complementary slackness and equilibria in competitive economic environments.

3.2.2.8   The Simplex Algorithm

Linear programming is challenging in high-dimensional settings, partly because the linear objective function implies that solutions are not interior. The first efficient solution methods for linear programs appeared in the 1930s and 1940s, starting with the simplex method of Kantorovich and Dantzig. As the simplex method began to prove its worth, linear programming grew into a technique of enormous practical importance. Operations research, communication, and production systems began to make heavy use of linear programs.

The simplex algorithm makes use of the following result, which is proved in Theorem 2.7 of Bertsimas and Tsitsiklis (1997).

THEOREM 3.2.3   *If the linear program* (3.12) *has an optimal solution, then it also has an optimal solution that is an extreme point of the feasible set.*

(An extreme point of a polyhedron was defined in §A.5.1. The feasible set was shown to be a polyhedron in Exercise 3.2.3.)

The simplex algorithm makes use of Theorem 3.2.3 by walking along the edges of the polyhedron that forms the feasible set, from one extreme point to another, seeking at each step a new extreme point (which coincides with a vertex of the polyhedron) that strictly lowers the value of the objective function. Details can be found in Bertsimas and Tsitsiklis (1997) and Matousek and Gärtner (2007).

3.3   Optimal Transport

Next we turn to optimal flows across networks. One simple – but computationally nontrivial – example of a network flow problem is the linear assignment problem we analyzed in §3.2.1. There, the vertices are either workers or jobs, and the edges are assignments, chosen optimally to minimize aggregate cost. More general network flow problems extend these ideas, allowing endogenous formation of networks in more sophisticated settings. The general structure is that vertices are given, while edges and weights are chosen to optimize some criterion. There are natural applications of these ideas in trade, transportation, and communication, as well as less obvious applications within economics, finance, statistics, and machine learning.

In our study of network flows, we begin with the optimal transport problem, which is the most important special case of the general network flow problem. (In fact, as we show in §3.3.4.3, there exists a technique by which the general network flow problem can always be reduced to an optimal transport problem.)

3.3.1   The Monge–Kantorovich Problem

Optimal transport is a classic problem dating back to the work of Gaspard Monge (1746–1818), who studied, among many other things, the transport of earth for the construction of forts. This simple-sounding problem – how to transport a pile of a given shape into a new pile of a given shape at minimum cost – can, after normalization, be identified with the problem of least-cost transformation of one distribution into another distribution. Figure 3.10 gives a visualization of transforming one distribution into another in one dimension (although the cost function is not specified).

It turns out that, by varying the notion of cost, this transportation problem provides a highly flexible method for comparing the distance between two distributions, with the essential idea being that distributions are regarded as "close" if one can be transformed into the other at low cost. The resulting distance metric finds wide-ranging and important applications in statistics, machine learning, and various branches of applied mathematics.[2]

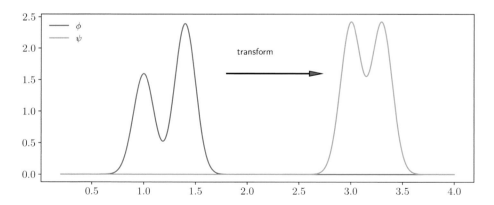

Figure 3.10 Transforming distribution φ into distribution ψ

[2] For example, in image processing, two images might be regarded as close if the cost of transforming one into the other by altering individual pixels is small. Even now, in image processing and some branches of machine learning, one of the metrics over the set of probability distributions arising from optimal transport methods is referred to as "earth mover's distance" in honor of the work of Monge.

In economics, optimal transport has important applications in transportation and trade networks, as well as in matching problems, econometrics, finance, and so on (see, e.g., Galichon (2018)). As such, it is not surprising that economists have contributed a great deal to the optimal transport problem, with deep and fundamental work being accomplished by the great Russian mathematical economist Leonid Kantorovich (1912–1986), as well as the Dutch economist Tjalling Koopmans (1910–1985), who shared the Nobel Prize with Kantorovich in 1975 for their work on linear programming and optimal transport.[3]

We start our discussion with a straightforward presentation of the mathematics. Then, in §3.3.3, we will connect the mathematics to economic problems, and show the deep connections between transport, duality, complementary slackness, and competitive equilibria.

3.3.1.1 Monge's Formulation

We start with the classical problem of Monge, which is simple to explain. We take as given two finite sets X and Y, paired with distributions $\varphi \in \mathcal{D}(X)$ and $\psi \in \mathcal{D}(Y)$. Elements of X and Y are called **locations**. To avoid tedious side cases, we assume throughout that φ and ψ are strictly positive on their domains. In addition, we are supplied with a cost function $c \colon X \times Y \to \mathbb{R}_+$. Our goal is to "transport" φ into ψ at minimum cost. That is, we seek to solve

$$\min_T \sum_x c(x, T(x)) \qquad (3.17)$$

over the set of all maps T from X onto Y satisfying

$$\sum_x \varphi(x) \mathbb{1}\{T(x) = y\} = \psi(y) \quad \text{for all } y \in Y. \qquad (3.18)$$

The constraint says T must be such that, for each target location y, the sum of all probability mass sent to y is equal to the specified quantity $\psi(y)$. The symbol $\sum_x$ is short for $\sum_{x \in X}$. In this context, T is often called a **Monge map**.

EXERCISE 3.3.1. While we required T to map X *onto* Y, meaning that every $y \in Y$ has some preimage, this condition is already implied by (3.18). Explain why.

The problem is easily illustrated in the current discrete setting. Figure 3.11 gives a visualization when locations are enumerated as $X = \{x_1, \ldots, x_7\}$ and $Y = \{y_1, y_2, y_3, y_4\}$, with both X and Y being subsets of $\mathbb{R}^2$. For simplicity, $\varphi(x_i)$ is written as φ_i and similarly for $\psi(y_j)$. Vertex size is proportional to probability mass assigned to the vertex. The edges represent one feasible Monge map.

---

[3] The optimal transport problem continues to attract the interest of many brilliant mathematicians and economists, with two recent Fields Medals being awarded for work on optimal transport. The first was awarded to Cedric Villani in 2010, while the second was to Alessio Figalli in 2018. Note that the Fields Medal is only awarded every four years (unlike the Nobel Prize, which is annual).

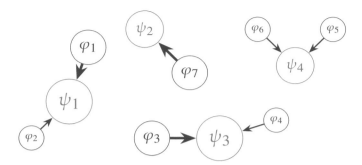

Figure 3.11 A Monge map transporting φ to ψ

Discreteness and lack of convexity in the constraint (3.18) imply that the Monge problem is, in general, hard to solve. Truly fundamental progress had to wait until Kantorovich showed how convexification can greatly simplify the problem. The convexification process requires shifting the problem to a higher-dimensional space, but the cost of higher dimensions is outweighed by the regularization provided by convexity and lack of discreteness. We study the Kantorovich formulation in §3.3.1.3.

EXERCISE 3.3.2. Another issue with the Monge formulation of optimal transport is that existence of a solution can easily fail. Provide an example where no Monge map exists in the setting where X and Y are finite.

3.3.1.2 Assignment as Optimal Transport

The linear assignment problem studied in §3.2.1, with cost $c(i, j)$ of training worker i for job j, is a special case of optimal transport. All we have to do is set X = Y = $[n]$ and take φ and ψ to be discrete uniform distributions on $[n]$.

EXERCISE 3.3.3. Show that, in this setting, T is a Monge map if and only if T is a bijection from $[n]$ to itself.

Since T must be a bijection on $[n]$, which is also a permutation of $[n]$, the objective of the optimal transport problem under the current configuration is

$$\min_{T \in \mathscr{P}} \sum_{i=1}^{n} c(i, T(i)), \tag{3.19}$$

where $\mathscr{P}$ is the set of all permutations of $[n]$. This is the same optimization problem as the linear assignment problem in (3.7).

3.3.1.3 Kantorovich's Relaxation of the Monge Problem

The basic idea in Kantorovich's relaxation of the Monge problem is to allow mass located at arbitrary $x \in$ X to be mapped to multiple locations in Y, rather than just one. This means that we are no longer seeking a function T, since, by definition, a

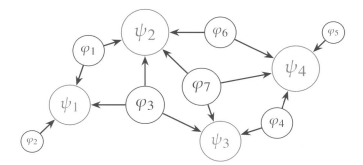

Figure 3.12 Kantorovich relaxation of the Monge problem

function can map a given point to only one image. Instead, we seek a "transport plan" that sends some fraction $\pi(x, y)$ of the mass at x to y. The plan is constrained by the requirement that, for all x and y,

(i) total probability mass sent to y is $\psi(y)$ and
(ii) total probability mass sent from x is $\varphi(x)$.

These constraints on this transport plan mean that it takes the form of a "coupling," which we define below.

Figure 3.12 illustrates a feasible transport plan in the discrete setting. As with Figure 3.11, $\varphi(x_i)$ is written as φ_i and similarly for $\psi(y_j)$, while vertex size is proportional to probability mass. Unlike the Monge setting of Figure 3.11, the mass at each vertex φ_i can be shared across multiple ψ_j, as long as the constraints are respected.

Let's write the constraints more carefully. We recall that, in probability theory, a coupling is a joint distribution with specific marginals. More precisely, given φ in $\mathscr{D}(\mathsf{X})$ and ψ in $\mathscr{D}(\mathsf{Y})$, a **coupling** of (φ, ψ) is an element π of $\mathscr{D}(\mathsf{X} \times \mathsf{Y})$ with marginals φ and ψ. This restriction on marginals means that

$$\sum_y \pi(x, y) = \varphi(x) \quad \text{for all } x \in \mathsf{X} \quad \text{and} \tag{3.20}$$

$$\sum_x \pi(x, y) = \psi(y) \quad \text{for all } y \in \mathsf{Y} \tag{3.21}$$

The constraints in (3.20)–(3.21) require that

(i) for any $x \in \mathsf{X}$, the total amount of probability mass flowing out of x is $\varphi(x)$ and
(ii) for any $y \in \mathsf{Y}$, the total amount of probability mass flowing into y is $\psi(y)$.

In the present setting, a coupling is also called a **transport plan**.

EXERCISE 3.3.4. The constraints (3.20)–(3.21), which define a coupling π of φ and ψ, generalize the Monge constraint in (3.18). To see this, let T be a map satisfying (3.18), and set

$$\pi(x, y) = \varphi(x)\mathbb{1}\{T(x) = y\}$$

on $X \times Y$, so that π is the joint distribution that puts all mass on the image of T. Prove that (3.20)–(3.21) both hold.

Let $\Pi(\varphi, \psi)$ be the set of all couplings of ψ and φ. Taking φ, ψ and the cost function c as given, the general **Monge–Kantorovich problem**, also called the **optimal transport problem**, is to solve

$$P := \min_{\pi} \langle c, \pi \rangle_F \quad \text{subject to} \quad \pi \in \Pi(\varphi, \psi), \tag{3.22}$$

where

$$\langle c, \pi \rangle_F := \sum_x \sum_y c(x, y) \pi(x, y)$$

is the **Frobenius inner product** of c and π, treated as $|X| \times |Y|$ matrices. The sum in $\langle c, \pi \rangle_F$ measures the total cost of transporting φ into ψ under the plan π. There is linearity embedded in this cost formulation, since doubling the amount sent from x to y scales the associated cost at rate $c(x, y)$.

We call any π solving (3.22) an **optimal plan**. Since we are maximizing over a finite set, at least one such plan exists.

REMARK 3.3.1 *The problem (3.22) is sometimes expressed in terms of random variables, as follows. In this setting, a coupling π in $\Pi(\varphi, \psi)$ is identified with a pair of random elements (X, Y) such that $X \overset{d}{=} \varphi$ and $Y \overset{d}{=} \psi$. We can then write*

$$P = \min_{(X,Y)} \mathbb{E}\, c(X, Y) \quad \text{subject to} \quad (X, Y) \in \mathcal{D}(X \times Y) \text{ with } X \overset{d}{=} \varphi \text{ and } Y \overset{d}{=} \psi.$$

EXERCISE 3.3.5. One of the most important features of the Kantorovich relaxation is that, for given φ and ψ, the constraint set is convex. To verify this, we let $n = |X|$ and $m = |Y|$, associate each $x \in X$ with some $i \in [n]$, associate each $y \in Y$ with some $j \in [m]$, and treat c and π as $n \times m$ matrices, with typical elements c_{ij} and π_{ij}. The constraints are

$$\pi \mathbb{1}_m = \varphi \quad \text{and} \quad \pi^\top \mathbb{1}_n = \psi, \tag{3.23}$$

where $\mathbb{1}_k$ is a $k \times 1$ vector of ones. With this notation, prove that the set $\Pi(\varphi, \psi)$ of $\pi \in \mathbb{M}^{n \times m}$ satisfying the constraints is convex, in the sense that

$$\pi, \hat{\pi} \in \Pi(\varphi, \psi) \text{ and } \alpha \in [0, 1] \implies \alpha \pi + (1 - \alpha)\hat{\pi} \in \Pi(\varphi, \psi).$$

3.3.1.4   Optimal Transport as a Linear Program

With some relatively simple manipulations, the general optimal transport problem can be mapped into a standard equality form linear program. This provides two significant benefits. First, we can apply duality theory, which yields important insights. Second, on the computational side, we can use linear program solvers to calculate optimal plans.

To map the optimal transport problem into a linear program, we need to convert matrices into vectors. We will use the vec operator, which takes an arbitrary $A \in \mathbb{M}^{n \times m}$ and maps it to a vector in $\mathbb{R}^{nm}$ by stacking its columns vertically. For example,

$$\text{vec} \begin{pmatrix} a_{11} & a_{12} \\ a_{21} & a_{22} \end{pmatrix} = \begin{pmatrix} a_{11} \\ a_{21} \\ a_{12} \\ a_{22} \end{pmatrix}.$$

In this section we adopt the notational conventions in Exercise 3.3.5. The objective function $\langle c, \pi \rangle_F$ for the optimal transport problem can now be expressed as $\text{vec}(c)^\top \text{vec}(\pi)$.

To rewrite the constraints in terms of $\text{vec}(\pi)$, we use the Kronecker product, which is denoted by $\otimes$ and defined as follows. Suppose A is an $m \times s$ matrix with entries (a_{ij}) and that B is an $n \times t$ matrix. The **Kronecker product** $A \otimes B$ of A and B is the $mn \times st$ matrix, defined, in block matrix form, by

$$A \otimes B = \begin{pmatrix} a_{11}B & a_{12}B & \cdots & a_{1s}B \\ a_{21}B & a_{22}B & \cdots & a_{2s}B \\ & & \vdots & \\ a_{m1}B & a_{m2}B & \cdots & a_{ms}B \end{pmatrix}.$$

It can be shown that Kronecker products and the vec operator are connected by the following relationship: For conformable matrices A, B, and M, we have

$$\text{vec}(AMB) = (B^\top \otimes A)\,\text{vec}(M). \tag{3.24}$$

Using (3.24) and the symbol I_k for the $k \times k$ identity matrix, we can rewrite the first constraint in (3.23) as

$$\varphi = I_n \pi \mathbb{1}_m = \text{vec}(I_n \pi \mathbb{1}_m) = (\mathbb{1}_m^\top \otimes I_n)\,\text{vec}(\pi). \tag{3.25}$$

EXERCISE 3.3.6. Show that the second constraint in (3.23) can be expressed as

$$\psi = (I_m \otimes \mathbb{1}_n^\top)\,\text{vec}(\pi). \tag{3.26}$$

Now, using block matrix notation and setting

$$A := \begin{pmatrix} \mathbb{1}_m^\top \otimes I_n \\ I_m \otimes \mathbb{1}_n^\top \end{pmatrix} \quad \text{and} \quad b := \begin{pmatrix} \varphi \\ \psi \end{pmatrix},$$

the optimal transport problem can be expressed as the standard equality form linear program

$$\min_x \text{vec}(c)^\top x \quad \text{over } x \in \mathbb{R}_+^{nm} \text{ such that } Ax = b. \tag{3.27}$$

Finally, for a given solution x, the transport plan is recovered by inverting $x = \text{vec}(\pi)$.

3.3.1.5   Implementation

Listing 1 is a function that implements the above steps, given flat (one-dimensional) arrays `phi` and `psi` representing the distributions over the source and target locations, plus a two-dimensional array `c` representing transport costs. (The `method` argument `highs-ipm` tells `linprog` to use a particular interior point method, details of which can be found in the `linprog` documentation. Simplex and other methods give similar results.)

```python
import numpy as np
from scipy.optimize import linprog

def ot_solver(phi, psi, c, method='highs-ipm'):
    """
    Solve the OT problem associated with distributions phi, psi
    and cost matrix c.

    Parameters
    ----------
    phi : 1-D array
        Distribution over the source locations.
    psi : 1-D array
        Distribution over the target locations.
    c : 2-D array
        Cost matrix.
    """
    n, m = len(phi), len(psi)

    # Vectorize c
    c_vec = c.reshape((m * n, 1), order='F')

    # Construct A and b
    A1 = np.kron(np.ones((1, m)), np.identity(n))
    A2 = np.kron(np.identity(m), np.ones((1, n)))
    A  = np.vstack((A1, A2))
    b  = np.hstack((phi, psi))

    # Call solver
    res = linprog(c_vec, A_eq=A, b_eq=b, method=method)

    # Invert the vec operation to get the solution as a matrix
    pi = res.x.reshape((n, m), order='F')
    return pi
```

Listing 1: Function to solve a transport problem via linear programming

Notice that in Listing 1, the reshape order is specified to F. This tells NumPy to reshape with Fortran **column-major** order, which coincides with the definition of the vec operator described in §3.3.1.4. (The Python vectorize operation defaults to **row-major** order, which concatenates rows rather than stacking columns. In contrast, Julia uses column-major by default.)

Let's call this function for the very simple problem

$$\varphi = \begin{pmatrix} 0.5 \\ 0.5 \end{pmatrix}, \quad \psi = \begin{pmatrix} 1 \\ 0 \end{pmatrix}, \quad \text{and} \quad c = \begin{pmatrix} 1 & 1 \\ 1 & 1 \end{pmatrix}.$$

With these primitives, all mass from φ_1 and φ_2 should be sent to ψ_1. To implement this problem, we set

```
phi = np.array((0.5, 0.5))
psi = np.array((1, 0))
c = np.ones((2, 2))
```

and then call ot_solver via

```
ot_solver(phi, psi, c)
```

The output is as expected:

```
array([[0.5, 0. ],
       [0.5, 0. ]])
```

3.3.1.6   Python Optimal Transport

In the case of Python, the steps above have been automated by the Python Optimal Transport (POT) package, due to Flamary et al. (2021). For the simple problem from §3.3.1.5, we run

```
import ot
ot.emd(phi, psi, c)     # Use simplex method via the emd solver
```

The output is again equal to

```
array([[0.5, 0. ],
       [0.5, 0. ]])
```

Figure 3.13 shows an example of an optimal transport problem solved using the POT package. The interpretation is similar to Figure 3.12, although the number of vertices is larger. In addition, the edges show the optimal transport configuration, in the sense that π^*, the optimal transport plan, is treated as the adjacency matrix for the graph. (The figure shows the unweighted graph, with an arrow drawn from φ_i to ψ_j whenever $\pi^*_{ij} > 0$.) The optimal transport plan is obtained by converting the transport problem into a linear program, as just described, and applying the simplex method. Although there are 32 nodes of each type, the problem is solved by the simplex routine in less than 1 millisecond.

3.3.1.7   Kantorovich Relaxation and Linear Assignment

We showed in §3.3.1.2 that the linear assignment problem studied in §3.2.1 is a special case of optimal transport, where φ and ψ become discrete uniform distributions on $[n]$. Moreover, as we have just seen, Kantorovich's relaxation method allows us to apply linear programming. This leads to fast solutions.

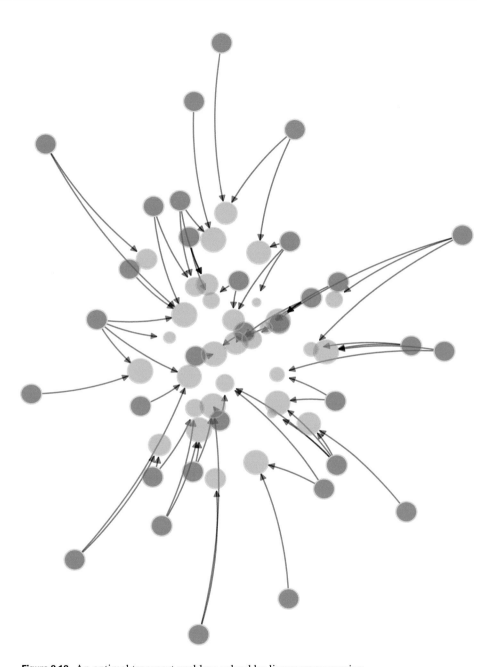

Figure 3.13 An optimal transport problem solved by linear programming

In the discussion in §3.2.1 we used $n = 40$. Let's start here with $n = 4$, to illustrate the method, and then try with $n = 40$. The matrix $c(i, j)$ of costs, which is the only other primitive, will be generated randomly as an independent array of uniform random variables. Then we apply the POT library, as in §3.3.1.6.

Here is our set up:

```
import numpy as np
import ot

n = 4
phi = np.ones(n)
psi = np.ones(n)
```

We have broken the rule that φ and ψ should sum to one. This could be fixed easily by using `np.ones(n)/n` instead of `np.ones(n)`, but the POT library does not care (as long as `np.sum(phi)` equals `np.sum(psi)`), and, moreover, the idea of putting unit mass everywhere is natural, since each element of φ represents one worker, and each element of ψ represents one job.

Now we build the cost matrix:

```
c = np.random.uniform(size=(n, n))
```

The output is

```
array([[0.03841, 0.32896, 0.55989, 0.41682],
       [0.91527, 0.24566, 0.26022, 0.64510],
       [0.96275, 0.44089, 0.79274, 0.93065],
       [0.40454, 0.87307, 0.43555, 0.54903]])
```

(For example, the cost of retraining worker 1 for job 2 is 0.32896.) Finally, we call the solver:

```
ot.emd(phi, psi, c)
```

The output is

```
array([[1., 0., 0., 0.],
       [0., 0., 1., 0.],
       [0., 1., 0., 0.],
       [0., 0., 0., 1.]])
```

This is a permutation matrix, which provides another way to express a permutation of $[n]$. The first row tells us that worker 1 is assigned to job 1, the second tells us that worker 2 is assigned to job 3, and so on.

If we now set $n = 40$ and rerun the code. The line `ot.emd(phi, psi, c)`, which calls the simplex-based solver, runs in less than 1 millisecond on a mid-range laptop. This is a remarkable improvement on the 2.5×10^{30}-year estimate for the brute force solver we obtained in §3.2.1.

3.3.1.8 Tight Relaxation

Notice that the solution we obtained for the linear assignment problem using the simplex method does not split mass, as permitted by the Kantorovich relaxation. For example, we do not send half of a worker to one job and the other half to another. This is convenient, but why does it hold?

While we omit the details, the basic idea is that a general Kantorovich transport plan is a bistochastic matrix, and all such matrices can be formed as convex combinations of permutation matrices. (This is called Birkhoff's theorem.) In other words, the permutation matrices are extreme points of the set of bistochastic matrices. Moreover, Theorem 3.2.3 tells us that any optimizer of a linear program will be an extreme point – in this case, a permutation matrix.

3.3.2 Kantorovich Duality

One of the greatest achievements of Kantorovich was to show that the optimal transport problem can be connected to a dual problem, and how that dual problem can be used to characterize solutions. This work anticipated much of the later development of duality theory for arbitrary linear programs.

Throughout this section, in stating the main results, we use the notation

$$\langle f, \varphi \rangle = \sum_x f(x)\varphi(x) \quad \text{for } f \in \mathbb{R}^{\mathsf{X}} \text{ and } \varphi \in \mathscr{D}(\mathsf{X}).$$

This is just the usual inner product, when we think of f and φ as vectors in $\mathbb{R}^{|\mathsf{X}|}$. Also, given a cost function c on $\mathsf{X} \times \mathsf{Y}$, let $\mathscr{F}_c$ be all pairs (w, p) in $\mathbb{R}^{\mathsf{X}} \times \mathbb{R}^{\mathsf{Y}}$ such that

$$p(y) \leqslant c(x, y) + w(x) \text{ on } \mathsf{X} \times \mathsf{Y}. \tag{3.28}$$

One part of Kantorovich's duality results runs as follows.

THEOREM 3.3.1   *For all $\varphi \in \mathscr{D}(\mathsf{X})$ and $\psi \in \mathscr{D}(\mathsf{Y})$, we have $P = D$, where*

$$D := \max_{(w, p)} \left\{ \langle p, \psi \rangle - \langle w, \varphi \rangle \right\} \quad \textit{subject to} \quad (w, p) \in \mathscr{F}_c. \tag{3.29}$$

Theorem 3.3.1 can now be understood as a special case of the more general result that strong duality holds for linear programs, which we stated in Theorem 3.2.1. In that spirit, let us verify Theorem 3.3.1 using Theorem 3.2.1, by working with the linear programming formulation of the optimal transport problem provided in §3.3.1.4.

To do this, we take that formulation, which is stated in (3.27), and apply the dual formula in (3.13), which yields

$$D = \max_{\theta \in \mathbb{R}^{n+m}} \begin{pmatrix} \varphi \\ \psi \end{pmatrix}^{\mathsf{T}} \theta \text{ subject to } \begin{pmatrix} \mathbb{1}_m^{\mathsf{T}} \otimes I_n \\ I_m \otimes \mathbb{1}_n^{\mathsf{T}} \end{pmatrix}^{\mathsf{T}} \theta \leqslant \text{vec}(c).$$

If we write the argument $\theta \in \mathbb{R}^{n+m}$ as $(-w, p)$, so that we now maximize over the two components $-w \in \mathbb{R}^n$ and $p \in \mathbb{R}^m$, as well as transposing the constraint, we get

$$\max_{w,\, p} \left\{ p^\top \psi - w^\top \varphi \right\} \quad \text{subject to} \quad p^\top (I_m \otimes \mathbb{1}_n^\top) - w^\top (\mathbb{1}_m^\top \otimes I_n) \leqslant \operatorname{vec}(c)^\top,$$

where $w \in \mathbb{R}^n$ and $p \in \mathbb{R}^m$. By using the definition of the Kronecker product and carefully writing out the individual terms, it can be shown that the constraint in this expression is equivalent to requiring that $p_j - w_i \leqslant c_{ij}$ for all $(i, j) \in [n] \times [m]$. Recalling that X has been mapped to $[n]$ and Y has been mapped to $[m]$; this is exactly the same restriction as (3.28).

At this point it is clear that (3.29) is nothing but the dual of the linear program formed from the optimal transport problem. The claims in Theorem 3.3.1 now follow directly from the strong duality of linear programs (Theorem 3.2.1).

EXERCISE 3.3.7. Show that

$$\langle c, \pi \rangle \geqslant \langle p, \psi \rangle - \langle w, \varphi \rangle \quad \text{whenever } \pi \in \Pi(\varphi, \psi) \text{ and } (w, p) \in \mathscr{F}_c. \tag{3.30}$$

Use this fact to provide a direct proof that weak duality holds for the optimal transport problem, in the sense that $D \leqslant P$. (Here P is defined in the primal problem (3.22), and D is defined in the dual problem (3.29).)

3.3.3 Optimal Transport and Competitive Equilibria

The other major achievement of Kantorovich in the context of duality theory for optimal transport was to connect optimality of transport plans with the existence of functions w, p from the dual problem such that a version of the complementary slackness conditions holds. Here we present this result, not in the original direct formulation but rather through the lens of a competitive equilibrium problem. In doing so, we illustrate some of the deep connections between prices, decentralized equilibria, and efficient allocations.

3.3.3.1 The Advisor's Problem

We imagine the following scenario. Iron is mined at a finite collection of sites, which we denote by X. We identify an element $x \in \mathsf{X}$ with a point $(a, b) \in \mathbb{R}^2$, which can be understood as the location of the mine in question on a map. At the wish of the queen, who seeks to defend the empire from greedy rivals, this iron is converted to swords by blacksmiths. There are a number of talented blacksmiths in this country, located at sites given by Y. As for X, each $y \in \mathsf{Y}$ indicates a point in $\mathbb{R}^2$. Henceforth, we refer to "mine x" rather than "the mine at x," and so on.

Each month, mine x produces $\varphi(x)$ ounces of iron ore, while blacksmith y consumes $\psi(y)$ ounces. We take these quantities as fixed. We assume that total supply equals total demand, so that $\sum_x \varphi(x) = \sum_y \psi(y)$. For convenience, we normalize this sum to unity. As a result, φ and ψ are elements of $\mathcal{D}(\mathsf{X})$ and $\mathcal{D}(\mathsf{Y})$, respectively.

The cost of transporting from x to y is known and given by $c(x, y)$ per ounce. The queen's chief advisor is tasked with allocating and transporting iron from the mines to the blacksmiths, such that each blacksmith y receives their desired quantity $\psi(y)$, at minimum cost. A small amount of thought will convince you that the advisor's problem is a version of the optimal transport problem (3.22). We call this the primal problem in what follows.

Operating in the days before Kantorovich, Dantzig, and the electronic computer, the advisor employs a large team of bean counters, instructing them to find the allocation with least cost by trying different combinations. However, after a few days, she realizes the futility of the task. (With infinite divisibility, which corresponds to our mathematical model, the number of allocations is infinite. If we replace infinite divisibility with a finite approximation, the scale can easily be as large as that of the matching problem discussed in §3.2.1, with only a moderate number of mines and blacksmiths.)

3.3.3.2   The Guild's Problem

At this point she has another idea. There is a guild of traveling salespeople, who buy goods in one town and sell them in another. She seeks out the guild master and asks him to bid for the project along the following lines. The guild will pay the queen's treasury $w(x)$ per ounce for iron ore at mine x. It will then sell the iron at price $p(y)$ per ounce to the queen's representative at blacksmith y. The difference can be pocketed by the guild, as long as all blacksmiths are provided with their desired quantities. The guild master is asked to propose price functions w and p.

The guild master sees at once that p and w must satisfy $p(y) - w(x) \leqslant c(x, y)$ at each x, y, for otherwise the advisor, who is no one's fool, will see immediately that money could be saved by organizing the transportation herself. Given this constraint, the guild master seeks to maximize aggregate profits, which is $\sum_y p(y)\psi(y) - \sum_x w(x)\varphi(x)$. At this point it will be clear to you that the problem of the guild master is exactly that of Kantorovich's dual problem, as given in Theorem 3.3.1.

Since the advisor has given up on her team of bean counters, the guild master employs them and asks them to produce the optimal pair of prices. The bean counters set to work, trying different combinations of prices that satisfy the constraints. However, without a systematic methodology to follow or fast computers to turn to, their progress is slow. The advisor begins to fear that the coming war will be over before the guild master replies.

3.3.3.3   Decentralized Equilibrium

At this point, it occurs to the advisor that yet another approach exists: privatize the mines, abolish the guild, and let the traveling salespeople, mine owners, and blacksmiths make individual choices in order to maximize their profits. Purchase and sales prices, as well as quantities transported from each mine to each blacksmith, will be determined by the free market.

Although the advisor predates Kantorovich, she reasons that competition will prevent each salesperson from profiteering, while the desire for profits will encourage high levels of transportation and minimal waste. It turns out that this idea works amazingly well, in the sense that we now describe.

For the record, we define a **competitive equilibrium** for this market as a pair of price vectors (w, p) in $\mathbb{R}^X \times \mathbb{R}^Y$ and a set of quantities $\pi : X \times Y \to \mathbb{R}_+$ such that the following three conditions hold: For all (x, y) in $X \times Y$,

$$\sum_{v \in Y} \pi(x, v) = \varphi(x) \text{ and } \sum_{u \in X} \pi(u, y) = \psi(y) \tag{RE}$$

$$p(y) \leqslant c(x, y) + w(x) \tag{NA}$$

$$p(y) = c(x, y) + w(x) \text{ whenever } \pi(x, y) > 0. \tag{IC}$$

Condition (RE) is a resource constraint that builds in the assumption that no ore is wasted or disposed. Condition (NA) imposes no arbitrage. If it is violated along route (x, y), then another salesperson, of which we assume there are many, will be able to gain business without suffering losses by offering a slightly higher purchase price at x or a slightly lower sales price at y. Finally, condition (IC) is an incentive constraint, which says that, whenever a route is active (in the sense that a nonzero quantity is transported), prices are such that the salespeople do not lose money.

We do not claim that a competitive equilibrium will hold immediately and at every instant in time. However, we reason, as the advisor does, that competitive equilibrium has natural stability properties, as described in the previous paragraph. As such, we predict it as a likely outcome of decentralized trade, provided that private property rights are enforced (e.g., bandits are eliminated from the routes) and noncompetitive behaviors are prevented (e.g., collusion by mine owners is met by suitably painful punishments).

Taking c, φ, and ψ as given, we can state the following key theorem, which states that any competitive equilibrium simultaneously solves both the advisor's quantity problem *and* the guild master's price problem.

THEOREM 3.3.2   *If prices (w, p) and $\pi \in \mathbb{M}^{n \times m}$ form a competitive equilibrium, then*

(i) π is an optimal transport plan, solving the primal problem (3.22); and
(ii) (w, p) solves the Kantorovich dual problem (3.29).

To prove the theorem, we will use the results from the next exercise.

EXERCISE 3.3.8. Let A and B be nonempty sets. Let f and g be real-valued on A and B such that $f(a) \geqslant g(b)$ for all $(a, b) \in A \times B$, and, in addition, $\min_{a \in A} f(a) = \max_{b \in B} g(b)$. Prove the following statement: If there exist $\bar{a} \in A$ and $\bar{b} \in B$ such that $f(\bar{a}) = g(\bar{b})$, then $\bar{a}$ is a minimizer of f on A, and $\bar{b}$ is a maximizer of g on B.

We will use Exercise 3.3.8 in the following way. Let $A = \Pi(\varphi, \psi)$ and $B = \mathscr{F}_c$. Let f be the value of the primal and g be the value of the dual. By (3.30), the ordering $f(\pi) \geqslant g(w, p)$ holds over all feasible $\pi \in A$ and $(w, p) \in B$ pairs. By strong duality, we also have $\min_{\pi \in A} f(\pi) = \max_{(w, p) \in B} g(w, p)$. Hence we need only show that, when (w, p) and π form a competitive equilibrium, we have $f(\pi) = g(w, p)$.

Proof of Theorem 3.3.2   Suppose that (w, p) and π form a competitive equilibrium. From (RE) we know that π is feasible for the primal problem. From (NA) we know that (w, p) is feasible for the dual. Since the equality in the (IC) condition holds when $\pi(x, y) > 0$, we can multiply both sides of this equality by $\pi(x, y)$ and sum over all x, y to obtain

$$\sum_{x, y} c(x, y)\pi(x, y) = \sum_y p(y)\psi(y) - \sum_x w(x)\psi(x). \tag{3.31}$$

The result of Exercise 3.3.8 now applies, so π attains the minimum in the primal problem, and (w, p) attains the maximum in the dual.   □

We also have the following converse:

THEOREM 3.3.3   *If π is an optimal transport plan, then there exists a pair $(w, p) \in \mathbb{R}^X \times \mathbb{R}^Y$ such that the quantities determined by π and the prices in (w, p) form a competitive equilibrium.*

Proof   Let π be an optimal plan. To be optimal, π must be feasible, so $\pi \in \Pi(\varphi, \psi)$, which implies that (RE) holds.

By Kantorovich's duality theorem (Theorem 3.3.1), we can obtain $(w, p) \in \mathscr{F}_c$ such that (3.31) holds. Since $(w, p) \in \mathscr{F}_c$, (NA) holds. From (NA) we have $c(x, y) + w(x) - p(y) \geqslant 0$ for all x, y. From this and (3.31) we see that (IC) must be valid. We conclude that π and (w, p) form a competitive equilibrium.   □

3.3.4   The General Flow Problem

We now describe a general network flow problem that can be used to analyze a large range of applications, from international trade to communication and assignment. This general problem includes optimal transport as a special case.

Once we have introduced the problem, we show two results. First, the problem can easily be formulated as a linear program and solved using standard linear programming methods. Second, even though optimal transport is a strict subset of the general flow problem, every general flow problem can be solved using a combination of optimal transport and shortest path methods.

3.3.4.1   Problem Statement

We are interested in the flow of a good or service across a network with n vertices. This network can be understood as a weighted directed graph (V, E, c). To simplify

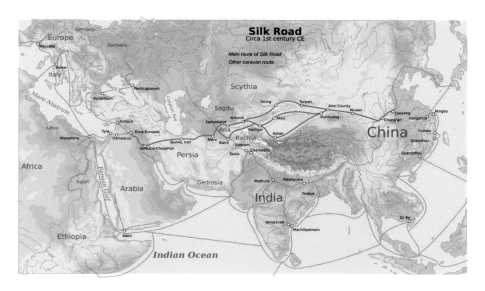

Figure 3.14 The Silk Road (Source: Wikimedia Commons)

notation, we label the nodes from 1 to n and let $V = [n]$. Existence of an edge $e = (i, j) \in E$ with weight $c(i, j)$ indicates that the good can be shipped from i to j at cost $c(i, j)$. We recall from §1.4.1 that $\mathcal{I}(i)$ is the set of direct predecessors of vertex i (all $u \in V$ such that $(u, i) \in E$) and $\mathcal{O}(i)$ is the set of direct successors (all $j \in V$ such that $(i, j) \in E$).

A classic example is the famous Silk Road of antiquity, part of which is illustrated in Figure 3.14. Silk was produced in Eastern cities such as Loyang and Changan, and then transported westward to satisfy final demand in Rome, Constantinople, and Alexandria. Towns such as Yarkand acted as trade hubs. Rather than covering the whole route, traders typically traveled backward and forward between one pair of hubs, where they knew the language and customs.[4]

Returning to the model, we allow for both **initial supply** of and **final demand** for the good at every node (although one or both could be zero). Let $s(i)$ and $d(i)$ be supply and demand at node i, respectively. Aggregate supply and demand over the network are assumed to be equal, so that

$$\sum_{i \in V} s(i) = \sum_{i \in V} d(i). \tag{3.32}$$

This can be understood as an equilibrium condition: Prices have adjusted to equalize initial supply and final demand in aggregate. We assume throughout that the vectors s and d are nonnegative with at least one positive element.

---

[4] Our use of the Silk Road as an example of a network flow problem is not original. Galichon (2018) provides a highly readable treatment in the context of optimal transport.

Let $q(i, j)$ be the amount of the good shipped from node i to node j for all $i, j \in V$. The minimum cost network flow problem is to minimize **total shipping cost**

$$\sum_{i \in V} \sum_{j \in V} c(i, j) q(i, j), \tag{3.33}$$

subject to the restriction that $q \geqslant 0$ and

$$s(i) + \sum_{v \in \mathscr{I}(i)} q(v, i) = d(i) + \sum_{j \in \mathscr{O}(i)} q(i, j) \quad \text{for all } i \in V. \tag{3.34}$$

The left-hand side of (3.34) is total supply to node i (initial supply plus inflow from other nodes), while the right-hand side is total demand (final demand plus outflow to other nodes).

EXERCISE 3.3.9. Although we presented them separately, the node-by-node restriction (3.34) implies the aggregate restriction (3.32). Explain why this is the case.

3.3.4.2   Optimality

There are several ways to transform the network flow problem into a linear program. We follow the presentation in Bertsimas and Tsitsiklis (1997). We take $m = |E|$ to be the total number of edges and enumerate them (in any convenient way) as $e_1, \ldots, e_m$. Let's say that e_k **leaves** node i if $e_k = (i, j)$ for some $j \in [n]$, and that e_k **enters** node i if $e_k = (\ell, i)$ for some $\ell \in [n]$. Then we define the $n \times m$ **node–edge incidence matrix** A by

$$A = (a_{ik}) \quad \text{with} \quad a_{ik} := \begin{cases} 1 & \text{if } e_k \text{ leaves } i \\ -1 & \text{if } e_k \text{ enters } i \\ 0 & \text{otherwise.} \end{cases}$$

Example 3.3.1: Consider the very simple minimum cost flow problem in Figure 3.15. The shipment costs $c(i, j)$ are listed next to each existing edge. Initial supply is 10 at node 1 and zero elsewhere. Final demand is 10 at node 4 and zero elsewhere. We enumerate the edges as

$$E = \{e_1, \ldots, e_4\} = \{(1, 2), (1, 4), (2, 3), (3, 4)\}. \tag{3.35}$$

The node–edge incidence matrix is

$$A = \begin{pmatrix} 1 & 1 & 0 & 0 \\ -1 & 0 & 1 & 0 \\ 0 & 0 & -1 & 1 \\ 0 & -1 & 0 & -1 \end{pmatrix}.$$

Now, returning to the general case, we rearrange q and c into $m \times 1$ vectors (q_k) and (c_k), where q_k is the amount shipped along edge k, and c_k is the cost. For example, if

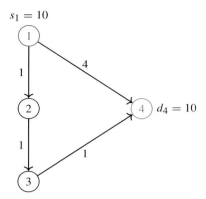

Figure 3.15 A simple network flow problem

$e_k = (i, j)$, then $q_k = q(i, j)$ and $c_k = c(i, j)$. In addition, we set b to be the vector in $\mathbb{R}^n$ with i-th element $s(i) - d(i)$, which is net exogenous supply at node i.

EXERCISE 3.3.10. In this set up, show that (3.34) is equivalent to $Aq = b$ in the special case of Example 3.3.1.

EXERCISE 3.3.11. Let $(Aq)(i)$ be the i-th row of Aq. Show that

$$(Aq)(i) = \sum_{j \in \mathcal{O}(i)} q(i, j) - \sum_{v \in \mathcal{I}(i)} q(v, i). \tag{3.36}$$

Equation (3.36) tells us that the i-th row of Aq give us the net outflow from node i under the transport plan q. Now, with $\langle c, q \rangle := \sum_{k=1}^{m} c_k q_k$, the minimum cost network flow problem can now be expressed as

$$\min \langle c, q \rangle \quad \text{s.t.} \quad q \geqslant 0 \text{ and } Aq = b. \tag{3.37}$$

This is a linear program in standard equality form, to which we can apply any linear programming solver. For Example 3.3.1, we run the following:

```
A = (( 1,   1,   0,   0),
     (-1,   0,   1,   0),
     ( 0,   0,  -1,   1),
     ( 0,  -1,   0,  -1))

b = (10,  0,  0,  -10)
c = (1,  4,  1,  1)

result = linprog(c, A_eq=A, b_eq=b, method='highs-ipm')
print(result.x)
```

The output is [10. 0. 10. 10.]. Recalling the order of the paths in (3.35), this means that the optimal transport plan is $q(1,4) = 0$ and $q(1,2) = q(2,3) = q(3,4) = 10$, as our intuition suggests.

EXERCISE 3.3.12. Some network flow problems have **capacity constraints**, which can be modeled as a map $g\colon E \to [0,\infty]$, along with the restriction $q(e) \leqslant g(e)$ for all $e \in E$. (If $g(e) = +\infty$, there is no capacity constraint over shipping on edge e.) Formulate this as a linear program, and modify the code above, which solves Example 3.3.1, to include the capacity constraint $g(1,2) = 5$. Solve for the optimal plan.

EXERCISE 3.3.13. Explain how the generic optimal transport problem treated in §3.3.1 is a special case of the minimum cost network flow problem.

3.3.4.3   Reduction to Optimal Transport

In Exercise 3.3.13, we saw how every optimal transport problem is a special kind of minimum cost network flow problem. There is a sense in which the converse is also true. In particular, we can use optimal transport methods to solve any network flow problem, provided that we first modify the network flow problem via an application of shortest paths.

To explain how this works, we take the abstract network flow problem described in §3.3.4.1, on the weighted digraph (V, E, c), with $V = [n]$, initial supply vector $s \in \mathbb{R}^n_+$ and final demand vector $d \in \mathbb{R}^n_+$. For the purposes of this section, we agree to call a node i with $s(i) - d(i) > 0$ a **net supplier**. A node i with $d(i) - s(i) > 0$ will be called a **net consumer**. Nodes with $s(i) = d(i)$ will be called **trading stations**.

Example 3.3.2: In the left-hand side of Figure 3.16, nodes 1 and 2 are net suppliers, 3 is a trading station, and 4 and 5 are net consumers.

Example 3.3.3: In the Silk Road application, Rome would be a net consumer, where final demand is large and positive, while initial supply is zero. A city such as Yarkand should probably be modeled as a trading station, with $s(i) = d(i) = 0$.

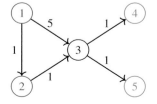   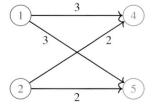

Figure 3.16 Reducing minimum cost optimal flow to optimal transport

The idea behind the reduction is to treat the net supplier nodes as source locations and the net consumer nodes as target locations in an optimal transport problem. The next step is to compute the shortest path (if there are multiple paths, pick any one) from each net supplier i to each net consumer j. Let $\rho(i, j)$ denote this path, represented as a sequence of edges in E. The cost of traversing $\rho(i, j)$ is

$$\hat{c}(i, j) := \sum_{k=1}^{m} c_k \mathbb{1}\{e_k \in \rho(i, j)\}.$$

Now the trading stations are eliminated, and we solve the optimal transport problem with

- $\mathsf{X} =$ the set of net suppliers,
- $\mathsf{Y} =$ the set of net consumers,
- $\varphi(i) = s(i) - d(i)$ on X,
- $\psi(j) = d(j) - s(j)$ on Y, and
- cost function $\hat{c}(i, j)$ as defined above.[5]

After we find the optimal transport plan π, the network minimum cost flow q_k along arbitrary edge $e_k \in E$ is recovered by setting

$$q_k = \sum_{i \in \mathsf{X}} \sum_{j \in \mathsf{Y}} \pi(i, j) \mathbb{1}\{e_k \in \text{ the shortest path from } i \text{ to } j\}.$$

EXERCISE 3.3.14. Recalling our assumptions on s and d, prove that $\sum_{i \in \mathsf{X}} \varphi(i) = \sum_{j \in \mathsf{Y}} \psi(j)$ and that this sum is nonzero.

REMARK 3.3.2   *We have not imposed $\sum_i \varphi(i) = \sum_j \psi(j) = 1$, as required for the standard formulation of the optimal transport problem. But this normalization is only used for convenience in exposition, and most solvers do not require it.*

Figure 3.16 illustrates the method. Trading station 3 is eliminated after the shortest paths are computed.

3.4   Chapter Notes

Our treatment of shortest paths can be understood as a simplified version of both the Bellman–Ford algorithm and Dijkstra's algorithm, which are routinely used to solve large shortest path planning problems. Our approach is intended to emphasize recursive solution methods, which are valuable for analyzing a vast range of economic problems, from intertemporal modeling (see, e.g., Lucas and Stokey (1989) or Ljungqvist and Sargent (2018)) to production chains (Kikuchi et al., 2021).

---

[5] If no path exists from i to j, then we set $\hat{c}(i, j) = \infty$. Such settings can be handled in linear programming solvers by adding capacity constraints. See, for example, Peyré et al. (2019), section 10.3.

Betweenness centrality has been used to quantify the notion of "too connected to fail," which gained attention after the 2007–2008 global financial crisis. For example, Huang et al. (2016) examine how betweenness centrality affects systemic risk. Betweenness centrality is used to examine liquidity shocks in the inter-bank market by Chiu et al. (2020). Relatedly, Yun et al. (2019) propose a measure of "too central to fail" based on the PageRank algorithm.

For a more in-depth treatment of linear programming, we recommend the excellent textbooks by Bertsimas and Tsitsiklis (1997) and Matousek and Gärtner (2007). For bedtime reading, Cook (2011) provides an entertaining introduction to some of the main ideas and applications to network problems, including a review of computation.

While §3.2.1 provided a rather whimsical introduction to matching and assignment problems, such problems have great real world importance. Examples include assigning kidney donors to recipients, mothers to maternity wards, doctors to hospitals, students to schools, delivery drivers to orders, and autonomous vehicles to riders.[6] A brief history of assignment, matching problems, and combinatorial optimization can be found in Schrijver (2005). Greinecker and Kah (2021) study the existence of stable matchings in a setting with many agents.

Villani (2008) and Vershik (2013) provide extensive historical background on the optimal transport problem. Vershik (2013) mentions some of the problems that Kantorovich faced, as a Soviet mathematician working in the time of Stalin and Khrushchev, given that his main duality theorem for optimal transport can be seen as a proof that competitive market equilibria attain the maximal transport plan.

In §3.3.2, we mentioned that Kantorovich's work anticipated much of the later development of duality theory for arbitrary linear programs. In fact, according to Vershik (2013), Kantorovich anticipated much of the general theory of linear programming itself, including providing a version of the simplex algorithm later rediscovered and extended by Dantzig.

Optimal transport has a remarkably wide variety of applications, spread across economics, econometrics, finance, statistics, artificial intelligence, machine learning, and other fields. Within economics, Galichon (2018) provides an excellent overview. Charpentier et al. (2019) and Fajgelbaum and Schaal (2020) consider optimal transport in spatial equilibria. Ocampo (2022) applies optimal transport measures to the study of tasks and occupations. Beiglböck et al. (2022) review some of the major milestones of modern finance theory and show their connections via optimal transport. Connections to machine learning are surveyed in Kolouri et al. (2017).

The computational theory of optimal transport is now a major field. A high-quality exposition can be found in Peyré et al. (2019). Blanchet et al. (2018) use computational optimal transport to solve for Cournot–Nash equilibria in mean-field-type games.

---

[6] The latter problem occurs in the field of autonomous mobility on demand (AMoD). See, for example, Ascenzi and Palanza (2021) or Simonetto et al. (2019).

4 Markov Chains and Networks

Markov chains evolving on finite sets are a foundational class of stochastic processes. These processes have been employed in quantitative economics to study stochastic systems ranging from labor income to harvest outputs, firm productivity, stock prices, unemployment dynamics, policy regimes, interest rates, and social mobility. Fortunately, we are now well placed to study Markov chains, since such chains are most naturally viewed as a special kind of weighted digraph. Moreover, graph-theoretic properties such as connectedness and periodicity are key determinants of their dynamics. In this chapter we investigate these ideas.

4.1 Markov Chains as Digraphs

We begin with fundamental definitions and then investigate dynamics.

4.1.1 Markov Models

A **finite Markov model** is a weighted directed graph $\mathcal{M} = (S, E, p)$, where S is the (finite) set of vertices, E is the set of edges, and p is the weight function, with the additional restriction that

$$\sum_{y \in \mathcal{O}(x)} p(x, y) = 1 \quad \text{for all } x \in S. \tag{4.1}$$

Figure 1.15 on page 32 presented an example of such a digraph.

The set of vertices S of a finite Markov model $\mathcal{M} = (S, E, p)$ is also called the **state space** of the model, and vertices are called **states**. The two standard interpretations are

(i) S is a set of possible states for some random element (the state), and the weight $p(x, y)$ represents the probability that the state moves from x to y in one step.

(ii) S is a set of possible values for some measurement over a large population (e.g., hours worked per week measured across a large cross-section of households), and $p(x, y)$ is the fraction of agents that transition from state x to state y in one unit of time.

These two perspectives are related in ways that we explore below.

4.1.1.1   Transition Matrices

If $\mathcal{M}$ is a finite Markov model, then the restriction (4.1) is equivalent to the statement that the adjacency matrix associated with $\mathcal{M}$ is stochastic (see §1.3.1.3 for the definition). Identifying $S = \{poor, middle, rich\}$ with $\{1, 2, 3\}$, the adjacency matrix for this weighted digraph is

$$P_a = \begin{pmatrix} 0.9 & 0.1 & 0.0 \\ 0.4 & 0.4 & 0.2 \\ 0.1 & 0.1 & 0.8 \end{pmatrix}. \tag{4.2}$$

Since $P_a \geqslant 0$ and rows sum to unity, P_a is stochastic as required. In the context of finite Markov models, the adjacency matrix of $\mathcal{M}$ is also called the **transition matrix**.

Regarding notation, when S has typical elements x, y, it turns out to be convenient to write elements of the transition matrix P as $P(x, y)$ rather than P_{ij} or similar. We can think of P as extending the weight function p from E to the set of all (x, y) pairs in $S \times S$, assigning zero whenever $(x, y) \notin E$. As such, for every possible choice of (x, y), the value $P(x, y)$ represents the probability of transitioning from x to y in one step.

The requirement that P is stochastic can now be written as $P \geqslant 0$ and

$$\sum_{y \in S} P(x, y) = 1 \text{ for all } x \in S. \tag{4.3}$$

The restriction in (4.3) just says that the state space is "complete": after arriving at $x \in S$, the state must now move to some $y \in S$.

Using notation from §1.3.1, to say that P is stochastic is the same as requiring that each row of P is in $\mathcal{D}(S)$.

Example 4.1.1: A Markov model is estimated in the international growth dynamics study of Quah (1993). The state is real GDP per capita in a given country relative to the world average. Quah discretizes the possible values to 0–1/4, 1/4–1/2, 1/2–1, 1–2, and 2–∞, calling these states 1 to 5, respectively. The transitions are over a one-year period. Estimated one-step transition probabilities are represented as a weighted digraph in Figure 4.1, where

- $S = \{1, \ldots, 5\}$ is the state space;
- the set of edges E is represented by arrows; and
- transition probabilities are identified with weights attached to these edges.

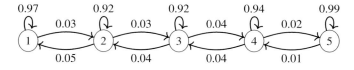

Figure 4.1 Cross-country GDP dynamics as a digraph

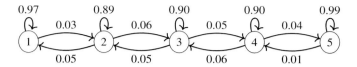

Figure 4.2 Cross-country GDP dynamics as a digraph, updated data

The transition matrix for the Markov model in Example 4.1.1 is

$$P_Q = \begin{pmatrix} 0.97 & 0.03 & 0.00 & 0.00 & 0.00 \\ 0.05 & 0.92 & 0.03 & 0.00 & 0.00 \\ 0.00 & 0.04 & 0.92 & 0.04 & 0.00 \\ 0.00 & 0.00 & 0.04 & 0.94 & 0.02 \\ 0.00 & 0.00 & 0.00 & 0.01 & 0.99 \end{pmatrix}. \tag{4.4}$$

Note the large values on the principal diagonal of P_Q. These indicate strong persistence: The state stays constant from period to period with high probability.

Quah (1993) estimated P_Q by maximum likelihood, pooling transitions over the years 1960–1984. (In this case, maximum likelihood estimation amounts to recording the relative frequency of transitions between states.) Figure 4.2 shows how the numbers change if we repeat the exercise using World Bank GDP data from 1985–2019. The numbers are quite stable relative to the earlier estimate. Below we will examine how long-run predictions are affected.

As another example, Benhabib et al. (2019) estimate the following transition matrix for intergenerational social mobility:

$$P_B := \begin{pmatrix} 0.222 & 0.222 & 0.215 & 0.187 & 0.081 & 0.038 & 0.029 & 0.006 \\ 0.221 & 0.22 & 0.215 & 0.188 & 0.082 & 0.039 & 0.029 & 0.006 \\ 0.207 & 0.209 & 0.21 & 0.194 & 0.09 & 0.046 & 0.036 & 0.008 \\ 0.198 & 0.201 & 0.207 & 0.198 & 0.095 & 0.052 & 0.04 & 0.009 \\ 0.175 & 0.178 & 0.197 & 0.207 & 0.11 & 0.067 & 0.054 & 0.012 \\ 0.182 & 0.184 & 0.2 & 0.205 & 0.106 & 0.062 & 0.05 & 0.011 \\ 0.123 & 0.125 & 0.166 & 0.216 & 0.141 & 0.114 & 0.094 & 0.021 \\ 0.084 & 0.084 & 0.142 & 0.228 & 0.17 & 0.143 & 0.121 & 0.028 \end{pmatrix} \tag{4.5}$$

Here the states are percentiles of the wealth distribution. In particular, with the states represented by $1, 2, \ldots, 8$, the corresponding percentiles are

0–20%, 20–40%, 40–60%, 60–80%, 80–90%, 90–95%, 95–99%, 99–100% .

Transition probabilities are estimated from US 2007–2009 Survey of Consumer Finances data. Relative to the highly persistent matrix P_Q, less weight on the principal diagonal suggests more mixing – the influence of initial conditions is relatively short-lived.

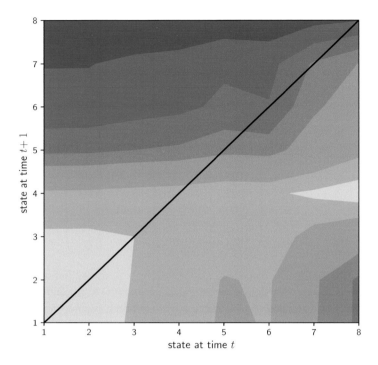

Figure 4.3 Contour plot of transition matrix P_B

Additional insight about the dynamics can be obtained from a contour plot of the matrix P_B, as in Figure 4.3. Here P_B is plotted as a heat map after rotating it 90 degrees anticlockwise. The rotation is so that the dynamics are comparable to the 45-degree diagrams often used to understand discrete time dynamic systems. A vertical line from state x corresponds to the next period conditional distribution $P(x, \cdot)$.

In this case, we see that, for example, lower states are quite persistent, whereas households in the highest state tend to fall back toward the middle.

EXERCISE 4.1.1. Let $\mathcal{M}$ be a finite Markov model with state space S and transition matrix P. Show that $U \subset S$ is absorbing (see §1.4.1.3) for the digraph $\mathcal{M}$ if and only if

$$\sum_{y \in U} P(x, y) = 1 \quad \text{for all} \quad x \in U. \tag{4.6}$$

4.1.1.2 Markov Chains

Consider a finite Markov model $\mathcal{M}$ with state space S and transition matrix P. As before, $P(x, y)$ indicates the probability of transitioning from x to y in one step. Another way to say this is that, when in state x, we update to a new state by choosing it from S via the distribution $P(x, \cdot)$. The resulting stochastic process is called a Markov chain.

We can state this more formally as follows. Let $(X_t)_{t \in \mathbb{Z}_+}$ be a sequence of random variables taking values in S. We say that (X_t) is a **Markov chain** on S if there exists a stochastic matrix P on S such that

$$\mathbb{P}\{X_{t+1} = y \mid X_0, X_1, \ldots, X_t\} = P(X_t, y) \quad \text{for all} \quad t \geqslant 0, \ y \in S. \tag{4.7}$$

To simplify terminology, we also call (X_t) P-**Markov** when it satisfies (4.7) . We call either X_0 or its distribution ψ_0 the **initial condition** of (X_t) depending on context.

The definition of a Markov chain says two things:

(i) When updating to X_{t+1} from X_t, earlier states are not required.
(ii) The matrix P encodes all of the information required to perform the update, given X_t.

One way to think about Markov chains is algorithmically: Let P be a stochastic matrix and let ψ_0 be an element of $\mathscr{D}(S)$. Now generate (X_t) via Algorithm 3. The resulting sequence is P-Markov with initial condition ψ_0.

---

1 set $t = 0$ and draw X_t from ψ_0
2 while $t < \infty$ **do**
3 $\quad$ draw X_{t+1} from the distribution $P(X_t, \cdot)$
4 $\quad$ let $t = t + 1$
5 end

Algorithm 3: Generation of P-Markov (X_t) with initial condition ψ_0

4.1.1.3 Simulation

For both simulation and theory, it is useful to be able to translate Algorithm 3 into a stochastic difference equation governing the evolution of $(X_t)_{t \geqslant 0}$. We now outline the procedure, which uses inverse transform sampling (see §1.3.1.2). For simplicity, we assume that $S = [n]$, with typical elements i, j. The basic idea is to apply the inverse transform method to each row of P and then sample by drawing a uniform random variable at each update.

To this end, we set

$$F(i, u) := \sum_{j=1}^{n} j \mathbb{1}\{q(i, j-1) < u \leqslant q(i, j)\} \quad (i \in S, \ u \in (0, 1)),$$

where, for each $i, j \in S$, the value $q(i, j)$ is defined recursively by

$$q(i, j) := q(i, j-1) + P(i, j) \quad \text{with } q(i, 0) = 0.$$

Let $U(0, 1)$ represent the uniform distribution on $(0, 1)$, and take

$$X_{t+1} = F(X_t, U_{t+1}), \quad \text{where } (U_t) \overset{\text{IID}}{\sim} U(0, 1). \tag{4.8}$$

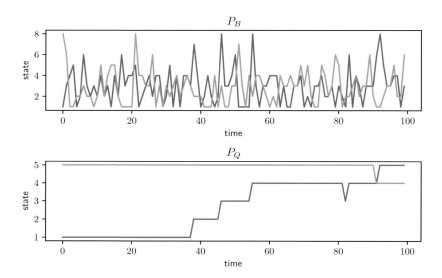

Figure 4.4 Wealth percentile over time

If X_0 is an independently drawn random variable with distribution ψ_0 on S, then (X_t) is P-Markov on S with initial condition ψ_0, as Exercise 4.1.2 asks you to show.

EXERCISE 4.1.2. Conditional on $X_t = i$, show that, for given $j \in S$,

(i) $X_{t+1} = j$ if and only if U_{t+1} lies in the interval $(q(i, j - 1), q(i, j)]$.
(ii) This event has probability $P(i, j)$.

Conclude that X_{t+1} in (4.8) is a draw from $P(i, \cdot)$.

Each subfigure in Figure 4.4 shows realizations of two Markov chains, both generated using the stochastic difference equation (4.8). Each sequence is generated with its own independent sequence of draws (U_t). The underlying transition matrices are P_B from (4.5) in the top panel and P_Q from (4.4) in the bottom panel. In both panels, one chain starts from the lowest state and the other from the highest. Notice that time series generated by P_B mix faster than those generated by P_Q: The difference in initial states is not a strong predictor of outcomes after an initial "burn in" period. We discuss mixing and its connection to stability below.

4.1.1.4 Higher-Order Transition Matrices

Given a finite Markov model $\mathscr{M}$ with state space S and transition matrix P, define $(P^k)_{k \in \mathbb{N}}$ by $P^{k+1} = P P^k$ for all k, with the understanding that $P^0 = I =$ the identity matrix. In other words, for each k, the matrix P^k is the k-th power of P. If we spell out the matrix product $P^{k+1} = P P^k$ element-by-element, we get

$$P^{k+1}(x, y) := \sum_z P(x, z) P^k(z, y) \qquad (x, y \in S, \ k \in \mathbb{N}). \qquad (4.9)$$

EXERCISE 4.1.3. Prove that P^k is a stochastic matrix on S for all $k \in \mathbb{N}$.

In this context, P^k is called the k-**step transition matrix** corresponding to P. The k-step transition matrix has the following interpretation: If (X_t) is P-Markov, then, for any $t, k \in \mathbb{N}$ and $x, y \in S$,

$$P^k(x, y) = \mathbb{P}\{X_{t+k} = y \mid X_t = x\}. \tag{4.10}$$

In other words, P^k provides the k-step transition probabilities for the P-Markov chain (X_t), as suggested by its name.

This claim can be verified by induction. Fix $t \in \mathbb{N}$ and $x, y \in S$. The claim is true by definition when $k = 1$. Suppose the claim is also true at k, and now consider the case $k + 1$. By the law of total probability, we have

$$\mathbb{P}\{X_{t+k+1} = y \mid X_t = x\} = \sum_z \mathbb{P}\{X_{t+k+1} = y \mid X_{t+k} = z\}\mathbb{P}\{X_{t+k} = z \mid X_t = x\}.$$

The induction hypothesis allows us to use (4.10), so the last equation becomes

$$\mathbb{P}\{X_{t+k+1} = y \mid X_t = x\} = \sum_z P(z, y)P^k(x, z) = P^{k+1}(x, y).$$

This completes our proof by induction.

A useful identity for the higher-order Markov matrices is

$$P^{j+k}(x, y) = \sum_z P^k(x, z)P^j(z, y) \qquad ((x, y) \in S \times S), \tag{4.11}$$

which holds for any j, k in $\mathbb{N}$. This is called the **Chapman–Kolmogorov equation**. Note that

- (4.9) is a special case of (4.11); and
- (4.11) is a special case of (1.27) on page 36, written with different notation.

To provide probabilistic intuition for the validity of the Chapman–Kolmogorov equation, let $X_0 = x$ and let $y \in S$ be given. Using the law of total probability again, we have

$$\mathbb{P}\{X_{j+k} = y \mid X_0 = x\} = \sum_z \mathbb{P}\{X_{j+k} = y \mid X_0 = x, X_k = z\}\mathbb{P}\{X_k = z \mid X_0 = x\}.$$

By Markov property (4.7), the future and past are independent given the present, so

$$\sum_z \mathbb{P}\{X_{j+k} = y \mid X_0 = x, X_k = z\} = \sum_z \mathbb{P}\{X_{j+k} = y \mid X_k = z\}.$$

As a result of this fact and (4.10), the equation before this one can be rewritten as (4.11).

4.1.2   Distribution Dynamics

Let $\mathcal{M}$ be a finite Markov model with state space S and transition matrix P. Let (X_t) be P-Markov, and, for each $t \geqslant 0$, let $\psi_t \in \mathscr{D}(S)$ be defined by

$$\psi_t := \mathbb{P}\{X_t = \cdot\} = \text{ the distribution of } X_t.$$

The vector ψ_t is called the **marginal distribution** of X_t. While (X_t) is random, the sequence (ψ_t) is deterministic. In this section we investigate its dynamics.

4.1.2.1   Updating Marginal Distributions

The key idea for this section is that there is a simple link between successive marginal distributions: By the law of total probability, we have

$$\mathbb{P}\{X_{t+1} = y\} = \sum_x \mathbb{P}\{X_{t+1} = y \mid X_t = x\} \cdot \mathbb{P}\{X_t = x\},$$

which can be rewritten as

$$\psi_{t+1}(y) = \sum_x P(x, y)\psi_t(x) \qquad (y \in S). \tag{4.12}$$

This fundamental expression tells us how to update marginal distributions given the transition matrix P.

When each ψ_t is interpreted as a row vector, we can write (4.12) as

$$\psi_{t+1} = \psi_t P. \tag{4.13}$$

(Henceforth, in expressions involving matrix algebra, distributions are row vectors unless otherwise stated). Some authors refer to (4.13) as the **forward equation** associated with P, while $\psi \mapsto \psi P$ is called the **forward operator**, by analogy with the Kolmogorov forward equation from continuous time.

Think of (4.13) as a difference equation in distribution space. Iterating backwards,

$$\psi_t = \psi_{t-1}P = (\psi_{t-2}P)P = \psi_{t-2}P^2 = \cdots = \psi_0 P^t.$$

Given any $\psi_0 \in \mathscr{D}(S)$ and $t \in \mathbb{N}$, we have

$$\psi_0 P^t = \text{ the distribution of } X_t \text{ given } X_0 \overset{d}{=} \psi_0.$$

Example 4.1.2: As an illustration, let's take the matrix P_Q estimated by Quah (1993) using 1960–1984 data and use P_Q^t to update the 1985 distribution $t = 2019 - 1985 = 34$ times, in order to obtain a prediction for the countrywide income distribution in 2019. Figure 4.5 shows how this prediction fares compared to the realized 2019 distribution, calculated from World Bank GDP data.[1]

---

[1] Example 4.1.2 is intended as an illustration of the mechanics of updating distributions. While the methodology in Quah (1993) is thought-provoking, it struggles to make plausible long-run predictions about something as complex as the countrywide income distribution. Indeed, the Kullback–Leibler deviation between the predicted and realized 2019 distributions is actually larger than the

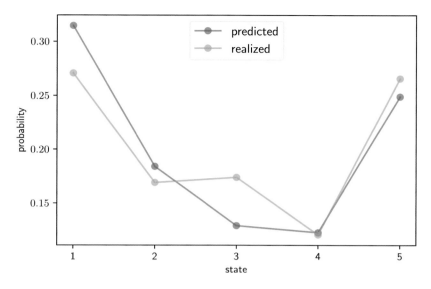

Figure 4.5 Predicted vs. realized cross-country income distributions for 2019

4.1.2.2 Trajectories in the Long Run

One of the main subfields of Markov chain analysis is asymptotics of distribution sequences. This topic turns out to be important for network theory as well. In §4.2.2 we will investigate asymptotics in depth. In this section we build some intuition via simulations.

Figure 4.6 shows the trajectory (ψP_a^t) when $S = \{1, 2, 3\}$, $\psi = (0, 0, 1)$, and P_a is the transition matrix displayed in (4.2). The blue triangle is the unit simplex in $\mathbb{R}^3_+$, consisting of all row vectors $\psi \in \mathbb{R}^3$ such that $\psi \geqslant 0$ and $\psi \mathbb{1} = 1$. The unit simplex can be identified with $\mathcal{D}(S)$ when $S = \{1, 2, 3\}$. Red dots in the figure are distributions in the sequence (ψP_a^t) for $t = 0, \ldots, 20$. Figure 4.7 shows distribution dynamics for P_a that start from initial condition $\psi = (0, 1/2, 1/2)$.

It seems that both of the sequences are converging. This turns out to be the case – the black dot in the figures is the limit of both sequences, and, moreover, this point is a stationary distribution for P_a, as defined in §1.3.1.3. In fact we can – and will – also show that no other stationary distribution exists and that ψP_a^t converges to the stationary distribution regardless of the choice of $\psi \in \mathcal{D}(S)$. This is due to certain properties of P_a, related to connectivity and aperiodicity.

Figure 4.8 provides another view of a distribution sequence, this time generated from the matrix P_B in (4.5). The initial condition ψ_0 was uniform. Each distribution shown was calculated as ψP_Q^t for different values of t. The distribution across wealth classes converges rapidly to what appears to be a long-run limit. Below we confirm

Kullback–Leibler deviation between the 1985 and 2019 distributions. Evidently, a naive estimate "nothing will change" model predicts better than Quah's. Most of the focus in this text is on short-term forecasts and scenarios, where the system is approximately stationary after suitable transformations, rather than heroic long-term predictions where nonstationary change is hard to quantify.

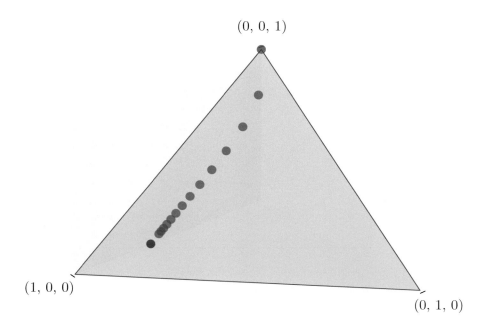

Figure 4.6 A trajectory from $\psi_0 = (0,0,1)$

that this is so and that the limit is independent of the initial condition. The rapid rate of convergence is due to the high level of mixing in the transition dynamics.

4.1.3   Stationarity

In this section we examine stationary distributions and their properties. As we will see, stationary distributions can be regarded as steady states for the evolution of the sequence of marginal distributions. (Later, when we study ergodicity, stationary distributions will acquire another important interpretation.)

4.1.3.1   Stationary Distributions

Recall from §1.3.1.3 that if P is a stochastic matrix and $\psi \in \mathbb{R}_+^n$ is a row vector such that $\psi \mathbb{1} = 1$ and $\psi P = \psi$, then ψ is called stationary for P. So now let $\mathcal{M}$ be a finite Markov model with state space S and transition matrix P. Translating to the notation of Markov chains, a distribution $\psi^* \in \mathcal{D}(S)$ is **stationary** for $\mathcal{M}$ if

$$\psi^*(y) = \sum_{x \in S} P(x, y)\psi^*(x) \quad \text{for all } y \in S.$$

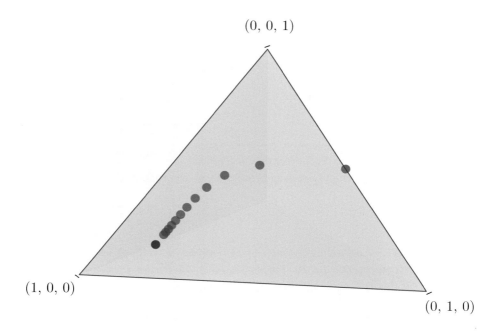

Figure 4.7 A trajectory from $\psi_0 = (0, 1/2, 1/2)$

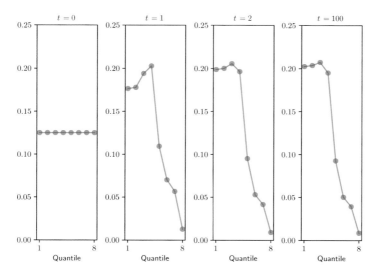

Figure 4.8 Distribution projections from P_B

We also write this expression as $\psi^* = \psi^* P$ and understand ψ^* as a fixed point of the map $\psi \mapsto \psi P$ that updates distributions (cf. Equation (4.13)).

If $X_t \stackrel{d}{=} \psi^*$, then, for any $j \in \mathbb{N}$, the fixed point property implies that $X_{t+j} \stackrel{d}{=} \psi^* P^j = \psi^*$. Hence

$$X_t \stackrel{d}{=} \psi^* \implies X_{t+j} \stackrel{d}{=} \psi^* \text{ for all } j \in \mathbb{N}.$$

Example 4.1.3: Suppose workers are hired at rate α and fired at rate β, transitioning between unemployment and employment according to

$$P_w = \begin{pmatrix} 1 - \alpha & \alpha \\ \beta & 1 - \beta \end{pmatrix}. \tag{4.14}$$

In §1.2.3.3 we showed that $\alpha + \beta > 0$ implies $\psi = (\beta/(\alpha+\beta), \alpha/(\alpha+\beta))$ is a dominant left eigenvector for P_w. Since $r(P_w) = 1$, the Perron–Frobenius theorem tells us that ψ is stationary for P_w. One implication is that, if the distribution of workers across the two employment states is given by ψ, and updates obey the dynamics encoded in P_w, then no further change is observed in the unemployment rate.

Example 4.1.4: The black dot in each of Figures 4.6 and 4.7, indicating the limit of the marginal sequences, is a stationary distribution for the Markov matrix P_a displayed in (4.2), page 130. We discuss its calculation in §4.1.3.4.

EXERCISE 4.1.4. Let $\mathcal{M}$ be a finite Markov model with state space $|S| = n$ and transition matrix P. Let $\psi \equiv 1/n$ be the uniform distribution on S. Prove that ψ is stationary for P if and only if P is **doubly stochastic** (i.e., has unit column sums as well as unit row sums).

In Figures 4.6 and 4.7, all trajectories converge toward the stationary distribution. Not all stationary distributions have this "attractor" property, and in general there can be many stationary distributions. The next example illustrates.

EXERCISE 4.1.5. Let $\mathcal{M} = (S, E, p)$ be a finite Markov model with $(x, y) \in E$ if and only if $x = y$. Describe the implied weight function and corresponding transition matrix. Show that every distribution in $\mathcal{D}(S)$ is stationary for $\mathcal{M}$.

4.1.3.2   Existence and Uniqueness

From the Perron–Frobenius theorem we easily obtain the following fundamental result.

THEOREM 4.1.1 (Existence and Uniqueness of Stationary Distributions)   *Every finite Markov model $\mathcal{M} = (S, E, p)$ has at least one stationary distribution ψ^* in $\mathcal{D}(S)$. If* the digraph (S, E) is strongly connected, then ψ^* is unique and everywhere positive on S.

Proof   Let $\mathcal{M}$ be a finite Markov model. Since the corresponding adjacency matrix P is stochastic, existence follows from Exercise 1.3.7 in §1.3.1.3. By Theorem 1.4.3 on page 36, strong connectedness of $\mathcal{M}$ implies irreducibility of P. When P is irreducible, uniqueness and everywhere positivity of the stationary distribution follows from the Perron–Frobenius theorem (page 13).   □

The basic idea behind the uniqueness part of Theorem 4.1.1 is as follows: Suppose to the contrary that $\mathcal{M}$ is strongly connected and yet two distinct stationary distributions ψ^* and ψ^{**} exist in $\mathscr{A}(S)$. Since a P-Markov chain started at ψ^* always has marginal distribution ψ^* and likewise for ψ^{**}, different initial conditions lead to different long-run outcomes. This contradicts strong connectedness in the following way: Strong connectedness implies that both chains traverse the whole state space. Moreover, being Markov chains, they forget the past once they arrive at any state, so the starting draws should eventually be irrelevant.

(Actually, the story in the last paragraph is incomplete. Initial conditions *can* determine long-run outcomes under strong connectedness in one sense: A "periodic" Markov model can traverse the whole space but *only at specific times* that depend on the starting location. If we rule out such periodicity, we get results that are even stronger than Theorem 4.1.1. This topic is treated in §4.2.2.)

4.1.3.3   Brouwer's Theorem

Another way to prove the existence claim in Theorem 4.1.1 is via the famous fixed point theorem of L. E. J. Brouwer (1881–1966).

THEOREM 4.1.2 (Brouwer)   *If C is a convex compact subset of $\mathbb{R}^n$ and G is a continuous self-map on C, then G has at least one fixed point in C.*

The proof of Theorem 4.1.2 in one dimension is not difficult, while the proof in higher dimensions is challenging. See, for example, Aliprantis and Border (1999).

EXERCISE 4.1.6. Prove Brouwer's fixed point theorem for the case $C = [0, 1]$ by applying the intermediate value theorem.

One advantage of Brouwer's fixed point theorem is that its conditions are quite weak. One disadvantage is that it provides only existence, without uniqueness or stability. Figure A.4 provides an example of how multiple fixed points can coexist under the conditions of the theorem.[2]

EXERCISE 4.1.7. Prove the first part of Theorem 4.1.1 (existence of a stationary distribution) using Brouwer's fixed point theorem.

---

[2] There are many useful extensions to Brouwer's theorem, such as one for set-valued functions due to Kakutani (1941). These results have many applications in economics (see, for example, Nash (1950)). Another paper, due to Schauder (1930), extends Brouwer's result to infinite-dimensional spaces.

4.1.3.4   Computation

Let's consider how to compute stationary distributions. While $\psi^* P = \psi^*$ is a finite set of linear equations that we might hope to solve directly for ψ^*, there are problems with this idea. For example, $\psi^* = 0$ is a solution that fails to lie in $\mathscr{D}(S)$.

To restrict the solution to $\mathscr{D}(S)$, we proceed as follows: Suppose $|S| = n$, and note that row vector $\psi \in \mathscr{D}(S)$ is stationary if and only if $\psi(I - P) = 0$, where I is the $n \times n$ identity matrix. Let $\mathbb{1}_n$ be the $1 \times n$ row vector $(1, \ldots, 1)$. Let $\mathbb{1}_{n \times n}$ be the $n \times n$ matrix of ones.

EXERCISE 4.1.8. Consider the linear system

$$\mathbb{1}_n = \psi(I - P + \mathbb{1}_{n \times n}), \tag{4.15}$$

where ψ is a row vector. Show that

(i) every solution ψ of (4.15) lies in $\mathscr{D}(S)$; and
(ii) ψ is stationary for P if and only if (4.15) holds.

Solving the linear system (4.15) produces a stationary distribution in any setting where the stationary distribution is unique. When this is not the case, problems can arise.

EXERCISE 4.1.9. Give a counterexample to the claim that $(I - P + \mathbb{1}_{n \times n})$ is always nonsingular when P is a stochastic matrix.

There are also graph-theoretic algorithms for computing all of the stationary distributions of an arbitrary stochastic matrix. (The Python and Julia libraries `QuantEcon.py` and `QuantEcon.jl` have efficient implementations of this type.)

4.2   Asymptotics

In this section we turn to long-run properties of Markov chains, including ergodicity. With these ideas in hand, we will then investigate the evolution of information over social networks.

4.2.1   Ergodicity

Let's begin with the fascinating and important topic of ergodicity. The simplest way to understand ergodicity is as an extension of the law of large numbers from IID sequences to more general settings, where the IID property holds only in a limiting sense.

4.2.1.1   Harmonic Functions

Let $\mathscr{M}$ be a finite Markov model with state space S and transition matrix P. Fix $h \in \mathbb{R}^S$, and let

$$Ph(x) := \sum_{y \in S} P(x, y)h(y) \qquad (x \in S). \qquad (4.16)$$

If h is understood as a column vector in $\mathbb{R}^{|S|}$, then $Ph(x)$ is just element x of the vector Ph. The map $h \mapsto Ph$ is sometimes called the "conditional expectation operator," since, given that $P(x, y) = \mathbb{P}\{X_{t+1} = y \mid X_t = x\}$, we have

$$\sum_{y \in S} P(x, y)h(y) = \mathbb{E}[h(X_{t+1}) \mid X_t = x].$$

A function $h \in \mathbb{R}^S$ is called P-**harmonic** if $Ph = h$ pointwise on S. Thus, P-harmonic functions are fixed points of the conditional expectation operator $h \mapsto Ph$.

If h is P-harmonic and (X_t) is P-Markov, then

$$\mathbb{E}[h(X_{t+1}) \mid X_t] = (Ph)(X_t) = h(X_t). \qquad (4.17)$$

(A stochastic process with this property – i.e., that the current value is the best predictor of next period's value – is called a *martingale*. Martingales are one of the foundational concepts in probability, statistics, and finance.)

Example 4.2.1: Let $\mathcal{M}$ be a finite Markov model with state space S and transition matrix P. If $A \subset S$ and $A^c := S \setminus A$ are both absorbing for $\mathcal{M}$, then $\mathbb{1}_A$ and $\mathbb{1}_{A^c}$ are both P-harmonic. To see this, we apply Exercise 4.1.1 to obtain

$$(P\mathbb{1}_A)(x) = \sum_{y \in S} P(x, y)\mathbb{1}_A(y) = \sum_{y \in A} P(x, y) = \begin{cases} 1 & \text{if } x \in A \\ 0 & \text{if } x \in A^c. \end{cases}$$

In other words, $P\mathbb{1}_A = \mathbb{1}_A$. A similar argument gives $P\mathbb{1}_{A^c} = \mathbb{1}_{A^c}$.

EXERCISE 4.2.1. Let $\mathcal{M}$ be a finite Markov model with state space S and transition matrix P. Show that every constant function in $\mathbb{R}^S$ is P-harmonic.

4.2.1.2 Definition and Implications

Let $\mathcal{M}$ be a finite Markov model with state space S and transition matrix P. We know that every constant function in $\mathbb{R}^S$ is P-harmonic. We call $\mathcal{M}$ **ergodic** if the only P-harmonic functions in $\mathbb{R}^S$ are the constant functions.

Example 4.2.2: If $P(x, y) = \varphi(y)$ for all x, y in S, where φ is some fixed distribution on S, then P generates an IID Markov chain, since the next period draw has no dependence on the current state. Any model $\mathcal{M}$ with an adjacency matrix of this type is ergodic. Indeed, if P has this property and $h \in \mathbb{R}^S$ is P-harmonic, then, for any $x \in S$, we have

$$h(x) = (Ph)(x) = \sum_y P(x, y)h(y) = \sum_y \varphi(y)h(y).$$

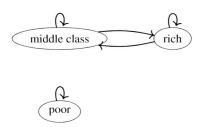

Figure 4.9 A poverty trap

Hence, h is constant. This proves that any P-harmonic function is a constant function.

Example 4.2.3: A laborer is either unemployed (state 1) or employed (state 2). In state 1 they are hired with probability α. In state 2 they are fired with probability β. The corresponding Markov model $\mathcal{M}$ has state and transition matrix given by

$$S = \{1,2\} \quad \text{and} \quad P_w = \begin{pmatrix} 1 - \alpha & \alpha \\ \beta & 1 - \beta \end{pmatrix}.$$

The statement $P_w h = h$ becomes

$$\begin{pmatrix} 1 - \alpha & \alpha \\ \beta & 1 - \beta \end{pmatrix} \begin{pmatrix} h(1) \\ h(2) \end{pmatrix} = \begin{pmatrix} h(1) \\ h(2) \end{pmatrix}.$$

The first row is $(1 - \alpha)h(1) + \alpha h(2) = h(1)$, or $\alpha h(1) = \alpha h(2)$. Thus, $\mathcal{M}$ is ergodic whenever $\alpha > 0$. By a similar argument, $\mathcal{M}$ is ergodic whenever $\beta > 0$.

Example 4.2.4: Let $\mathcal{M}$ be any finite Markov model with state space S and transition matrix P. It is immediate from Example 4.2.1 that if S can be partitioned into two nonempty absorbing sets, then $\mathcal{M}$ is not ergodic. Hence, the poverty trap model in Figure 4.9 is not ergodic. Similarly, if $\alpha = \beta = 0$ in the matrix P_w discussed in Example 4.2.3, then $P_w = I$, and each state is a disjoint absorbing set. Ergodicity fails.

The examples discussed above suggest that, for a finite Markov model $\mathcal{M}$, ergodicity depends on the connectivity properties of the digraph. The next result confirms this.

PROPOSITION 4.2.1   *If $\mathcal{M}$ is strongly connected, then $\mathcal{M}$ is ergodic.*

Proof Let $\mathcal{M}$ be a strongly connected Markov model with state space S and transition matrix P. Let h be P-harmonic, and let $x \in S$ be the maximizer of h on S. Let $m = h(x)$. Suppose there exists a y in S with $h(y) < m$. Since $\mathcal{M}$ is strongly connected, we can choose a $k \in \mathbb{N}$ such that $P^k(x, y) > 0$. Since h is P-harmonic, we have $h = P^k h$, and hence

$$m = h(x) = \sum_z P^k(x,z)h(z) = P^k(x,y)h(y) + \sum_{z \neq y} P^k(x,z)h(z) < m.$$

This contradiction shows that h is constant. Hence $\mathcal{M}$ is ergodic. □

The implication in Proposition 4.2.1 is one way, as the next exercise asks you to confirm.

EXERCISE 4.2.2. Provide an example of a finite Markov model that is ergodic but not strongly connected.

4.2.1.3   Implications of Ergodicity

One of the most important results in probability theory is the **law of large numbers** (LLN). In the finite state setting, the classical version of this theorem states that

$$\mathbb{P}\left\{ \lim_{k \to \infty} \frac{1}{k} \sum_{t=0}^{k-1} h(X_t) = \sum_{x \in S} h(x)\varphi(x) \right\} = 1$$

when $(X_t)_{t \geq 0}$ is an IID sequence of random variables with common distribution $\varphi \in \mathcal{D}(S)$ and h is an arbitrary element of $\mathbb{R}^S$.

This version of the LLN is classical in the sense that the IID assumption is imposed. It turns out that the IID assumption can be weakened to allow for a degree of dependence between observations, which leads us to ask whether or not the LLN holds for Markov chains as well.

The answer to this question is yes, provided that dependence between observations dies out fast enough. One candidate for this condition is ergodicity. In fact, it turns out that ergodicity is the exact necessary and sufficient condition required to extend the law of large numbers to Markov chains. The next theorem gives details.

THEOREM 4.2.2   *Let $\mathcal{M}$ be any finite Markov model with state space S and transition matrix P. The following statements are equivalent:*

(i) *$\mathcal{M}$ is ergodic.*
(ii) *$\mathcal{M}$ has a unique stationary distribution ψ^*, and, for any P-Markov chain (X_t) and any $h \in \mathbb{R}^S$,*

$$\mathbb{P}\left\{ \lim_{k \to \infty} \frac{1}{k} \sum_{t=0}^{k-1} h(X_t) = \sum_{x \in S} h(x)\psi^*(x) \right\} = 1. \tag{4.18}$$

The proof of Theorem 4.2.2 is given in Chapter 17 of Meyn and Tweedie (2009). We skip the proof but provide intuition through the following examples.

Example 4.2.5: Recall the IID case from Example 4.2.2. We showed that $\mathcal{M}$ is ergodic. By Theorem 4.2.2, the convergence in (4.18) holds with $\psi^* = \varphi$. This is consistent with the LLN for IID sequences.

Example 4.2.6: Let $\mathscr{M}$ be a finite Markov model with $S = \{1, 2\}$ and $P = I$, the identity matrix. Markov chains generated by P are constant. Since every $h \in \mathbb{R}^2$ satisfies $Ph = h$, we see that $\mathscr{M}$ is not ergodic. This means that the LLN result in (4.18) fails. But this is exactly what we would expect, since a constant chain (X_t) implies $\frac{1}{k} \sum_{t=0}^{k-1} X_t = X_0$ for all k. In particular, if X_0 is drawn from a nondegenerate distribution, then the sample mean does not converge to any constant value.

Example 4.2.7: Consider again the poverty trap model in Figure 4.9. Say that $h(x)$ is earnings in state x and that $h(\text{poor}) = 1$, $h(\text{middle}) = 2$, and $h(\text{rich}) = 3$. Households that start with $X_0 = \text{poor}$ will always be poor, so $\frac{1}{k} \sum_{t=0}^{k-1} h(X_t) = 1$ for all k. Households that start with X_0 in $\{\text{middle, rich}\}$ remain in this absorbing set forever, so $\frac{1}{k} \sum_{t=0}^{k-1} h(X_t) \geqslant 2$ for all k. In particular, the limit of the sum depends on the initial condition. This violates part (ii) of Theorem 4.2.2, which states that the limit is independent of the distribution of X_0.

4.2.1.4   Reinterpreting the Stationary Distribution

Ergodicity has many useful implications. One is a new *interpretation* for the stationary distribution. To illustrate this, let $\mathscr{M}$ be an ergodic Markov model with state space S and transition matrix P. Let (X_t) be a P-chain, and let

$$\hat{\psi}_k(y) := \frac{1}{k} \sum_{t=1}^{k} \mathbb{1}\{X_t = y\} \qquad (y \in S).$$

The value $\hat{\psi}_k(y)$ measures the fraction of time that the P-chain spends in state y over the time interval $1, \ldots, k$. Under ergodicity, for fixed $y \in S$, we can use (4.18) with $h(x) = \mathbb{1}\{x = y\}$ to obtain

$$\hat{\psi}_k(y) \to \sum_{x \in S} \mathbb{1}\{x = y\} \psi^*(x) = \psi^*(y). \qquad (4.19)$$

Turning (4.19) around, we see that

$$\psi^*(y) \approx \text{ the fraction of time that any } P\text{-chain } (X_t) \text{ spends in state } y. \qquad (4.20)$$

Figure 4.10 illustrates this idea for a simulated Markov chain (X_t) generated from the matrix P_B introduced in (4.5). The figure compares $\hat{\psi}_k$ and ψ^* for different values of k. As $k \to \infty$, the convergence claimed in (4.19) occurs.

Of course, we must remember that (4.20) is only valid under ergodicity. For example, if $P = I$, the identity, then every distribution is stationary, every P-Markov chain is constant, and (4.20) does not hold.

Notice that, in view of Theorem 4.2.2, the convergence in (4.18) occurs for *any* initial condition. This gives us, under ergodicity, a way of computing the stationary distribution via simulation (and (4.19)). While this method is slower than algebraic

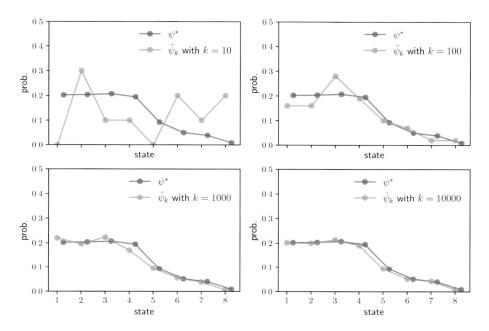

Figure 4.10 Convergence of the empirical distribution to ψ^*

techniques (see, e.g., §4.1.3.4) for small problems, it can be the only feasible option when $|S|$ is large.

4.2.2 Aperiodicity and Stability

In §4.2.1 we discussed sample path properties of Markov chains, finding that strong connectivity is sufficient for the stability of time series averages. Next we turn to marginal distributions of the chain and their long-run properties, which we examined informally in §4.1.2.2. We will see that, to guarantee convergence of these sequences, we also need a condition that governs periodicity.

4.2.2.1 Convergence of Marginals

Let $\mathcal{M}$ be a finite Markov model with state space S and transition matrix P. We call $\mathcal{M}$ **globally stable** if there is only one stationary distribution ψ^* in $\mathcal{D}(S)$, and, moreover,

$$\lim_{t \to \infty} \psi P^t = \psi^* \quad \text{for all } \psi \in \mathcal{D}(S). \tag{4.21}$$

In other words, marginal distributions of every P-Markov chain converge to the unique stationary distribution of the model.

There is a useful connection between global stability and absorbing sets. Intuitively, if $\mathcal{M}$ is globally stable and has an absorbing set A that can be reached from any $x \in S$, then any Markov chain generated by these dynamics will eventually arrive in A and never leave. Hence, the stationary distribution must put all of its mass on A. The next exercise asks you to confirm this.

EXERCISE 4.2.3. Let $\mathcal{M}$ be a finite Markov model with state space S and transition matrix P. Let A be a nonempty absorbing subset of S. Assume that

(a) $\mathcal{M}$ is globally stable with unique stationary distribution ψ^*; and
(b) for each $x \in A^c := S \setminus A$, there exists an $a \in A$ such that a is accessible from x.

Show that, under the stated conditions, there exists an $\varepsilon > 0$ such that $\sum_{y \in A^c} P^n(x, y) \leqslant 1 - \varepsilon$ for all $x \in S$, where $n = |S|$. Using this fact, show in addition that $\sum_{y \in A} \psi^*(y) = 1$.

4.2.2.2   A Key Theorem

From Theorem 4.1.1 we saw that strong connectedness is sufficient for uniqueness of the stationary distribution. One might hope that strong connectedness is enough for global stability too, but this is not true. To see why, suppose for example that $S = \{0, 1\}$ and $E = \{(0, 1), (1, 0)\}$. The transition matrix is

$$P_d = \begin{pmatrix} 0 & 1 \\ 1 & 0 \end{pmatrix}. \tag{4.22}$$

While this model is strongly connected, global stability fails. Indeed, if (X_t) is P_d-Markov and starts at 0, then (X_t) will visit state 1 on odd dates and state 0 on even dates. That is, $P_d^t \delta_0 = \delta_{t \bmod 2}$. This sequence does not converge.

The issue with P_d is that, even though the chain traverses the whole state space, the distribution of X_t will affect that of X_{t+j} for all j due to periodicity. This causes stability to fail. If, however, we rule out periodicity, then we have enough for stability to hold. This line of reasoning leads to the following famous theorem.

THEOREM 4.2.3   *Let $\mathcal{M}$ be a finite Markov model. If $\mathcal{M}$ is strongly connected and aperiodic, then $\mathcal{M}$ is globally stable.*

Proof   Let $\mathcal{M}$ be a finite Markov model with state S and transition matrix P. Suppose $\mathcal{M}$ is aperiodic and strongly connected. Let ψ^* be the unique stationary distribution of $\mathcal{M}$. By Theorem 1.4.4, P is primitive. Hence we can apply the last part of the Perron–Frobenius theorem (see page 13). Using $r(P) = 1$, this result tells us that $P^t \to e_r e_\ell^\top$ as $t \to \infty$, where e_r and e_ℓ are the unique right and left eigenvectors of P corresponding to the eigenvalue $r(P) = 1$ that also satisfy the normalization $\langle e_\ell, e_r \rangle = 1$.

Now observe that ψ^* obeys $\psi^* = \psi^* P$ and, in addition, $P\mathbb{1} = \mathbb{1}$. Hence ψ^* and $\mathbb{1}$ are left and right eigenvectors corresponding to $r(P) = 1$. Moreover, $\langle \psi^*, \mathbb{1} \rangle = 1$. Hence $e_r = \mathbb{1}$ and $e_\ell^\top = \psi^*$.

Combining these facts leads to

$$\lim_{t \to \infty} P^t = P^*, \quad \text{where} \quad P^* := \mathbb{1}\psi^*. \tag{4.23}$$

If we pick any $\psi \in \mathscr{D}(S)$, then, by (4.23), we get $\psi P^t \to \langle \psi, \mathbb{1} \rangle \psi^* = \psi^*$. Hence global stability holds. □

Example 4.2.8: The Markov models P_Q and P_B in §4.1.1 are both aperiodic by the results in §1.4.1.4. Being strongly connected, they are also globally stable.

The aperiodicity condition in Theorem 4.2.3 is, in general, not stringent. On the other hand, the strong connectedness requirement is arguably quite strict. Weaker conditions for global stability are available, as we shall see in §4.2.3.

4.2.2.3 Rates of Convergence: Spectral Gap

While global stability is a very useful property, the implications are qualitative rather than quantitative. In practice, we usually want to know something about the *rate* of convergence. There are several ways of looking at this. We cover the two most common in this section and the next.

As a first step, fixing a Markov model $\mathscr{M}$ with state space S and transition matrix P, we use (1.5) on page 10 to write P^t as

$$P^t = \sum_{i=1}^{n-1} \lambda_i^t e_i \varepsilon_i^\top + \mathbb{1}\psi^*, \tag{4.24}$$

where each λ_i is an eigenvalue of P, and e_i and ε_i are the right and left eigenvectors corresponding to λ_i. We have also ordered the eigenvalues from smallest to largest and used the Perron–Frobenius theorem to infer that $\lambda_n = r(P) = 1$, as well as the arguments in the proof of Theorem 4.2.3 that showed $e_n = \mathbb{1}$ and $\varepsilon_n^\top = \psi^*$.

Premultiplying P^t by arbitrary $\psi \in \mathscr{D}(S)$ and rearranging now gives

$$\psi P^t - \psi^* = \sum_{i=1}^{n-1} \lambda_i^t \psi e_i \varepsilon_i^\top. \tag{4.25}$$

Recall that eigenvalues are ordered from smallest to largest. Moreover, by the Perron–Frobenius theorem, $\lambda_i < 1$ for all $i < n$ when P is primitive (i.e., $\mathscr{M}$ is strongly connected and aperiodic). Hence, after taking the Euclidean norm deviation, we obtain

$$\|\psi P^t - \psi^*\| = O(\eta^t), \quad \text{where} \quad \eta := |\lambda_{n-1}| < 1. \tag{4.26}$$

Thus, the rate of convergence is governed by the modulus of the second-largest eigenvalue.

The difference between the largest and second-largest eigenvalue of a nonnegative matrix is often called the **spectral gap**. For this reason, we can also say that, for primitive stochastic matrices, the rate of convergence is determined by the (nonzero) spectral gap.

Example 4.2.9: When studying the worker model with hiring rate α and firing rate β in §1.2.1.3, we found that the eigenvalues of the transition matrix P_w are $\lambda_1 = 1 - \alpha - \beta$ and $\lambda_2 = 1$. Hence the spectral gap is $\alpha + \beta$ and the rate of convergence is $O((1 - \alpha - \beta)^t)$. High hiring and firing rates both produce faster convergence. In essence, this is because higher hiring and firing rates mean workers do not stay in any state for long, so initial conditions die out faster.

4.2.3   The Markov–Dobrushin Coefficient

The rate of convergence of ψP^t to ψ^* given in §4.2.2.3 restricts the Euclidean distance between these vectors as a function of t. There are, however, other metrics we could use in studying rates of convergence, and sometimes these other metrics give more convenient results. In fact, as we show in this section, a good choice of metric leads us to a more general stability result than the (better known) aperiodicity-based result in §4.2.2.

4.2.3.1   An Alternative Metric

For the purposes of this section, For $\varphi, \psi \in \mathscr{D}(S)$, we set

$$\rho(\varphi, \psi) := \|\varphi - \psi\|_1 := \sum_{x \in S} |\varphi(x) - \psi(x)|,$$

which is just the ℓ_1 deviation between φ and ψ (see §2.3.1.1).

EXERCISE 4.2.4. Show that, for any $\varphi, \psi \in \mathscr{D}(S)$, we have

(i) $\rho(\varphi, \psi) \leqslant 2$;

(ii) $\rho(\varphi P, \psi P) \leqslant \rho(\varphi, \psi)$ for any stochastic matrix P.

Property (ii) is called the **nonexpansiveness property** of stochastic matrices under the ℓ_1 deviation. As we will see, we can tighten this bound when P satisfies certain properties.

As a first step we note that, for the ℓ_1 deviation, given any stochastic matrix P, we have

$$\rho(\varphi P, \psi P) \leqslant (1 - \alpha(P))\rho(\varphi, \psi), \tag{4.27}$$

where

$$\alpha(P) := \min \left\{ \sum_{y \in S} [P(x, y) \wedge P(x', y)] : (x, x') \in S \times S \right\}. \tag{4.28}$$

Here $a \wedge b := \min\{a,b\}$ when $a,b \in \mathbb{R}$. We call $\alpha(P)$ the **Markov–Dobrushin coefficient** of P, although other names are also used in the literature. A proof of the bound in (4.27) can be found in Stachurski (2022a) or Seneta (2006a).[3]

EXERCISE 4.2.5. Consider the stochastic matrix

$$P_w = \begin{pmatrix} 1 - \alpha & \alpha \\ \beta & 1 - \beta \end{pmatrix}.$$

Show that $\alpha(P_w) = 0$ if and only if $\alpha = \beta = 0$ or $\alpha = \beta = 1$.

How should the Markov–Dobrushin coefficient be understood? The coefficient is large when the rows of P are relatively similar. For example, if rows $P(x,\cdot)$ and $P(x',\cdot)$ are identical, the $\sum_{y \in S}[P(x,y) \wedge P(x',y)] = 1$. Similarity of rows is related to stability. The next exercise helps to illustrate this.

EXERCISE 4.2.6. Let P be such that all rows are identical and equal to $\varphi \in \mathscr{D}(S)$. Prove that global stability holds in one step, in the sense that φ is the unique stationary distribution, and $\psi P = \varphi$ for all $\psi \in \mathscr{D}(S)$.

EXERCISE 4.2.7. Using (4.27), show that, for any $\varphi, \psi \in \mathscr{D}(S)$, we have

$$\rho(\varphi P^t, \psi P^t) \leqslant (1 - \alpha(P))^t \rho(\varphi, \psi) \quad \text{for all } t \in \mathbb{N}. \tag{4.29}$$

Since powers of stochastic matrices are again stochastic, and since (4.27) is valid for any stochastic matrix, the bound in (4.29) can be generalized by replacing P with P^k for any given $k \in \mathbb{N}$, which gives (with t replaced by τ)

$$\rho(\varphi P^{\tau k}, \psi P^{\tau k}) \leqslant (1 - \alpha(P^k))^\tau \rho(\varphi, \psi) \quad \text{for all } \tau \in \mathbb{N}.$$

Now observe that, for any $t \in \mathbb{N}$, we can write $t = \tau k + j$, where $\tau \in \mathbb{Z}_+$ and $j \in \{0, \ldots, k-1\}$. Fixing t and choosing j to make this equality hold, we get

$$\rho(\varphi P^t, \psi P^t) = \rho(\varphi P^{\tau k+j}, \psi P^{\tau k+j}) \leqslant \rho(\varphi P^{\tau k}, \psi P^{\tau k}) \leqslant (1 - \alpha(P^k))^\tau \rho(\varphi, \psi),$$

where the second inequality is due to the nonexpansive property of stochastic matrices (Exercise 4.2.4). Since τ is an integer satisfying $\tau = \lfloor t/k \rfloor$, where $\lfloor \cdot \rfloor$ is the floor function, we can now state the following.

THEOREM 4.2.4 *Let $\mathscr{M}$ be a finite Markov model with state space S and transition matrix P. For all $\varphi, \psi \in \mathscr{D}(S)$ and all $k,t \in \mathbb{N}$, we have*

$$\rho(\varphi P^t, \psi P^t) \leqslant (1 - \alpha(P^k))^{\lfloor t/k \rfloor} \rho(\varphi, \psi). \tag{4.30}$$

In particular, if there exists a $k \in \mathbb{N}$ such that $\alpha(P^k) > 0$, then $\mathscr{M}$ is globally stable.

---

[3] Seneta (2006a) also discusses the history of Andrey Markov's work, from which originated the kinds of contraction-based arguments used in this section.

To see why the global stability implication stated in Theorem 4.2.4 holds, suppose there exists a $k \in \mathbb{N}$ such that $\alpha(P^k) > 0$. Now substitute arbitrary $\psi \in \mathscr{D}(S)$ and any stationary distribution ψ^* for P into (4.30) to obtain

$$\rho(\psi P^t, \psi^*) \leqslant (1 - \alpha(P^k))^{\lfloor t/k \rfloor} \rho(\psi, \psi^*) \leqslant 2(1 - \alpha(P^k))^{\lfloor t/k \rfloor} \tag{4.31}$$

for all $t \in \mathbb{N}$, where the second bound is due to Exercise 4.2.4.

EXERCISE 4.2.8. In the preceding discussion, the distribution ψ^* was taken to be any stationary distribution of P. Using (4.31), prove that P has only one stationary distribution when $\alpha(P^k) > 0$.

One of the major advantages of Theorem 4.2.4 is that strong connectivity of $\mathscr{M}$ is not required. In the next section we will see an example of a finite Markov model $\mathscr{M}$ where (i) strong connectivity fails but (ii) the conditions of Theorem 4.2.4 are satisfied.[4]

EXERCISE 4.2.9. Let $\mathscr{M}$ be a finite Markov model with state space S and transition matrix P. Prove the existence of a $k \in \mathbb{N}$ with $\alpha(P^k) > 0$ whenever $\mathscr{M}$ is strongly connected and aperiodic.

4.2.3.2   Sufficient Conditions

While the Markov–Dobrushin coefficient $\alpha(P^k)$ can be calculated for any given k on a computer by stepping through all pairs of rows in P^k, this calculation is computationally intensive when S is large. When applicable, the following lemma simplifies the problem by providing a sufficient condition for $\alpha(P^k) > 0$.

LEMMA 4.2.5   *Let k be a natural number, and let $\mathscr{M}$ be a finite Markov model with state space S and transition matrix P. If there is a state $z \in S$ such that, for every $x \in S$, there exists a directed walk from x to z of length k, then $\alpha(P^k) > 0$.*

Proof   Let $k \in \mathbb{N}$ and $z \in S$ be such that, for every $x \in S$, there exists a directed walk from x to z of length k. By Proposition 1.4.2, we then have $r := \min_{x \in S} P^k(x, z) > 0$. Since, for any $x, x' \in S$,

$$\sum_{y \in S} [P^k(x, y) \wedge P^k(x', y)] \geqslant P^k(x, z) \wedge P^k(x', z) \geqslant r > 0,$$

strict positivity of $\alpha(P^k)$ now follows from the definition of the Markov–Dobrushin coefficient. $\square$

Example 4.2.10: Consider the digraph in Figure 4.11. This digraph is not strongly connected because node 4 is not accessible from anywhere. However, there exists a

---

[4] It can be shown that the condition $\alpha(P^k) > 0$ for some $k \in \mathbb{N}$ is both necessary and sufficient for global stability of a finite Markov model. Hence the conditions of Theorem 4.2.4 are strictly weaker than strong connectedness plus aperiodicity, as used in Theorem 4.1.1.

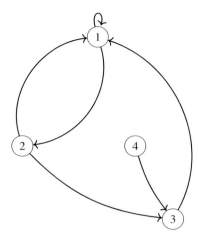

Figure 4.11 A digraph with walk of length 2 from any node to 1

directed walk from any vertex to vertex 1 in $k = 2$ steps. For example, from node 2 we can choose $2 \to 1$ and then $1 \to 1$, from node 1 we can choose $1 \to 1$ and then $1 \to 1$, etc. Hence, if Figure 4.11 is the digraph of a finite Markov model with transition matrix P, then $\alpha(P^2) > 0$.

Example 4.2.11: Consider the Markov dynamics suggested in Figure 1.10 on page 25. Although there are no weights, we can see that poor is accessible from every state in one step, so $\mathcal{M}$ must be globally stable. In addition, poor is, by itself, an absorbing set. Hence, by Exericse 4.2.3, for any choice of weights compatible with these edges, the stationary distribution will concentrate all its mass on poor.

REMARK 4.2.1   *As was pointed out in the proof of Lemma 4.2.5, under the conditions of that lemma, we have $P^k(x, z) > 0$ for all $x \in S$. This means that $\alpha(P^k) > 0$ whenever P^k has a strictly positive column.*

4.2.3.3   Application: PageRank

In §1.4.3 we discussed centrality measures for networks. Centrality measures provide a ranking of vertices in the network according to their "centrality" or "importance." One of the most important applications of ranking of vertices in a network is ranking the importance of web pages on the internet. Historically, the most prominent example of a ranking mechanism for the internet is PageRank, which transformed Google from a minor start-up to a technology behemoth. In this section we provide a simple introduction to the original form of PageRank and connect it to previously discussed measures of centrality.

Consider a finite collection of web pages W, and let L be the hyperlinks between them. We understand (W, L) as a digraph $\mathcal{G}$, where W is the set of vertices and L is

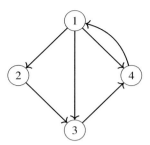

Figure 4.12 A digraph with walk of length 2 from any node to 1

the set of edges. Let A be the associated adjacency matrix, so that $A(u, v) = 1$ if there is a link from u to v and zero otherwise. We set $n = |W|$, so that A is $n \times n$.

To start our analysis, we consider the case where $\mathcal{G}$ is strongly connected, such as the small network in Figure 4.12. Furthermore, we introduce a second matrix P in which each row of A has been normalized so that it sums to one. For the network in Figure 4.12, this means that

$$A = \begin{pmatrix} 0 & 1 & 1 & 1 \\ 0 & 0 & 1 & 0 \\ 0 & 0 & 0 & 1 \\ 1 & 0 & 0 & 0 \end{pmatrix} \quad \text{and} \quad P = \begin{pmatrix} 0 & 1/3 & 1/3 & 1/3 \\ 0 & 0 & 1 & 0 \\ 0 & 0 & 0 & 1 \\ 1 & 0 & 0 & 0 \end{pmatrix}.$$

Now consider an internet surfer who, once per minute, randomly clicks on one of the k outgoing links on a page, each link selected with uniform probability $1/k$. The idea of PageRank is to assign to each page $u \in W$ a value $g(u)$ equal to the fraction of time that this surfer spends on page u over the long run. Intuitively, a high value for $g(u)$ indicates a heavily visited and hence important site.

The vector g is easy to compute, given our knowledge of Markov chains. Let $\mathcal{M}$ be the finite Markov model associated with the random surfer, with state space W and adjacency matrix given by P. Since $\mathcal{M}$ is strongly connected, the ergodicity theorem (page 145) tells us that P has a unique stationary distribution ψ^*, and that the fraction of time the surfer spends at page u is equal to the probability assigned to u under the stationary distribution (see, in particular, (4.20)). Hence $g = \psi^*$.

As g is stationary and $r(P) = 1$, we can write $g = (1/r(P))gP$. Taking transposes gives $g^\top = (1/r(P))P^\top g^\top$. Comparing with (1.34) on page 43, we see that, for this simple case, the PageRank vector g is just the authority-based eigenvector centrality measure of $\mathcal{M}$. Thus, PageRank gives high ranking to pages with many inbound links, attaching high value to inbound links from pages that are themselves highly ranked.

There are two problems with the preceding analysis. First, we assumed that the internet is strongly connected, which is clearly violated in practice (we need only one page with no outbound links). Second, internet users sometimes select pages without using hyperlinks, by manually entering the URL.

The PageRank solution to this problem is to replace P with the so-called **Google matrix**

$$G := \delta P + (1 - \delta)\frac{1}{n}\mathbb{1},$$

where $\mathbb{1}$ is the $n \times n$ matrix of ones. The value $\delta \in (0, 1)$ is called the **damping factor**.

EXERCISE 4.2.10. Prove that G is a stochastic matrix for all $\delta \in (0, 1)$.

The Markov dynamics embedded in the stochastic matrix G can be understood as follows: The surfer begins by flipping a coin with heads probability δ. (See Exercise 1.3.6 and its solution for the connection between convex combinations and coin flips.) If the coin is heads, then the surfer randomly selects and follows one of the links on the current page. If not, then the surfer randomly selects and moves to any page on the internet.

For given δ, the PageRank vector for this setting is adjusted to be the stationary distribution of the Google matrix G.

EXERCISE 4.2.11. Verify that the digraph associated with the transition probabilities in G is always strongly connected (assuming, as above, that $\delta \in (0, 1)$).

As a result of Exercise 4.2.11, we can always interpret the stationary of G as telling us the fraction of time that the surfer spends on each page in the long run.

EXERCISE 4.2.12. Use (4.31) to obtain a rate of convergence of ψG^t to the adjusted PageRank vector g^* (i.e., the unique stationary distribution g^* of G), where ψ is an arbitrary initial distribution on W. (Set $k = 1$.)

4.2.4 Information and Social Networks

In recent years, the way that opinions spread across social networks has become a major topic of concern in many countries around the globe. A well-known mathematical model of this phenomenon is **DeGroot learning**, which was originally proposed in DeGroot (1974). This mechanism has linear properties that make it relatively easy to analyze (although large and complex underlying networks can cause significant challenges).

In DeGroot learning, a group of agents, labeled from 1 to n, is connected by a social or information network of some type. Connections are indicated by a **trust matrix** T, where, informally,

$$T(i, j) = \text{amount that } i \text{ trusts the opinion of } j.$$

In other words, $T(i, j)$ is large if agent i puts a large positive weight on the opinion of agent j. The matrix T is assumed to be stochastic.

We can view the trust matrix as an adjacency matrix for a weighed digraph $\mathcal{S}$ with vertex set $V := [n]$ and edges

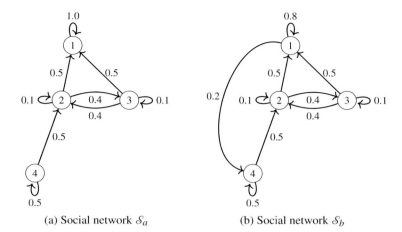

(a) Social network $\mathcal{S}_a$ (b) Social network $\mathcal{S}_b$

Figure 4.13 Two social networks

$$E = \{(i, j) \in V \times V : T(i, j) > 0\}.$$

Figure 4.13 shows two social networks $\mathcal{S}_a$ and $\mathcal{S}_b$ with trust matrices given by

$$T_a = \begin{pmatrix} 1 & 0 & 0 & 0 \\ 0.5 & 0.1 & 0.4 & 0 \\ 0.5 & 0.4 & 0.1 & 0 \\ 0 & 0.5 & 0 & 0.5 \end{pmatrix} \quad \text{and} \quad T_b = \begin{pmatrix} 0.8 & 0 & 0 & 0.2 \\ 0.5 & 0.1 & 0.4 & 0 \\ 0.5 & 0.4 & 0.1 & 0 \\ 0 & 0.5 & 0 & 0.5 \end{pmatrix},$$

respectively. In network A, agent 1 places no trust in anyone's opinion but their own. In network B, they place at least some trust in the opinion of agent 4. Below we show how these differences matter for the dynamics of beliefs.

4.2.4.1   Learning

At time zero, all agents have an initial subjective belief concerning the validity of a given statement. Belief takes values in $[0, 1]$, with 1 indicating complete (subjective) certainty that the statement is true. Let $b_0(i)$ be the belief of agent i at time zero.

An agent updates beliefs sequentially based on the beliefs of others, weighted by the amount of trust placed in their opinion. Specifically, agent i updates their belief after one unit of time to $\sum_{j=1}^{n} T(i, j)b_0(j)$. More generally, at time $t + 1$, beliefs update to

$$b_{t+1}(i) = \sum_{j=1}^{n} T(i, j)b_t(j) \quad (i \in V). \tag{4.32}$$

In matrix notation this is $b_{t+1} = Tb_t$, where each b_t is treated as a column vector.

(Notice that this update rule is similar but not identical to the marginal distribution updating rule for Markov chains (the forward equation) discussed on page 136. Here we are postmultiplying by a column vector rather than premultiplying by a row vector.)

EXERCISE 4.2.13. If some subgroup of agents $U \subset V$ is an absorbing set for the digraph $\mathcal{S}$, indicating that members of this group place no trust in outsiders, then the initial beliefs $\{b_0(i)\}_{i \in U^c}$ of the outsiders (members of $U^c = V \setminus U$) have no influence on the beliefs of the insiders (members of U) at any point in time. Prove that this is true.

4.2.4.2 Consensus

A social network $\mathcal{S}$ is said to lead to **consensus** if $|b_t(i) - b_t(j)| \to 0$ as $t \to \infty$ for all $i, j \in V$. Consensus implies that all agents eventually share the same belief. An important question is, what conditions on the network lead to a consensus outcome?

PROPOSITION 4.2.6 *If there exists a $k \in \mathbb{N}$ such that $\alpha(T^k) > 0$, then consensus is obtained. In particular,*

$$|b_t(i) - b_t(j)| \leqslant 2(1 - \alpha(T^k))^{\lfloor t/k \rfloor} \quad \text{for all } t \in \mathbb{N} \text{ and } i, j \in V. \tag{4.33}$$

Proof Fix $i, j \in V$ and $t \in \mathbb{N}$. Let $b = b_0$. For any $\varphi, \psi \in \mathscr{D}(V)$, an application of the triangle inequality gives

$$|\varphi T^t b - \psi T^t b| = \left| \sum_j (\varphi T^t)(j) b(j) - \sum_j (\psi T^t)(j) b(j) \right| \leqslant \sum_j |(\varphi T^t)(j) - (\psi T^t)(j)|,$$

where we have used the fact that $|b(j)| = b(j) \leqslant 1$. Applying the definition of the ℓ_1 deviation and (4.30), we obtain the bound

$$|\varphi T^t b - \psi T^t b| \leqslant (1 - \alpha(T^k))^{\lfloor t/k \rfloor} \rho(\varphi, \psi) \leqslant 2(1 - \alpha(T^k))^{\lfloor t/k \rfloor}. \tag{4.34}$$

Since this bound is valid for any choice of $\varphi, \psi \in \mathscr{D}(V)$, we can specialize to $\varphi = \delta_i$ and $\psi = \delta_j$ and, applying $T^t b = b_t$, we get

$$|b_t(i) - b_t(j)| = |\delta_i T^t b - \delta_j T^t b| \leqslant 2(1 - \alpha(T^k))^{\lfloor t/k \rfloor}. \qquad \square$$

Proposition 4.2.6 can be applied to the two social networks $\mathcal{S}_a$ and $\mathcal{S}_b$ in Figure 4.13. For example, in network $\mathcal{S}_a$, for every node i, there exists a walk of length 2 from node i to node 1. Hence, by Lemma 4.2.5, we have $\alpha(T^2) > 0$. In network $\mathcal{S}_b$, the same is true.

EXERCISE 4.2.14. Let $\mathcal{S}$ be a social network with trust (and adjacency) matrix T. Use Proposition 4.2.6 to show that $\mathcal{S}$ leads to consensus whenever $\mathcal{S}$ is strongly connected and aperiodic.

4.2.4.3 Influence of Authorities

Now let's consider what beliefs converge to when consensus emerges. In particular, we are interested in discovering whose opinions are most influential under DeGroot learning, for a given trust matrix.

To answer the question, let $\mathscr{S}$ be a given social network with trust matrix T. Suppose that $\alpha(T^k) > 0$ for some $k \in \mathbb{N}$. By Theorem 4.2.4, the network $\mathscr{S}$ is globally stable when viewed as a finite Markov model. Let ψ^* be the unique stationary distribution, so that $\psi^* = \psi^* T$.

Applying (4.34) with $\varphi = \delta_i$ and $\psi = \psi^*$ yields

$$\left| b_t(i) - b^* \right| \leqslant (1 - \alpha(T^k))^{\lfloor t/k \rfloor} \rho(\varphi, \psi) \leqslant 2(1 - \alpha(T^k))^{\lfloor t/k \rfloor},$$

where

$$b^* := \sum_{j \in V} \psi^*(j) b_0(j).$$

We conclude that the belief of every agent converges geometrically to b^*, which is a weighted average of the initial beliefs of all agents. In particular, those agents with high weighting under the stationary distribution have a large influence on these equilibrium beliefs.

We can interpret this through notions of centrality. Since $r(T) = 1$, we have $(\psi^*)^\top = (1/r(T)) T^\top (\psi^*)^\top$, so ψ^* is the authority-based eigenvector centrality measure on $\mathscr{S}$. Thus, the influence of each agent on long-run beliefs is proportional to their authority-based eigenvector centrality. This makes sense because such agents are highly trusted by many agents who are themselves highly trusted.

EXERCISE 4.2.15. For network $\mathscr{S}_a$ in Figure 4.13, show that $b^* = b_0(1)$. That is, all agents' beliefs converge to the belief of agent 1.

EXERCISE 4.2.16. Using a computer, show that the stationary distribution for $\mathscr{S}_b$, rounded to two decimal places, is $\psi^* = (0.56, 0.15, 0.07, 0.22)$. (Notice how the relatively slight change in network structure from $\mathscr{S}_a$ to $\mathscr{S}_b$ substantially reduces the influence of agent 1.)

4.3   Chapter Notes

High quality treatments of finite-state Markov dynamics include Norris (1998), Häggström et al. (2002), and Privault (2013). For the general state case see Meyn and Tweedie (2009).

A review of DeGroot learning is available in Jackson (2010). Some interesting extensions related to the "wisdom of crowds" phenomenon are provided in Golub and Jackson (2010). Molavi et al. (2018) provide a theory of social learning that includes DeGroot learning as a special case. Acemoglu et al. (2021a) study misinformation and echo chambers in information networks. Board and Meyer-ter Vehn (2021) analyze learning dynamics in continuous time on large social networks. Shiller (2020) provides an interesting discussion of how ideas spread across social networks and shape economic outcomes. In a large-scale empirical study, Chetty et al. (2022)

analyze how cross-class friendships influence social mobility. Acemoglu et al. (2023) consider the effect of strong and weak links on Bayesian learning in a social network. Dasaratha et al. (2022) analyze how Bayesian agents learn about a changing state by interacting with their neighbors. While the resulting dynamics are similar to those of the DeGroot model, they are generated as an equilibrium outcome rather than imposed as a behavioral assumption.

5   Nonlinear Interactions

Much of what makes network analysis interesting is how ramifications of choices flow across networks. In general, decisions made at a given node i affect responses of neighboring nodes and, through them, neighbors of neighboring nodes, and so on. As these consequences flow across the network, they in turn affect choices at i. This is a tail-chasing scenario, which can be unraveled through fixed point theory.

In some network settings, such as the input–output model in §2.1, interactions are linear, and fixed point problems reduce to a system of linear equations. In other settings, interactions are inherently nonlinear, and, as a result, we need more sophisticated fixed point theory.

This chapter is dedicated to the study of networks with nonlinear interactions. We begin with relevant fixed point theory and then apply it to a sequence of problems that arise in the analysis of economic networks, including production models with supply constraints and financial networks.

5.1   Fixed Point Theory

Let S be any set. Recall from §A.1.6 that, given a self-map G on S, a point $x \in S$ is called a fixed point of G if $Gx = x$. (A self-map on S is a function G from S to itself. When working with self-maps, it is common to abbreviate $G(x)$ to Gx.) In this chapter, we will say that G is **globally stable** on S if G has a unique fixed point $x^* \in S$, and $G^k x \to x^*$ as $k \to \infty$ for all $x \in S$. In other words, under this property, the fixed point is not only unique but also globally attracting under iteration of G.

We have already discussed fixed points, indirectly or directly, in multiple contexts:

- In Chapter 2 we studied the equation $x = Ax + d$, where x is an output vector, A is a matrix of coefficients, and d is a demand vector. A solution x to this equation can also be thought of as a fixed point of the affine map $Fx = Ax + d$.
- In Chapter 4 we learned that a stationary distribution of a finite Markov model with state space S and adjacency matrix P is a $\psi \in \mathscr{D}(S)$ with $\psi = \psi P$. In other words, ψ is a fixed point of $\psi \mapsto \psi P$ in $\mathscr{D}(S)$.
- In Chapter 3 we studied the Bellman equation $q(x) = \min_{y \in \mathscr{O}(x)} \{c(x, y) + q(y)\}$ and introduced an operator, the Bellman operator T, with the property that its fixed points exactly coincide with solutions to the Bellman equation.

In each case, when we introduced these fixed point problems, we immediately needed to consider questions of the existence and uniqueness of fixed points. Now we address these same issues more systematically in an abstract setting.

5.1.1 Contraction Mappings

In Chapter 2 we studied solutions of the system $x = Ax + b$ that are fixed points of the affine map $Fx = Ax + b$ on $\mathbb{R}^n$ studied in Example 5.1.1. The Neumann series lemma on page 11 is, in essence, a statement about the existence and uniqueness of fixed points of this map. Here we investigate another fixed point theorem, due to Stefan Banach (1892–1945), that can be thought of as extending the Neumann series lemma to nonlinear systems.

5.1.1.1 Contractions

Let S be a nonempty subset of $\mathbb{R}^n$. A self-map F on S is called **contracting** or a **contraction of modulus** λ on S if there exist a $\lambda < 1$ and a norm $\| \cdot \|$ on $\mathbb{R}^n$ such that

$$\|Fu - Fv\| \leqslant \lambda \|u - v\| \quad \text{for all} \quad u, v \in S. \tag{5.1}$$

EXERCISE 5.1.1. Let F be a contraction of modulus λ on S. Show that

(i) F is continuous on S and
(ii) F has at most one fixed point on S.

Example 5.1.1: Let $S = \mathbb{R}^n$, paired with the Euclidean norm $\| \cdot \|$. Let $Fx = Ax + b$, where $A \in \mathbb{M}^{n \times n}$ and $b \in \mathbb{R}^n$. If $\|A\| < 1$, where $\| \cdot \|$ is the operator norm on $\mathbb{M}^{n \times n}$, then F is a contraction of modulus $\|A\|$, since, for any $x, y \in S$,

$$\|Ax + b - Ay - b\| = \|A(x - y)\| \leqslant \|A\| \|x - y\|.$$

The next example uses a similar idea but is based on a different norm.

Example 5.1.2: In (2.22) we studied the system $\rho = A^{\top}\rho - \varepsilon$, where $A = (a_{ij})$ is a matrix of coefficients satisfying $\sum_i a_{ij} = 1 - \alpha$ for some $\alpha \in (0, 1)$, the vector ε is given, and ρ is unknown. Solutions can be viewed as fixed points of the map $F : \mathbb{R}^n \to \mathbb{R}^n$ defined by $Fp = A^{\top}p - \varepsilon$. Under the $\| \cdot \|_\infty$ norm, F is a contraction of modulus $1 - \alpha$ on $\mathbb{R}^n$. Indeed, for any $p, q \in \mathbb{R}^n$,

$$\|Fp - Fq\|_\infty = \max_j \left| \sum_{i=1}^{n} a_{ij}(p_i - q_i) \right| \leqslant \max_j \sum_{i=1}^{n} a_{ij} |p_i - q_i|.$$

Since $|p_i - q_i| \leqslant \|p - q\|_\infty$, we obtain

$$\|Fp - Fq\|_\infty \leqslant \max_j \sum_{i=1}^{n} a_{ij} \|p - q\|_\infty = (1 - \alpha)\|p - q\|_\infty.$$

Consider again Example 5.1.1. For the affine map $Fx = Ax + b$, the condition $\|A\| < 1$ used to obtain contraction is stronger than the condition $r(A) < 1$ used to obtain a unique fixed point in the Neumann series lemma (see Exercise 2.3.11 on page 82). Furthermore, the Neumann series lemma provides a geometric series representation of the fixed point. On the other hand, as we now show, the contraction property can be used to obtain unique fixed points when the map in question is not affine.

5.1.1.2   Banach's Theorem

The fundamental importance of contractions stems from the following theorem.

THEOREM 5.1.1 (Banach's contraction mapping theorem)   *If S is closed in $\mathbb{R}^n$ and F is a contraction of modulus λ on S, then F has a unique fixed point u^* in S, and*

$$\|F^n u - u^*\| \leqslant \lambda^n \|u - u^*\| \quad \text{for all } n \in \mathbb{N} \text{ and } u \in S. \tag{5.2}$$

In particular, F is globally stable on S.

We complete a proof of Theorem 5.1.1 in stages.

EXERCISE 5.1.2. Let S and F have the properties stated in Theorem 5.1.1. Fix $u_0 \in S$ and let $u_m := F^m u_0$. Show that

$$\|u_m - u_k\| \leqslant \sum_{i=m}^{k-1} \lambda^i \|u_0 - u_1\|$$

holds for all $m, k \in \mathbb{N}$ with $m < k$.

EXERCISE 5.1.3. Using the results in Exercise 5.1.2, prove that (u_m) is a Cauchy sequence in $\mathbb{R}^n$ (see §A.3.2 for notes on the Cauchy property).

EXERCISE 5.1.4. Using Exercise 5.1.3, argue that (u_m) hence has a limit $u^* \in \mathbb{R}^n$. Prove that $u^* \in S$.

Proof of Theorem 5.1.1   In the exercises we proved the existence of a point $u^* \in S$ such that $F^m u \to u^*$. The fact that u^* is a fixed point of F now follows from Lemma A.3.4 on page 194 and Exercise 5.1.1. Uniqueness is implied by Exercise 5.1.1. The bound (5.2) follows from iteration on the contraction inequality (5.1) while setting $v = u^*$. □

5.1.1.3   Eventual Contractions

Let S be a nonempty subset of $\mathbb{R}^n$. A self-map F on S is called **eventually contracting** if there exists a $k \in \mathbb{N}$ such that F^k is a contraction on S. Significantly, most of the conclusions of Banach's theorem carry over to the case where F is eventually contracting.

THEOREM 5.1.2   *Let F be a self-map on $S \subset \mathbb{R}^n$. If S is closed and F is eventually contracting, then F is globally stable on S.*

EXERCISE 5.1.5. Prove Theorem 5.1.2.[1]

There is a close connection between Theorem 5.1.2 and the Neumann series lemma (NSL). If $S = \mathbb{R}^n$ and $Fx = Ax + b$ with $r(A) < 1$, then the NSL implies a unique fixed point. We can also obtain this result from Theorem 5.1.2, since, for any $k \in \mathbb{N}$,

$$\|F^k x - F^k y\| = \|A^k x - A^k y\| = \|A^k(x - y)\| \leqslant \|A^k\| \|x - y\|.$$

As $r(A) < 1$, we can choose k such that $\|A^k\| < 1$ (see §2.3.3). Hence F is eventually contracting, and Theorem 5.1.2 applies.

As mentioned above, contractions and eventual contractions have much wider scope than the NSL, since they can also be applied in nonlinear settings. At the same time, the NSL is preferred when its conditions hold, since it also gives inverse and power series representations of the fixed point.

5.1.1.4   A Condition for Eventual Contractions

The result below provides a useful test for the eventual contraction property. (In the statement, the absolute value of a vector is defined pointwise, as in §A.2.2.)

PROPOSITION 5.1.3   *Let F be a self-map on $S \subset \mathbb{R}^n$ such that, for some $n \times n$ matrix A,*

$$|Fx - Fy| \leqslant A|x - y| \quad \text{for all } x, y \in S.$$

If, in addition, $A \geqslant 0$ and $r(A) < 1$, then F is eventually contracting on S with respect to the Euclidean norm.

Proof   Our first claim is that, under the conditions of the proposition,

$$|F^k x - F^k y| \leqslant A^k|x - y| \quad \text{for all } k \in \mathbb{N} \text{ and } x, y \in S. \tag{5.3}$$

This is true at $k = 1$ by assumption. If it is true at $k - 1$, then

$$|F^k x - F^k y| \leqslant A|F^{k-1}x - F^{k-1}y| \leqslant AA^{k-1}|x - y|, \tag{5.4}$$

where the second inequality uses the induction hypothesis and $A \geqslant 0$ (so that $u \leqslant v$ implies $Au \leqslant Av$). Hence (5.3) holds.

It follows from the definition of the Euclidean norm that $\||u|\| = \|u\|$ for any vector u. Also, for the same norm, $|u| \leqslant |v|$ implies $\|u\| \leqslant \|v\|$. Hence, for all $k \in \mathbb{N}$ and $x, y \in S$,

$$\|F^k x - F^k y\| \leqslant \|A^k|x - y|\| \leqslant \|A^k\|_o \|x - y\|.$$

---

[1] Hint: Theorem 5.1.1 is self-improving: It implies this seemingly stronger result. The proof is not trivial, but see if you can get it started. You might like to note that F^k has a unique fixed point u^* in S. (Why?) Now consider the fact that $\|Fu^* - u^*\| = \|FF^{nk}u^* - u^*\|$ for all $n \in \mathbb{N}$.

In the second inequality, we used $\| \cdot \|_o$ for the operator norm, combined with the fact that $\|Au\| \leqslant \|A\|_o \|u\|$ always holds, as discussed in §2.3.2.3.

By Gelfand's lemma (see in particular Exercise 2.3.18 on page 83), we obtain the existence of a $\lambda \in (0, 1)$ and a $k \in \mathbb{N}$ with $\|A^k\|_o \leqslant \lambda < 1$. Hence, for this k,

$$\|F^k x - F^k y\| \leqslant \lambda \|x - y\|.$$

Since λ does not depend on x or y, we have shown that F is an eventual contraction on S with respect to the Euclidean norm. $\square$

5.1.2   Shortest Paths Revisited

Consider again the shortest path problem introduced in §3.1. One modification that sometimes appears in applications is the addition of discounting during travel between vertices. For example, if the vertices are international ports and travel takes place by sea, then port-to-port travel time is measured in weeks or even months. It is natural to apply time discounting to future costs associated with that travel, to implement the idea that paying a given dollar amount in the future is preferable to paying it now.

EXERCISE 5.1.6. Suppose it is possible to borrow and lend risk-free at a positive interest rate r. Explain why it is always preferable to have \$100 now than \$100 in a year's time in this setting.

Recall that, without discounting, the Bellman equation for the shortest path problem takes the form $q(x) = \min_{y \in \mathcal{O}(x)}\{c(x, y) + q(y)\}$ for all $x \in V$, where c is the cost function, V is the set of vertices, and q is a candidate for the cost-to-go function. We showed that the minimum cost-to-go function q^* satisfies the Bellman equation and is the unique fixed point of the Bellman operator.

The Bellman equation neatly divides the problem into current costs, embedded in the term $c(x, y)$, and future costs embedded in $q(y)$. To add discounting, we need only discount $q(y)$. We do this by multiplying it by a **discount factor** $\beta \in (0, 1)$. The Bellman equation is then $q(x) = \min_{y \in \mathcal{O}(x)}\{c(x, y) + \beta q(y)\}$ for all $x \in V$, and the Bellman operator is

$$Tq(x) = \min_{y \in \mathcal{O}(x)} \{c(x, y) + \beta q(y)\} \qquad (x \in V). \qquad (5.5)$$

In §3.1.2, without discounting, we had to work hard to show that the Bellman operator has a unique fixed point in U, the set of all $q : V \to \mathbb{R}_+$ with $q(d) = 0$. With discounting, the proof is easier, since we can leverage the Banach contraction mapping theorem.

In what follows, we identify the vertices in V with integers $1, \ldots, n$, where d is identified with n. We then understand U as all nonnegative vectors q in $\mathbb{R}^n$ with $q(n) = 0$. (We continue to write $q(x)$ for the x-th element of the vector q, but now x is in $[n]$.)

EXERCISE 5.1.7. Prove that U is a closed subset of $\mathbb{R}^n$.

EXERCISE 5.1.8. Prove that T is order-preserving on U with respect to the pointwise order.

EXERCISE 5.1.9. Prove that, for any $q \in U$ and $\alpha \in \mathbb{R}_+$, we have $T(q + \alpha\mathbb{1}) = Tq + \beta\alpha\mathbb{1}$.

Now let $\|\cdot\|_\infty$ be the supremum norm on $\mathbb{R}^n$ (see §2.3.1). We claim that T is a contraction on U of modulus β. To see that this is so, fix $p, q \in U$ and observe that, pointwise,

$$Tq = T(p + q - p) \leqslant T(p + \|q - p\|_\infty\mathbb{1}) \leqslant Tp + \beta\|q - p\|_\infty\mathbb{1},$$

where the first inequality is by the order-preserving of T, and the second follows from Exercise 5.1.9. Hence

$$Tq - Tp \leqslant \beta\|q - p\|_\infty\mathbb{1}.$$

Reversing the roles of p and q gives the reverse inequality. Hence

$$|Tq(x) - Tp(x)| \leqslant \beta\|q - p\|_\infty$$

for all $x \in [n]$. Taking the maximum on the left-hand side yields $\|Tq - Tp\|_\infty \leqslant \beta\|q - p\|_\infty$, which shows that T is a contraction of modulus β. Hence Banach's theorem applies, and a unique fixed point exists.

5.1.3 Supply Constraints

While the input–output model from §2.1.2 has many useful applications, its linear structure can be a liability. One natural objection to linearity is supply constraints: if sector j doubles its orders from sector i, we cannot always expect that sector i will quickly meet this jump in demand.

In this section we investigate the impact of supply constraints on equilibrium. These constraints introduce nonlinear relationships between nodes that affect equilibria and make analysis more challenging.

We recall from §2.1.2 that d_i is the final demand for good i, x_i is the total sales of sector i, z_{ij} is the inter-industry sales from sector i to sector j, and $a_{ij} = z_{ij}/x_j$ is the dollar value of inputs from i per dollar output from j.

Departing from our previous formulation of equilibrium in the input–output model, suppose that, in the short run, the total output value of sector i is constrained by a positive constant $\bar{x}(i)$. Holding prices fixed (in the short run), this means that sector i has a capacity constraint in terms of unit output. For the purposes of our model, the vector of capacity constraints $\bar{x} := (\bar{x}(i))_{i=1}^n$ can be any vector in $\mathbb{R}_+^n$.

For each sector i, we modify the accounting identity (2.1) from page 56 to

$$x_i = \min\left\{\sum_{j=1}^{n} o_{ij} + d_i, \, \bar{x}(i)\right\}, \tag{5.6}$$

where o_{ij} is the value of orders from sector i made by sector j. Thus, if the capacity constraint in sector i is not binding, then output is the sum of orders from other sectors and orders from final consumers. If $\bar{x}(i)$ is less than this sum, however, then sector i produces to capacity $\bar{x}(i)$.

An equilibrium for this model is one where all orders are met, subject to capacity constraints. The fact that orders are met means that $o_{ij} = z_{ij} = a_{ij}x_j$. Substituting this equality into (5.6) and rewriting as a vector equality, (5.6) can equivalently be formulated as

$$x = Gx, \quad \text{where} \quad Gx := (Ax + d) \wedge \bar{x}. \tag{5.7}$$

The following exercise is key to solving the fixed point problem (5.7).

EXERCISE 5.1.10. Prove that, for any $x, y \in \mathbb{R}^n_+$ and $k \in \mathbb{N}$, we have

$$|Gx - Gy| \leqslant A|x - y|. \tag{5.8}$$

We are now ready to prove the existence of a unique fixed point under the assumption that every sector has positive value added.

PROPOSITION 5.1.4   *If Assumption 2.1.1 holds, then G is globally stable in $\mathbb{R}^n_+$. In particular, the constrained production model has a unique equilibrium $x^* \in \mathbb{R}^n_+$.*

Proof   As shown in Exercise 2.1.2, Assumption 2.1.1 yields $r(A) < 1$. Moreover, $A \geqslant 0$. Hence, by Exercise 5.1.10 and Proposition 5.1.3, G is eventually contracting on $\mathbb{R}_+$. In consequence, a unique equilibrium exists.   □

REMARK 5.1.1   *In Proposition 5.1.4, the weaker conditions on production discussed in §2.3.4.1 can be used in place of Assumption 2.1.1, which requires positive value added in every sector. As explained in §2.3.4.1, for $r(A) < 1$ it is enough that value added is nonnegative in each sector and, in addition, every sector has an upstream supplier with positive value added.*

5.1.4   Fixed Points and Monotonicity

Banach's fixed point theorem and its extensions are foundations of many central results in pure and applied mathematics. For our purposes, however, we need to search a little further, since not all mappings generated by network models have the contraction property. In this section, we investigate two fixed point results that drop contractivity in favor of monotonicity.

5.1.4.1 Existence

Without contractivity, one needs to work harder to obtain even existence of fixed points, let alone uniqueness and convergence. This is especially true if the map in question fails to be continuous. If, however, the map is order-preserving, then existence can often be obtained via some variation on the Knaster–Tarski fixed point theorem.

Here we present a version of this existence result that is optimized to our setting, while avoiding unnecessary excursions into order theory. In stating the theorem, we recall that a **closed order interval** in $\mathbb{R}^n$ is a set of the form

$$[a,b] := \{x \in \mathbb{R}^n : a \leqslant x \leqslant b\},$$

where a and b are vectors in $\mathbb{R}^n$. Also, we call $(x_k) \subset \mathbb{R}^n$ **increasing** (resp., **decreasing**) if $x_k \leqslant x_{k+1}$ (resp., $x_k \geqslant x_{k+1}$) for all k.

EXERCISE 5.1.11. Let $[a,b]$ be a closed order interval in $\mathbb{R}^n$, and let G be an order-preserving self-map on $[a,b]$. Prove the following:

(i) $(G^k a)$ is increasing and $(G^k b)$ is decreasing.
(ii) If x is a fixed point of G in $[a,b]$, then $G^k a \leqslant x \leqslant G^k b$ for all $k \in \mathbb{N}$.

For a self-map G on $S \subset \mathbb{R}^n$, we say that x^* is a **least fixed point** (resp., **greatest fixed point**) of G on S if x^* is a fixed point of G in S and $x^* \leqslant x$ (resp., $x \leqslant x^*$) for every fixed point x of G in S. Finally, we say that G is

- **continuous from below** if $x_k \uparrow x$ in S implies $Gx_k \uparrow Gx$ in S;
- **continuous from above** if $x_k \downarrow x$ in S implies $Gx_k \downarrow Gx$ in S.

Here $x_k \uparrow x$ means that (x_k) is increasing and $x_k \to x$. The definition of $x_k \downarrow x$ is analogous. In the next theorem, $S := [a,b]$ is a closed order interval in $\mathbb{R}^n$, and G is a self-map on S.

THEOREM 5.1.5   *If G is order-preserving on S, then G has a least fixed point x^* and a greatest fixed point x^{**} in S. Moreover,*

(i) *if G is continuous from below, then $G^k a \uparrow x^*$; and*
(ii) *if G is continuous from above, then $G^k b \downarrow x^{**}$.*

REMARK 5.1.2   *As alluded to above, fixed point results for order-preserving maps can be obtained in more general settings than the ones used in Theorem 5.1.5 (see, e.g., Davey and Priestley (2002), Theorem 2.35). Theorem 5.1.5 is sufficient for our purposes, given our focus on finite networks.*

Proof of Theorem 5.1.5   Under the stated conditions, the existence of least and greatest fixed points x^* and x^{**} follows from the Knaster–Tarski fixed point theorem. (This holds because $[a,b]$ is a complete lattice. For a definition of complete lattices and a proof of the Knaster–Tarski theorem, see, e.g., Davey and Priestley (2002).)

Regarding claim (i), suppose that G is continuous from below, and consider the sequence $(x_k) := (G^k a)_{k \geqslant 1}$. Since G is order-preserving (and applying Exercise 5.1.11), this sequence is increasing and bounded above by x^*. Since bounded monotone sequences in $\mathbb{R}$ converge, each individual component of the vector sequence x^k converges in $\mathbb{R}$. Hence, by Lemma 2.3.1, the vector sequence x^k converges in $\mathbb{R}^n$ to some $\bar{x} \in [a, x^*]$. Finally, by continuity from below, we have

$$\bar{x} = \lim_k G^k a = \lim_k G^{k+1} a = G \lim_k G^k a = G\bar{x},$$

so that $\bar{x}$ is a fixed point.

We have now shown that $(G^k a)$ converges up to a fixed point $\bar{x}$ of G satisfying $\bar{x} \leqslant x^*$. Since x^* is the least fixed point of G in S, we also have $x^* \leqslant \bar{x}$. Hence $\bar{x} = x^*$.

The proof of claim (ii) is similar to that of claim (i) and is hence omitted.   □

REMARK 5.1.3   *In the preceding theorem, x^* and x^{**} can be equal, in which case G has only one fixed point in S.*

EXERCISE 5.1.12. Consider the map $Gx = (Ax + d) \wedge \bar{x}$ from the constrained production model. In §5.1.3, we showed that G has a unique fixed point in $\mathbb{R}^n_+$ when $r(A) < 1$. Show now that G has at least one fixed point in $\mathbb{R}^n_+$, even when $r(A) < 1$ fails. (Continue to assume that $A \geqslant 0$, $d \geqslant 0$, and $\bar{x} \geqslant 0$.)

5.1.4.2   Du's Theorem

Theorem 5.1.5 is useful because of its relatively weak assumptions. At the same time, it fails to deliver uniqueness. Hence its conclusions are considerably weaker than the results we obtained from contractivity assumptions in §5.1.1.

In order to recover uniqueness without imposing contractivity, we now consider order-preserving maps that have additional shape properties. In doing so, we use the definition of concave and convex functions in §A.5.2.

THEOREM 5.1.6 (Du)   *Let G be an order-preserving self-map on order interval $S = [a, b] \subset \mathbb{R}^n$. In this setting, if either*

(i) G is concave and $Ga \gg a$ or
(ii) G is convex and $Gb \ll b$,

then G is globally stable on S.

A proof of Theorem 5.1.6 was obtained in a more abstract setting in Du (1990). Interested readers can consult that article for a proof.

To illustrate how these results can be applied, consider the constrained production model without assuming positive value added, so that $r(A) < 1$ is not enforced. In Exercise 5.1.12 we obtained existence. With Theorem 5.1.6 in hand, we can also show uniqueness whenever $d \gg 0$ and $\bar{x} \gg 0$.

Indeed, we have already seen that G is a self-map on $S := [0, \bar{x}]$, and when this last condition holds, we have $G0 = d \wedge \bar{x} \gg 0$. Hence the conclusions of Theorem 5.1.6 will hold if we can establish that G is concave.

EXERCISE 5.1.13. Prove that G is concave on S. [Hint: Review §A.5.2.]

Here is a small extension of Du's theorem that will prove useful soon:

COROLLARY 5.1.7 *Let G be an order-preserving self-map on $S = [a, b]$. If G is concave and there exists an $\ell \in \mathbb{N}$ such that $G^\ell a \gg a$, then G is globally stable on S.*

Proof Assume the conditions of Corollary 5.1.7. Since compositions of increasing concave operators are increasing and concave, Theorem 5.1.6 implies that G^ℓ is globally stable on $[a, b]$. Denote its fixed point by $\bar{v}$. Since $\{G^m a\}_{m \in \mathbb{N}}$ is increasing and since the subsequence $\{G^{m\ell} a\}_{m \in \mathbb{N}}$ converges up to $\bar{v}$ as $m \to \infty$, we must have $G^m a \to \bar{v}$. A similar argument gives $G^m b \to \bar{v}$. For any $v \in [a, b]$ we have $G^m a \leqslant G^m v \leqslant G^m b$, so $G^m v \to \bar{v}$ as $m \to \infty$.

The last step is to show that $\bar{v}$ is the unique fixed point of G. From Theorem 5.1.5, we know that at least one fixed point exists. Now suppose $v \in [a, b]$ is such a point. Then $v = G^m v$ for all m. At the same time, $G^m v \to \bar{v}$ by the results just established. Hence $v = \bar{v}$. The proof is now complete. ☐

5.2 Financial Networks

Given the long history of crises in financial markets around the globe, economists and business analysts have developed many tools for assessing the credit-worthiness of banks and other financial institutions. After the major financial crisis of 2007–2008, originating in the subprime market in the USA and the sudden collapse of Lehmann Brothers, it became clear that the financial health of individual institutions cannot be assessed in isolation. Rather, it is essential to analyze solvency and credit-worthiness in terms of the entire network of claims and liabilities within a highly interconnected financial system. In this section, we review financial crises and apply network analysis to study how they evolve.

5.2.1 Contagion

Some financial crises have obvious causes external to the banking sector. A prominent example is the hyperinflation that occurred in Weimar Germany around 1921–1923, which was driven by mass printing of bank notes to meet war reparations imposed under the Treaty of Versailles. Here the monetary authority played the central role, while the actions of private banks were more passive.

Other crises seem to form within the financial sector itself, driven by interactions between banks, hedge funds, and asset markets. In many cases, the crisis follows a boom, where asset prices rise and economic growth is strong. Typically, the seeds of the crisis are laid during this boom phase, when banks extend loans and firms raise capital on the basis of progressively more speculative business plans. At some point it becomes clear to investors that these businesses will fail to meet expectations, leading to a rush for the exit.

The last phase of this cycle is painful for the financial sector, since rapidly falling asset values force banks and other financial institutions to generate short-term capital by liquidating long-term loans, typically with large losses, as well as selling assets in the face of falling prices, hoarding cash, and refusing to roll over or extend short-term loans to other institutions in the financial sector. The financial crisis of 2007–2008 provides a textbook example of these dynamics.

One key aspect of the financial crisis of 2007–2008, as well as other similar crises, is **contagion**, which refers to the way that financial stress spreads across a network of financial institutions. If one institution becomes stressed, that stress will often spread to investors or counterparties to which this institution is indebted. The result of this process is not easy to predict, since, like equilibrium in the production networks studied in Chapter 2, there is a tail-chasing problem: Stress spreads from institution A to institutions B, C, and D, which may in turn increase stress on A, and so on.

In this section we study financial contagion, beginning with a now-standard model of default cascades.

5.2.2   Default Cascades

Default cascades are a form of financial contagion, in which default by a node in a network leads to default by some of its counterparties, which then spreads across the network. Below we present a model of default cascades and analyze its equilibria.

5.2.2.1   Network Valuation

Consider a financial network $\mathscr{G} = (V, E, w)$, where $V = [n]$ is a list of n financial institutions called *banks*, with an edge $(i, j) \in E$ indicating that j has extended credit to i. The size of that loan is $w(i, j)$. Thus, an edge points in the direction of a liability, as in Figure 1.17 on page 35: Edge (i, j) indicates a liability for i and an asset for j. As in §1.4.1, the set of all direct predecessors of $i \in V$ will be written as $\mathscr{I}(i)$, while the set of all direct successors will be denoted $\mathscr{O}(i)$.

Banks in the network have both internal and external liabilities, as well as internal and external assets. Internal (i.e., inter-bank) liabilities and assets are given by the weight function w, in the sense that $w(i, j)$ is a liability for i, equal to the size of its loan from j, and also an asset for j. Positive weights indicate the presence of counterparty risk: When j holds an asset of book value $w(i, j)$, whether or not the loan is repaid in full depends on the stress placed on bank i and rules that govern repayment in the event of insolvency.

We use the following notation for the primitives of the model: $x_i := \sum_{j \in \mathscr{O}(i)} w(i, j)$ is total inter-bank liabilities of bank i,

$$\Pi_{ij} := \begin{cases} w(i, j)/x_i & \text{if } x_i > 0 \\ 0 & \text{otherwise} \end{cases} \tag{5.9}$$

is the matrix of relative inter-bank liabilities, a_i is external assets held by bank i, and d_i is external liabilities.

When considering the inter-bank assets of bank j, we need to distinguish between the book value $\sum_{i \in \mathscr{I}(j)} w(i, j)$ of its claims on other banks and the realized value in the face of partial or complete default by its counterparties $\mathscr{I}(j)$. To this end, we introduce a clearing vector $p \in \mathbb{R}_+^n$, which is a list of proposed payments by each bank in the network. In particular, p_i is total payments made by bank i to its counterparties within the banking sector. Under the choice of a particular clearing vector, the actual payments received by bank j on its internal loan portfolio are $\sum_{i \in V} p_i \Pi_{ij}$.

The last statement is an assumption about the legal framework for the banking sector. It means that the actual payment $p_i \Pi_{ij}$ from i to j is proportional to the amount that i owes j, relative to its total inter-bank obligations. The idea is that all counterparties in the banking sector have equal seniority, so that residual funds are spread across claimants according to the relative size of the claims.

Let $\hat{p}_j$ be the amount of funds bank j makes available to repay all of its debts, both inter-bank and external. This quantity is

$$\hat{p}_j = \min \left\{ a_j + \sum_{i \in V} p_i \Pi_{ij}, \, d_j + x_j \right\}. \tag{5.10}$$

The right-hand term inside the min operator is the total debts of bank j. The left-hand side is the amount on hand to repay those debts, including external assets and repayments by other banks. The bank repays up to – but not beyond – its ability to pay.

External liabilities are assumed to be senior to inter-bank liabilities, which means that for bank j we also have

$$p_j = \max\{\hat{p}_j - d_j, \, 0\}. \tag{5.11}$$

Thus, inter-bank payments by j are a remainder after external debts are settled. If these debts exceed the bank's ability to pay, the bank becomes insolvent and pays nothing to internal creditors. This is a form of limited liability.

Combining (5.10) and (5.11) and rearranging slightly yields

$$p_j = \max \left\{ \min \left\{ a_j - d_j + \sum_{i \in V} p_i \Pi_{ij}, \, x_j \right\}, \, 0 \right\}.$$

Now let's take p, a, d, and x as row vectors in $\mathbb{R}^n$ and write this collection of equations, indexed by j, in vector form. With max and min taken pointwise, and using the symbols $\vee$ and $\wedge$ for max and min, we get

$$p = ((a - d + p\Pi) \wedge x) \vee 0. \tag{5.12}$$

A solution to this equation is called an **equilibrium clearing vector** for the banking system.

REMARK 5.2.1   *An equilibrium clearing vector captures the impacts of contagion within the specified banking system, in the sense that it traces out the full network effects of inter-bank lending within the model. We shall study this equilibrium while also recognizing that the model is restrictive in the sense that it assumes a specific form for seniority and implicitly rules out some kinds of nonlinear phenomena. We return to this theme in §5.2.3.*

5.2.2.2   Existence and Uniqueness of Fixed Points

In order to analyze the existence and uniqueness of equilibria, we introduce the operator $T : \mathbb{R}^n \to \mathbb{R}^n$ defined by

$$Tp = ((e + p\Pi) \wedge x) \vee 0, \tag{5.13}$$

where $e := a - d$ represents net external assets. Evidently $p \in \mathbb{R}^n_+$ is an equilibrium clearing vector if and only if it is a fixed point of T.

EXERCISE 5.2.1. Prove that the operator T is continuous on $\mathbb{R}^n$.

Using this operator, establishing the existence of at least one equilibrium clearing vector is not problematic for this model, regardless of the values of the primitives and configuration of the network:

EXERCISE 5.2.2. Show that the banking model described above always has at least one equilibrium clearing vector. What else can you say about equilibria in this general case?

While existence is automatic in this model, uniqueness is not:

Example 5.2.1: If $n = 2$, $e = (0,0)$ and $(1,1)$ and $\Pi = \begin{pmatrix} 0 & 1 \\ 1 & 0 \end{pmatrix}$, then $Tp = p$ is equivalent to

$$\begin{pmatrix} p_1 \\ p_2 \end{pmatrix} = \begin{pmatrix} p_2 \\ p_1 \end{pmatrix} \wedge \begin{pmatrix} 1 \\ 1 \end{pmatrix}.$$

Both $p = (1,1)$ and $p = (0,0)$ solve this equation.

There are several approaches to proving the uniqueness of fixed points of T. Here is one:

EXERCISE 5.2.3. Prove that T is globally stable on $S := [0, x]$ whenever $r(\Pi) < 1$.[2]

---

[2] Here's a hint, if you get stuck: Show that $r(\Pi) < 1$ implies T is an eventual contraction on $[0, x]$ using one of the propositions presented in this chapter.

This leads us to the following result:

PROPOSITION 5.2.1   *Let $\mathscr{G}$ be a financial network. If, for each bank $i \in V$, there exists a bank $j \in V$ with $i \to j$ and such that j has zero inter-bank liabilities, then T is globally stable on S, and $\mathscr{G}$ has a unique equilibrium clearing vector.*

Proof   By construction, the matrix Π is substochastic. Suppose that Π is also weakly chained substochastic. Then, by Proposition 2.3.5, we have $r(\Pi) < 1$, and, by Exercise 5.2.3, T is globally stable on S. Hence the proof will be complete if we can show that, under the stated conditions, Π is weakly chained substochastic.

To see that this is so, let $\mathscr{G}$ be a financial network that satisfies the conditions of Proposition 5.2.1. Now fix $i \in V$. We know that there exists a bank $j \in V$ with $i \to j$ and j has no inter-bank liabilities. If $w(i, j) > 0$, then $\Pi_{ij} > 0$, so $i \to j$ under digraph $\mathscr{G}$ implies $i \to j$ in the digraph induced by the substochastic matrix Π. Also, since j has no inter-bank liabilities, we have $x_j = 0$, and hence row j of Π is identically zero. In particular, $\sum_k \Pi_{jk} = 0$. Hence Π is weakly chained substochastic, as required. $\square$

REMARK 5.2.2   *The proof of Proposition 5.2.1 also shows that T is eventually contracting, so we can compute the unique fixed point by taking the limit of $T^k p$ for any choice of $p \in S$.*

There are several possible assumptions about the structure of the bank network $\mathscr{G}$ that imply the conditions of Proposition 5.2.1. For example, it would be enough that $\mathscr{G}$ is strongly connected and has at least one bank with zero inter-bank liabilities. Below we investigate another sufficient condition, related to cyclicality.

EXERCISE 5.2.4. Let $\mathscr{G}$ be a financial network. Show that $\mathscr{G}$ has a unique equilibrium clearing vector whenever $\mathscr{G}$ is a directed acyclic graph.

5.2.2.3   Nonnegative External Equity

In this section we investigate the special case in which

(E1) each bank has nonzero inter-bank debt, so that Π is a stochastic matrix, and
(E2) external net assets are nonnegative, in the sense that $e = a - d \geqslant 0$.

In view of (E1), we cannot hope to use Proposition 5.2.1, since we always have $r(\Pi) = 1$ when Π is stochastic. Nonetheless, we can still obtain global stability under certain restrictions on e and the topology of the network. Here is a relatively straightforward example, which we will later try to refine:

EXERCISE 5.2.5. Let $\mathscr{G}$ be a financial network such that (E1) and (E2) hold. Using Du's theorem (page 168), prove that T has a unique fixed point in $S := [0, x]$ whenever $e \gg 0$.

The condition $e \gg 0$ is rather strict. Fortunately, it turns out that we can obtain global stability under significantly weaker conditions. To this end, we will say that node j in a financial system $\mathscr{G}$, is *cash accessible* if there exists an $i \in V$ such that $i \to j$ and $e(i) > 0$. In other words, j is downstream in the liability chain from at least one bank with positive net assets outside of the banking sector.

EXERCISE 5.2.6. Prove the following result: If (E1) and (E2) hold and every node in $\mathscr{G}$ is cash-accessible, then $T^k 0 \gg 0$ for some $k \in \mathbb{N}$. (This is a relatively challenging exercise.)

With the result from Exercise 5.2.6 in hand, the next lemma is easy to establish.

LEMMA 5.2.2   *If (E1) and (E2) hold and every node in $\mathscr{G}$ is cash accessible, then T is globally stable and $\mathscr{G}$ has a unique clearing vector $p^* \gg 0$.*

Proof   Let $\mathscr{G}$ be as described. By Corollary 5.1.7, it suffices to show that T is an order-preserving concave self-map on $[0, x]$ with $T^k 0 \gg 0$ for some $k \in \mathbb{N}$. The solution to Exercise 5.2.5 shows that T is order-preserving and concave. The existence of a $k \in \mathbb{N}$ with $T^k 0 \gg 0$ was verified in Exercise 5.2.6.   □

Stronger results are available, with a small amount of effort. In fact, under (E1) and (E2), there is a strong sense in which uniqueness of the fixed point is obtained without any further assumptions, provided that we rule out an ambiguity related to what happens when $e = 0$. That ambiguity is discussed in the next exercise, and further references can be found in §5.3.

EXERCISE 5.2.7. Conditions (E1) and (E2) cannot by themselves pin down outcomes for the extreme case where every firm in the network has zero net external assets. Illustrate this with an example.[3]

Although Exercise 5.2.7 suggests ambiguity about outcomes when $e = 0$, it is natural to adopt the convention that the equilibrium clearing vector p^* obeys $p^* = 0$ whenever $e = 0$. If the entire banking sector has no zero net assets, then no positive payment sequence can be initiated (without outside capital).

In the next exercise, we say that $U \subset V$ is *accessible* from $i \in V$ if there exists a $j \in U$ such that j is accessible from i.

EXERCISE 5.2.8. Let P be the set of all nodes in V that are cash accessible. Let A be all i in P^c such that P is accessible from i. Let N be all i in P^c such that P is not accessible from i. Note that $V = P \cup A \cup N$ and that these sets are disjoint. Show that N and P are both absorbing sets.

---

[3] Hint: Every stochastic matrix has at least one stationary distribution.

5.2.3   Equity Cross-Holdings

In this section we analyze the model of default cascades constructed by Elliott et al. (2014). The model differs from the one studied in §5.2.2 in several ways. One is that financial institutions are linked by share cross-holdings: Firm i owns a fraction c_{ij} of firm j for $i, j \in V := [n]$. This implies that failure of firm j reduces the market value of firm i, which in turn reduces the market value of other firms, and so on.

The second – and ultimately more significant – difference is the introduction of failure costs, which add significant nonlinearities to the model. Failure costs reinforce the impact of each firm failure, leading to greater shock propagation across the network. This feature ties into the intuitive idea that, when many firms are financially stressed, a failure by one firm can trigger a wave of bankruptcies.

5.2.3.1   Book and Market Value

We now describe the features of the model. Let $C = (c_{ij})_{i,j\in V}$ be the matrix of fractional cross-holdings, as mentioned above, with $0 \leqslant c_{ij} \leqslant 1$ for all i, j.

ASSUMPTION 5.2.1   *The matrix of cross-holdings satisfies $\sum_k c_{ki} < 1$ for all $i \in V$.*

Assumption 5.2.1 implies that firms are not solely owned by other firms in the network: Investors outside the network hold at least some fraction of firm i for all i.

The **book value** of firm i is given by

$$b_i = e_i + \sum_j c_{ij} b_j \qquad (i \in V). \qquad (5.15)$$

Here the first term $e_i \geqslant 0$ is the external assets of firm i and the second represents the value of firm i's cross-holdings. In vector form, the last equation becomes $b = e + Cb$.

EXERCISE 5.2.9. Let I be the $n \times n$ identity. Prove that, under Assumption 5.2.1, the matrix $I - C$ is invertible, and the equation $b = e + Cb$ has the unique solution

$$b = (I - C)^{-1} e. \qquad (5.16)$$

Prove also that $b \geqslant 0$.

EXERCISE 5.2.10. Provide a weaker condition on C such that $I - C$ is invertible.

There is a widely used argument that cross-holdings artificially inflate the value of firms, in the sense that the sum of book values of firms exceeds $\sum_i e_i$, the sum of underlying equity values. The next exercise illustrates this:

EXERCISE 5.2.11. Show that $e \gg 0$ and $\min_{i,j} c_{ij} > 0$ implies $\sum_i b_i > \sum_i e_i$.

Due to this artificial inflation, we distinguish between the book value b_i of a firm and its **market value** $\bar{v}_i$, which is defined as $r_i b_i$ with $r_i := 1 - \sum_k c_{ki}$. The value r_i, which gives the share of firm i held by outsider investors, is strictly positive for all i

by Assumption 5.2.1. With $R := \mathrm{diag}(r_1, \ldots, r_n)$, we can write the vector of market values as $\bar{v} = Rb$. Substituting in (5.16) gives

$$\bar{v} := Ae, \quad \text{where} \quad A := R(I - C)^{-1}. \tag{5.17}$$

5.2.3.2 Failure Costs

So far the model is very straightforward, with the market value of firms being linear in external assets e. However, since bankruptcy proceedings are expensive, it is reasonable to assume that firm failures are costly. Moreover, when the market value of a firm falls significantly, the firm will experience difficulty raising short-term funds and will often need to cease revenue generating activities and sell illiquid assets well below their potential value.

We now introduce failure costs. As before, $\bar{v}_i$ is market value without failure costs, as determined in (5.17), while v_i will represent market value in the presence of failure costs. Failure costs for firm i are modeled as a threshold function

$$f(v_i) = \beta \mathbb{1}\{v_i < \theta \bar{v}_i\} \quad (i = 1, \ldots, n),$$

where $\theta \in (0,1)$ and $\beta > 0$ are parameters. Thus, costs are zero when v_i is large and $-\beta$ when they fall below the threshold $\theta \bar{v}_i$. In particular, a discrete failure cost of $-\beta$ is incurred when firm value falls far enough below the no-failure market value $\bar{v}_i$. The larger is θ, the more prone the firm is to failure.

The book value of firm i without failure costs was defined in (5.15). The book value of firm i in the presence of failure costs is defined as

$$b_i = e_i + \sum_j c_{ij} b_j - f(v_i).$$

Written in vector form, with f applied pointwise to the vector v, we get $b = e + Cb - f(v)$. Solving for b gives $b = (I - C)^{-1}(e - f(v))$. The corresponding market value is

$$v = Rb = A(e - f(v)). \tag{5.18}$$

Notice that, when no firms fail, we have $v_i = \bar{v}_i$, as expected.

5.2.3.3 Equilibria

Equation (5.18) is a nonlinear equation in n unknowns. A vector $v \in \mathbb{R}^n$ solves (5.18) if and only if it is a fixed point of the operator $T: \mathbb{R}^n \to \mathbb{R}^n$ defined by

$$Tv = A(e - f(v)). \tag{5.19}$$

In what follows we set $d := A(e - \beta \mathbb{1})$ and $S := [d, \bar{v}]$.

PROPOSITION 5.2.3 T is a self-map on S with least fixed point v^* and greatest fixed point v^{**} in S. Moreover,

(i) the sequence $(T^k d)_{k \in \mathbb{N}}$ converges up to v^* in a finite number of steps and
(ii) the sequence $(T^k \bar{v})_{k \in \mathbb{N}}$ converges down to v^{**} in a finite number of steps.

Note that $v^* = v^{**}$ is a possibility, in which case T has a unique fixed point in S.

EXERCISE 5.2.12. Prove the first claim (first sentence) in Proposition 5.2.3.

Why does $(T^k d)_{k \in \mathbb{N}}$ converge up to v^* in a finite number of steps? First, as you saw in the solution to Exercise 5.2.12, the map T is an order-preserving self-map on $[d, \bar{v}]$, so $Td \in [d, \bar{v}]$. In particular, $d \leqslant Td$. Iterating on this inequality and using the order-preserving property gives $d \leqslant Td \leqslant T^2 d \leqslant \cdots$, so $(T^k d)$ is indeed increasing. Moreover, the range of T is a finite set, corresponding to all vectors of the form

$$u = A(e - \beta w),$$

where w is an n-vector containing only zeros and ones. Finiteness holds because there are only finitely many binary sequences of length n.

EXERCISE 5.2.13. Given the above facts, prove that $(T^k d)_{k \in \mathbb{N}}$ converges up to v^* in a finite number of steps.

Similar logic can be applied to prove that $(T^k \bar{v})_{k \in \mathbb{N}}$ converges down to v^{**} in a finite number of steps.

If we set $v^0 = \bar{v}$ and $v^{k+1} = Tv^k$, we can consider the sequence of valuations (v^k) as a dynamic process, and the number of currently failing firms $m^k := \sum_i \mathbb{1}\{v_i^k < \theta\}$ can be understood as tracking waves of bankruptcies. Failures of firms in the first wave put stress on otherwise healthy firms that have exposure to the failed firms, which in turn causes further failures, and so on.

EXERCISE 5.2.14. Prove that the sequence (m_k) is monotone increasing.

As discussed in Proposition 5.2.3, the sequence (v^k), which can also be written as $(T^k \bar{v})$, is decreasing pointwise. In other words, the value of each firm is non-increasing. Hence, if $v_i^k < \theta$ for some k, then $v_i^{k+j} < \theta$ for all $j \geqslant 0$.

Figure 5.1 illustrates a growing wave of failures that can arise in a financial network. Firms with lighter colors have better balance sheets. Black firms have failed. The code for generating this figure, along with details on parameters, can be found in the code book.

5.3   Chapter Notes

Shin (2010) gives an excellent overview of systemic risk and the financial crisis of 2007–2008. Battiston et al. (2012) study connectedness in financial networks and introduce a measure of systemic impact called DebtRank. Bardoscia et al. (2015) provide a dynamic theory of instability related to DebtRank. Demange (2018) provides a threat index for contagion in financial networks related to Katz centrality. Bardoscia et al. (2019) analyze the risks associated with solvency contagion during crises. Jackson and Pernoud (2019) study investment in risky portfolios by banks in financial

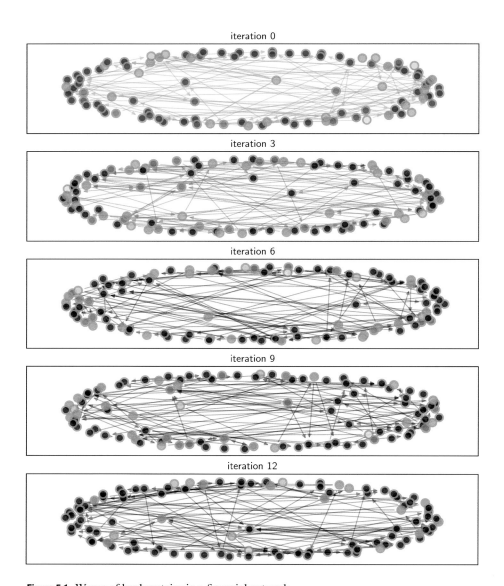

Figure 5.1 Waves of bankruptcies in a financial network

networks with debt and equity interdependencies. Jackson and Pernoud (2020) analyze optimal bailouts in financial networks. Amini and Minca (2020) offer an introduction to the modeling of clearing systems, analyzing equilibria for network payments and asset prices. Jackson and Pernoud (2021) provide a survey of the relationship between financial networks and systemic risk.

The setting in §5.2.2.3 was investigated by Eisenberg and Noe (2001), one of the first papers on a network approach to default cascades. Additional details on stability properties can be found in Stachurski (2022b). As already mentioned, §5.2.3

is based on Elliott et al. (2014), which also includes an interesting discussion of how the level of integration across a network affects equilibria. Klages-Mundt and Minca (2021) discuss optimal intervention in economic networks via influence maximization methods, using Elliott et al. (2014) as an example. Acemoglu et al. (2021b) study how anticipation of future defaults can result in "credit freezes."

A general discussion of contraction maps and related fixed point theory can be found in Goebel and Kirk (1990) and Cheney (2013). For more on fixed point methods for order-preserving operators, see, for example, Guo et al. (2004), Zhang (2012), Marinacci and Montrucchio (2019) or Deplano et al. (2020).

Appendix A Math Review

This appendix provides a brief review of basic analysis and linear algebra. The material contained here should be covered in intermediate mathematical economics courses or, if not, in math boot camp at the very start of a graduate program.

(For those who want a slower treatment of the analysis section, we recommend Bartle and Sherbert (2011), which is carefully constructed and beautifully written. High quality texts on linear algebra at the right level for this course include Jänich (1994), Meyer (2000), Aggarwal (2020), and Cohen (2021).)

A.1 Sets and Functions

As a first step, let's clarify elementary terminology and notation.

A.1.1 Sets

A **set** is an arbitrary collection of objects. Individual objects are called **elements** of the set. We assume the reader is familiar with basic set operations such as intersections and unions. If A is a finite set, then $|A|$ is the number of elements in A. Powers applied to sets indicate **Cartesian products**, so that

$$A^2 := A \times A := \{(a, a') : a \in A, \ a' \in A\}, \ \text{etc.}$$

Throughout, $\wp(A)$ is the **power set** of A, consisting of all subsets of A. For example,

$$A = \{1, 2\} \quad \implies \quad \wp(A) = \{\varnothing, \{1\}, \{2\}, A\}.$$

Let $\mathbb{N}$ be the natural numbers, $\mathbb{Z}$ be the integers, $\mathbb{Q}$ be the rational numbers, and $\mathbb{R}$ be the reals (i.e., the union of the rational and irrational numbers). For x, y in $\mathbb{R}$, we let

$$x \vee y := \max\{x, y\} \quad \text{and} \quad x \wedge y := \min\{x, y\}. \tag{A.1}$$

Absolute value is $|x| := x \vee (-x)$. For $n \in \mathbb{N}$ we set $[n] := \{1, \ldots, n\}$.
We make use of the following elementary facts: For all $a, b, c \in \mathbb{R}$,

- $|a + b| \leqslant |a| + |b|$.
- $(a \wedge b) + c = (a + c) \wedge (b + c)$ and $(a \vee b) + c = (a + c) \vee (b + c)$.

- $(a \vee b) \wedge c = (a \wedge c) \vee (b \wedge c)$ and $(a \wedge b) \vee c = (a \vee c) \wedge (b \vee c)$.
- $|a \wedge c - b \wedge c| \leqslant |a - b|$.
- $|a \vee c - b \vee c| \leqslant |a - b|$.

The first item is called the **triangle inequality**. Also, if $a, b, c \in \mathbb{R}_+$, then

$$(a + b) \wedge c \leqslant (a \wedge c) + (b \wedge c). \tag{A.2}$$

EXERCISE A.1.1. Prove: For all $a, b, c \in \mathbb{R}_+$, we have $|a \wedge c - b \wedge c| \leqslant |a - b| \wedge c$.

A.1.2 Equivalence Classes

Let S be any set. A **relation** $\sim$ on S is a nonempty subset of $S \times S$. It is customary to write $x \sim y$ rather than $(x, y) \in \sim$ to indicate that (x, y) is in $\sim$. A relation $\sim$ on S is called an **equivalence relation** if, for all $x, y, z \in S$, we have

(**reflexivity**) $x \sim x$,
(**symmetry**) $x \sim y$ implies $y \sim x$ and
(**transitivity**) $x \sim y$ and $y \sim z$ implies $x \sim z$.

Any equivalence relation on S induces a partition of S into a collection of mutually disjoint subsets such that their union exhausts S. These subsets are called **equivalence classes**. They can be constructed by taking, for each $x \in S$, the set of all elements that are equivalent to x.

Example A.1.1: Let S be the set of all people in the world. If $x \sim y$ indicates that x and y live in the same country, then $\sim$ is an equivalence relation. (Check the axioms.) The equivalence classes are the populations of each country. The partition induced on S is the set of these classes, which we can identify with the set of all countries in the world.

A.1.3 Functions

A **function** f from set A to set B is a rule, written $f : A \to B$ or $a \mapsto f(a)$, that associates each element a of A with one and only one element $f(a)$ of B. The set A is called the **domain** of f, and B is called the **codomain**. The **range** or **image** of f is

$$\text{range}(f) := \{b \in B : b = f(a) \text{ for some } a \in A\}.$$

A function $f : A \to B$ is called

- **one-to-one** if $f(a) = f(a')$ implies $a = a'$;
- **onto** if range$(f) = B$; and
- a **bijection** or **one-to-one correspondence** if f is both onto and one-to-one.

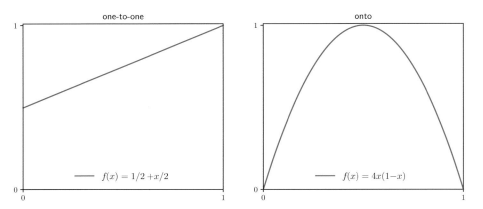

Figure A.1 Different types of functions on $(0, 1)$

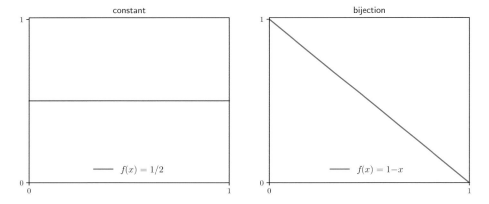

Figure A.2 Some functions are bijections and some are not

Example A.1.2: If S is a nonempty set, then the **identity map** on S is the map
$I : S \rightarrow S$ such that $I(x) = x$ for all $x \in S$. The identity map is a bijection for any
choice of S.

The left panel of Figure A.1 shows a one-to-one function on $(0, 1)$. This function is
not onto, however. For example, there exists no $x \in (0, 1)$ with $f(x) = 1/4$. The right
panel of Figure A.1 shows an onto function, with range$(f) = (0, 1)$. This function is
not one-to-one, however. For example, $f(1/4) = f(3/4) = 3/4$.

The left panel of Figure A.2 gives an example of a function that is neither one-to-
one nor onto. The right panel of Figure A.2 gives an example of a bijection.

A.1.4   Inverse Functions

One motivation for our interest in the basic properties of functions is that we wish to
solve inverse problems. For an arbitrary nonempty set S and a function $f : S \rightarrow S$, an
abstraction of an inverse problem is solving $y = f(x)$ for $x \in S$.

Prior to stating the next result, we recall that an **inverse function** for $f: S \to S$ is a function $g: S \to S$ such that $f \circ g = g \circ f = I$, where I is the identity map on S. The inverse function of f is often written as f^{-1}.

LEMMA A.1.1 *For $f: S \to S$, the following statements are equivalent:*

(i) *f is a bijection on S.*
(ii) *For each $y \in S$, there exists a unique $x \in S$ such that $f(x) = y$.*
(iii) *f has an inverse on S.*

Proof ((i) $\implies$ (ii)) Fix $y \in S$. Since f is onto, there exists an $x \in S$ such that $f(x) = y$. Since f is one-to-one, there is at most one such x.

((ii) $\implies$ (iii)) Let $g: S \to S$ map each $y \in S$ into the unique $x \in S$ such that $f(x) = y$. By the definition of g, for fixed $x \in S$, we have $g(f(x)) = x$. Moreover, for each $y \in S$, the point $g(y)$ is the point that f maps to y, so $f(g(y)) = y$.

((iii) $\implies$ (i)) Let g be the inverse of f. To see that f must be onto, pick any $y \in S$. Since $f \circ g$ is the identity, we have $f(g(y)) = y$. Hence there exists a point $g(y)$ in S that is mapped into $y \in S$. To see that f is one-to-one, fix $x, y \in S$. If $f(x) = f(y)$, then $g(f(x)) = g(f(y))$. But $g \circ f$ is the identity, so $x = y$. □

Here is a nice logical exercise that turns out to be useful when we solve linear inverse problems.

EXERCISE A.1.2. Let S and T be nonempty sets. For $f: S \to T$, a function $g: T \to S$ is called a **left inverse** of f if $g \circ f = I$, where I is the identity on S. Prove that f is one-to-one if and only if f has a left inverse.

A.1.5 Real-Valued Functions

If S is any set and $f: S \to \mathbb{R}$, we call f a **real-valued function**. The set of all real-valued functions on S is denoted $\mathbb{R}^S$. When S has n elements, $\mathbb{R}^S$ is the same set as $\mathbb{R}^n$ expressed in different notation. The next lemma clarifies.

LEMMA A.1.2 *If $|S| = n$, then*

$$\mathbb{R}^S \ni h = (h(x_1), \dots, h(x_n)) \quad \longleftrightarrow \quad \begin{pmatrix} h_1 \\ \vdots \\ h_n \end{pmatrix} \in \mathbb{R}^n \tag{A.3}$$

is a one-to-one correspondence between $\mathbb{R}^n$ and the function space $\mathbb{R}^S$.

The lemma just states that a function h can be identified by the set of values that it takes on S, which is an n-tuple of real numbers. We use this identification routinely in what follows.

The **indicator function** of logical statement P is denoted $\mathbb{1}\{P\}$ and takes value 1 (resp., 0) if P is true (resp., false).

Example A.1.3: If $x, y \in \mathbb{R}$, then

$$\mathbb{1}\{x \leqslant y\} = \begin{cases} 1 & \text{if } x \leqslant y \\ 0 & \text{otherwise.} \end{cases}$$

If $A \subset S$, where S is any set, then $\mathbb{1}_A(x) := \mathbb{1}\{x \in A\}$ for all $x \in S$.

A nonempty set S is called **countable** if it is finite or can be placed in one-to-one correspondence with the natural numbers $\mathbb{N}$. In the second case we can enumerate S by writing it as $\{x_1, x_2, \ldots\}$. Any nonempty set S that fails to be countable is called **uncountable**. For example, $\mathbb{Z}$ and $\mathbb{Q}$ are countable, whereas $\mathbb{R}$ and every nontrivial interval in $\mathbb{R}$ are uncountable.

In general, if f and g are real-valued functions defined on some common set S and α is a scalar, then $f + g, \alpha f, fg$, etc., are functions on S defined by

$$(f + g)(x) = f(x) + g(x), \quad (\alpha f)(x) = \alpha f(x), \quad \text{etc.} \tag{A.4}$$

for each $x \in S$. Similarly, $f \vee g$ and $f \wedge g$ are functions on S defined by

$$(f \vee g)(x) = f(x) \vee g(x) \quad \text{and} \quad (f \wedge g)(x) = f(x) \wedge g(x). \tag{A.5}$$

Figure A.3 illustrates.

If $f: A \to B$ and $g: B \to C$, then $g \circ f$ is called the **composition** of f and g. It is the function mapping $a \in A$ to $g(f(a)) \in C$.

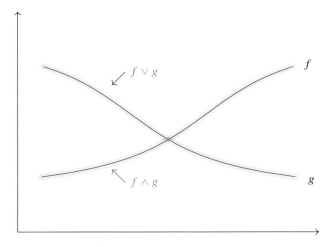

Figure A.3 Functions $f \vee g$ and $f \wedge g$ when defined on a subset of $\mathbb{R}$

A.1.6   Fixed Points

Let S be any set. A **self-map** on S is a function G from S to itself. When working with self-maps in arbitrary sets, it is common to write the image of x under G as Gx rather than $G(x)$. We often follow this convention.

Given a self-map G on S, a point $x \in S$ is called a **fixed point** of G if $Gx = x$.

Example A.1.4: Every point of arbitrary S is fixed under the identity map $I : x \mapsto x$.

Example A.1.5: If $S = \mathbb{N}$ and $Gx = x + 1$, then G has no fixed point.

Figure A.4 shows another example, for a self-map G on $S = [0, 2]$. The fixed points are numbers $x \in [0, 2]$ where G meets the 45 degree line. In this case there are three.

One of the most common techniques for solving systems of nonlinear equations in applied mathematics – and quantitative economics – is to convert them into fixed point problems and then apply fixed point theory. We will see many applications of this technique.

EXERCISE A.1.3. Let S be any set, and let G be a self-map on S. Suppose there exist an $\bar{x} \in S$ and an $m \in \mathbb{N}$ such that $G^k x = \bar{x}$ for all $x \in S$ and $k \geqslant m$. Prove that, under this condition, $\bar{x}$ is the unique fixed point of G in S.

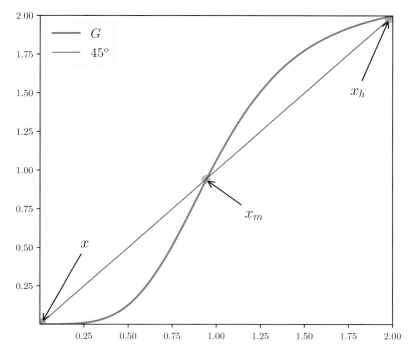

Figure A.4 Graph and fixed points of $G : x \mapsto 2.125/(1 + x^{-4})$

A.1.7   Vectors

An n-vector x is a tuple of n numbers $x = (x_1, \ldots, x_n)$, where $x_i \in \mathbb{R}$ for each $i \in [n]$. In general, x is neither a row vector nor a column vector – which coincides with the perspective of most scientific computing environments, where the basic vector structure is a flat array. When using matrix algebra, vectors are treated as column vectors unless otherwise stated.

The two most fundamental vector operations are vector addition and scalar multiplication. These operations act pointwise, so that, when $\alpha \in \mathbb{R}$ and $x, y \in \mathbb{R}^n$,

$$x + y = \begin{pmatrix} x_1 \\ x_2 \\ \vdots \\ x_n \end{pmatrix} + \begin{pmatrix} y_1 \\ y_2 \\ \vdots \\ y_n \end{pmatrix} := \begin{pmatrix} x_1 + y_1 \\ x_2 + y_2 \\ \vdots \\ x_n + y_n \end{pmatrix} \quad \text{and} \quad \alpha x := \begin{pmatrix} \alpha x_1 \\ \alpha x_2 \\ \vdots \\ \alpha x_n \end{pmatrix}.$$

We let $\mathbb{R}^n$ be the set of all n-vectors and $\mathbb{M}^{n \times k}$ be all $n \times k$ matrices. If A is a matrix then $A^\top$ is its transpose.

- The **inner product** of $x, y \in \mathbb{R}^n$ is defined as $\langle x, y \rangle := \sum_{i=1}^n x_i y_i$.
- The **Euclidean norm** of $x \in \mathbb{R}^n$ is $\|x\| := \sqrt{\langle x, x \rangle}$.

The norm and inner product satisfy the **triangle inequality** and **Cauchy–Schwarz inequality**, which state that, respectively,

$$\|x + y\| \leqslant \|x\| + \|y\| \quad \text{and} \quad |\langle x, y \rangle| \leqslant \|x\|\|y\| \quad \text{for all } x, y \in \mathbb{R}^n.$$

A.1.8   Complex Numbers

We recall some elementary facts about $\mathbb{C}$, the set of complex numbers.

Each element of $\mathbb{C}$ can be understood as a point $(a, b) \in \mathbb{R}^2$. In fact $\mathbb{C}$ is just $\mathbb{R}^2$ endowed with a special form of multiplication. The point (a, b) is more often written as $a + ib$. We elaborate below.

The first and second projections of (a, b) are written as $\mathrm{Re}(a, b) = a$ and $\mathrm{Im}(a, b) = b$ and called the **real** and **nonreal** (or **imaginary**) parts, respectively. The symbol i represents the point $(0, 1) \in \mathbb{C}$. As is traditional, in the context of complex numbers, the complex number $(a, 0) \in \mathbb{C}$ is often written more simply as a. With addition and scalar multiplication defined pointwise, this means that, as expected,

$$(a, b) = (a, 0) + (0, b) = (a, 0) + (0, 1)b = a + ib.$$

Let $z = (a, b)$. The **modulus** of z is written $|z|$ and defined as the Euclidean norm $(a^2 + b^2)^{1/2}$ of the tuple (a, b). The two-dimensional Euclidean space is then endowed with a new operation called **multiplication**, which is defined by

$$(a, b)(c, d) = (ac - bd, ad + bc). \tag{A.6}$$

Note that, under this rule and our conventions, $i^2 = (0,1)(0,1) = (-1,0) = -1$.

As in the real case, the exponential e^z is defined for $z \in \mathbb{C}$ by $\sum_{k \geqslant 0} z^k/(k!)$. It can be shown that, under this extension, the exponential function continues to enjoy the additive property $e^{z_1+z_2} = e^{z_1}e^{z_2}$. As a result, $e^{a+ib} = e^a e^{ib}$.

Rather than providing its coordinates, another way to represent a vector $z = (a,b) \in \mathbb{R}^2$, and hence in $\mathbb{C}$, is by providing a pair (r,φ) where $r > 0$ is understood as the length of the vector and $\varphi \in [0, 2\pi)$ is the angle. This translates to Euclidean coordinates via

$$a + ib = (a,b) = (r\cos\varphi, r\sin\varphi) = r(\cos\varphi + i\sin\varphi).$$

The representation (r, φ) is called the **polar form** of the complex number. By **Euler's formula** $\cos(\varphi) + i\sin(\varphi) = e^{i\varphi}$, we can also write

$$r(\cos\varphi + i\sin\varphi) = re^{i\varphi}.$$

Figure A.5 translates $\mathbb{C} \ni (1, \sqrt{3}) = 1 + i\sqrt{3}$ into polar coordinates $2e^{i(\pi/3)}$.

The advantage of these representations is clear when we multiply, since the rule

$$re^{i\varphi} se^{i\psi} = rs\, e^{i(\varphi+\psi)} \tag{A.7}$$

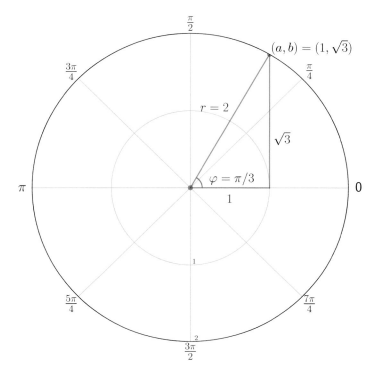

Figure A.5 The complex number $(a,b) = re^{i\varphi}$

is easier to remember and apply than (A.6). Calculating the modulus is also easy, since, by the trigonometric formula $\cos^2 \varphi + \sin^2 \varphi = 1$,

$$|re^{i\varphi}| = |r(\cos(\varphi) + i\sin(\varphi))| = r\left(\cos^2 \varphi + \sin^2 \varphi\right)^{1/2} = r. \qquad (A.8)$$

EXERCISE A.1.4. Show that, for any $u, v \in \mathbb{C}$ we have $|uv| = |u||v|$.

A.2   Order

Order structure is of great importance in economics – typically more so than in other fields such as physics or chemistry. Here we review the basics.

A.2.1   Partial Orders

It was mentioned in the preface that order-theoretic methods form a core part of the text. In this section we introduce some key concepts.

Let P be a nonempty set. A **partial order** on P is a relation $\preceq$ on $P \times P$ satisfying, for any p, q, r in P,

$p \preceq p$,	(reflexivity)
$p \preceq q$ and $q \preceq p$ implies $p = q$,	(antisymmetry)
and	(transitivity)
$p \preceq q$ and $q \preceq r$ implies $p \preceq r$.	

When paired with a partial order $\preceq$, the set P (or the pair $(P, \preceq)$) is called a **partially ordered set**.

Example A.2.1: The usual order $\leqslant$ on $\mathbb{R}$ is a partial order on $\mathbb{R}$. Unlike other partial orders we consider, it has the additional property that either $x \leqslant y$ or $y \leqslant x$ for every x, y in $\mathbb{R}$. For this reason, $\leqslant$ is also called a **total order** on $\mathbb{R}$.

EXERCISE A.2.1. Let P be any set, and consider the relation induced by equality, so that $p \preceq q$ if and only if $p = q$. Show that this relation is a partial order on P.

EXERCISE A.2.2. Let M be any set. Show that $\subset$ is a partial order on $\wp(M)$, the set of all subsets of M.

Example A.2.2: (**Pointwise order over functions**) Let S be any set. For f, g in $\mathbb{R}^S$, we write

$$f \leqslant g \text{ if } f(x) \leqslant g(x) \text{ for all } x \in S.$$

This relation $\leqslant$ on $\mathbb{R}^S$ is a partial order called the **pointwise order** on $\mathbb{R}^S$.

A subset B of a partially ordered set $(P, \preceq)$ is called

- **increasing** if $x \in B$ and $x \preceq y$ implies $y \in B$;
- **decreasing** if $x \in B$ and $y \preceq x$ implies $y \in B$.

EXERCISE A.2.3. Describe the set of increasing sets in $(\mathbb{R}, \leqslant)$.

Example A.2.3: (Pointwise order over vectors) For vectors $x = (x_1, \ldots, x_d)$ and $y = (y_1, \ldots, y_d)$, we write

- $x \leqslant y$ if $x_i \leqslant y_i$ for all $i \in [d]$ and
- $x \ll y$ if $x_i < y_i$ for all $i \in [d]$.

The statements $x \geqslant y$ and $x \gg y$ are defined analogously.[1] The relation $\leqslant$ is a partial order on $\mathbb{R}^n$, also called the **pointwise order**. (In fact, the present example is a special case of Example A.2.2 under the identification in Lemma A.1.2 (page 183).) On the other hand, $\ll$ is not a partial order on $\mathbb{R}^n$. (Which axiom fails?)

EXERCISE A.2.4. Recall from Example A.3.2 that limits in $\mathbb{R}$ preserve weak inequalities. Prove that the same is true in $\mathbb{R}^d$. In particular, show that, for vectors $a, b \in \mathbb{R}^d$ and sequence (x_n) in $\mathbb{R}^d$, we have $a \leqslant x_n \leqslant b$ for all $n \in \mathbb{N}$, and $x_n \to x$ implies $a \leqslant x \leqslant b$.

A.2.2   Pointwise Operations on Vectors

In this text, operations on real numbers such as $|\cdot|$ and $\vee$ are applied to vectors pointwise. For example, for vectors $a = (a_i)$ and $b = (b_i)$ in $\mathbb{R}^d$, we set

$$|a| = (|a_i|), \quad a \wedge b = (a_i \wedge b_i), \quad \text{and} \quad a \vee b = (a_i \vee b_i).$$

(The last two are special cases of (A.5).)

A small amount of thought will convince you that, with this convention plus the pointwise order over vectors, the order-theoretic inequalities and identities listed in §A.1.1 also hold for vectors in $\mathbb{R}^d$. (For example, $|a + b| \leqslant |a| + |b|$ for any $a, b, c \in \mathbb{R}^d$.)

EXERCISE A.2.5. Prove: If B is $m \times k$ and $B \geqslant 0$, then $|Bx| \leqslant B|x|$ for all $k \times 1$ column vectors x.

A.2.3   Monotonicity

Given two partially ordered sets $(P, \preceq)$ and $(Q, \unlhd)$, a function G from P to Q is called **order-preserving** if

---

[1] The notation $x \leqslant y$ over vectors is standard, while $x \ll y$ is less so. In some fields, $n \ll k$ is used as an abbreviation for "n is much smaller than k." Our usage lines up with most of the literature on partially ordered vector spaces. See, e.g., Zhang (2012).

$$p, q \in P \text{ and } p \preceq q \quad \Longrightarrow \quad Gp \lhd Gq. \tag{A.9}$$

Example A.2.4: Let $\mathscr{C}$ be all continuous functions from $S = [a, b]$ to $\mathbb{R}$, and let $\leqslant$ be the pointwise partial order on $\mathscr{C}$. Define

$$I : \mathscr{C} \ni f \to \int_a^b f(x)dx \in \mathbb{R}.$$

Since $f \leqslant g$ implies $\int_a^b f(x)dx \leqslant \int_a^b g(x)dx$, the integral map I is order-preserving on $\mathscr{C}$.

EXERCISE A.2.6. Let X be a random variable mapping Ω to finite S. Define $\ell : \mathbb{R}^S \to \mathbb{R}$ by $\ell h = \mathbb{E}h(X)$. Show that ℓ is order-preserving when $\mathbb{R}^S$ has the pointwise order.

If $P = Q = \mathbb{R}$, and $\preceq$ and $\lhd$ are both equal to $\leqslant$, the standard order on $\mathbb{R}$, then the order-preserving property reduces to the usual notion of an **increasing function** (i.e., nondecreasing function), and we will use the terms "increasing" and "order-preserving" interchangeably in this setting.[2]

In addition, if $S = g$ maps $A \subset \mathbb{R}$ into $\mathbb{R}$, then we will call g

- **strictly increasing** if $x < y$ implies $g(x) < g(y)$ and
- **strictly decreasing** if $x < y$ implies $g(x) > g(y)$.

A.3   Convergence

Let's now recall the basics of convergence and continuity.

Given any set S, an S-valued **sequence** $(x_n) := (x_n)_{n \in \mathbb{N}}$ is a function $n \mapsto x_n$ from $\mathbb{N}$ to S. If $S = \mathbb{R}$, we call (x_n) a **real-valued sequence**. A **subsequence** of $(x_n)_{n \in \mathbb{N}}$ is a sequence of the form $(x_{\sigma(n)})_{n \in \mathbb{N}}$, where σ is a strictly increasing function from $\mathbb{N}$ to itself. You can think of forming a subsequence from a sequence by deleting some of its elements – while still retaining infinitely many.

In computer science and statistics, it is common to classify sequences according to their asymptotic behavior. Often this is done via **big O notation**, where, for a real-valued sequence (x_n), we write $(x_n) = O(g_n)$ if there exists a nonnegative sequence (g_n) and a constant $M < \infty$ such that $|x_n| \leqslant Mg_n$ for all $n \in \mathbb{N}$.

EXERCISE A.3.1. Let $x_n = -5n + n^2$ for all $n \in \mathbb{N}$. Show that $(x_n) = O(n^2)$ holds but $(x_n) = O(n)$ fails.

---

[2] Other common terms for order-preserving in the literature include "monotone increasing," "monotone," and "isotone."

A.3.1   Metric Properties of the Real Line

The following definition is fundamental to what follows: A real-valued sequence (x_n) **converges** to $x \in \mathbb{R}$, and we write $x_n \to x$, if

for each $\varepsilon > 0$, there is an $N \in \mathbb{N}$ such that $|x_n - x| < \varepsilon$ whenever $n \geqslant N$.

Example A.3.1: If $x_n = 1 - 1/n$, then $x_n \to 1$. Indeed, for any $\varepsilon > 0$, the statement $|x_n - 1| < \varepsilon$ is equivalent to $n > 1/\varepsilon$. This clearly holds whenever n is sufficiently large.

EXERCISE A.3.2. Prove: If $a, b \in \mathbb{R}$, $x_n \to a$ and $x_n \to b$, then $a = b$.

Let's state some elementary limit laws that are used without comment throughout. (You can review the proofs in sources such as Bartle and Sherbert (2011)).

A sequence (x_n) is called **bounded** if there is an $M \in \mathbb{R}$ such that $|x_n| \leqslant M$ for all $n \in \mathbb{N}$. It is called

- **monotone increasing** if $x_n \leqslant x_{n+1}$ for all $n \in \mathbb{N}$ and
- **monotone decreasing** if $x_n \geqslant x_{n+1}$ for all n.

The sequence is called **monotone** if it is either monotone increasing or decreasing. The next theorem, concerning monotone sequences, is a deep result about the structure of $\mathbb{R}$.

THEOREM A.3.1   *A real-valued monotone sequence converges in $\mathbb{R}$ if and only if it is bounded.*

The intuitive meaning of the "if" part of Theorem A.3.1 is that monotone bounded sequences always converge to some point in $\mathbb{R}$ because $\mathbb{R}$ contains no gaps. This statement is closely related to the "completeness" property of the real line, which is discussed in Bartle and Sherbert (2011) and many other texts on real analysis.

Next let's consider **series**. Given a sequence (x_n) in $\mathbb{R}$, we set

$$\sum_{n \geqslant 1} x_n := \lim_{N \to \infty} \sum_{n=1}^{N} x_n \text{ whenever the limit exists in } \mathbb{R}.$$

More generally, given arbitrary countable S and $g \in \mathbb{R}^S$, we write $\sum_{x \in S} g(x) = M$ if there exists an enumeration $(x_n)_{n \in \mathbb{N}}$ of S such that $\sum_{n \geqslant 1} |g(x_n)|$ is finite and, in addition, $\sum_{n \geqslant 1} g(x_n) = M$.[3]

EXERCISE A.3.3. Show that, if S is countable, $g \in \mathbb{R}^S$, and there exist $x', x'' \in S$ such that $g(x') > 0$ and $g(x'') < 0$, then $\left| \sum_{x \in S} g(x) \right| < \sum_{x \in S} |g(x)|$.[4]

---

[3] This definition is not ambiguous because every possible enumeration leads to the same value when the absolute sum is finite (see, e.g., the rearrangement theorem in Bartle and Sherbert (2011), §9.1).
[4] Hint: Start with the case $|S| = 2$. Argue that the case with n elements follows from this case and the ordinary (weak) triangle inequality $|\sum_{x \in S} g(x)| \leqslant \sum_{x \in S} |g(x)|$.

A.3.2   Metric Properties of Euclidean Space

Now we review the metric properties of $\mathbb{R}^d$, for some $d \in \mathbb{N}$, when distance between vectors $x, y \in \mathbb{R}^d$ is understood in terms of Euclidean norm deviation $\|x - y\|$. The notion of convergence for real-valued sequences extends naturally to this setting: Sequence (x_n) in $\mathbb{R}^d$ is said to **converge** to $x \in \mathbb{R}^d$ if

> for each $\varepsilon > 0$, there is an $N \in \mathbb{N}$ such that $\|x_n - x\| < \varepsilon$ whenever $n \geqslant N$.

In this case we write $x_n \rightarrow x$. Figure A.6 shows a sequence converging to the origin in $\mathbb{R}^3$, with colder colors being later in the sequence.

EXERCISE A.3.4. Prove that limits in $\mathbb{R}^d$ are unique. In other words, show that, if (x_n) is a sequence converging to $x \in \mathbb{R}^d$ and $y \in \mathbb{R}^d$, then $x = y$.

Given any point $u \in \mathbb{R}^d$ and $\varepsilon > 0$, the ε-**ball** around u is the set

$$B_\varepsilon(u) := \{v \in \mathbb{R}^d : \|u - v\| < \varepsilon\}.$$

With this terminology, we can say that (x_n) converges to $x \in \mathbb{R}^d$ if the sequence (x_n) is eventually in any ε-ball around x.

PROPOSITION A.3.2   *If (x_n) and (y_n) are sequences in $\mathbb{R}^d$ with $x_n \rightarrow x$ and $y_n \rightarrow y$, then*

(i) $x_n + y_n \rightarrow x + y$, *and* $x_n y_n \rightarrow xy$;
(ii) $x_n \leqslant y_n$ *for all* $n \in \mathbb{N}$ *implies* $x \leqslant y$;
(iii) $\alpha x_n \rightarrow \alpha x$ *for any* $\alpha \in \mathbb{R}$;
(iv) $x_n \vee y_n \rightarrow x \vee y$, *and* $x_n \wedge y_n \rightarrow x \wedge y$.

A sequence $(x_n) \subset \mathbb{R}^d$ is called **Cauchy** if, for all $\varepsilon > 0$, there exists an $N \in \mathbb{N}$ with $|x_n - x_m| < \varepsilon$ whenever $n, m \geqslant N$.

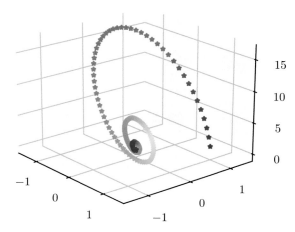

Figure A.6 Convergence of a sequence to the origin in $\mathbb{R}^3$

EXERCISE A.3.5. Let $d = 1$ and suppose $x_n = 1/n$. Prove that (x_n) is Cauchy.

EXERCISE A.3.6. Prove that every convergent sequence in $\mathbb{R}^d$ is Cauchy.

It is a fundamental result of analysis, stemming from axiomatic properties of the reals, that the converse is also true:

THEOREM A.3.3   *A sequence in $\mathbb{R}^d$ converges to a point in $\mathbb{R}^d$ if and only if it is Cauchy.*

A.3.3   Topology

A point $u \in A \subset \mathbb{R}^d$ is called **interior** to A if there exists an $\varepsilon > 0$ such that $B_\varepsilon(u) \subset A$.

EXERCISE A.3.7. Let $d = 1$ so that $\|x - y\| = |x - y|$. Show that 0.5 is interior to $A := [0, 1)$ but 0 is not. Show that $\mathbb{Q}$, the set of rational numbers in $\mathbb{R}$, contains no interior points.

A subset G of $\mathbb{R}^d$ is called **open** in $\mathbb{R}^d$ if every $u \in G$ is interior to G. A subset F of $\mathbb{R}^d$ is called **closed** if, given any sequence (x_n) satisfying $x_n \in F$ for all $n \in \mathbb{N}$ and $x_n \to x$ for some $x \in \mathbb{R}^d$, the point x is in F. In other words, F contains the limit points of all convergent sequences that take values in F.

Example A.3.2: Limits in $\mathbb{R}$ preserve orders, so $a \leqslant x_n \leqslant b$ for all $n \in \mathbb{N}$, and $x_n \to x$ implies $a \leqslant x \leqslant b$. Thus, any closed interval $[a, b]$ in $\mathbb{R}$ is closed in the standard (one-dimensional Euclidean) metric.

EXERCISE A.3.8. Prove that $G \subset \mathbb{R}^d$ is open if and only if G^c is closed.

A subset B of $\mathbb{R}^d$ is called **bounded** if there exists a finite M such that $\|b\| \leqslant M$ for all $b \in B$. A subset K of $\mathbb{R}^d$ is called **compact** in $\mathbb{R}^d$ if every sequence in K has a subsequence converging to some point in K. The Bolzano–Weierstrass theorem tells us that K is compact if and only if K is closed and bounded.

A.3.4   Continuity in Vector Space

If $A \subset \mathbb{R}^d$, then $f : A \to \mathbb{R}^k$ is called **continuous** at $x \in A$ if, for each sequence $(x_n) \subset A$ with $x_n \to x$, we have $f(x_n) \to f(x)$ in $\mathbb{R}^k$. If f is continuous at all $x \in A$, then we call f **continuous on** A.

Example A.3.3: If $f(x) = x^2$ on $A = \mathbb{R}$, then f is continuous at all $x \in \mathbb{R}$ because, by Proposition A.3.2, $x_n \to x$ implies $x_n^2 = x_n \cdot x_n \to x \cdot x = x^2$.

More generally, every polynomial function is continuous on $\mathbb{R}$. The elementary functions sin, cos, exp, and log are all continuous on their domains.

EXERCISE A.3.9. Prove: If $\alpha, \beta \in \mathbb{R}$ and f, g are continuous functions from $A \subset \mathbb{R}^d$ to $\mathbb{R}^k$, then so is $\alpha f + \beta g$.

EXERCISE A.3.10. Fix $a \in \mathbb{R}^d$. Prove that $f, g \colon \mathbb{R}^d \to \mathbb{R}^d$ defined by $f(x) = x \wedge a$ and $g(x) = x \vee a$ are both continuous functions on $\mathbb{R}^d$.

The next lemma is helpful in locating fixed points.

LEMMA A.3.4   *Let F be a self-map on $S \subset \mathbb{R}^d$. If $F^m u \to u^*$ as $m \to \infty$ for some pair $u, u^* \in S$ and, in addition, F is continuous at u^*, then u^* is a fixed point of F.*

Proof   Assume the hypotheses of Lemma A.3.4, and let $u_m := F^m u$ for all $m \in \mathbb{N}$. By continuity and $u_m \to u^*$, we have $F u_m \to F u^*$. But the sequence $(F u_m)$ is just (u_m) with the first element omitted, so, given that $u_m \to u^*$, we must have $F u_m \to u^*$. Since limits are unique, it follows that $u^* = F u^*$.   □

A.4   Linear Algebra

Next we review fundamental concepts and definitions from linear algebra.

A.4.1   Subspaces and Independence

A subset E of $\mathbb{R}^n$ is called a **linear subspace** of $\mathbb{R}^n$ if

$$x, y \in E \text{ and } \alpha, \beta \in \mathbb{R} \implies \alpha x + \beta y \in E.$$

In other words, E is **closed** under the operations of addition and scalar multiplication; that is, (i) $\alpha \in \mathbb{R}$ and $x \in E$ implies $\alpha x \in E$ and (ii) $x, y \in E$ implies $x + y \in E$.

EXERCISE A.4.1. Fix $c \in \mathbb{R}^n$ and $C \in \mathbb{M}^{n \times k}$. Show that

- $H := \{x \in \mathbb{R}^n \colon \langle c, x \rangle = 0\}$ and
- range $C := \{y \in \mathbb{R}^n \colon y = Cx \text{ for some } x \in \mathbb{R}^k\}$

are linear subspaces of $\mathbb{R}^n$. Show that $S := \{x \in \mathbb{R}^n \colon \langle c, x \rangle \geqslant 0\}$ is not.

A **linear combination** of vectors $v_1, \ldots, v_k$ in $\mathbb{R}^n$ is a vector of the form

$$\alpha_1 v_1 + \cdots + \alpha_k v_k, \text{ where } (\alpha_1, \ldots, \alpha_k) \in \mathbb{R}^k.$$

The set of all linear combinations of elements of $F \subset \mathbb{R}^n$ is called the **span** of F and written as span F.

Example A.4.1: The set range C in Exercise A.4.1 is the span of the columns of the matrix C, viewed as a set of vectors in $\mathbb{R}^n$. The set range C is also called the **column space** of C.

EXERCISE A.4.2. Let F be a nonempty subset of $\mathbb{R}^n$. Prove that

(i) span F is a linear subspace of $\mathbb{R}^n$ and
(ii) span F is the intersection of all linear subspaces $S \subset \mathbb{R}^n$ with $S \supset F$.

Figure A.7 shows the linear subspace spanned by the three vectors

$$u = \begin{pmatrix} 3 \\ 4 \\ 1 \end{pmatrix}, \quad v = \begin{pmatrix} 3 \\ -4 \\ 0.2 \end{pmatrix}, \quad \text{and } w = \begin{pmatrix} -3.5 \\ 3 \\ -0.4 \end{pmatrix}. \tag{A.10}$$

The subspace H in which these vectors lie is, in fact, the set of all $x \in \mathbb{R}^3$ such that $\langle x, c \rangle = 0$, with $c = (-0.2, -0.1, 1)$. This plane is a two-dimensional object. While we make this terminology precise in §A.4.2, the key idea is that

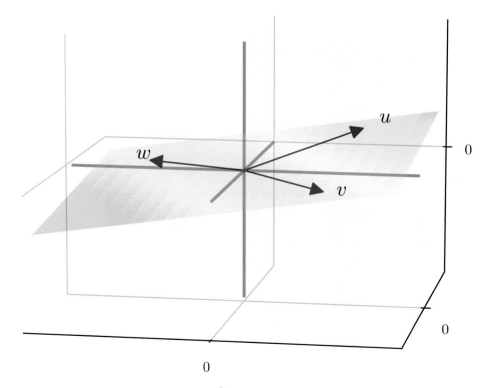

Figure A.7 The span of vectors u, v, w in $\mathbb{R}^3$

- at least two vectors are required to span H and
- any additional vectors will not increase the span.

A finite set of vectors $F := \{v_1, \ldots, v_k\} \subset \mathbb{R}^n$ is called **linearly independent** if, for real scalars $\alpha_1, \ldots, \alpha_k$,

$$\alpha_1 v_1 + \cdots + \alpha_k v_k = 0 \implies \alpha_1 = \cdots = \alpha_k = 0.$$

If F is not linearly independent, it is called **linearly dependent**.

EXERCISE A.4.3. Show that F is linearly dependent if and only if there exists a vector in F that can be written as a linear combination of other vectors in F.

EXERCISE A.4.4. Prove the following:

(i) Every subset of a linearly independent set in $\mathbb{R}^n$ is linearly independent.[5]
(ii) Every finite superset of a linearly dependent set in $\mathbb{R}^n$ is linearly dependent.

Example A.4.2: It is easy to check that the set $E := \{\delta_1, \ldots, \delta_n\} \subset \mathbb{R}^n$ defined by

$$\delta_1 := \begin{pmatrix} 1 \\ 0 \\ \vdots \\ 0 \end{pmatrix}, \quad \delta_2 := \begin{pmatrix} 0 \\ 1 \\ \vdots \\ 0 \end{pmatrix}, \quad \cdots, \quad \delta_n := \begin{pmatrix} 0 \\ 0 \\ \vdots \\ 1 \end{pmatrix}$$

is linearly independent. Its elements are called the **canonical basis vectors** of $\mathbb{R}^n$.

The span of the canonical basis vectors in $\mathbb{R}^n$ is equal to all of $\mathbb{R}^n$. In particular, each $x \in \mathbb{R}^n$ can be expressed as

$$x = \sum_{i=1}^{n} \alpha_i \delta_i, \quad \text{where } \alpha_i := \langle x, \delta_i \rangle. \tag{A.11}$$

On the other hand, we cannot omit an element of the basis $\{\delta_1, \ldots, \delta_n\}$ and still span $\mathbb{R}^n$. The next theorem generalizes this idea.

THEOREM A.4.1   *If $E = \{u_1, \ldots, u_n\}$ is a set of n vectors in $\mathbb{R}^n$, then* span $E = \mathbb{R}^n$ *if and only if E is linearly independent.*

See, for example, Jänich (1994). Theorem A.4.1 captures the notion that linear independence of a set of vectors means linear diversity, which allows the span to be large.

EXERCISE A.4.5. The **null space** or **kernel** of a matrix $A \in \mathbb{M}^{n \times k}$ is the set

$$\text{null } A := \{x \in \mathbb{R}^k : Ax = 0\}.$$

---

[5] By the law of the excluded middle, the empty set must be linearly independent too.

Show that (i) null A is a linear subspace of $\mathbb{R}^k$ and (ii) null $A = \{0\}$, where 0 is the origin in $\mathbb{R}^k$, if and only if the columns of A form a linearly independent subset of $\mathbb{R}^n$.

A.4.2   Basis Vectors and Dimension

Let V be a linear subspace of $\mathbb{R}^n$. A set $B \subset V$ is called a **basis** for V if B is linearly independent and span $B = V$.

The key idea behind a basis is this: If $S = \{v_1, \ldots, v_k\}$ spans some linear subspace V, then each element of V can be written as a linear combination of elements of S. If S is, in addition, linearly independent (and hence a basis), then this representation is *unique*: For each $u \in V$, there is exactly one $(\alpha_1, \ldots, \alpha_k) \in \mathbb{R}^k$ such that

$$u = \alpha_1 v_1 + \cdots + \alpha_k v_k.$$

Indeed, if $u = \beta_1 v_1 + \cdots + \beta_k v_k$ is another representation, then, subtracting this equality from the last, we have

$$(\alpha_1 - \beta_1)v_1 + \cdots + (\alpha_k - \beta_k)v_k = 0.$$

Because S is assumed to be linearly independent, this yields $\alpha_i = \beta_i$ for all $i \in [k]$.

Not surprisingly, given their name, the canonical basis vectors $E := \{\delta_1, \ldots, \delta_n\}$ serve as a basis for the whole space $\mathbb{R}^n$. The representation (A.11), with coefficients $\alpha_i = \langle x, \delta_i \rangle$, is unique.

THEOREM A.4.2   *If V is a nonzero linear subspace of $\mathbb{R}^n$, then*

 (i) V has at least one basis and
(ii) every basis of V has the same number of elements.

Theorem A.4.2 is a relatively deep result. See, for example, Jänich (1994). The common number of bases in (ii) is called the **dimension** of V and written as dim V.

The "nonzero" qualification in Theorem A.4.2 is included for the case $V = \{0\}$, which is a linear subspace that lacks any basis. It is sensible, and standard, to agree that the linear subspace $\{0\} \subset \mathbb{R}^n$ has dimension zero.

Dimensionality is one measure of the "size" of a linear subspace. To illustrate, consider the system $Ax = b$, where $A \in \mathbb{M}^{n \times k}$, $x \in \mathbb{R}^k$, and $b \in \mathbb{R}^n$. Is there an x that solves this system? This will be more likely if the column space of A is large (see Example A.4.1). A large span will be obtained when the columns are linearly "diverse." In other words, our hope is that there exists a large subset of the columns of A that is linearly independent, which in turn will be true when the span of A is high-dimensional.

To quantify these ideas, we define the **rank** of A as

$$\text{rank } A := \dim(\text{range } A) = \text{ dimension of the column space of } A.$$

THEOREM A.4.3   *For any matrix A, the following quantities are equal:*

   (i) rank *A*,
   (ii) *the maximal number of linearly independent columns of A, and*
   (iii) *the maximal number of linearly independent rows of A.*

See, for example, chapter 2 of Aggarwal (2020) or chapter 5 of Jänich (1994). In view of Exercise A.4.6, for $A \in \mathbb{M}^{n \times k}$, we have rank $A \leqslant k$. If rank $A = k$, then A is said to have **full column rank**.

In general, a linear subspace V contains within itself many other linear subspaces. (For example, a plane passing through the origin contains many lines that pass through the origin, each one of which is a linear subspace.) However, there is no proper subspace of V (i.e., no linear subspace contained in and distinct from V) with the same dimension as V. The next theorem records this fact.

THEOREM A.4.4   *If U, V are linear subspaces of $\mathbb{R}^n$, then $U \subset V$ implies $\dim U \leqslant \dim V$, with equality if and only if $U = V$.*

EXERCISE A.4.6. Let U be a linear subspace of $\mathbb{R}^n$. Using the results given above, prove the following statements:

   (i) The only n-dimensional linear subspace of $\mathbb{R}^n$ is $\mathbb{R}^n$.
   (ii) If $A \subset U$ is finite and $|A| > \dim U$, then A is linearly dependent.

Part (ii) is related to Figure A.7. The plane in that figure is two-dimensional, as we confirm in §A.4.3 below. Any three vectors lying in the plane are linearly dependent.

A.4.3   Linear Maps Are Matrices

We will see in the following chapters that many nonlinear dynamic models and estimation problems can be expressed in terms of linear operations in high-dimensional spaces. We now state the definition of linear maps and their connection to matrices.

A function $u \mapsto Au$ from $\mathbb{R}^k$ to $\mathbb{R}^n$ is called **linear** if

$$A(\alpha u + \beta v) = \alpha Au + \beta Av \quad \text{for all } \alpha, \beta \in \mathbb{R} \text{ and all } u, v \text{ in } \mathbb{R}^k.$$

In this context, A is sometimes called an **operator** rather than a function, but the meaning is the same.

EXERCISE A.4.7. Fix $s, t \in \mathbb{R}$. Show that $A: \mathbb{R} \to \mathbb{R}$ defined by $Au = su + t$ is a linear function on $\mathbb{R}$ if and only if $t = 0$.

EXERCISE A.4.8. Let $A: \mathbb{R}^n \to \mathbb{R}^n$ be a linear bijection. By Lemma A.1.1, the operator A has an inverse A^{-1} mapping $\mathbb{R}^n$ to itself. Prove that A^{-1} is linear.

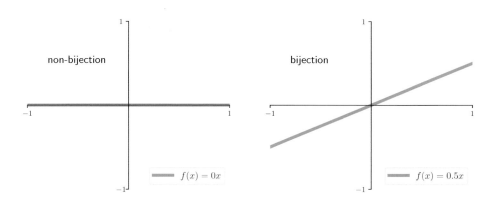

Figure A.8 Equivalence of the onto and one-to-one properties

One of the most striking and useful properties of linear operators is that the one-to-one property and the onto property are equivalent when the domain and codomain agree:

THEOREM A.4.5 *Let $A \colon \mathbb{R}^n \to \mathbb{R}^n$ be linear. The operator A is a one-to-one function if and only if it is onto.*

The proof can be found in Jänich (1994) or Stachurski (2016). Figure A.8 illustrates in the one-dimensional case. The linear map $f(x) = \alpha x$ is onto if and only if it is one-to-one, which occurs if and only if $\alpha \neq 0$.

A matrix $A \in \mathbb{M}^{n \times k}$ is a linear function from $\mathbb{R}^k$ to $\mathbb{R}^n$ when identified with the mapping that sends a (column) vector u in $\mathbb{R}^k$ into the vector Au in $\mathbb{R}^n$. In fact it is fundamental that, for *every* linear map $A \colon \mathbb{R}^k \to \mathbb{R}^n$, there exists a unique $M_A \in \mathbb{M}^{n \times k}$ such that

$$Au = M_A u \quad \text{for all} \quad u \in \mathbb{R}^k \tag{A.12}$$

(see, e.g., Kreyszig (1978), §2.9). Thus, the set of linear maps and the set of matrices are in one-to-one correspondence in the finite-dimensional setting.

A.4.4 Linear Hyperplanes

In Exercise A.4.1, you confirmed that, for a given nonzero $c \in \mathbb{R}^n$, the subset of $\mathbb{R}^n$ defined by $H := \{x \in \mathbb{R}^n \colon \langle c, x \rangle = 0\}$ is a linear subspace of $\mathbb{R}^n$. Any set H of this form is called a **linear hyperplane** in $\mathbb{R}^n$. The vector c is called the **normal vector** of the hyperplane.

THEOREM A.4.6 (Rank–Nullity Theorem) *For each $A \in \mathbb{M}^{n \times k}$, we have*

$$\operatorname{rank} A + \dim(\operatorname{null} A) = k.$$

Example A.4.3: If A has linearly independent columns, then rank $A = k$, and A is said to have full column rank. Recall from Exercise A.4.5 that this is precisely the setting where null $A = \{0\}$. Hence dim(null A) $= 0$, and Theorem A.4.6 holds.

In the discussion after Figure A.7, we claimed that the linear hyperplane showed there is a two-dimensional subset of $\mathbb{R}^3$. The next example generalizes this idea.

Example A.4.4: A linear hyperplane $H = \{x \in \mathbb{R}^n : \langle x, c \rangle = 0\}$ with $c \neq 0$ has dimension $n - 1$. To see this, just set A in Theorem A.4.6 to c, treated as a $1 \times n$ row vector. Then $H = $ null A, and

$$\dim H = \dim \text{null } A = n - \text{rank } A = n - 1.$$

(Here rank $A = 1$ follows from Theorem A.4.3.)

A.4.5   Nonsingular Linear Systems

A crucial task in applied modeling is solving linear systems such as $Ax = b$, where A is a matrix and x and b are conformable column vectors. The system can be underdetermined, overdetermined, or exactly determined (i.e., the same number of equations as unknowns). In this section we consider the last case, where the theory is straightforward.

Let A and B be in $\mathbb{M}^{n \times n}$, and suppose that $AB = BA = I$. Then B is called the **inverse** of A, written as A^{-1}, while A is said to be **invertible** or **nonsingular**.

The next theorem states that, for square matrices, the property of having either a left or a right inverse is equivalent to nonsingularity.

THEOREM A.4.7   *Given A in $\mathbb{M}^{n \times n}$, the following statements are equivalent:*

(i) There exists an $L \in \mathbb{M}^{n \times n}$ such that $LA = I$.
(ii) There exists an $R \in \mathbb{M}^{n \times n}$ such that $AR = I$.

If one and hence both of these statements hold, then A is nonsingular and $L = R = A^{-1}$.

Proof Fix A in $\mathbb{M}^{n \times n}$, and suppose first that (i) holds. This implies that A has a left inverse. In view of Exercise A.1.2, it must be that $x \mapsto Ax$ is one-to-one on $\mathbb{R}^n$. By Theorem A.4.5, this means that the same function is onto. Hence $x \mapsto Ax$ is a bijection and therefore invertible (Lemma A.1.1). By Exercise A.4.8, the inverse function is linear and hence can be represented by a matrix. We denote it A^{-1}. For the left inverse L we have $L = A^{-1}$, since $L = L(AA^{-1}) = (LA)A^{-1} = A^{-1}$.

Now suppose there exists an $R \in \mathbb{M}^{n \times n}$ such that $AR = I$. Then, A is the left inverse of R, and, by the previous argument, R is invertible with $A = R^{-1}$.

Pre-multiplying both sides by R gives $RA = I$, so R is also a left inverse of A. As we now know, this means that A is nonsingular and $R = A^{-1}$.

In summary, if either (i) or (ii) holds, then A is nonsingular, with left and right inverses both equal to A^{-1}.   □

Consider the linear system $Ax = b$, where $A \in \mathbb{M}^{n \times n}$ and $b \in \mathbb{R}^n$. We seek a solution $x \in \mathbb{R}^n$. The next theorem provides conditions under which such an x is always uniquely identified.

THEOREM A.4.8   *The following statements are equivalent:*

  (i) *For each $b \in \mathbb{R}^n$, the equation $Ax = b$ has a unique solution.*
 (ii) *The columns of A are linearly independent.*
(iii) *The columns of A form a basis of $\mathbb{R}^n$.*
(iv) null $A = \{0\}$.
 (v) rank $A = n$.
(vi) det A *is nonzero.*
(vii) A *is nonsingular.*

The symbol det A represents the **determinant** of A. For the definition, see, for example, Jänich (1994) or Cohen (2021). We note only that, for $n \times n$ matrices A and B,

- $\det(AB) = \det(A)\det(B)$;
- $\det(\alpha A) = \alpha^n \det A$ for all $\alpha \in \mathbb{R}$; and
- $\det(A^{-1}) = (\det A)^{-1}$ whenever A is nonsingular.

Most of the equivalences in Theorem A.4.8 can be established from the results presented above. The key idea is that, under these equivalent conditions, the columns of A form a basis of $\mathbb{R}^n$, and hence any $b \in \mathbb{R}^n$ can be expressed uniquely as a linear combination of elements of these columns. In other words, there exists a unique $x \in \mathbb{R}^n$ with $Ax = b$. The remaining points are just equivalent ways of saying that the columns of A form a basis of $\mathbb{R}^n$.

EXERCISE A.4.9. Let A and B be conformable in the sense that AB is well defined. Show that rank$(AB) \leqslant$ rank A, with equality if and only if B is nonsingular. [Hint: Use Theorem A.4.4.]

A.4.6   Orthogonality

We recall that vectors u, v in $\mathbb{R}^n$ are called **orthogonal** and we write $u \perp v$ if $\langle u, v \rangle = 0$. For a linear subspace L of $\mathbb{R}^n$, we call $u \in \mathbb{R}^n$ **orthogonal to** L and write $u \perp L$ whenever $u \perp v$ for all $v \in L$.

EXERCISE A.4.10. The **orthogonal complement** of linear subspace L is defined as $L^\perp := \{v \in \mathbb{R}^n : v \perp L\}$. Show that $L^\perp$ is a linear subspace of $\mathbb{R}^n$.

EXERCISE A.4.11. Prove: for any linear subspace $L \subset \mathbb{R}^n$, we have $L \cap L^{\perp} = \{0\}$.

A set of vectors $O \subset \mathbb{R}^n$ is called an **orthogonal set** if any two distinct elements of O are orthogonal. For any orthogonal set O, the **Pythagorean law**

$$\left\| \sum_{u \in O} u \right\|^2 = \sum_{u \in O} \|u\|^2$$

always holds.

EXERCISE A.4.12. Prove: Orthogonality implies linear independence in the sense that

$$O \subset \mathbb{R}^n \text{ is orthogonal and } 0 \notin O \implies O \text{ is linearly independent.}$$

An orthogonal set $O \subset \mathbb{R}^n$ is called an **orthonormal set** if $\|u\| = 1$ for all $u \in O$. If L is a linear subspace of $\mathbb{R}^n$, O is orthonormal in L, and span $O = L$, then O is called an **orthonormal basis** of L. For example, the canonical basis $\{e_1, \dots, e_n\}$ forms an orthonormal basis of $\mathbb{R}^n$.

EXERCISE A.4.13. Explain why an orthonormal basis O of a subspace L is, in fact, a basis of L, in the sense of the definition in §A.4.2.

A matrix M is called an **orthonormal matrix** if $M \in \mathbb{M}^{n \times n}$ for some $n \in \mathbb{N}$, and, in addition, the columns of M form an orthonormal set in $\mathbb{R}^n$. These kinds of matrices will be important to us when we analyze singular value decomposition. Notice that,

- by definition, every orthonormal matrix is square, and
- the n columns of an orthonormal matrix M in $\mathbb{R}^n$ form a basis of $\mathbb{R}^n$, since they are nonzero and orthogonal.

The second point tells us that M is nonsingular. The next lemma summarizes important properties of orthonormal matrices.

LEMMA A.4.9   *Fix $M \in \mathbb{M}^{n \times n}$ and let I be the $n \times n$ identity. The following statements are equivalent:*

(i) *M is an orthonormal matrix.*
(ii) *$M^{\top} M = I$.*
(iii) *$M M^{\top} = I$.*
(iv) *$M^{\top} = M^{-1}$.*

The equivalence of (ii) and (iii) is quite striking. It tells us that a square matrix with orthonormal columns automatically has orthonormal rows.

Proof   Clearly (i) and (ii) are equivalent, since they are two ways of writing the same thing. Equivalence of (ii)–(iv) follows from Theorem A.4.7 on page 200.   □

A.5 Convexity and Concavity

Convexity and concavity are structures of enormous significance in economics and finance, in terms of both computation and theory. In this section we note the key definitions and provide exercises that help build familiarity.

A.5.1 Convexity and Polyhedra

Convexity plays a central role in optimization and fixed point theory. As usual, a subset C of $\mathbb{R}^n$ is called **convex** if

$$u, v \in C \text{ and } \lambda \in [0, 1] \implies \lambda u + (1 - \lambda)v \in C.$$

EXERCISE A.5.1. Show that"

(i) The unit simplex in $\mathbb{R}^n$ is a convex subset of $\mathbb{R}^n$.
(ii) For all $a \in \mathbb{R}^n$ and $\varepsilon > 0$, the sphere $B = \{x \in \mathbb{R}^n : \|x - a\| < \varepsilon\}$ is convex.
(iii) The intersection of an arbitrary number of convex sets in $\mathbb{R}^n$ is again convex.

In economic optimization problems, the convex sets within which we seek extrema are usually polyhedra. A **polyhedron** in $\mathbb{R}^n$ is a set of the form

$$P = \{x \in \mathbb{R}^n : Ax \leqslant b\} \quad \text{for some } A \in \mathbb{M}^{k \times n} \text{ and } b \in \mathbb{R}^k. \tag{A.13}$$

Equivalently, P is a polyhedron in $\mathbb{R}^n$ if there exist scalars $b_1, \ldots, b_k$ and n-dimensional vectors $a_1, \ldots, a_k$ such that $x \in P$ if and only if $a_i^\top x \leqslant b_i$ for $i = 1, \ldots, k$.

Example A.5.1: A budget set of the form $B = \{x \in \mathbb{R}_+^n : p^\top x \leqslant m\}$, where $m \geqslant 0$ and $p \in \mathbb{R}_+^n$, is a polyhedron. Here p is a vector of prices and x is a consumption bundle. Indeed, B can be expressed as the set of all $x \in \mathbb{R}^n$ such that $p^\top x \leqslant m$ and, for the nonnegativity constraints, $-\delta_i^\top x \leqslant 0$ for $i = 1, \ldots, n$, where δ_i is the i-th canonical basis vector in $\mathbb{R}^n$. This meets the definition of a polyhedron.

Given $b \in \mathbb{R}$ and nonzero $c \in \mathbb{R}^n$,

- $H_0 := \{x \in \mathbb{R}^n : x^\top c = b\}$ is called a **hyperplane** in $\mathbb{R}^n$, while
- $H_1 := \{x \in \mathbb{R}^n : x^\top c \leqslant b\}$ is called a **halfspace** in $\mathbb{R}^n$.

Note our convention. In §A.4.4 we defined *linear* hyperplanes, which correspond to H_0 when $b = 0$. Thus linear hyperplanes are a special kind of hyperplane. You will be able to confirm that the hyperplane H_0 is a linear subspace of $\mathbb{R}^n$ if and only if $b = 0$.

EXERCISE A.5.2. Show that H_0 and H_1 are both convex in $\mathbb{R}^n$.

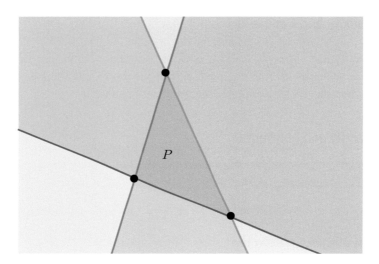

Figure A.9 A polyhedron P represented as intersecting halfspaces

It is immediate from the definition that $P \subset \mathbb{R}^n$ is a polyhedron if and only if P is the intersection of k halfspaces in $\mathbb{R}^n$ for some $k \in \mathbb{N}$. Figure A.9 helps illustrate this idea.

An **extreme point** of a polyhedron P is a point $p \in P$ that cannot be realized as the convex combination of other points in P. In other words, we cannot find two points $x, y \in P$ that are distinct from p and satisfy $\lambda x + (1 - \lambda)y = p$ for some $\lambda \in [0, 1]$. The extreme points of P in Figure A.9 are represented as black dots.

EXERCISE A.5.3. Show that every polyhedron in $\mathbb{R}^n$ is convex.

A **cone** in $\mathbb{R}^n$ is a set $C \subset \mathbb{R}^n$ such that $x \in C$ implies $\alpha x \in C$ for all $\alpha > 0$.

EXERCISE A.5.4. Show that (i) the intersection of any two cones is again a cone and (ii) a cone $C \subset \mathbb{R}^n$ is convex (i.e., C is a **convex cone**) if and only if it is closed under addition (i.e, $x, y \in C$ implies $x + y \in C$).

EXERCISE A.5.5. The **positive cone** of $\mathbb{R}^n$ is the set

$$\mathbb{R}^n_+ := \{x \in \mathbb{R}^n : x \geqslant 0\}.$$

Show that, for the partially ordered set $(\mathbb{R}^n, \leqslant)$, the positive cone is an increasing subset of $\mathbb{R}^n$. Show in addition that $\mathbb{R}^n_+$ is a convex cone.

A.5.2   Convex and Concave Functions

A function g from a convex subset C of $\mathbb{R}^n$ to $\mathbb{R}^k$ is called **convex** if

$$g(\lambda u + (1 - \lambda)v) \leqslant \lambda g(u) + (1 - \lambda)g(v) \quad \text{whenever } u, v \in C \text{ and } 0 \leqslant \lambda \leqslant 1$$

and **concave** if $-g$ is convex. Concavity of g is obviously equivalent to

$$g(\lambda u + (1 - \lambda)v) \geq \lambda g(u) + (1 - \lambda)g(v) \quad \text{whenever } u, v \in C \text{ and } 0 \leq \lambda \leq 1.$$

When $k = 1$, the function g is called, respectively, **strictly convex** or **strictly concave** if, in addition, the inequalities become strict whenever u, v are distinct and $0 < \lambda < 1$.

EXERCISE A.5.6. Give an example of a function g from $\mathbb{R}^n$ to $\mathbb{R}^n$ that is both convex and concave.

These properties of functions are closely related to the convexity of sets. For example, the same function g is convex if and only if its **epigraph**

$$\text{epi}(g) := \{(x, g(x)) \in \mathbb{R}^{n+1} : x \in C\}$$

is convex.

EXERCISE A.5.7. If C is a convex subset of $\mathbb{R}^n$ and $g \colon \mathbb{R}^n \to \mathbb{R}$ is convex, then **Jensen's inequality** states that, for any vectors $\{x_1, \ldots, x_k\} \subset C$ and weights $\{\lambda_1, \ldots, \lambda_k\} \subset \mathbb{R}$ with $0 \leq \lambda_i \leq 1$ and $\sum_i \lambda_i = 1$, we have

$$g\left(\sum_{i=1}^{k} x_i \lambda_i\right) \leq \sum_{i=1}^{k} g(x_i) \lambda_i.$$

If g is concave then the reverse inequality holds. Prove Jensen's inequality for the case where g is convex when $k = 3$.

In the next exercise, if $\{y_i\}$ is a finite collection of vectors in $\mathbb{R}^k$, then $\max_i y_i$ is the vector in $\mathbb{R}^k$ obtained by taking the maximum pointwise. The minimum $\min_i y_i$ is defined in a similar way.

EXERCISE A.5.8. Fix $m \in \mathbb{N}$ and let $\{g_i\}_{i \in [m]}$ be a collection of $\mathbb{R}^k$-valued functions defined on a convex subset C of $\mathbb{R}^n$. Show that:

(i) If g_i is convex for every i in $[m]$, then g defined at each x in C by
$g(x) := \max_{i \in [m]} g_i(x)$ is also convex on C.
(ii) If g_i is concave for every i in $[m]$, then g defined at each x in C by
$g(x) := \min_{i \in [m]} g_i(x)$ is also concave on C.

EXERCISE A.5.9. Let f and g map C to $\mathbb{R}$, where $C \subset \mathbb{R}^n$ is convex and so are f and g. Show that (i) $f + g$ is convex and (ii) $f + g$ is strictly convex if, in addition, either f or g is strictly convex.

Important examples of concave and convex scalar-valued functions include certain kinds of quadratic forms. For the following you should recall that a symmetric $n \times n$ matrix A is called

- **positive semidefinite** if $x^\top A x \geqslant 0$ for any x in $\mathbb{R}^n$;
- **positive definite** if $x^\top A x > 0$ for any nonzero x in $\mathbb{R}^n$;
- **negative semidefinite** if $x^\top A x \leqslant 0$ for any x in $\mathbb{R}^n$; and
- **negative definite** if $x^\top A x < 0$ for any nonzero x in $\mathbb{R}^n$.

It's important to remember (but easy to forget) that symmetry is part of the definition of these properties. You probably remember that

- A is positive definite (resp., semidefinite) if and only if all its eigenvalues are strictly positive (resp., nonnegative) and
- A is positive definite (resp., semidefinite) $\implies$ its determinant is strictly positive (resp., nonnegative).

The second statement follows from the first, since the determinant of a matrix equals the product of its eigenvalues.

The **quadratic form** $q(x) = x^\top A x$ is

- convex if and only if A is positive semidefinite;
- strictly convex if and only if A is positive definite;
- concave if and only if A is negative semidefinite; and
- strictly concave if and only if A is negative definite.

See, for example, Simon (1994).

EXERCISE A.5.10. Let X be $n \times k$. Prove the following:

(i) $X^\top X$ is positive semidefinite.
(ii) If, in addition, X has full column rank, then $X^\top X$ is positive definite.

A.6   Optimization

In this section we review some key topics in optimization theory.

A.6.1   Definitions and Existence

A number m contained in a subset A of $\mathbb{R}$ is called the **maximum** of A and we write $m = \max A$ if $a \leqslant m$ for every $a \in A$. It is called the **minimum** of A, written as $m = \min A$, if $m \in A$ and $a \geqslant m$ for every $a \in A$.

Given an arbitrary set D and a function $f : D \to \mathbb{R}$, define

$$\max_{x \in D} f(x) := \max\{f(x) : x \in D\} \quad \text{and} \quad \min_{x \in D} f(x) := \min\{f(x) : x \in D\}.$$

A point $x^* \in D$ is called

- a **maximizer** of f on D if $x^* \in D$ and $f(x^*) \geqslant f(x)$ for all $x \in D$ and
- a **minimizer** of f on D if $x^* \in D$ and $f(x^*) \leqslant f(x)$ for all $x \in D$.

Equivalently, $x^* \in D$ is a maximizer of f on D if $f(x^*) = \max_{x \in D} f(x)$ and a minimizer if $f(x^*) = \min_{x \in D} f(x)$. We define

$$\operatorname*{argmax}_{x \in D} f(x) := \{x^* \in D : f(x^*) \geqslant f(x) \text{ for all } x \in D\}.$$

The set $\operatorname{argmin}_{x \in D} f(x)$ is defined analogously.

Example A.6.1: If $f(x) = x^2$ and $D = [-1, 1]$, then $\operatorname{argmax}_{x \in D} f(x) = \{-1, 1\}$, while $\operatorname{argmin}_{x \in D} f(x) = \{0\}$. In the second case, where the solution set is a singleton, that is, a set with exactly one element, we write $\operatorname{argmin}_{x \in D} f(x) = 0$ as well.

EXERCISE A.6.1. Let $f : D \to A \subset \mathbb{R}$ be any given function. Prove the following:

(i) If $g : A \to \mathbb{R}$ is a strictly increasing function, then x^* is a maximizer of f on D if and only if x^* is a maximizer of $g \circ f$ on A.
(ii) If $g : A \to \mathbb{R}$ is a strictly decreasing function, then x^* is a maximizer of f on D if and only if x^* is a minimizer of $g \circ f$ on A.

One important special case of part (ii) is that $x^* \in D$ is a maximizer of f on D if and only if x^* is a minimizer of $-f$ on D. Hence, any maximization problem can be converted into a minimization problem and vice-versa.

A.6.2   Convexity and Extrema

§ A.6.1 discussed the existence of optimizers. In this section we consider uniqueness. The key observation is that, for convex and concave functions, local optimizers are global optimizers.

If $C \subset \mathbb{R}^n$ and f is a real-valued function on C, then $u^* \in C$ is a **local minimizer** of f on C if there exists an open set G in C such that $u^* \in G$ and $f(u^*) \leqslant f(u)$ whenever $u \in G$. A **local maximizer** is defined analogously.

The next exercise highlights one of the most important facts concerning computation of solutions to optimization problems in real-world applications. It is especially valuable in high-dimensional settings, where optimization problems can be very challenging.

EXERCISE A.6.2. Show that, if $C \subset \mathbb{R}^n$ is convex, f is convex and u^* is a local minimizer of f on C, then u^* is a minimizer of f on C.

Similarly, if f is concave on C, then any local maximizer is a global maximizer.

A.6.3   Multivariate Quadratic Objectives

§ 1.4.2.3 treated a one-dimensional quadratic optimization problem. Next we treat n-dimensional problems of the same type.

LEMMA A.6.1   *If $H \in \mathbb{M}^{n \times n}$ is positive definite, then, for any $b \in \mathbb{R}$ and $a \in \mathbb{R}^n$,*

$$u^* := H^{-1}a \text{ is the unique minimizer of } q(u) := u^\top H u - 2u^\top a + b \text{ in } \mathbb{R}^n.$$

EXERCISE A.6.3. Prove that any local minimizer of q in Lemma A.6.1 is also a global minimizer. [Hint: Use Exercise A.5.9.]

EXERCISE A.6.4. Complete the proof of Lemma A.6.1 by showing that u^* is a local minimizer. It suffices to show that the derivative of q at u^* is zero. Use the following facts from matrix calculus:

$$a \in \mathbb{R}^n \text{ and } H \in \mathbb{M}^{n \times n} \quad \Longrightarrow \quad \frac{d}{du}u^\top a = a \text{ and } \frac{d}{du}u^\top H u = (H + H^\top)u.$$

A.7   Lagrangian Duality

If you have studied undergraduate economics, you will have used Lagrangian methods to solve constrained optimization problems. The objective of this section is to supply insight on when and why the method works, as well as to highlight the connection between an original constrained problem and a so-called "dual problem." This connection yields deep insights in economics, finance, statistical learning, artificial intelligence, and many other fields.

A.7.1   Theory

Let E be a subset of $\mathbb{R}^n$, and let f map E to $\mathbb{R}$. We aim to solve

$$\min_{x \in E} f(x) \text{ subject to } g(x) = 0 \text{ and } h(x) \leqslant 0. \tag{A.14}$$

Here g maps E to $\mathbb{R}^m$ and h maps E to $\mathbb{R}^k$. For example, the zero symbol in the statement $g(x) = 0$ is a vector of zeros, and the meaning is that $g_i(x) = 0$ in $\mathbb{R}$ for i in $1, \ldots, m$. The interpretation of the second constraint is analogous.

Any $x \in E$ that satisfies the constraints in (A.14) is called **feasible**. Let $F(g,h)$ be the set of all feasible $x \in E$. A feasible point that attains the minimum in (A.14) is called **optimal** for – or a **solution** to – the optimization problem.

Our first claim is that the constrained optimization problem (A.14) is equivalent to the *un*constrained problem

$$P = \min_{x \in E} \max_{\theta \in \Theta} L(x, \theta), \tag{A.15}$$

where $\theta := (\lambda, \mu)$ and

$$L(x, \theta) = L(x, \lambda, \mu) := f(x) + \sum_{i=1}^{m} \lambda_i g_i(x) + \sum_{i=1}^{k} \mu_i h_i(x). \qquad \text{(A.16)}$$

Here $\theta \in \Theta$ combines the vectors of **Lagrange multipliers** $\lambda \in \mathbb{R}^m$ and $\mu \in \mathbb{R}^k_+$, where $\Theta := \mathbb{R}^m \times \mathbb{R}^k_+$. By *equivalent to*, we mean that

(i) $\hat{f}(x) := \max_{\theta \in \Theta} L(x, \theta)$ satisfies $\hat{f} = f$ on $F(g, h)$;
(ii) $\hat{f} = +\infty$ on the complement of $F(g, h)$; and
(iii) together $\hat{f}$ and f satisfy

$$P := \min_{x \in E} \hat{f}(x) = \min_{x \in F(g,h)} \hat{f}(x) = \min_{x \in F(g,h)} f(x). \qquad \text{(A.17)}$$

The first equality in (A.17) is by definition. The second two follow from (ii) and (i), respectively. Hence we need only verify (i) and (ii).

EXERCISE A.7.1. Show that (i) and (ii) both hold. You can assume that extrema exist.

The function L in problem (A.16) is usually called the **Lagrangian**. The P in (A.15) stands for **primal**. So far we have shown that the original constrained problem and the primal problem are the same. The next step is to pair the primal problem with its **dual** problem, which is obtained by reversing the order of min and max in the primal:

$$D = \max_{\theta \in \Theta} \min_{x \in E} L(x, \theta). \qquad \text{(A.19)}$$

The dual problem has two attractive features. One is that, when minimizing with respect to x, we do not need to concern ourselves with the constraints on x in the original formulation (A.14). The second is that, since $L(x, \theta)$ is linear in θ, and since we are minimizing a family of these functions with respect to x, the minimizer is a concave function (see page 205). Concavity assists maximization, which is the next step in solving D.

EXERCISE A.7.2. Show that $D \leqslant P$ always holds.

The result $D \leqslant P$ in Exercise A.7.2 is called **weak duality**. If $P = D$, then **strong duality** is said to hold. Unlike weak duality, strong duality requires conditions on the primitives.

Evidently strong duality holds if and only if it is valid to reverse the order of the min and max operators in the definition of the primal (or the dual). Results of this kind are called *min-max theorems*. Such theorems hold at "saddle points" of the function L. The next section explains.

A.7.2   Saddle Points and Duality

We seek necessary and sufficient conditions for strong duality, which will lead to a characterization of minimizers for the original constrained problem. To do so, we again take $\theta := (\lambda, \mu)$ and $\Theta := \mathbb{R}^m \times \mathbb{R}_+^k$, so that

$$P = \min_{x \in E} \max_{\theta \in \Theta} L(x, \theta) \quad \text{and} \quad D = \max_{\theta \in \Theta} \min_{x \in E} L(x, \theta). \tag{A.20}$$

A pair (x^*, θ^*) in $E \times \Theta$ is called a **saddle point** of L if

$$L(x^*, \theta) \leqslant L(x^*, \theta^*) \leqslant L(x, \theta^*) \quad \text{for all} \quad (x, \theta) \in E \times \Theta. \tag{A.21}$$

A depiction of a saddle point of a given bivariate function $(x, \theta) \mapsto L(x, \theta) \in \mathbb{R}$ is given in Figure A.10. The left-hand side of the top panel is a 3D visualization, and the right-hand side is a contour plot of the same function. The saddle point is at the center.

When the extrema in (A.20) exist, we have the following result:

THEOREM A.7.1   *If L has a saddle point (x^*, θ^*) in $E \times \Theta$, then strong duality holds. Moreover, $P = D = L(x^*, \theta^*)$, and x^* solves the constrained optimization problem* (A.14).

Proof   Let (x^*, θ^*) be a saddle point (x^*, θ^*) of L in $E \times \Theta$. We have, for all $(x, \theta) \in E \times \Theta$,

$$P \leqslant \max_{\theta} L(x^*, \theta) \leqslant L(x^*, \theta^*) \leqslant \min_{x} L(x, \theta^*),$$

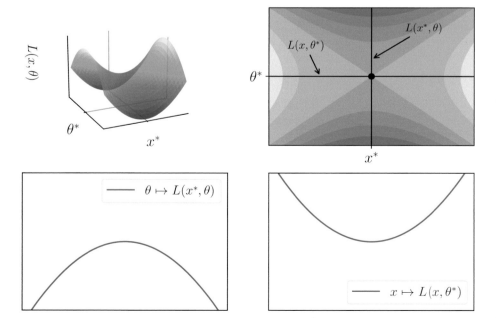

Figure A.10 A saddle point (x^*, θ^*) of the function L

where the first inequality is by definition and the second two are by the saddle point property. The last term is clearly dominated by D, so we conclude that $P \leqslant L(x^*, \theta^*) \leqslant D$. But, by weak duality, we also have $D \leqslant P$, so $P = L(x^*, \theta^*) = D$.

Finally, to confirm that x^* solves the original constrained problem, suppose to the contrary that there exists an $x_0 \in E$ that satisfies the constraints and yields $f(x_0) < f(x^*)$. Since the constraints are satisfied at both x_0 and x^*, we can apply (A.18) on page 233 to obtain $\max_{\theta \in \Theta} L(x_0, \theta) = f(x_0)$ and $\max_{\theta \in \Theta} L(x^*, \theta) = f(x^*)$. Hence the second inequality of the saddle point condition implies

$$f(x^*) = \max_{\theta \in \Theta} L(x^*, \theta) \leqslant \max_{\theta \in \Theta} L(x_0, \theta) = f(x_0).$$

This contradicts the hypothesis that $f(x_0) < f(x^*)$. □

Theorem A.7.1 tells us that to solve the constrained optimization problem and establish strong duality, we need only obtain a saddle point of the Lagrangian.

A.7.3   Karush, Kuhn, and Tucker

For well-behaved problems, saddle points can be identified via well-known first-order conditions, called the **Karush–Kuhn–Tucker** (KKT) conditions. To state them, we return to the original problem (A.14) and write θ explicitly as (λ, μ), so that $(x^*, \lambda^*, \mu^*) \in E \times \mathbb{R}^m \times \mathbb{R}_+^k$ satisfies the saddle point condition if

$$L(x^*, \lambda, \mu) \leqslant L(x^*, \lambda^*, \mu^*) \leqslant L(x, \lambda^*, \mu^*) \quad \text{for all} \quad x \in E, \lambda \in \mathbb{R}^m \text{ and } \mu \in \mathbb{R}_+^k.$$

The **KKT conditions** are met by $(x^*, \lambda^*, \mu^*) \in E \times \mathbb{R}^m \times \mathbb{R}_+^k$ if $x^* \in F(g, h)$,

$$\nabla f(x^*) + \sum_{i=1}^m \lambda_i^* \nabla g_i(x^*) + \sum_{i=1}^k \mu_i^* \nabla h_i(x^*) = 0, \quad \text{and} \qquad \text{(A.22)}$$

$$\mu_i^* h_i(x^*) = 0 \quad \text{for all } i \in [k]. \qquad \text{(A.23)}$$

Here we are requiring that f, g, h are all differentiable at x^*, and, for a given function $q \colon E \to \mathbb{R}$, we use ∇ to represent the vector of partial derivatives. Equation (A.22) requires that the derivative of the Lagrangian with respect to x is zero at x^*. The second condition is called the **complementary slackness** condition.

The KKT conditions are nothing more than saddle point conditions. Condition (A.22) is the first-order condition for an interior minimizer of the Lagrangian with respect to x, at the point (x^*, θ^*), which tries to identify the local minimum visualized in the lower right panel of Figure A.10. The complementary slackness condition is also needed because if $\mu_i^* h_i(x^*) = 0$ fails at some i, then $\mu_i^* h_i(x^*) < 0$ must hold, in which case we could strictly increase the Lagrangian by shifting μ_i^* to 0. This violates the saddle point property.

If enough regularity conditions hold, then the KKT conditions exactly identify extremal points. Here is one example, which is proved in Chapter 8 of Matousek and Gärtner (2007).

THEOREM A.7.2 (Karush–Kuhn–Tucker)   *If E is open, f is continuously differentiable and convex, and both g and h are affine functions, then x^* minimizes f on $F(g,h)$ if and only if there exists a pair $(\lambda^*, \mu^*) \in \mathbb{R}^m \times \mathbb{R}^k_+$ such that the KKT conditions hold.*

Appendix B Solutions to Selected Exercises

Solution to Exercise 1.2.1. For $\lambda_1 = i$, we have

$$Ae_1 = \begin{pmatrix} 0 & -1 \\ 1 & 0 \end{pmatrix} \begin{pmatrix} -1 \\ i \end{pmatrix} = \begin{pmatrix} -i \\ -1 \end{pmatrix} = \lambda_1 e_1.$$

Similarly for $\lambda_2 = -i$, we have

$$Ae_2 = \begin{pmatrix} 0 & -1 \\ 1 & 0 \end{pmatrix} \begin{pmatrix} -1 \\ -i \end{pmatrix} = \begin{pmatrix} i \\ -1 \end{pmatrix} = \lambda_2 e_2.$$

Solution to Exercise 1.2.2. Fix an eigenpair (λ, e) of A and a nonzero scalar α. We have

$$A(\alpha e) = \alpha A e = \lambda(\alpha e).$$

Hence αe is an eigenvector and λ is an eigenvalue, as claimed.

Solution to Exercise 1.2.3. Fix $A \in \mathbb{M}^{n \times n}$ and $\tau > 0$. If $\lambda \in \sigma(A)$, then $\tau^n \det(A - \lambda I) = 0$, or $\det(\tau A - \tau \lambda I) = 0$. Hence $\tau \lambda \in \sigma(\tau A)$. To obtain the converse implication, multiply by $1/\tau$.

Solution to Exercise 1.2.4. If $p(\lambda) := \det(A - \lambda I)$ has n distinct roots, then $|\sigma(A)| = n$. For each $\lambda_i \in \sigma(A)$, let e_i be a corresponding eigenvector. It suffices to show that $\{e_i\}_{i=1}^n$ is linearly independent. To this end, let k be the largest number such that $\{e_1, \ldots, e_k\}$ is independent. Seeking a contradiction, suppose that $k < n$. Then $e_{k+1} = \sum_{i=1}^k \alpha_i e_i$ for suitable scalars $\{\alpha_i\}$. Hence, by $Ae_{k+1} = \lambda_{k+1} e_{k+1}$, we have

$$\sum_{i=1}^k \alpha_i \lambda_i e_i = \sum_{i=1}^k \alpha_i \lambda_{k+1} e_i \quad \Longleftrightarrow \quad \sum_{i=1}^k \alpha_i (\lambda_i - \lambda_{k+1}) e_i = 0.$$

Since $\{e_1, \ldots, e_k\}$ is independent, we have $\alpha_i(\lambda_i - \lambda_{k+1}) = 0$ for all i. At least one α_i is nonzero, so $\lambda_i = \lambda_{k+1}$ for some $i \leqslant k$. Contradiction.

Solution to Exercise 1.2.5. Suppose to the contrary that there is one zero column vector in P. Then P is not nonsingular. Contradiction.

Solution to Exercise 1.2.6. Let A be as stated, with $A = PDP^{-1}$. Using elementary properties of the trace and determinant, we have

$$\text{trace}(A) = \text{trace}(PDP^{-1}) = \text{trace}(DPP^{-1}) = \text{trace}(D) = \sum_i \lambda_i$$

and

$$\det(A) = \det(P)\det(D)\det(P^{-1}) = \det(P)\det(D)\det(P)^{-1} = \det(D) = \prod_i \lambda_i.$$

Solution to Exercise 1.2.8. If I is the identity and $Ie = \lambda e$ for some nonzero e, then $e = \lambda e$ and hence $\lambda = 1$. Hence $\sigma(A) = \{1\}$. At the same time, I is diagonalizable, since $I = IDI^{-1}$ when $D = I$.

Solution to Exercise 1.2.19. Fix $A \in \mathbb{M}^{n \times n}$ and $b \in \mathbb{R}^n$, where $r(A) < 1$. We can write $x = Ax + b$ as $(I - A)x = b$. Since $r(A) < 1$, $I - A$ is invertible and hence the linear system $(I - A)x = b$ has unique solution $x^* = (I - A)^{-1}b$. The expression $x^* = \sum_{m=0}^{\infty} A^m b$ follows from the Neumann series lemma.

Solution to Exercise 1.2.20. In what follows, P_w is as defined in (1.2), and, for any matrix Q, the symbol $Q(i, j)$ denotes the i, j-th element.

((i), ($\Rightarrow$)) Suppose that P_w is irreducible and yet $\alpha = 0$. Then, by the expression for P_w^m in (1.3), we have $P_w^m(1, 2) = 0$ for all m. This contradicts irreducibility, so $\alpha > 0$ must hold. A similar argument shows that $\beta > 0$.

((i), ($\Leftarrow$)) If $\alpha, \beta > 0$, then the off-diagonal elements of P_w are strictly positive. Moreover, the diagonal elements of P_w^2 are strictly positive. Hence $P_w + P_w^2 \gg 0$ and P_w is irreducible.

((ii), ($\Rightarrow$)) Suppose that P_w is primitive. Then P_w is irreducible, so $0 < \alpha, \beta \leqslant 1$ holds. It remains only to show that $\min\{\alpha, \beta\} < 1$. Suppose to the contrary that $\alpha = \beta = 1$. Then P_w^m has zero diagonal elements when m is odd and zero off-diagonal elements when m is even. This contradicts the primitive property, so $\min\{\alpha, \beta\} < 1$ must hold.

((ii), ($\Leftarrow$)) Suppose that $0 < \alpha, \beta \leqslant 1$ and $\alpha < 1$. Some algebra shows that $P_w^2 \gg 0$. The same is true when $0 < \alpha, \beta \leqslant 1$ and $\beta < 1$. Hence P_w is primitive.

Solution to Exercise 1.2.22. Fix $A \in \mathbb{M}^{n \times k}$ with $A \geqslant 0$, along with $x, y \in \mathbb{R}^k$. From $x \leqslant y$ we have $y - x \geqslant 0$, so $A(y - x) \geqslant 0$. But then $Ay - Ax \geqslant 0$, or $Ax \leqslant Ay$.

Solution to Exercise 1.3.2. For the first claim, fix $x \in S$ and $z \in (0, 1]$. If $\kappa(z) = x$, then, since all elements of S are distinct, the definition of κ implies $z \in I(x)$. Conversely, if $z \in I(x)$, then, since all intervals are disjoint, we have $\kappa(z) = x$.

For the second claim, pick any $x \in S$, and observe that, by the first claim, $\kappa(W) = x$ precisely when $W \in I(x)$. The probability of this event is the length of the interval

$I(x)$, which, by construction, is $\varphi(x)$. Hence $\mathbb{P}\{\kappa(W) = x\} = \varphi(x)$ for all $x \in S$ as claimed.

Solution to Exercise 1.3.3. Fix $j \in [n]$. Observe that $Y := \mathbb{1}\{\kappa(W) = j\}$ is a Bernoulli random variable. The expectation of such a Y equals $\mathbb{P}\{Y = 1\}$. As $\kappa(W) \overset{d}{=} \varphi$, this is $\varphi(j)$.

Solution to Exercise 1.3.5. Draw U uniformly on $(0, 1]$ and set the coin to heads if $U \leqslant \delta$. The probability of this outcome is $\mathbb{P}\{U \leqslant \delta\} = \delta$.

Solution to Exercise 1.3.6. For the solution we assume that S is finite, although the argument can easily be extended to densities. On the computer, we flip a biased coin $B \in \{0, 1\}$ with $\mathbb{P}\{B = 0\} = \delta$ and then

(i) draw Y from φ if $B = 0$, or
(ii) draw Y from ψ if $B = 1$.

With this set up, by the law of total probability,

$$\mathbb{P}\{Y = s\} = \mathbb{P}\{Y = s \mid B = 0\}\mathbb{P}\{B = 0\} + \mathbb{P}\{Y = s \mid B = 1\}\mathbb{P}\{B = 1\}$$
$$= \delta\varphi(s) + (1 - \delta)\psi(s).$$

In other words, $Y \overset{d}{=} f$.

Solution to Exercise 1.3.7. Let P and Q be as stated. Evidently $PQ \geqslant 0$. Moreover, $PQ\mathbb{1} = P\mathbb{1} = \mathbb{1}$, so PQ is stochastic. That $r(P) = 1$ follows directly from Lemma 1.2.7. By the Perron–Frobenius theorem, there exists a nonzero, nonnegative row vector φ satisfying $\varphi P = \varphi$. Rescaling φ to $\varphi/(\varphi\mathbb{1})$ gives the desired vector ψ.

Solution to Exercise 1.3.8. Fix $p > 0$ and let X be $LN(\mu, \sigma^2)$. We have

$$\mathbb{E}|X|^p = \mathbb{E}X^p = \mathbb{E}\exp(p\mu + p\sigma Z) \quad \text{for } Z \overset{d}{=} N(0, 1).$$

Since $p\mu + p\sigma Z \overset{d}{=} N(p\mu, p^2\sigma^2)$, we can apply the formula for the mean of a lognormal distribution to obtain $m_p = \exp(p\mu + (p\sigma)^2/2) < \infty$.

Solution to Exercise 1.3.9. Let X have a Pareto tail with tail index α, and let G be its CCDF. Fix $r \geqslant \alpha$. Under the Pareto tail assumption, we can take positive constants b and $\bar{x}$ such that $G(t) \geqslant bt^{-\alpha}$ whenever $t \geqslant \bar{x}$. Using (1.14) we have

$$\mathbb{E}X^r = r\int_0^\infty t^{r-1}G(t)\,dt \geqslant r\int_0^{\bar{x}} t^{r-1}G(t)\,dt + r\int_{\bar{x}}^\infty t^{r-1}bt^{-\alpha}\,dt.$$

But $\int_{\bar{x}}^\infty t^{r-\alpha-1}\,dt = \infty$ whenever $r - \alpha - 1 \geqslant -1$. Since $r \geqslant \alpha$, we have $\mathbb{E}X^r = \infty$.

Solution to Exercise 1.3.10. Fix $\lambda > 0$ and suppose $X \overset{d}{=} \mathrm{Exp}(\lambda)$. A simple integration exercise shows that $\mathbb{P}\{X > t\} = \mathrm{e}^{-\lambda t}$. Now fix $\alpha > 0$. Since $\lim_{t \to \infty} t^{\alpha} \mathrm{e}^{-\lambda t} = 0$, the random variable X does not obey a power law.

Solution to Exercise 1.3.11. Let p and the constants $\gamma, c > 0$ and $\bar{x} \in \mathbb{R}_+$ be as described in the exercise. Pick any $t \geqslant \bar{x}$. By the usual rules of integration,

$$\mathbb{P}\{X > t\} = c \int_t^\infty u^{-\gamma} \, \mathrm{d}u = -\frac{c}{1-\gamma} t^{1-\gamma}.$$

With $\alpha := \gamma - 1$, we then have $t^{\alpha} \mathbb{P}\{X > t\} = c/\alpha$, and X is Pareto-tailed with tail index α.

Solution to Exercise 1.4.1. Let $\mathscr{G}$ be a directed acyclic graph and fix u in $\mathscr{G}$. Suppose to the contrary that every node reachable from u has positive out-degree. In this case, we can construct a directed walk from u of arbitrary length. But $\mathscr{G}$ has only finitely many nodes, so any such walk must eventually cycle. Contradiction.

Solution to Exercise 1.4.3. If (V, E) is undirected, then the adjacency matrix is symmetric.

Solution to Exercise 1.4.4. Let $A^{\top} = (a'_{ij})$, so that $a'_{ij} = a_{ji}$ for each i, j. By definition, we have

$$(j, k) \in E' \iff a'_{jk} > 0 \iff a_{kj} > 0 \iff (k, j) \in E,$$

which proves (i). Regarding (ii), to say that k is accessible from j in $\mathscr{G}'$ means that we can find vertices $i_1, \ldots, i_m$ that form a directed path from j to k under $\mathscr{G}'$, in the sense that $i_1 = j$, $i_m = k$, and each successive pair $(i_\ell, i_{\ell+1})$ is in E'. But then, by (i), $i_m, \ldots, i_1$ provides a directed path from k to j under $\mathscr{G}$, since each successive pair $(i_{\ell+1}, i_\ell)$ is in E.

Solution to Exercise 1.4.5. Recalling that $\partial/(\partial x_k) x^{\top} A x = (x^{\top} A)_k$, the first-order condition corresponding to (1.26), taking the actions of other players as given, is

$$x_k = \alpha(x^{\top} A)_k + \varepsilon_k \qquad (k \in [n]).$$

Concatenating into a row vector and then taking the transpose yields $x = \alpha A x + \varepsilon$, where we used the fact that A is symmetric. Since $r(\alpha A) = \alpha r(A)$, the condition $r(A) < 1/\alpha$ implies that $r(\alpha A) < 1$, so, by the Neumann series lemma, the unique solution is $x^* = (I - \alpha A)^{-1} \varepsilon$.

Solution to Exercise 1.4.6. When A is strongly connected, the Perron–Frobenius theorem tells us that $r(A) > 0$ and A has a unique (up to a scalar multiple) dominant right eigenvector satisfying $r(A)e = Ae$. Rearranging gives (1.32).

Solution to Exercise 1.4.10. When $\beta < 1/r(A)$ we have $r(\beta A) < 1$. Hence, we can express (1.36) as $\kappa = \mathbb{1} + \beta A \kappa$ and employ Theorem 1.2.5 to obtain the stated result.

Solution to Exercise 2.1.1. Fix $j \in [n]$. Since $a_{ij} = z_{ij}/x_j$, we have $\eta_j = \frac{\sum_{i=1}^{n} z_{ij}}{x_j}$. Hence, if $v_j > 0$, then $\eta_j < 1$.

Solution to Exercise 2.1.2. It follows easily from Assumption 2.1.1 that $\eta(A) < 1$. Moreover, since $A \geqslant 0$, the results in §1.2.3.4 imply that $r(A)$ is dominated by the maximum of the column sums of A. But this is precisely $\eta(A)$. Hence $r(A) \leqslant \eta(A) < 1$.

Solution to Exercise 2.1.3. Let (A, d) be as stated. When A is irreducible, $L := \sum_{i=1}^{\infty} A^i \gg 0$ and $x^* = Ld$. Since d is nontrivial, $x^* \gg 0$ follows from $L \gg 0$ and the definition of matrix multiplication.

Solution to Exercise 2.1.4. If $r(A) < 1$, then $I - A$ is nonsingular. At the same time, for the nontrivial solution x, we have $(I - A)x = 0$. Contradiction. If, on the other hand, $r(A) = 1$, then, since $r(A)$ is an eigenvalue (by the Perron–Frobenius theorem), we have $Ax = x$ for some $x \gg 0$. The uniqueness claim follows from the Perron–Frobenius theorem.

Solution to Exercise 2.1.7. Let λ be an eigenvalue of A, and let e be the corresponding eigenvector. Then, for all $i \in [n]$, we have

$$\sum_j a_{ij} e_j = \lambda e_i \quad \Longleftrightarrow \quad \sum_j \frac{z_{ij}}{x_j} e_j = \lambda e_i \quad \Longleftrightarrow \quad \sum_j f_{ij} \frac{e_j}{x_j} = \lambda \frac{e_i}{x_i},$$

where we have used the fact that $x \gg 0$. It follows that λ is an eigenvalue of F. The same logic runs in reverse, so A and F share eigenvalues. Hence $r(A) = r(F)$.

Solution to Exercise 2.2.2. We need to show that $\mathbb{1}^\top A^m \mathbb{1} = n(1 - \alpha)^m$ for any m. We prove this by induction, noting that $\mathbb{1}^\top A = (1 - \alpha)\mathbb{1}^\top$ by the CRS assumption. It follows immediately that $\mathbb{1}^\top A \mathbb{1} = n(1 - \alpha)$. Now suppose also that $\mathbb{1}^\top A^m \mathbb{1} = n(1 - \alpha)^m$ holds. Then

$$\mathbb{1}^\top A^{m+1} \mathbb{1} = \mathbb{1}^\top A A^m \mathbb{1} = (1 - \alpha)\mathbb{1}^\top A^m \mathbb{1} = n(1 - \alpha)^{m+1},$$

where the last step is by the induction hypothesis.

Solution to Exercise 2.2.3. Inserting (2.18) into (2.19) and differentiating with respect to ℓ_j and q_{ij} leads to the first-order conditions given in (2.20). It can be shown that these local maximizers are global maximizers, although we omit the details.

Solution to Exercise 2.2.5. By Exercise 2.2.1 we have $r(A) < 1$. Hence $L = (I - A)^{-1}$ is well defined, and, moreover, we can solve (2.22) using the Neumann series lemma, yielding $\rho = -(I - A^\top)^{-1}\varepsilon$. Since the inverse of the transpose is the transpose of the inverse, we can write this as $\rho = -L^\top \varepsilon$. Unpacking gives the equation stated in the exercise.

Solution to Exercise 2.2.7. Equation (2.24) can be expressed as $h_i = n^{-1} + \sum_j a_{ij} h_j$. Letting $h = (h_i)$ be a column vector in $\mathbb{R}^n$ and letting $\mathbb{1}$ be a column vector of ones, these n equations become $h = n^{-1}\mathbb{1} + Ah$. Since $r(A) < 1$, the unique solution is $h = n^{-1}(I - A)^{-1}\mathbb{1} = n^{-1}L\mathbb{1}$. Unpacking the vector equation gives the stated result.

Solution to Exercise 2.2.8. From the result in Exercise 2.2.2, we have

$$\mathbb{1}^\top h = \frac{1}{n}\mathbb{1}^\top \sum_{m \geqslant 0} A^m \mathbb{1} = \frac{1}{n} \sum_{m \geqslant 0} \mathbb{1}^\top A^m \mathbb{1} = \frac{1}{n} n \sum_{m \geqslant 0} (1 - \alpha)^m.$$

The last expression evaluates to $1/\alpha$, as was to be shown.

Solution to Exercise 2.2.9. This expression follows easily from the definition of variance and the independence of firm-level shocks, which allows us to pass the variance through the sum.

Solution to Exercise 2.2.11. Let $h^* := 1/(\alpha n)$. The claim is that h^* is the minimizer of $\|h\|$ on $\mathbb{R}^n_+$ under the constraint $\sum_{i=1}^n h_i = 1/\alpha$. Squaring the objective function and substituting the constraint into the objective by taking $h_n = 1/\alpha - h_1 - \cdots - h_{n-1}$, we are led to the equivalent problem of finding the minimizer of

$$f(h_1, \ldots, h_{n-1}) := h_1^2 + \cdots + h_{n-1}^2 + \left(\frac{1}{\alpha} - h_1 - \cdots - h_{n-1}\right)^2.$$

Since f is convex, any local minimizer is a global minimizer. Moreover, the first-order conditions give

$$h_i = \left(\frac{1}{\alpha} - h_1 - \cdots - h_{n-1}\right) = h_n.$$

for all i. Hence, the solution vector is constant over i. Letting c be this constant and using the constraint gives $nc = 1/\alpha$. The claim follows.

Solution to Exercise 2.2.12. Let h^* be an n-vector with $h_k^* = 1/\alpha$ for some k and $h_j^* = 0$ for other indices. Clearly $\|h^*\| = 1/\alpha$. Hence it suffices to show that, for any $h \in \mathbb{R}^n_+$ with $\sum_{i=1}^n h_i = 1/\alpha$, we have $\|h\| \leqslant 1/\alpha$.

Fix $h \in \mathbb{R}^n_+$ with $\sum_{i=1}^n h_i = 1/\alpha$. Since we are splitting $1/\alpha$ into n parts, we can express h as $(w_1/\alpha, \ldots, w_n/\alpha)$, where $0 \leqslant w_i \leqslant 1$ and $\sum_i w_i = 1$. By Jensen's inequality (Exercise A.5.7), we have

$$\sum_i \left(\frac{w_i}{\alpha}\right)^2 \leqslant \left(\sum_i \frac{w_i}{\alpha}\right)^2 = \frac{1}{\alpha^2}.$$

Taking the square root gives $\|h\| \leqslant 1/\alpha$, as was to be shown.

Solution to Exercise 2.3.3. For $\alpha > 0$ we always have $\|\alpha u\|_0 = \|u\|_0$, which violates positive homogeneity.

Solution to Exercise 2.3.6. Let $\|\cdot\|$ be a norm on $\mathbb{R}^n$, let (u_m) be a sequence in $\mathbb{R}^n$, and let u be a point in $\mathbb{R}^n$. To show that (i) implies (ii), we fix $a \in \mathbb{R}^n$ and observe that

for all $m \in \mathbb{N}$, $\ |\langle a, u_m \rangle - \langle a, u \rangle| = |\langle a, u_m - u \rangle| \leqslant \|u_m - u\|_1 \max_i |a_i|$.

Hence convergence in ℓ_1 norm implies (ii). In view of Exercise 2.3.5, convergence in $\|\cdot\|$ implies convergence in ℓ_1, so (i) $\implies$ (ii) is confirmed.

To show that (ii) implies (iii) at the j-th component, we just specialize a to the j-th canonical basis vector. Finally, to show that (iii) implies (i), we first note that, by the equivalence of norms, it is enough to show that pointwise convergence implies ℓ_1 convergence; that is,

$$\text{(iii)} \implies \|u_m - u\|_1 = \sum_{j \in [n]} |\langle \delta_j, u_m - u \rangle| \to 0,$$

where δ_j is the j-th canonical basis vector. To prove that this sum converges to zero, it suffices to show that every element of the sum converges to zero (see §A.3.2), which is true by (iii).

Solution to Exercise 2.3.7. Consider the claim that $u_m \to x$ and $v_m \to y$ in $\mathbb{R}^n$ implies $u_m + v_m \to x + y$. We know this is true in the scalar case $n = 1$. Moreover, Lemma 2.3.1 tells us that convergence in $\mathbb{R}^n$ holds if and only if it holds componentwise – which is just the scalar case. The rest of the proof is similar.

Solution to Exercise 2.3.8. The Frobenius norm reduces to the Euclidean norm for column and row vectors, so (2.32) requires that $|\langle A, B \rangle_F| \leqslant \|A\|_F \|B\|_F$. This bound certainly holds: It is the Cauchy–Schwarz inequality.

Solution to Exercise 2.3.9. Let

$$a := \sup_{u \neq 0} f(u), \quad \text{where} \quad f(u) := \frac{\|Au\|}{\|u\|}, \quad \text{and let } b := \sup_{\|u\|=1} \|Au\|.$$

Evidently $a \geqslant b$ because the supremum is over a larger domain. To see the reverse, fix $\varepsilon > 0$ and let u be a nonzero vector such that $f(u) > a - \varepsilon$. Let $\alpha := 1/\|u\|$ and let $u_b := \alpha u$. Then

$$b \geqslant \|Au_b\| = \frac{\|Au_b\|}{\|u_b\|} = \frac{\|\alpha Au\|}{\|\alpha u\|} = \frac{\alpha}{\alpha} \frac{\|Au\|}{\|u\|} = f(u) > a - \varepsilon.$$

Since ε was arbitrary, we have $b \geqslant a$.

Solution to Exercise 2.3.10. Let A and B be elements of $\mathbb{M}^{n \times k}$ and $\mathbb{M}^{n \times j}$, respectively. Fix $v \in \mathbb{R}^n$. Since $\|Au\| \leqslant \|A\| \cdot \|u\|$ for any vector u, we have $\|ABv\| \leqslant \|A\| \cdot \|Bv\| \leqslant \|A\| \cdot \|B\| \cdot \|v\|$, from which (2.32) easily follows.

Solution to Exercise 2.3.15. Let (A_m) and (B_m) have the stated properties. Regarding (i), we use the triangle inequality to obtain

$$\|A_m - A\| = \|A_m - B_m + B_m - A\| \leqslant \|A_m - B_m\| + \|B_m - A\|.$$

Both terms on the right converge to zero, which completes the proof.

Regarding (ii), we use the submultiplicative property to obtain $\|BA_mC - BAC\| \leqslant \|B\| \|A_m - A\| \|C\| \to 0$.

Solution to Exercise 2.3.17. Let $\| \cdot \|_a$ and $\| \cdot \|_b$ be two norms on $\mathbb{M}^{n \times n}$. By the results in §2.3.2.5, these norms are equivalent, so there exist constants M, N such that $\|A^k\|_a \leqslant M \|A^k\|_b \leqslant N \|A^k\|_a$ for all $k \in \mathbb{N}$.

$$\therefore \quad \|A^k\|_a^{1/k} \leqslant M^{1/k} \|A^k\|_b^{1/k} \leqslant N^{1/k} \|A^k\|_a^{1/k}$$

for all $k \in \mathbb{N}$. Taking $k \to \infty$, we see that the definition of the spectral radius is independent of the choice of norm.

Solution to Exercise 2.3.18. Since $r(A) < 1$, we can find a constant K and an $\varepsilon > 0$ such that $k \geqslant K$ implies $\|A^k\| < (1 - \varepsilon)^k$. Setting $M := \max_{k \leqslant K} \|A^k\|$ and $\delta := 1 - \varepsilon$ produces the desired constants.

Solution to Exercise 2.3.19. Suppose $r(A) < 1$. Iterating backwards on $x_t = Ax_{t-1} + d$ yields $x_t = d + Ad + \cdots + A^{t-1}d + A^t x_0$. By the Neumann series lemma, we have $x^* = \sum_{t \geqslant 0} A^t d$, so

$$x^* - x_t = \sum_{j > t} A^j d - A^t x_0.$$

Hence, with $\| \cdot \|$ as both the Euclidean vector norm and the matrix operator norm, we have

$$\|x^* - x_t\| = \left\| \sum_{j > t} A^j d - A^t x_0 \right\| \leqslant \sum_{j > t} \|A^j\| \|d\| - \|A^t\| \|x_0\|.$$

Using $r(A) < 1$ again, it now follows from Exercise 2.3.18 that $\|x^* - x_t\| \to 0$ as $t \to \infty$.

Solution to Exercise 2.3.20. We have $\|A^m\|_1 = n(1 - \alpha)^m$ and so $\|A^m\|_1^{1/m} = n^{1/m}(1 - \alpha)$. Taking $m \to \infty$ gives $r(A) = 1 - \alpha$.

Solution to Exercise 2.3.21. Let $\| \cdot \|$ be a norm on $\mathbb{R}^n$. From the Perron–Frobenius theorem (Theorem 1.2.6), when A is primitive, $\| r(A)^{-m} A^m x \| \rightarrow c$ as $m \rightarrow \infty$, where $c > 0$ whenever $x \gg 0$. Hence $\lim_{m \to \infty} \| A^m x \|^{1/m} = \lim_{m \to \infty} r(A) c^{1/m} = r(A)$.

Solution to Exercise 2.3.22. We prove only that the stated conditions on A imply that $A^\top$ is weakly chained substochastic, since the proof of the reverse implication is very similar. We set $a'_{ij} := a_{ji}$, so that $A^\top = (a'_{ij})$.

Let A have the stated properties. Since A has less than unit column sums, $A^\top$ has less than unit rows, so $A^\top$ is substochastic.

Now fix $m \in [n]$ and take $i \in [n]$ such that $i \rightarrow m$ under A and $\sum_k a_{ki} < 1$. By Exercise 1.4.4 on page 34, $i \rightarrow m$ under A is equivalent to $m \rightarrow i$ under $A^\top$. Moreover, $\sum_k a_{ki} < 1$ is equivalent to $\sum_k a'_{ik} < 1$. Hence $A^\top$ is weakly chained substochastic.

Solution to Exercise 2.3.23. Let A be the adjacency matrix of an input–output network such that value added is nonnegative in each sector. In what follows, we write a'_{ij} for the i,j-th element of $A^\top$, so that $a'_{ij} = a_{ji}$.

Let's say that A has property U if, for each sector in the network, there exists an upstream supplier with positive value added. Property U is equivalent to the statement that, for all $m \in [n]$, there is an $i \in [n]$ with $i \rightarrow m$ under A and $\sum_k a_{ki} < 1$. By Exercise 2.3.22, this is equivalent to the statement that $A^\top$ is weakly chained substochastic. Since $A^\top$ is substochastic, this is, in turn, equivalent to $r(A^\top) < 1$. But $r(A) = r(A^\top)$, so property U is equivalent to $r(A) < 1$.

Solution to Exercise 2.3.25. Let $A = \mathrm{diag}(a, 1)$, where $0 < a < 1$. Clearly $r(A) = 1$. Let $b^\top = (1,0)$, and let $x^\top = (1/(1-a), 0)$. Simple algebra shows that $x = Ax + b$.

Solution to Exercise 3.1.1. If the path fails to reach d in $n - 1$ steps, then, since $|V| = n$, there exists a vertex $x \in V$ that appears twice in $(x_1, \ldots, x_n)$. This means there exists a cycle from x, which contradicts our assumption that $\mathcal{G}$ is a directed acyclic graph.

Solution to Exercise 3.1.2. Fix $q \in U$ and $\sigma \in \Sigma$. Nonnegativity of $T_\sigma q$ is obvious. Also, $(T_\sigma q)(d) = c(d, d) + q(d) = 0$, where the first equality is by $\sigma(d) = d$ and the second is by $q(d) = 0$ and $c(d, d) = 0$. Hence $T_\sigma q \in U$, as required.

Solution to Exercise 3.2.1. Since prices are positive (more output means more revenue), we expect that both inequality constraints (see (3.10)) will hold with equality. Reading from the figure, the equalities are $2q_1 + 5q_2 = 30$ and $4q_1 + 2q_2 = 20$. Solving simultaneously leads to $q = (2.5, 5.0)$.

Solution to Exercise 3.2.3. The equality constraint $Ax = b$ can be replaced by the two inequality constraints $Ax \leq b$ and $-Ax \leq -b$. The constraint $x \geq 0$ can be replaced by $-x \leqslant 0$. If we unpack these matrix inequalities, row by row, we obtain a collection of constraints, each of which has the form $h^\top x \leqslant g$ for suitable $h \in \mathbb{R}^n$ and $g \in \mathbb{R}$. The claim now follows from the definition of a polyhedron on page 203.

Solution to Exercise 3.3.1. Fix $y \in \mathsf{Y}$. The distributions φ and ψ are assumed to be everywhere positive, so if (3.18) holds for T, then $\varphi(x)\mathbb{1}\{T(x) = y\} > 0$ for some location x. Hence, there exists an $x \in \mathsf{X}$ such that $T(x) = y$.

Solution to Exercise 3.3.2. One scenario where no Monge map exists is when $|\mathsf{Y}| > |\mathsf{X}|$. For example, suppose $\mathsf{X} = \{x_1\}$ and $\mathsf{Y} = \{y_1, y_2\}$, with $\varphi(x_1) = 1$ and $\psi(y_i) \in (0, 1)$ for $i = 1, 2$. Either x_1 is mapped to y_1 or it is mapped to y_2. In either case, the Monge map condition (3.18) fails for both y_1 and y_2.

Solution to Exercise 3.3.3. Let T be a self-map on $[n]$. If T is a Monge map, then, by the definition in (3.18), we must have $\sum_i (1/n)\mathbb{1}\{T(i) = j\} = 1/n$ for all j. If T is not a bijection, then there exist indices i, k, j such that $i \neq k$ and $T(i) = T(k) = j$. This clearly violates the previous equality.

Conversely, if T is a bijection on $[n]$, then T satisfies $\sum_i (1/n)\mathbb{1}\{T(i) = j\} = 1/n$ for all j. Hence T is a Monge map.

Solution to Exercise 3.3.6. Applying (3.24) on page 113, we have

$$\psi = \operatorname{vec}(\psi^\top) = \operatorname{vec}(\mathbb{1}_n^\top \pi I_m) = (I_m \otimes \mathbb{1}_n^\top)\operatorname{vec}(\pi).$$

Solution to Exercise 3.3.7. Let π be feasible for the primal problem, and let (w, p) be feasible for the dual. By dual feasibility, we have $c(x, y) \geqslant p(y) - w(x)$ for all x, y, so

$$\langle \pi, c \rangle \geqslant \sum_x \sum_y \pi(x, y)[p(y) - w(x)] = \sum_x \sum_y \pi(x, y)p(y) - \sum_x \sum_y \pi(x, y)w(x).$$

Rearranging and using primal feasibility now gives $\langle \pi, c \rangle \geqslant \langle p, \psi \rangle - \langle w, \varphi \rangle$. This proves the first claim.

To see that $D \leqslant P$ follows from the last inequality: Just fix $\pi \in \Pi(\varphi, \psi)$ and maximize over all feasible dual pairs to obtain $\langle \pi, c \rangle \geqslant D$. Now minimize over $\pi \in \Pi(\varphi, \psi)$.

Solution to Exercise 3.3.8. From $\min_{a \in A} f(a) = \max_{b \in B} g(b)$, we have $f(a) \geqslant g(b)$ for all $(a, b) \in A \times B$. Taking $(\bar{a}, \bar{b})$ with $f(\bar{a}) = g(\bar{b})$, we have $f(\bar{a}) = g(\bar{b}) \leqslant f(a)$ for any given $a \in A$. In particular, $\bar{a}$ minimizes f on A. The argument for $\bar{b}$ is similar.

Solution to Exercise 3.3.9. Since any outflow from some node i is matched by equal inflow into some node j, summing both sides of (3.34) across all $i \in V$ yields (3.32).

Solution to Exercise 3.3.11. Verifying the claim is just a matter of working with the definition of A. Fixing $i \in [n]$, we have

$$(Aq)(i) = \sum_{k=1}^{m} a_{ik} q_k = \sum_{k=1}^{m} \mathbb{1}\{e_k \text{ leaves } i\} q_k - \sum_{k=1}^{m} \mathbb{1}\{e_k \text{ points to } i\} q_k.$$

This is equal to $\sum_{j \in \mathcal{O}(i)} q(i, j) - \sum_{v \in \mathcal{I}(i)} q(v, i)$, as was to be shown.

Solution to Exercise 3.3.12. To the code that solves the original version of Example 3.3.1, we need to add

```
bounds = ((0, 5),
          (0, None),
          (0, None),
          (0, None))
```

and then change the function call to

```
result = linprog(c, A_eq=A, b_eq=b, method='highs-ipm', bounds=bounds)
print(result.x)
```

The output is `[5. 5. 5. 5.]`, which also agrees with our intuition.

Solution to Exercise 4.1.2. Point (i) is immediate from the definition of F. Regarding (ii), from $q(i, j) = q(i, j-1) + P(i, j)$ we have $P(i, j) = q(i, j) - q(i, j-1)$, which is the length of the interval $(q(i, j-1), q(i, j)]$. The probability that U_{t+1} falls in this interval is its length, which we just agreed is $P(i, j)$. The proof is now complete.

Solution to Exercise 4.1.3. P^k is stochastic for all $k \in \mathbb{N}$ by induction and the fact that the set of stochastic matrices is closed under multiplication (see §1.3.1.3).

Solution to Exercise 4.1.5. Let $\mathcal{M}$ be as described. In this setting, the requirement that the transition matrix P is stochastic implies that $p(x, x) = 1$ and $P(x, y) = \mathbb{1}\{x = y\}$. Thus, $P = I$, the $n \times n$ identity matrix. Every distribution is stationary because $\psi I = \psi$ for all $\psi \in \mathcal{D}(S)$.

Solution to Exercise 4.1.6. Let G be a continuous function from $[0, 1]$ to itself, and set $f(x) := Gx - x$. Since G is a self-map on $[0, 1]$, we have $f(0) = G0 \geqslant 0$ and $f(1) = G1 - 1 \leqslant 0$, so f is a continuous function on $[0, 1]$ satisfying $f(0) \geqslant 0$ and $f(1) \leqslant 0$. Existence of an x satisfying $f(x) = 0$ follows from the intermediate value theorem. The same x is a fixed point of G.

Solution to Exercise 4.1.7. Let P be a Markov matrix on finite set S. Suppose in particular that S has d elements, so we can identify functions in $\mathbb{R}^S$ with vectors in $\mathbb{R}^d$ and $\mathcal{D}(S)$ with the unit simplex in $\mathbb{R}^d$. The set $\mathcal{D}(S)$ is a closed, bounded, and convex subset of $\mathbb{R}^d$ that P maps into itself. As a linear matrix operation, the map $\psi \mapsto \psi P$ is continuous. Existence of a fixed point now follows from Brouwer's fixed point theorem (p. 141).

Solution to Exercise 4.2.2. Let $\mathcal{M}$ be a finite Markov model with states $S = \{1,2\}$ and edge set $E = \{(1,2),(2,2)\}$. Thus, the chain immediately moves to state 2 and stays there forever. The corresponding transition matrix is

$$P = \begin{pmatrix} 0 & 1 \\ 0 & 1 \end{pmatrix}.$$

If h is P-harmonic, then $h(x) = Ph(x) = h(2)$. Hence h is constant. This shows that P is ergodic. At the same time (S, E) is not strongly connected.

Solution to Exercise 4.2.3. Let $\mathcal{M}$ and A have the stated properties. Fix $x \in S$. Consider a P-chain (X_t) that starts at x. By property (b), there exists an $a \in A$ and a $k \leqslant n := |S|$ such that $\varepsilon_x := \mathbb{P}\{X_k = a\}$ is strictly positive. Once (X_t) enters A it never leaves, so $X_k = a$ implies $X_n \in A$. Hence $\mathbb{P}\{X_n \in A\} \geqslant \varepsilon_x$. With $\varepsilon := \min_{x \in S} \varepsilon_x > 0$, we then have $\mathbb{P}\{X_n \in A\} \geqslant \varepsilon$ for any initial condition x. Another way to state this is $\sum_{y \in A^c} P^n(x, y) \leqslant 1 - \varepsilon$ for all $x \in S$, which proves the first claim.

Regarding the second claim, fix $\psi \in \mathcal{D}(S)$ and let $\psi_t = \psi P^t$ for all t. Observe that, for fixed $m \in \mathbb{N}$, we have $\psi_{(m+1)n} = P^n \psi_{mn}$. As a result, for $y \in A^c$, we have

$$\psi_{(m+1)n}(y) = \sum_{x \in S} P^n(x, y)\psi_{mn}(x) = \sum_{x \in A^c} P^n(x, y)\psi_{mn}(x).$$

Summing over y gives

$$\sum_{y \in A^c} \psi_{(m+1)n}(y) = \sum_{y \in A^c} \sum_{x \in A^c} P^n(x, y)\psi_{mn}(x) = \sum_{x \in A^c} \left[\sum_{y \in A^c} P^n(x, y) \right] \psi_{mn}(x).$$

Let $\eta_t := \sum_{x \in A^c} \psi_t(x)$ be the amount of probability mass on A^c at time t. Using the first claim and the definition of η_t now gives $\eta_{(m+1)n} \leqslant (1 - \varepsilon)\eta_{mn}$. Hence $\eta_{mn} \to 0$ as $m \to \infty$. At the same time, $\psi_{mn} \to \psi^*$ as $m \to \infty$, so

$$\sum_{x \in A^c} \psi^*(x) = \lim_{m \to \infty} \sum_{x \in A^c} \psi_{mn}(x) = \lim_{m \to \infty} \eta_{mn} = 0.$$

The second claim is now verified.

Solution to Exercise 4.2.4. Regarding part (i), the triangle inequality, combined with the assumption that $\varphi, \psi \in \mathcal{D}(S)$, gives the bound

$$\sum_x |\varphi(x) - \psi(x)| \leqslant \sum_x |\varphi(x)| + \sum_x |\psi(x)| \leqslant 2.$$

Regarding part (ii), if P is a stochastic matrix, then

$$\rho(\varphi P, \psi P) = \sum_y \left| \sum_x P(x, y)\varphi(x) - \sum_x P(x, y)\psi(x) \right| \leqslant \sum_y \sum_x P(x, y) \left| \varphi(x) - \psi(x) \right|.$$

Swapping the order of summation and using $\sum_y P(x, y) = 1$ proves the claim.

Solution to Exercise 4.2.7. Fix $\varphi, \psi \in \mathscr{D}(S)$. From (4.27) we know that (4.29) is true when $t = 1$. Now suppose it is true at t. Then, using the fact that (4.27) holds for any pair of distributions,

$$\rho(\varphi P^{t+1}, \psi P^{t+1}) \leqslant (1 - \alpha(P))\rho(\varphi P^t, \psi P^t) \leqslant (1 - \alpha(P))^{t+1}\rho(\varphi, \psi),$$

where the last step uses the induction hypothesis. Hence (4.29) also holds at $t + 1$ and, by induction, at all $t \in \mathbb{N}$.

Solution to Exercise 4.2.9. If $\mathcal{M}$ is strongly connected and aperiodic, then P is primitive, in which case there exists a $k \in \mathbb{N}$ with $P^k \gg 0$. Clearly $\alpha(P^k) > 0$.

Solution to Exercise 4.2.11. All elements of G are strictly positive, so a directed edge exists between every pair of pages $u, v \in W$. This clearly implies strong connectedness.

Solution to Exercise 4.2.12. For any $u, u', v \in W$, we have $G(u, v) \wedge G(u', v) \geqslant 1 - \delta$. Hence $\alpha(G) \geqslant 1 - \delta$. Therefore, by (4.31), we have

$$\rho(\psi G^t, g^*) \leqslant 2\delta^t.$$

Solution to Exercise 4.2.14. If $\mathcal{S}$ is strongly connected and aperiodic, then the adjacency matrix T is primitive, so there exists a $k \in \mathbb{N}$ such that $T^k \gg 0$. Hence $\alpha(T^k) > 0$, and Proposition 4.2.6 applies.

Solution to Exercise 5.1.3. From the bound in Exercise 5.1.2, we obtain

$$\|u_m - u_k\| \leqslant \frac{\lambda^m}{1 - \lambda}\lambda^i\|u_0 - u_1\| \qquad (m, k \in \mathbb{N} \text{ with } m < k).$$

Hence (u_m) is Cauchy, as claimed.

Solution to Exercise 5.1.5. Let S be complete, let F be a self-map on S, and let F^k be a uniform contraction. Let u^* be the unique fixed point of F^k. Fix $\varepsilon > 0$. We can choose n such that $\|F^{nk}Fu^* - u^*\| < \varepsilon$. But then

$$\|Fu^* - u^*\| = \|FF^{nk}u^* - u^*\| = \|F^{nk}Fu^* - u^*\| < \varepsilon.$$

Since ε was arbitrary, we have $\|Fu^* - u^*\| = 0$, implying that u^* is a fixed point of F.

Regarding convergence, fix $u \in S$. Given $n \in \mathbb{N}$, there exist integers $j(n)$ and $i(n)$ such that $n = j(n)k + i(n)$, and $j(n) \to \infty$ as $n \to \infty$. Hence

$$\|F^n u - u^*\| = \|F^{j(n)k+i(n)}u - u^*\| = \|F^{j(n)k}F^{i(n)}u - u^*\| \to 0 \qquad (n \to \infty),$$

by the assumptions on F^k. Convergence implies uniqueness of the fixed point (why?).

Solution to Exercise 5.1.6. If the risk-free real interest rate r is positive, then \$100 received now can be converted with probability one into $(1 + r)100 > 100$ dollars in one year.

Solution to Exercise 5.1.7. Take $q_k \to q$, where (q_k) is a sequence of n-vectors contained in U. By Exercise A.2.4 on page 189, since $q_k \geqslant 0$ for all k, we must have $q \geqslant 0$. It remains only to show that $q(n) = 0$. As $q_k \in U$ for all k, we have $q_k(n) = 0$ for all k. By Lemma 2.3.1, we also have $q_k(n) \to q(n)$. Hence $q(n) = 0$.

Solution to Exercise 5.1.8. We need to show that if $p, q \in U$ and $p \leqslant q$, then $Tp \leqslant Tq$. This follows easily from the definition of T in (5.5).

Solution to Exercise 5.1.9. Fix $q \in U$, $\alpha \in \mathbb{R}_+$, and $x \in V$. By definition,

$$T(q + \alpha \mathbb{1})(x) = \min_{y \in \mathscr{O}(x)} \{c(x, y) + \beta q(y) + \alpha \beta\} = Tq(x) + \alpha \beta.$$

Hence $T(q + \alpha \mathbb{1}) = Tq + \beta \alpha \mathbb{1}$ as claimed.

Solution to Exercise 5.1.10. Fix $x, y \in \mathbb{R}_+^n$ and $k \in \mathbb{N}$. By the inequalities in §A.1.1, applied pointwise to vectors, we have

$$|Gx - Gy| = |(Ax + d) \wedge \bar{x} - (AGy + d) \wedge \bar{x}| \leqslant |Ax + d - (Ay + d)|.$$

This proves the claim because, by Exercise A.2.5,

$$|Ax + d - (Ay + d)| = |A(x - y)| \leqslant A|x - y|.$$

Solution to Exercise 5.1.11. Since G is a self-map on $[a, b]$, we have $Ga \in [a, b]$ and hence $a \leqslant Ga$. As G is order-preserving, applying G to this inequality yields $Ga \leqslant G^2 a$. Continuing in this way (or using induction) proves that $(G^k a)$ is increasing. The proof for $(G^k b)$ is similar.

If $Gx = x$ for some $x \in [a, b]$, then, since $a \leqslant x$, we have $Ga \leqslant Gx = x$. Iterating on this inequality gives $G^k a \leqslant x$ for all k.

Solution to Exercise 5.1.12. Clearly G is a self-map on $S := [0, \bar{x}]$. Since $A \geqslant 0$, we have $Gx \leqslant Gy$ for all $x, y \in S$. From this it follows easily that G is order-preserving. Theorem 5.1.5 now guarantees existence of at least one fixed point.

Solution to Exercise 5.1.13. By Exercise A.5.8, the minimum of two concave functions is concave. Since $Fx = \bar{x}$ and $Hx = Ax + b$ are both concave, the claim holds.

Solution to Exercise 5.2.1. In essence, this holds because compositions of continuous functions are continuous. Nonetheless, here is a more explicit proof: Recalling the inequalities in §A.1.1, applied pointwise to vectors, we have, for any $p, q \in \mathbb{R}^n$,

$$|Tp - Tq| \leqslant |(e + p\Pi) \wedge x) - (e + q\Pi) \wedge x)| \leqslant |(p - q)\Pi|.$$

Since, for the Euclidean norm, $\|\,|u|\,\| = \|u\|$ and $u, v \geqslant 0$ with $u \leqslant v$ implies $\|u\| \leqslant \|v\|$, we then have $\|Tp - Tq\| \leqslant \|(p - q)\Pi\| \leqslant \|p - q\| \|\Pi\|_o$. It follows easily that if $\|p_n - p\| \to 0$, then $\|Tp_n - Tp\| \to 0$ also holds.

Solution to Exercise 5.2.2. Since $\Pi \geqslant 0$, we always have $p\Pi \leqslant q\Pi$ whenever $p \leqslant q$. As a result, $p \mapsto a - d + p\Pi$ is order-preserving and hence so is T. Moreover, for any $p \in S := [0, x]$, we have $Tp \in S$. Hence, by Theorem 5.1.5, T has a fixed point in S.

What else can we say about equilibria in this setting? By the same theorem, T has a least fixed point p^* and a greatest fixed point p^{**} in S. Moreover, since T is continuous, $T^k 0 \uparrow p^*$ and $T^k x \downarrow p^{**}$.

Solution to Exercise 5.2.3. Fix $p, q \in S$. Using the inequalities for min and max in §A.1.1, applied pointwise, we have

$$|Tp - Tq| \leqslant |e + p\Pi - (e + q\Pi)| = |(p - q)\Pi| \leqslant |p - q|\Pi.$$

After transposing both sides of this equation, we see that, when $r(\Pi) < 1$, the conditions of of Proposition 5.1.3 hold. The result follows. (If you prefer, instead of taking transposes, just use the proof of Proposition 5.1.3 directly, modified slightly to use the fact that we are operating on row vectors.)

Solution to Exercise 5.2.4. Let $\mathscr{G} = (V, E, w)$ be a financial network and a directed acyclic graph. By Proposition 5.2.1, it suffices to show that, for each bank $i \in V$, there exists a bank $j \in V$ with $i \to j$ and such that j has zero inter-bank liabilities. To this end, fix $i \in V$. By the directed acyclic graph property, we know that there exists a $j \in V$ with $i \to j$ and $\mathscr{O}(j) = 0$. But if $\mathscr{O}(j) = 0$, then j has no inter-bank liabilities. The claim follows.

Solution to Exercise 5.2.5. Let $\mathscr{G}$ be a financial network such that (E1) and (E2) hold. Since $e \gg 0$, we have

$$p \in S \quad \Longrightarrow \quad Tp := ((e + p\Pi) \wedge x) \vee 0 = (e + p\Pi) \wedge x.$$

By an argument identical to that employed for Exercise 5.1.13 on page 169, T is a concave operator on $S = [0, x]$. Evidently T is order-preserving. Finally, by (E1), we have $x_i > 0$ for all i, so $x \gg 0$ and hence $T0 = e \wedge x \gg 0$. It now follows directly from Du's theorem that T has a unique fixed point in S.

Solution to Exercise 5.2.6. Let $\mathscr{G}$ be such that every node is cash-accessible. Set

$$\delta := \frac{1}{n^2} \cdot \min \left\{ \{x_i : i \in V\} \cup \{e_i : i \in V \text{ s.t. } e_i > 0\} \right\}.$$

Let $\hat{e}$ be defined by $\hat{e}_i = 1$ if $e_i > 0$ and zero otherwise. We claim that, for all $m \leqslant n$,

$$T^m 0 \geqslant \delta(\hat{e} + \hat{e}\Pi + \cdots + \hat{e}\Pi^{m-1}). \tag{5.14}$$

This holds at $m = 1$ because $T0 = e \wedge x \geqslant \delta \hat{e}$. Now suppose (5.14) holds at some $m \leqslant n - 1$. Then, since T is order-preserving, we obtain

$$T^{m+1}0 \geqslant (\delta(\hat{e} + \hat{e}\Pi + \cdots + \hat{e}\Pi^{m-1})\Pi + e) \wedge x$$

$$\geqslant (\delta(\hat{e} + \hat{e}\Pi + \cdots + \hat{e}\Pi^{m})) \wedge x.$$

Since $\hat{e} + \hat{e}\Pi + \cdots + \hat{e}\Pi^{m} \leqslant n^2 \mathbb{1}$, where $\mathbb{1}$ is a vector of ones, and since $(\delta n^2 \mathbb{1}) \leqslant x$ by the definition of δ, we have $T^{m+1}0 \geqslant \delta(\hat{e} + \hat{e}\Pi + \cdots + \hat{e}\Pi^{m})$. This argument confirms that (5.14) holds for all $m \leqslant n$.

We now claim that $T^n 0 \gg 0$. In view of (5.14), it suffices to show that, for any $j \in V$, there exists a $k < n$ with $(\hat{e}\Pi^k)(j) = \sum_{i \in V} \hat{e}_i \Pi^k_{ij} > 0$. Since every node in S is cash-accessible, we know there exists an $i \in V$ with $e_i > 0$, and j is accessible from i. For this i we can choose $k \in \mathbb{N}$ with $k < n$ and $\Pi^k_{ij} = \hat{e}_i \Pi^k_{ij} > 0$. We conclude that $T^n 0 \gg 0$, as claimed.

Solution to Exercise 5.2.7. Let ψ be a stationary distribution for Π. Suppose λ is a constant in $[0, 1]$, $p = \lambda \psi$, and $x = \psi$. Then $e = 0$ implies $Tp = (e + \lambda \psi \Pi) \wedge x = (\lambda \psi) \wedge \psi = \lambda \psi = p$. Since λ was arbitrary in $[0, 1]$, there is a continuum of equilibria.

Solution to Exercise 5.2.8. The set N is an absorbing set, since, by definition, P is not accessible from N, and A cannot be accessible because otherwise P would also be accessible. The set P is also absorbing because if $j \in P^c$ is accessible from some $i \in P$, then j is cash-accessible. But then $j \in P$, which is a contradiction.

Solution to Exercise 5.2.9. Since $C \geqslant 0$, Lemma 1.2.7, we have $r(C) \leqslant \max_j \text{colsum}_j(C)$. In view of Assumption 5.2.1, this maximum is strictly less than one. Hence $r(C) < 1$, and, by the Neumann series lemma, $I - C$ is invertible and $(I - C)^{-1} = \sum_{k \geqslant 0} C^k$. The last equality implies $b \geqslant 0$ when $b = (I - C)^{-1}e$.

Solution to Exercise 5.2.10. Consider the condition $\sum_{i \in V} c_{ij} \leqslant 1$ for all $j \in V$, with strict inequality for at least one j. Since $C \geqslant 0$, this implies that $C^\top$ is weakly chained substochastic, by Exercise 2.3.22. Hence $r(C) = r(C^\top) < 1$, by Proposition 2.3.5. Hence $I - C$ is invertible, by the Neumann series lemma.

Solution to Exercise 5.2.11. We have

$$\sum_i b_i = \mathbb{1}'b = \mathbb{1}'e + \mathbb{1}'Ce + \mathbb{1}'C^2e + \cdots \geqslant \mathbb{1}'e + \mathbb{1}'Ce.$$

Hence it suffices to show that $\mathbb{1}'Ce > 0$. This will be true if at least one column of Ce has a nonzero entry. Since $e \gg 0$, we require only that $c_{ij} > 0$ for some i, j, which is true by assumption.

Solution to Exercise 5.2.12. Observe that $v_i \leqslant v'_i$ implies $f(v_i) \geqslant f(v'_i)$. As a result, the vector-valued map $v \mapsto -f(v)$ is order-preserving, and hence so is T.

Moreover, for $v \in [d, \bar{v}]$, we have

$$d = A(e - \beta \mathbb{1}) \leqslant Tv := A(e - f(v)) \leqslant Ae = \bar{v},$$

so T is a self-map on $[d, \bar{v}]$. It follows directly from Theorem 5.1.5 that T has a least and greatest fixed point in S.

Solution to Exercise 5.2.13. First, $v_k := T^k d$ is increasing, as just discussed. Second, this sequence can take only finitely many values, since T has finite range. As (v_k) is increasing, it cannot cycle, so it must converge in finitely many steps. Let v' be this limiting value, and let K be the number of steps required for (v_k) to attain v'. Since $v_k = v'$ for all $k \geqslant K$, we have

$$Tv' = TT^K v' = T^{K+1} v' = v',$$

so v' is a fixed point of T in S. Moreover, if v'' is any other fixed point of T in S, then $d \leqslant v''$, and hence, by the order-preserving property, $v_k = T^k d \leqslant T^k v'' = v''$ for all k. Hence $v' \leqslant v''$. Thus, v' is the least fixed point of T.

Solution to Exercise A.1.1. Fix $a, b \in \mathbb{R}_+$ and $c \in \mathbb{R}$. By (A.2), we have

$$a \wedge c = (a - b + b) \wedge c \leqslant (|a - b| + b) \wedge c \leqslant |a - b| \wedge c + b \wedge c.$$

Thus, $a \wedge c - b \wedge c \leqslant |a - b| \wedge c$. Reversing the roles of a and b gives $b \wedge c - a \wedge c \leqslant |a - b| \wedge c$. This proves the claim in Exercise A.1.1.

Solution to Exercise A.1.2. Suppose first that f is one-to-one. We construct a left inverse g as follows. For $y \in \text{range}(f)$, let $g(y)$ be the unique x such that $f(x) = y$. (Uniqueness is by the one-to-one property.) For $y \notin \text{range}(f)$, let $g(y) = \bar{x}$, where $\bar{x}$ is any point in S. The function g is a left inverse of f because, for any $x \in S$, the point $y = f(x)$ is in $\text{range}(f)$, and $g(y) = x$. Hence $g(f(x)) = x$.

Suppose next that f has a left inverse g. Suppose further that x and x' are points in S with $f(x) = f(x')$. Then $g(f(x)) = g(f(x'))$. Since g is a left inverse, this yields $x = x'$. Hence f is one-to-one.

Solution to Exercise A.1.3. Let G and S be as stated in the exercise. Regarding uniqueness, suppose that G has two distinct fixed points x and y in S. Since $G^m x = \bar{x}$ and $G^m y = \bar{x}$, we have $G^m x = G^m y$. But x and y are distinct fixed points, so $x = G^m x$ must be distinct from $y = G^m y$. Contradiction.

Regarding the claim that $\bar{x}$ is a fixed point, we recall that $G^k x = \bar{x}$ for $k \geqslant m$. Hence $G^m \bar{x} = \bar{x}$ and $G^{m+1} \bar{x} = \bar{x}$. But then

$$G\bar{x} = GG^m \bar{x} = G^{m+1} \bar{x} = \bar{x},$$

so $\bar{x}$ is a fixed point of G.

Solution to Exercise A.1.4. In polar form, we have $u = re^{i\varphi}$ and $v = se^{i\psi}$, so $uv = rs\,e^{i(\varphi+\psi)}$. Hence $|uv| = rs$ (see (A.8)), which is equal to $|u||v|$.

Solution to Exercise A.2.5. Fix $B \in \mathbb{M}^{m \times k}$ with $b_{ij} \geqslant 0$ for all i, j. Pick any $i \in [m]$ and $x \in \mathbb{R}^k$. By the triangle inequality, we have $|\sum_j b_{ij} x_j| \leqslant \sum_j b_{ij} |x_j|$. Stacking these inequalities yields $|Bx| \leqslant B|x|$, as was to be shown.

Solution to Exercise A.3.1. Let $x_n = -5n + n^2$. Then $|x_n| \leqslant 5n + n^2 \leqslant 6n^2$. Hence $(x_n) = O(n^2)$. Regarding the second claim, suppose to the contrary that $(x_n) = O(n)$. Then we can take an M such that $|x_n| \leqslant Mn$ for all $n \in \mathbb{N}$. But then $x_n = -5n + n^2 \leqslant Mn$ for all n. Dividing by n yields $n \leqslant 5 + M$ for all n. Contradiction.

Solution to Exercise A.3.9. If $x_n \to x$ in $\mathbb{R}^d$ and f and g are continuous, then $f(x_n) \to f(x)$ and $g(x_n) \to g(x)$ in $\mathbb{R}^k$. But then, by Proposition A.3.2, $\alpha f(x_n) + \beta g(x_n)$ converges to $\alpha f(x) + \beta g(x)$ in $\mathbb{R}^k$, as was to be shown.

Solution to Exercise A.3.10. Here's the answer for f: Take (x_n) converging to x in $\mathbb{R}^d$. Applying the inequalities in §A.1.1 pointwise to vectors, we have

$$0 \leqslant |f(x_n) - f(x)| = |x_n \wedge a - x \wedge a| \leqslant |x_n - x|.$$

Taking the Euclidean norm over these vectors and using $|u| \leqslant |v|$ implies $\|u\| \leqslant \|v\|$ yields $\|f(x_n) - f(x)\| \leqslant \|x_n - x\| \to 0$. Similar arguments can be applied to g.

Solution to Exercise A.4.4. Regarding the first claim, let $E = \{u_1, \ldots, u_k\}$ be linearly independent. Suppose that $\{u_1, \ldots, u_m\}$ is linearly dependent for some $m < k$. Then we can find a nonzero vector $(\alpha_1, \ldots, \alpha_m)$ such that $\sum_{i=1}^m \alpha_i u_i = 0$. Setting $\alpha_i = 0$ for i in $\{m + 1, \ldots, k\}$ yields $\sum_{i=1}^k \alpha_i u_i = 0$, contradicting independence of E.

Regarding the second claim, suppose that $E \subset F$ and E is linearly dependent. If F is linearly independent, then we have a violation of the first claim. Hence F is linearly dependent.

Solution to Exercise A.4.5. Regarding (i), if $Ax = Ay = 0$, then $A(\alpha x + \beta y) = \alpha Ax + \beta Ay = 0$, so null A is a linear subspace. Regarding (ii), suppose that null $A = \{0\}$. This means that the only $x \in \mathbb{R}^k$ satisfying $Ax = 0$ is the zero vector, which is equivalent to linear independence of the columns of A.

Solution to Exercise A.4.6. For part (i) just set $V = \mathbb{R}^n$ in Theorem A.4.4. Regarding part (ii), let A and U be as stated, with $|A| =: m > \dim U$. Suppose to the contrary that A is linearly independent. Then A is a basis for span A, and, therefore, $\dim \text{span } A = m > \dim U$. At the same time, since $A \subset U$ and U is a linear subspace, we have span $A \subset U$. Hence, by Theorem A.4.4, we have $m \leqslant \dim U$. Contradiction.

Solution to Exercise A.4.8. Here's a proof by contradiction: Let A be as stated. Suppose to the contrary that A^{-1} fails to be linear. Then we can find $\alpha, \beta \in \mathbb{R}$ and $x, y \in \mathbb{R}^n$ such that $A^{-1}(\alpha x + \beta y)$ and $\alpha A^{-1}x + \beta A^{-1}y$ are distinct points. Since A is a bijection, their images under A are also distinct, so

$$\alpha x + \beta y \neq A(\alpha A^{-1}x + \beta A^{-1}y).$$

Linearity of A leads to a contradiction.

Solution to Exercise A.4.10. Fix $u, v \in L^{\perp}$ and $\alpha, \beta \in \mathbb{R}$. If $z \in L$, then

$$\langle \alpha u + \beta v, z \rangle = \alpha \langle u, z \rangle + \beta \langle v, z \rangle = \alpha \times 0 + \beta \times 0 = 0.$$

Hence $\alpha u + \beta v \in L^{\perp}$, as was to be shown.

Solution to Exercise A.4.13. If O is an orthonormal basis of L, then, by definition, O spans L. In addition, the elements of O are independent because they are orthogonal and nonzero.

Solution to Exercise A.5.1. For part (i), let $S = \{x \in \mathbb{R}^n_+ : \mathbb{1}^{\top} x \leqslant 1\}$ be the unit simplex, where $\mathbb{1}$ is a column vector of ones. Fix $u, v \in S$ and $\lambda \in [0, 1]$. We have

$$\lambda u + (1 - \lambda)v \geqslant 0$$

and

$$\mathbb{1}^{\top}(\lambda u + (1 - \lambda)v) = \lambda \mathbb{1}^{\top} u + (1 - \lambda)\mathbb{1}^{\top} v \leqslant \lambda + (1 - \lambda) = 1.$$

Hence S is a convex set.

For part (ii), fix $u, v \in B$, $\lambda \in [0, 1]$ and $a \in \mathbb{R}^n, \varepsilon > 0$. We have

$$\|\lambda u + (1 - \lambda)v - a\| = \|\lambda(u - a) + (1 - \lambda)(v - a)\| \leqslant \lambda\|u - a\| + (1 - \lambda)\|v - a\|$$
$$\leqslant \lambda\varepsilon + (1 - \lambda)\varepsilon = \varepsilon.$$

Hence B is convex.

Regarding part (iii), let (S_i) be a convex set for $i = 1, 2, \cdots, n$. Fix $u, v \in \cap_{i=1}^{n} S_i$ and $\lambda \in [0, 1]$. We have

$$z = \lambda u + (1 - \lambda)v \in S_i \qquad \text{for all } i.$$

This implies $z \in \cap_{i=1}^{n} S_i$, and hence $\cap_{i=1}^{n} S_i$ is convex.

Solution to Exercise A.5.2. Fix $u, v \in H_0$, $\lambda \in [0, 1]$, $b \in \mathbb{R}$ and nonzero $c \in \mathbb{R}^n$. Then

$$(\lambda u + (1 - \lambda)v)^{\top} c = \lambda u^{\top} c + (1 - \lambda)v^{\top} c = \lambda b + (1 - \lambda)b = b.$$

Thus H_0 is convex. The proof that H_1 is convex is similar.

Solution to Exercise A.5.4. Regarding part (i), let C and D be two cones. Fix $x \in C \cap D$ and $\alpha > 0$. Since $x \in C$ and $x \in D$, and since both are cones, we have $\alpha x \in C \cap D$. Hence $C \cap D$ is a cone.

Regarding part (ii), suppose first that C is a convex cone, and fix $x, y \in C$. Since C is convex, it must be that $(1/2)(x + y) \in C$. Since C is a cone, we can scale by 2 without leaving C. Hence $x + y \in C$. Suppose next that C is a cone and closed under addition. Fix $\alpha \in (0, 1)$ and $x, y \in C$. Since C is a cone, we have $\alpha x \in C$ and $(1 - \alpha)y \in C$. Since C is closed under addition, it follows that $\alpha x + (1 - \alpha)y \in C$. Hence C is convex.

Solution to Exercise A.5.6. Every linear function is both convex and concave.

Solution to Exercise A.5.8. It suffices to prove these results in the scalar case $n = k = 1$, since the vector results are just element-by-element extensions of the scalar case. We focus on the setting where each g_i is convex, as the concave case is similar.

In general, for scalars $\{a_i\}_{i=1}^m$ and $\{b_i\}_{i=1}^m$, we always have

$$\max_i \{a_i + b_i\} \leqslant \max_i \{a_i\} + \max_i \{b_i\}.$$

Hence, in the scalar case, when all g_is are convex, we have, for any $\lambda \in [0, 1]$ and $x, y \in C$,

$$\max_i \{g_i(\lambda x + (1 - \lambda)y)\} \leqslant \max_i \{\lambda g_i(x) + (1 - \lambda)g_i(y)\} \leqslant \lambda \max_i g_i(x) + (1 - \lambda) \max_i g_i(y).$$

This proves the scalar case (and, by extension, the vector case).

Solution to Exercise A.6.1. Regarding part (i), let f and g be as stated. Since g is strictly increasing, we have

$$f(x^*) \geqslant f(x), \quad \forall x \in D \qquad \Longleftrightarrow \qquad g(f(x^*)) \geqslant g(f(x)), \quad \forall x \in D.$$

This proves the equivalence claimed in part (i). (Note why the strictly increasing property of g cannot be weakened here.) The proof of (ii) is similar, with the second inequality reversed.

Solution to Exercise A.6.2. Let f and C be as described, and let u^* be a local minimizer. Suppose, contrary to the claim in the exercise, that there exists a point u in C such that $f(u) < f(u^*)$. Then, by convexity, for each λ in $[0, 1]$, we have

$$f(\lambda u + (1 - \lambda)u^*) \leqslant \lambda f(u) + (1 - \lambda)f(u^*) < f(u^*).$$

Taking $\lambda \to 0$, we can find a point $v := \lambda u + (1 - \lambda)u^*$ arbitrarily close to u^* such that $f(v) < f(u^*)$. This contradicts the definition of a local minimizer.

Solution to Exercise A.7.1. Regarding the first claim, suppose that $g(x) = 0$ and $h(x) \leqslant 0$, so that $x \in F(g, h)$. In this case,

$$\hat{f}(x) = \max_{\theta \in \Theta} L(x, \theta) = f(x) + \max_{\lambda \in \mathbb{R}^m} \sum_i \lambda_i g_i(x) + \max_{\mu \in \mathbb{R}_+^k} \sum_i \mu_i h_i(x) = f(x).$$

$$(\text{A.18})$$

Hence $\hat{f} = f$ on $F(g, h)$, and claim (i) is verified.

Regarding claim (ii), suppose that $g_i(x)$ deviates from zero for some i. Then $\max_{\lambda \in \mathbb{R}^m} \sum_i \lambda_i g_i(x)$ equals $+\infty$, so $\hat{f}(x) = +\infty$. In addition, if $h_i(x) > 0$ for some i, then $\max_{\mu \in \mathbb{R}_+^k} \sum_i \mu_i h_i(x) = +\infty$, so, once again $\hat{f}(x) = +\infty$. We have confirmed that $\hat{f} = +\infty$ whenever $x \notin F(g, h)$.

Solution to Exercise A.7.2. Pick any $x' \in E$ and $\theta \in \Theta$. We have $L(x', \theta) \geqslant \min_x L(x, \theta)$, so

$$\max_\theta L(x', \theta) \geqslant \max_\theta \min_x L(x, \theta).$$

$$\therefore \quad \min_x \max_\theta L(x, \theta) \geqslant \max_\theta \min_x L(x, \theta).$$

References

Acemoglu, D. and Azar, P. D. (2020). Endogenous production networks. *Econometrica*, 88(1):33–82.

Acemoglu, D., Carvalho, V. M., Ozdaglar, A., and Tahbaz-Salehi, A. (2012). The network origins of aggregate fluctuations. *Econometrica*, 80(5):1977–2016.

Acemoglu, D., Ozdaglar, A., and Pattathil, S. (2023). Learning, diversity and adaptation in changing environments: The role of weak links. Technical report, National Bureau of Economic Research.

Acemoglu, D., Ozdaglar, A., and Siderius, J. (2021a). Misinformation: Strategic sharing, homophily, and endogenous echo chambers. Technical report, National Bureau of Economic Research.

Acemoglu, D., Ozdaglar, A., Siderius, J., and Tahbaz-Salehi, A. (2021b). Systemic credit freezes in financial lending networks. *Mathematics and Financial Economics*, 15(1): 185–232.

Acemoglu, D., Ozdaglar, A., and Tahbaz-Salehi, A. (2016). Networks, shocks, and systemic risk. In *The Oxford Handbook of the Economics of Networks*. Oxford University Press.

Aggarwal, C. C. (2020). *Linear Algebra and Optimization for Machine Learning*. Springer.

Aliprantis, C. D. and Border, Kim, C. (1999). *Infinite Dimensional Analysis: A Hitchhiker's Guide*. Springer-Verlag, 2 edition.

Allouch, N. (2015). On the private provision of public goods on networks. *Journal of Economic Theory*, 157:527–552.

Amarasinghe, A., Hodler, R., Raschky, P., and Zenou, Y. (2020). Key players in economic development. Technical report, IZA Discussion Paper.

Amini, H. and Minca, A. (2020). Clearing financial networks: Impact on equilibrium asset prices and seniority of claims. *Tutorials in Operations Research*, pages 154–175. DOI https://doi.org/10.1287/educ.2020.0221.

Antràs, P. (2020). *Global Production: Firms, Contracts, and Trade Structure*. Princeton University Press.

Antràs, P., Chor, D., Fally, T., and Hillberry, R. (2012). Measuring the upstreamness of production and trade flows. *American Economic Review*, 102(3):412–416.

Ascenzi, E. and Palanza, F. (2021). How to control electric autonomous taxi fleets in an energy efficient way. Technical report, Chalmers University of Technology.

Atalay, E., Hortacsu, A., Roberts, J., and Syverson, C. (2011). Network structure of production. *Proceedings of the National Academy of Sciences*, 108(13):5199–5202.

Axtell, R. L. (2001). Zipf distribution of US firm sizes. *Science*, 293(5536):1818–1820.

Azimzadeh, P. (2019). A fast and stable test to check if a weakly diagonally dominant matrix is a nonsingular m-matrix. *Mathematics of Computation*, 88(316):783–800.

Bala, V. and Goyal, S. (2000). A noncooperative model of network formation. *Econometrica*, 68(5):1181–1229.

Ballester, C., Calvó-Armengol, A., and Zenou, Y. (2006). Who's who in networks. Wanted: The key player. *Econometrica*, 74(5):1403–1417.

Baqaee, D. R. (2018). Cascading failures in production networks. *Econometrica*, 86(5): 1819–1838.

Barabási, A.-L. and Albert, R. (1999). Emergence of scaling in random networks. *science*, 286(5439):509–512.

Bardoscia, M., Barucca, P., Codd, A. B., and Hill, J. (2019). Forward-looking solvency contagion. *Journal of Economic Dynamics and Control*, 108:103755.

Bardoscia, M., Battiston, S., Caccioli, F., and Caldarelli, G. (2015). Debtrank: A microscopic foundation for shock propagation. *PloS one*, 10(6):e0130406.

Barrot, J.-N. and Sauvagnat, J. (2016). Input specificity and the propagation of idiosyncratic shocks in production networks. *The Quarterly Journal of Economics*, 131(3):1543–1592.

Bartle, R. G. and Sherbert, D. R. (2011). *Introduction to Real Analysis*. Wiley, 4th edition.

Battiston, S., Puliga, M., Kaushik, R., Tasca, P., and Caldarelli, G. (2012). Debtrank: Too central to fail? Financial networks, the Fed and systemic risk. *Scientific Reports*, 2(1):1–6.

Beiglböck, M., Pammer, G., and Schachermayer, W. (2022). From Bachelier to Dupire via optimal transport. *Finance and Stochastics*, 26(1):59–84.

Belhaj, M., Bervoets, S., and Deroïan, F. (2016). Efficient networks in games with local complementarities. *Theoretical Economics*, 11(1):357–380.

Belhaj, M. and Deroïan, F. (2019). Group targeting under networked synergies. *Games and Economic Behavior*, 118:29–46.

Benhabib, J., Bisin, A., and Luo, M. (2019). Wealth distribution and social mobility in the US: A quantitative approach. *American Economic Review*, 109(5):1623–1647.

Benzi, M. and Klymko, C. (2015). On the limiting behavior of parameter-dependent network centrality measures. *SIAM Journal on Matrix Analysis and Applications*, 36(2):686–706.

Bernard, A. B., Dhyne, E., Magerman, G., Manova, K., and Moxnes, A. (2019). The origins of firm heterogeneity: A production network approach. Technical report, National Bureau of Economic Research.

Bertsimas, D. and Tsitsiklis, J. N. (1997). *Introduction to Linear Optimization*. Athena Scientific.

Blanchet, A., Carlier, G., and Nenna, L. (2018). Computation of Cournot–Nash equilibria by entropic regularization. *Vietnam Journal of Mathematics*, 46(1):15–31.

Board, S. and Meyer-ter-Vehn, M. (2021). Learning dynamics in social networks. *Econometrica*, 89(6):2601–2635.

Bollobás, B. (1999). *Linear Analysis: An Introductory Course*. Cambridge University Press.

Borgatti, S. P., Everett, M. G., and Johnson, J. C. (2018). *Analyzing Social Networks*. Sage.

Borovička, J. and Stachurski, J. (2020). Necessary and sufficient conditions for existence and uniqueness of recursive utilities. *The Journal of Finance*, 75(3):1457–1493.

Bramoullé, Y., Galeotti, A., and Rogers, B. W. (2016). *The Oxford Handbook of the Economics of Networks*. Oxford University Press.

Cai, J. and Szeidl, A. (2018). Interfirm relationships and business performance. *The Quarterly Journal of Economics*, 133(3):1229–1282.

Calvó-Armengol, A., Patacchini, E., and Zenou, Y. (2009). Peer effects and social networks in education. *The Review of Economic Studies*, 76(4):1239–1267.

Candogan, O., Bimpikis, K., and Ozdaglar, A. (2012). Optimal pricing in networks with externalities. *Operations Research*, 60(4):883–905.

Carvalho, V. M. (2014). From micro to macro via production networks. *Journal of Economic Perspectives*, 28(4):23–48.

Carvalho, V. M. and Grassi, B. (2019). Large firm dynamics and the business cycle. *American Economic Review*, 109(4):1375–1425.

Carvalho, V. M., Nirei, M., Saito, Y. U., and Tahbaz-Salehi, A. (2021). Supply chain disruptions: Evidence from the great east Japan earthquake. *The Quarterly Journal of Economics*, 136(2):1255–1321.

Carvalho, V. M. and Tahbaz-Salehi, A. (2019). Production networks: A primer. *Annual Review of Economics*, 11:635–663.

Charpentier, A., Galichon, A., and Vernet, L. (2019). Optimal transport on large networks, a practitioner's guide. *arXiv preprint arXiv:1907.02320*.

Cheney, W. (2013). *Analysis for Applied Mathematics*, volume 208. Springer Science & Business Media.

Chetty, R., Jackson, M. O., Kuchler, T., Stroebel, J., Hendren, N., Fluegge, R. B., Gong, S., Gonzalez, F., Grondin, A., and Jacob, M. (2022). Social capital I: Measurement and associations with economic mobility. *Nature*, 608(7921):108–121.

Chiu, J., Eisenschmidt, J., and Monnet, C. (2020). Relationships in the interbank market. *Review of Economic Dynamics*, 35:170–191.

Çınlar, E. (2011). *Probability and Stochastics*, volume 261. Springer Science & Business Media.

Cochrane, J. H. (1994). Shocks. In *Carnegie-Rochester Conference series on public policy*, volume 41, pages 295–364. Elsevier. DOI https://doi.org/10.1016/0167-2231(94)00024-7.

Cohen, M. X. (2021). *Linear Algebra: Theory, Intuition, Code*. sincXpress.

Cook, W. J. (2011). *In Pursuit of the Traveling Salesman*. Princeton University Press.

Coscia, M. (2021). The atlas for the aspiring network scientist. *arXiv preprint arXiv:2101.00863*.

Dantzig, G. B. (1951). Application of the simplex method to a transportation problem. In T. C. Koopmans (Ed.), *Activity Analysis of Production and Allocation*, pages 359–373. John Wiley and Sons.

Dasaratha, K., Golub, B., and Hak, N. (2022). Learning from neighbors about a changing state. Technical report, Northwestern University.

Davey, B. A. and Priestley, H. A. (2002). *Introduction to Lattices and Order*. Cambridge University Press.

De Masi, G., Fujiwara, Y., Gallegati, M., Greenwald, B., and Stiglitz, J. E. (2011). An analysis of the Japanese credit network. *Evolutionary and Institutional Economics Review*, 7(2): 209 –232.

DeGroot, M. H. (1974). Reaching a consensus. *Journal of the American Statistical Association*, 69(345):118–121.

Demange, G. (2017). Optimal targeting strategies in a network under complementarities. *Games and Economic Behavior*, 105:84–103.

Demange, G. (2018). Contagion in financial networks: A threat index. *Management Science*, 64(2):955–970.

Deplano, D., Franceschelli, M., and Giua, A. (2020). A nonlinear Perron–Frobenius approach for stability and consensus of discrete-time multi-agent systems. *Automatica*, 118:109025.

Dew-Becker, I. (2022). Tail risk in production networks. Technical report, Northwestern University.

Di Giovanni, J., Levchenko, A. A., and Mejean, I. (2014). Firms, destinations, and aggregate fluctuations. *Econometrica*, 82(4):1303–1340.

Du, Y. (1990). Fixed points of increasing operators in ordered Banach spaces and applications. *Applicable Analysis*, 38(01–02):1–20.

Du, Y., Lehrer, E., and Pauzner, A. (2015). Competitive economy as a ranking device over networks. *Games and Economic Behavior*, 91:1–13.

Dupor, B. (1999). Aggregation and irrelevance in multi-sector models. *Journal of Monetary Economics*, 43(2):391–409.

Durrett, R. (2007). *Random Graph Dynamics*. Cambridge University Press.

Easley, D. and Kleinberg, J., (2010). *Networks, Crowds, and Markets*, volume 8. Cambridge University Press.

Eisenberg, L. and Noe, T. H. (2001). Systemic risk in financial systems. *Management Science*, 47(2):236–249.

Elliott, M. and Golub, B. (2019). A network approach to public goods. *Journal of Political Economy*, 127(2):730–776.

Elliott, M. and Golub, B. (2022). Networks and economic fragility. *Annual Review of Economics*, 14:665–696.

Elliott, M., Golub, B., and Jackson, M. O. (2014). Financial networks and contagion. *American Economic Review*, 104(10):3115–3153.

Elliott, M., Golub, B., and Leduc, M. V. (2022). Supply network formation and fragility. *American Economic Review*, 112(8):2701–47.

Erdös, P. and Rényi, A. (1960). On the evolution of random graphs. *Publications of the Mathematical Institute of the Hungarian Academy of Sciences*, 5(1):17–60.

Fajgelbaum, P. D. and Schaal, E. (2020). Optimal transport networks in spatial equilibrium. *Econometrica*, 88(4):1411–1452.

Flamary, R., Courty, N., Gramfort, A., Alaya, M. Z., Boisbunon, A., Chambon, S., Chapel, L., Corenflos, A., Fatras, K., Fournier, N., Gautheron, L., Gayraud, N. T., Janati, H., Rakotomamonjy, A., Redko, I., Rolet, A., Schutz, A., Seguy, V., Sutherland, D. J., Tavenard, R., Tong, A., and Vayer, T. (2021). Pot: Python optimal transport. *Journal of Machine Learning Research*, 22(78):1–8.

Foss, S., Korshunov, D., and Zachary, S. (2011). *An Introduction to Heavy-Tailed and Subexponential Distributions*, volume 6. Springer.

Gabaix, X. (2011). The granular origins of aggregate fluctuations. *Econometrica*, 79(3): 733–772.

Galeotti, A., Golub, B., and Goyal, S. (2020). Targeting interventions in networks. *Econometrica*, 88(6):2445–2471.

Galeotti, A. and Goyal, S. (2010). The law of the few. *American Economic Review*, 100(4):1468–1492.

Galichon, A. (2018). *Optimal Transport Methods in Economics*. Princeton University Press.

Glynn, P. W. and Desai, P. Y. (2018). A probabilistic proof of the Perron–Frobenious theorem. Technical report, arXiv preprint 1808.04964.

Goebel, K. and Kirk, W. A. (1990). *Topics in Metric Fixed Point Theory*. Cambridge University Press.

Golub, B. and Jackson, M. O. (2010). Naive learning in social networks and the wisdom of crowds. *American Economic Journal: Microeconomics*, 2(1):112–149.

Goyal, S. (2023). *Networks: An Economics Approach*. MIT Press.

Graham, B. S. (2017). An econometric model of network formation with degree heterogeneity. *Econometrica*, 85(4):1033–1063.

Greinecker, M. and Kah, C. (2021). Pairwise stable matching in large economies. *Econometrica*, 89(6):2929–2974.

Guo, D., Cho, Y. J., and Zhu, J. (2004). *Partial Ordering Methods in Nonlinear Platforms*. Nova Publishers.

Häggström, O. (2002). *Finite Markov Chains and Algorithmic Applications*. Cambridge University Press.

Herskovic, B. (2018). Networks in production: Asset pricing implications. *The Journal of Finance*, 73(4):1785–1818.

Hojman, D. A. and Szeidl, A. (2008). Core and periphery in networks. *Journal of Economic Theory*, 139(1):295–309.

Holme, P. (2019). Rare and everywhere: Perspectives on scale-free networks. *Nature Communications*, 10(1):1–3.

Huang, W.-Q., Zhuang, X.-T., Yao, S., and Uryasev, S. (2016). A financial network perspective of financial institutions' systemic risk contributions. *Physica A: Statistical Mechanics and Its Applications*, 456:183–196.

Jackson, M. O. (2010). *Social and Economic Networks*. Princeton University Press.

Jackson, M. O. (2014). Networks in the understanding of economic behaviors. *Journal of Economic Perspectives*, 28(4):3–22.

Jackson, M. O. and Pernoud, A. (2019). Investment incentives and regulation in financial networks. Technical report, SSRN 3311839.

Jackson, M. O. and Pernoud, A. (2020). Credit freezes, equilibrium multiplicity, and optimal bailouts in financial networks. Technical report, arxiv 2012.12861.

Jackson, M. O. and Pernoud, A. (2021). Systemic risk in financial networks: A survey. *Annual Review of Economics*, 13:171–202.

Jackson, M. O. and Wolinsky, A. (1996). A strategic model of social and economic networks. *Journal of Economic Theory*, 71(1):44–74.

Jänich, K. (1994). Linear Algebra. In Undergraduate Texts in Mathematics. *Springer-Verlag*.

Kakutani, S. (1941). A generalization of Brouwer's fixed point theorem. *Duke Mathematical Journal*, 8(3):457–459.

Katz, L. (1953). A new status index derived from sociometric analysis. *Psychometrika*, 18(1):39–43.

Kepner, J. and Gilbert, J. (2011). *Graph Algorithms in the Language of Linear Algebra*. SIAM.

Kikuchi, T., Nishimura, K., Stachurski, J., and Zhang, J. (2021). Coase meets bellman: Dynamic programming for production networks. *Journal of Economic Theory*, 196:105287.

Kim, K., Kim, S. Y., and Ha, D.-H. (2007). Characteristics of networks in financial markets. *Computer Physics Communications*, 177(1–2):184–185.

Klages-Mundt, A. and Minca, A. (2021). Optimal intervention in economic networks using influence maximization methods. *European Journal of Operational Research*, 300(3): 1136–1148.

Kolouri, S., Park, S. R., Thorpe, M., Slepcev, D., and Rohde, G. K. (2017). Optimal mass transport: Signal processing and machine-learning applications. *IEEE Signal Processing Magazine*, 34(4):43–59.

Kondo, I. O., Lewis, L. T., and Stella, A. (2020). Heavy tailed, but not zipf: Firm and establishment size in the US. Technical report, Federal Reserve Bank of Minneapolis.

Krasnoselskii, M. (1964). *Positive Solutions of Operator Equations*. Noordhoff.

Kreyszig, E. (1978). *Introductory Functional Analysis with Applications*, volume 1. Wiley.

Kumamoto, S.-I. and Kamihigashi, T. (2018). Power laws in stochastic processes for social phenomena: An introductory review. *Frontiers in Physics*, 6:20.

La'O, J. and Tahbaz-Salehi, A. (2022). Optimal monetary policy in production networks. *Econometrica*, 90(3):1295–1336.

Leontief, W. W. (1941). *The Structure of American Economy, 1919–1929*. Harvard University Press.

Liu, E. (2019). Industrial policies in production networks. *The Quarterly Journal of Economics*, 134(4):1883–1948.

Liu, E. and Tsyvinski, A. (2020). Dynamical structure and spectral properties of input–output networks. Technical report, National Bureau of Economic Research.

Ljungqvist, L. and Sargent, T. J. (2018). *Recursive Macroeconomic Theory*. MIT press, 4th edition.

Lucas, R. and Stokey, N. (1989). *Recursive Methods in Dynamic Economics*. Harvard University Press.

Marinacci, M. and Montrucchio, L. (2019). Unique Tarski fixed points. *Mathematics of Operations Research*, 44(4):1174–1191.

Martin, T. and Otto, C. A. (2020). The downstream impact of upstream tariffs: Evidence from investment decisions in supply chains. Technical report, SSRN 2872662.

Matousek, J. and Gärtner, B. (2007). *Understanding and Using Linear Programming*. Springer Science & Business Media.

Menczer, F., Fortunato, S., and Davis, C. A. (2020). *A First Course in Network Science*. Cambridge University Press.

Meyer, C. D. (2000). *Matrix Analysis and Applied Linear Algebra*, volume 71. SIAM.

Meyer-Nieberg, P. (2012). *Banach Lattices*. Springer Science & Business Media.

Meyn, S. P. and Tweedie, R. L. (2009). *Markov Chains and Stochastic Stability*. Cambridge University Press.

Miller, R. E. and Blair, P. D. (2009). *Input-Output Analysis: Foundations and Extensions*. Cambridge University Press.

Miranda-Pinto, J. (2021). Production network structure, service share, and aggregate volatility. *Review of Economic Dynamics*, 39:146–173.

Molavi, P., Tahbaz-Salehi, A., and Jadbabaie, A. (2018). A theory of non-Bayesian social learning. *Econometrica*, 86(2):445–490.

Nair, J., Wierman, A., and Zwart, B. (2021). *The Fundamentals of Heavy Tails: Properties, Emergence, and Estimation*. Preprint, California Institute of Technology.

Nash, J. F. (1950). Equilibrium points in n-person games. *Proceedings of the National Academy of Sciences*, 36(1):48–49.

Newman, M. E. (2005). Power laws, Pareto distributions and Zipf's law. *Contemporary Physics*, 46(5):323–351.

Newman, M. E. (2018). *Networks*. Oxford University Press.

Nikaido, H. (1968). *Convex Structures and Economic Theory*. Academic Press.

Norris, J. R. (1998). *Markov Chains*. Cambridge University Press.

Ocampo, S. (2022). A task-based theory of occupations with multidimensional heterogeneity. Technical report, Western University.

Olabisi, M. (2020). Input–output linkages and sectoral volatility. *Economica*, 87(347):713–746.

Ou, Q., Jin, Y.-D., Zhou, T., Wang, B.-H., and Yin, B.-Q. (2007). Power-law strength-degree correlation from resource-allocation dynamics on weighted networks. *Physical Review E*, 75(2):021102.

Pearce, R. (2017). Triangle counting for scale-free graphs at scale in distributed memory. In *2017 IEEE High Performance Extreme Computing Conference (HPEC)*, Sept. 2017, Waltham, MA USA. Pages 1–4. IEEE.

Peyré, G. and Cuturi, M. (2019). Computational optimal transport: With applications to data science. *Foundations and Trends® in Machine Learning*, 11(5-6):355–607.

Polovnikov, K., Pospelov, N., and Skougarevskiy, D. (2022). Ownership concentration and wealth inequality in Russia. In *Proceedings of the 31st International Joint Conference on Artificial Intelligence*, July 2022, Vienna. Pages 5136–5142.

Privault, N. (2013). *Understanding Markov Chains. Examples and Applications*. Springer-Verlag Singapore, 357–358.

Punel, A. and Ermagun, A. (2018). Using twitter network to detect market segments in the airline industry. *Journal of Air Transport Management*, 73:67–76.

Quah, D. (1993). Empirical cross-section dynamics in economic growth. *European Economic Review*, 37(2-3.):426–434.

Rybski, D., Buldyrev, S. V., Havlin, S., Liljeros, F., and Makse, H. A. (2009). Scaling laws of human interaction activity. *Proceedings of the National Academy of Sciences*, 106(31):12640–12645.

Schauder, J. (1930). Der Fixpunktsatz in Funktionalräumen. *Studia Math*, 2:71–80.

Schrijver, A. (2005). On the history of combinatorial optimization (till 1960). *Handbooks in Operations Research and Management Science*, 12:1–68.

Seneta, E. (2006a). Markov and the creation of Markov chains. In *Markov Anniversary Meeting*, pages 1–20. Citeseer.

Seneta, E. (2006b). *Non-Negative Matrices and Markov Chains*. Springer Science & Business Media.

Sharkey, K. J. (2017). A control analysis perspective on Katz centrality. *Scientific reports*, 7(1):1–8.

Shiller, R. J. (2020). *Narrative Economics: How Stories Go Viral and Drive Major Economic Events*. Princeton University Press.

Shin, H. S. (2010). *Risk and Liquidity*. Oxford University Press.

Simon, C. P. (1994). *Mathematics for Economists*. Norton & Company, Inc.

Simonetto, A., Monteil, J., and Gambella, C. (2019). Real-time city-scale ridesharing via linear assignment problems. *Transportation Research Part C: Emerging Technologies*, 101: 208–232.

Stachurski, J. (2016). *A Primer in Econometric Theory*. MIT Press.

Stachurski, J. (2022a). *Economic Dynamics: Theory and Computation*. MIT Press, 2nd edition.

Stachurski, J. (2022b). Systemic risk in financial systems: Properties of equilibria. arXiv preprint. arXiv:2202.11183.

Vershik, A. M. (2013). Long history of the Monge–Kantorovich transportation problem. *The Mathematical Intelligencer*, 35(4):1–9.

Villani, C. (2008). *Optimal Transport: Old and New*, volume 338. Springer Science & Business Media.

Watts, A. (2001). A dynamic model of network formation. *Games and Economic Behavior*, 34(2):331–341.

Yun, T.-S., Jeong, D., and Park, S. (2019). "Too central to fail" systemic risk measure using Pagerank algorithm. *Journal of Economic Behavior & Organization*, 162:251–272.

Zenou, Y. (2016). Key Players. *Oxford Handbook on the Economics of Networks*, pages 244–274.

Zhang, Z. (2012). *Variational, Topological, and Partial Order Methods with Their Applications*, volume 29. Springer.

Index

Printed in the United States
by Baker & Taylor Publisher Services